The Autobiography of
JOHN ROY LYNCH

NEGRO AMERICAN

BIOGRAPHIES AND

AUTOBIOGRAPHIES

John Hope Franklin / Series Editor

Reminiscences of an Active Life

The Autobiography of JOHN ROY LYNCH

Edited and with an Introduction by
John Hope Franklin

The University of Chicago Press
CHICAGO AND LONDON

International Standard Book Number: 0-226-49818-2
Library of Congress Catalog Card Number: 70-110669
The University of Chicago Press, Chicago 60637
The University of Chicago Press, Ltd., London

Published 1970
Printed in the United States of America

CONTENTS

INTRODUCTION

When John Roy Lynch completed the writing of *Reminiscences of an Active Life*, he was already in his ninetieth year. His life encompassed a momentous era; and he had been a part of much that had occurred. Born on a Louisiana plantation in 1847, he knew about slavery from experience and observation. He knew the heartbreak of a slave mother when an Irish father died before completing the plans for emancipating her and her children. He knew her bitter disappointment when the father's friend broke his promise and kept them all in slavery. He had experienced the tragic breakup of the family, when he was sent to work on a plantation while the others remained in Natchez. He knew hard work, the rewards for doing the "right thing and staying in his place," and the punishments for precocity and for "conduct unbecoming a slave."

Long before he became paymaster in the United States

Army, Lynch knew what war was like. As a teenager, he saw the Union forces invade the lower Mississippi River Valley where he lived. This was, for him, a war of deliverance; and when the Union forces approached that area, he joined other slaves in the "general strike" and in the enjoyment of freedom long before the cessation of hostilities. Perhaps this early contact with soldiers—as a camp employee and a waiter on a naval vessel—had something to do with his seizing the opportunity, some thirty-five years later, to become a major in the United States Army. In 1863 and 1864, however, so lofty a rank in so grand an army was beyond his wildest dreams.

For Lynch, the postwar years were years of discovery. He had picked up a few odds and ends of the rudiments of an education as he served his owner and the guests at meals. The most valuable lesson he learned was that education was important; his mistress, he observed, became outraged when he displayed any knowledge at all. When the whites of Mississippi began to establish schools in 1865, they made no provisions for educating Negroes; and Lynch had to wait until a group of Northern teachers established a school for Negroes in 1866. It was an evening school, and Lynch attended for the four months that it remained open. After that, his education was, at best, informal—reading books and newspapers and listening to the recitations in the white school just across the alley from the photographic studio where he worked. Within a few years he had not only become quite literate but had also developed a capacity for expression that made a favorable impression on his listeners. He was developing talents and acquiring experience that would take him successively into politics, public service, the practice of law, and the pursuit of historical studies.

I

For Mississippi freedmen—indeed, for freedmen everywhere—the postwar years were exceedingly difficult. For more than two years after the Civil War, they had no economic opportunities that would set them on the road to real freedom and independence. Indeed, the great fear was that the freedmen might actually become independent, or dangerous in some other way; and everything was done to forestall any such grave eventuality. The black codes, especially those enacted by Mississippi in 1865, were in many respects reminiscent of the old slave codes. In the effort to prevent freedmen from becoming independent farmers, Mississippi went so far as to forbid the sale of land to Negroes, except in incorporated towns. Under the pretext of preserving the public peace the state also restricted the activities of the freedmen in a dozen different ways.

Meanwhile, Mississippi and the other states of the old Confederacy were governed at every level by whites, most of them native born and former Confederates. Political participation of Negroes, however well qualified, was beyond the thought of any responsible white leader in the South and, indeed, of most citizens in the country. The suggestion that they should become voters was greeted with the same kind of amused incredulity that greeted the suggestion that schools should be provided for the education of the freedmen.

Most Southerners seemed to feel that it was difficult enough to go down to defeat in the Civil War and to lose their slaves as well. It was too much to expect them to go beyond the acceptance of defeat and emancipation to regard the freedmen as political and social equals. They had reached the limit in making concessions. They would stand firm against the Freedmen's Bureau, which proposed not only to educate the freedmen but to encourage them to seek economic independence. They would be even more firm—if that was possible—against such groups as the Union League, which catechized Negroes in politics and held before them the prospect of social equality. Southern whites did their best, through laws, economic sanctions, and intimidation and violence, to hold the line. But their intransigence ignored the implications of the very concrete results of the Civil War. The victors would not, at least in 1866 and 1867, permit the vanquished to turn the clock back. Consequently, they insisted on a new dispensation in 1867, in which the freedmen were to enjoy political equality. Surely this was an indication that the old order was changing.

Lynch was scarcely twenty years old when new political opportunities came to him and the other freedmen with their enfranchisement in 1867. He would make the most of his opportunities. He became active in one of the local Republican clubs in Natchez and wrote and spoke in support of the new state constitution. Soon he displayed those talents that were to take him far in the political world. One of the first to recognize them was Governor Adelbert Ames, who, in 1869, appointed him to the office of justice of the peace. His own account of his experiences as a neophyte judge is a rare documentation of the efforts of freedmen to understand the intricacies of the law and their obligations and rights under it. The picture that Lynch gives of himself is that of a venerable sage, freely sharing his advice with the uninitiated who appeared before him. One almost forgets that at the time Lynch was only twenty-one.

Lynch was destined for higher public service, and before the end of his first year as justice of the peace he was elected to the House of Representatives of the Mississippi legislature, where he served until 1873. In his *Reminiscences* he has little to say about the deliberations of that body or his role in it. The journals of the legislature, however, make it clear that he was a most active and even popular member. In his first term he became a member of two important standing committees: the Committee on Military Affairs and the Committee on Elections. Immediately, he indicated a lively interest in the deliberations; and if he was not always successful in carrying the day for the measures he advocated, he succeeded in serving notice that he would not be ignored. He offered amendments to pending bills, presented riders to measures before the House, and dropped into the hopper his own bills covering a variety of matters.[1]

He was a much more important member in the next session of the legislature, which met in 1871. He even received one vote for the speakership. The new Speaker, H. W. Warren of Leake County, made good use of his erstwhile rival. He appointed him to the special committee on resolutions to express sympathy in the death of members of the House and to the joint special committee on printing rules for the use of the House and the Senate. Warren also appointed Lynch to the standing committees on public education and the judiciary and to the chairmanship of the Committee on Elections. Lynch soon established himself as one of the most important members of the legislature. Frequently he offered resolutions, motions, and bills. Apparently he assumed a responsibility that was tantamount to that of majority leader. It was Lynch who frequently offered the motion to consider the business that lay on the Speaker's desk; and invariably his motion carried. It was Lynch who offered amendments to pending legislation; and the amendments were supported by a majority of the House. The member from Adams County had clearly achieved a status that was in marked contrast to his position as neophyte and outsider in the previous session.[2]

When the legislature met on 2 January 1872, few would dispute the claim that John R. Lynch could become the most important member of the House. On the first day he gained a seat on the Committee on Credentials; and on the second day he was elected Speaker of the House. It is not difficult to believe that he had much to do with the election of his political ally, James Hill, as sergeant at arms of the House. As Speaker, Lynch generally voted with the majority and joined in the

1. See the *Journal of the House of Representatives of the State of Mississippi* (Jackson, 1870), pp. 98–99, 155, 159, 415, 776–77.

2. *Journal of the House of Representatives of the State of Mississippi at a Regular Session Thereof* (Jackson, 1871), pp. 7, 12, 24, 25, 30, 34, 263, 756–57, 1042.

efforts of the legislature to eliminate most of the laws of the pro-Confederate legislature of 1865–66. When the House was unable to agree on a plan for redistricting the state, the body placed the matter in the hands of the Speaker. Lynch then devised a plan that would make five districts safely and reliably Republican and one district Democratic. At the end of the session in April 1872, the House considered a resolution to tender thanks to "Hon. J. R. Lynch, for the able, efficient, and impartial manner in which he presided over the deliberations of this body during the present session." John Calhoun of Marshall County moved to strike the word "impartial," which was lost; and the resolution was adopted.[3]

Thus, Lynch was clearly becoming one of the state's outstanding and influential young leaders. Although only twenty-four years of age in 1872, he was ready for bigger things. That year his party sent him as a delegate to the Republican National Convention, where he served on the Committee on Resolutions.[4] Upon his return to the state, he and his friends decided that he should run for the lower house of Congress against the white Republican incumbent, L. W. Perce. Lynch described Perce as a "strong and able man" who had made a "creditable and satisfactory record." As a native New Yorker and as a veteran of the Union army, however, Perce was the object of bitter attacks in the Democratic press. When Lynch defeated him for the Republican nomination, one Mississippi newspaper called it "retributive justice." It gloated over Perce's defeat and said, "There is special satisfaction in the overthrow of Perce, whose malignant and slanderous accusations of the white people of Mississippi are familiar to the public."[5]

Lynch's campaign was conducted by three popular and re-

3. *Journal of the House of Representatives of the State of Mississippi at a Regular Session Thereof* (Jackson, 1872), pp. 3, 4, 9, 34, 333, 343, 863.

4. *Presidential Election, 1872: Proceedings of the National Union Republican Convention* (Washington, D.C., 1872), pp. 9, 33.

5. Jackson *Weekly Clarion*, 5 September 1872.

sourceful Negro Republicans, William McCary, Robert H. Wood, and Robert Fitzhugh. The contest was heated and exciting, but there was no bitterness and apparently no strong racial overtones. As far as one can ascertain, Lynch's principal reason for ousting Perce was not that Perce was white but that Lynch wanted the seat for himself. In the general election, his white Democratic opponent was Judge Hiram Cassidy. Although the congressional district that he sought to represent was safely Republican, Lynch would need the votes of white Republicans in order to defeat Judge Cassidy. After his nomination, Lynch received the support of all or most of Perce's supporters. On several occasions he and Judge Cassidy engaged in joint debates before enthusiastic crowds. When the returns were in, Lynch was the victor by a majority of more than five thousand, thereby becoming Mississippi's first black member of the United States House of Representatives.[6]

While congressman-elect, Lynch presided over the 1873 session of the lower house of the Mississippi legislature. It was a busy and productive session, dealing with matters varying from the changing of persons' names to regulating the sale of liquor to incorporating a large number of banks, industrial firms, and colleges. At the close of the session, the House unanimously adopted a resolution complimenting and thanking the Speaker for the manner in which he presided, "with becoming dignity, with uniform courtesy and impartiality, and with marked ability."[7] Later, J. H. Piles of Panola, the chairman of the Committee on Public Works, took the floor and made a presentation to Lynch. In part, he said:

> The members of the House over whom you have presided so long and so well, with so much impartiality and so much of the *debonair*, irrespective of party, have generously contributed, and

6. See below, pp. 99–106.

7. *Journal of the House of Representatives of the State of Mississippi, at a Regular Session Thereof, Held in the City of Jackson, 1873* (Jackson, 1873), p. 2055.

> complimentarily confided the agreeable task upon me of presenting to you the gold watch and chain, which I now send to your desk by the son of one of Mississippi's deceased Speakers.
>
> Believe me, sir, it is not for its intrinsic worth, nor for its extrinsic show, but rather as a memento of our high admiration and respect for you as a gentleman, citizen, and Speaker.
>
> Indeed, if it were possible to weld into one sentiment, and to emit by one impulse of the voice the sentiments of all, at this good hour, methinks it would be "God bless Hon. J. R. Lynch; he is an honest and fair man."...
>
> Doubtless we shall not all meet again this side of the All Hail Hereafter. We will miss you, Mr. Speaker. Be it my privilege now, on behalf of the House of Representatives, to bid you a long, lingering and affectionate farewell.

Another member of the House, R. W. Houston of Washington County, spoke of the many questions of parliamentary law that had arisen during the session and observed that the Speaker's decisions on those questions had given "no cause to murmur on account of urbanity or impartiality. And I ask, Mr. Speaker, that you accept my profoundest gratitude for the dignified courtesy and distinguished manliness and marked ability which have characterized your entire conduct as the chief honored officer of this body." Lynch replied that his leaving was "more than an ordinary separation . . . wherein we expect soon to meet again." He remarked that all members had been uniformly courteous. "For your manifestations of confidence and respect, accept my earnest and sincere thanks. In regard to your token of admiration, language is inadequate to express my thanks. I shall ever preserve it in grateful remembrance of the generous hearts of those who contributed to it."[8]

When Lynch took his seat at the opening of the Forty-third Congress in December 1873, he was, at twenty-six years of age, the youngest member of that body. He drew two committee assignments, the Committee on Mines and Mining and the Com-

8. *Journal of the House of Representatives of the State of Mississippi, at a Regular Session Thereof, Held in the City of Jackson, 1873* (Jackson, 1873), pp. 2057–58.

mittee on Expenditures in the Interior Department.[9] Despite his age, he had poise, self-confidence, and considerable legislative experience. On 9 December, eight days after he took his seat, Lynch made his maiden speech. He offered an amendment to the bill to repeal the increase of salaries of members of Congress. He spoke with grace and good humor; and although his amendment did not pass, he made a favorable impression on the members of the House.[10]

During his first term in Congress, Lynch was careful to attend to the needs of his constituents. He introduced bills for the relief of private persons, to donate the marine hospital at Natchez to the state of Mississippi, and to provide for an additional term of the United States District Court for the southern district of Mississippi. He also offered a bill to fix the time for the election of representatives to the Forty-fourth Congress from the state of Mississippi.[11] He was successful in securing the passage of most of these bills, and throughout his tenure his success continued with similar legislation.[12]

When the Civil Rights Bill was before the House in June 1874, Lynch plunged into the debate. He said that he had not been anxious to get into the fight but felt impelled to do so because of the extent of the discussion concerning the bill both in and out of Congress. He argued for the bill "not only because it is an act of simple justice, but because it will be instrumental in placing the colored people in a more independent position; because it will, in my judgment, be calculated to bring

9. U.S., Congress, House, *Congressional Record,* 43d Cong., 1st sess., 1873, pt. 1:74.

10. *Congressional Record,* 43d Cong., 1st sess., 1873, pt. 1:118–19; and James G. Blaine, *Twenty Years of Congress* (Norwich, 1886), 2:515.

11. *Congressional Record,* 43d Cong., 1st sess., 1873, pt. 1:370, 766; pt. 2: 1121; pt. 4:3770, 3990–91; pt. 5:455–46.

12. See, for example, U.S., Congress, House, *Congressional Record,* 44th Cong., 1st sess., 1875, pt. 1:206, 321; pt. 2:1203; and 47th Cong., 1st sess., 1882, pt. 4:3946, 4531.

about a friendly feeling between the two races in all sections of the country, and will place the colored people in a position where their identification with any party will be a matter of choice and not of necessity."[13]

In succeeding months Lynch engaged in the debate on the Civil Rights Bill whenever it was before the House. He sought to deal with the canard that civil rights meant social equality. He pleaded for the retention of the provision that would open all public schools to children of all races. He chided all Republicans who had not supported the bill. In February 1875, less than a month before the bill became law, Lynch made an impassioned plea for the passage of the bill. In part, he said:

> I appeal to all members of the House–republicans and democrats, conservatives and liberals–to join with us in the passage of this bill, which has for its object the protection of human rights. And when every man, woman, and child can feel and know that his, her, and their rights are fully protected by the strong arm of a generous and grateful Republic, then can all truthfully say that this beautiful land of ours, over which the Star Spangled Banner so triumphantly waves, is, in truth and in fact, the "land of the free and the home of the brave."[14]

Because of his vigorous support of the Civil Rights Act, many of the white citizens of Lynch's district were more determined than ever to unseat him. They were encouraged, moreover, by the national Democratic trend that had become clear in the elections of 1874. Their opportunity, they thought, would come in their own congressional elections–to be held in 1875 instead of 1874–and in the regular elections of 1876. While Lynch's renomination was assured, the nomination was no longer tantamount to election. Many white Republicans in Mississippi were going into the Democratic camp, either be-

13. *Congressional Record,* 43d Cong., 1st sess., 1873, pt. 5:4955.

14. *Congressional Record,* 43d Cong., 2d sess., 1875, pt. 2:947.

cause of intimidation or because they believed that the Democratic party served their own needs.[15]

Lynch was an active, even aggressive, candidate for reelection. His Democratic opponent was the popular Colonel Roderick Seal. Lynch stood by his record in Congress, pointing out how much he had done for his district and for the state. During September and October 1875 he campaigned vigorously throughout his district. When he spoke at Biloxi in early October, the local reporter said that he had been "agreeably impressed" with him. "His deportment and bearing were respectful and polite. . . . He at some length alluded to his record in Congress and gave his reasons for voting for several obnoxious measures, but felt no regret for what he had done."[16] Foul play may have been involved in his appearance in Vicksburg. In the course of his speech the lights went out, at which time a "pell mell stampede of the audience took place which was frightful to behold."[17]

The race was close, but Lynch was victorious. The Democrats, however, made a clean sweep of the other offices. Each side accused the other of misconduct and even fraud. One Mississippi paper exulted over the Lynch victory. The writer said, "Notwithstanding the fraud and intimidation practiced in Claiborne County to defeat the Republican ticket and the determined opposition made against Mr. Lynch on the Sea Coast, we are happy to chronicle the fact that the Republicans of Mississippi will have at least one representative in the Forty-Fourth Congress in the person of Hon. John R. Lynch."[18]

One of the first items on the agenda of the new Democratic legislature was the redistricting of the state. Five districts were to be safely Democratic; and a sixth—taking in every county

15. James W. Garner, *Reconstruction in Mississippi* (New York, 1901), p. 372 ff.

16. Quoted in ibid., 12 October 1875.

17. *Hinds County Gazette*, 25 October 1875.

18. *Weekly Mississippi Pilot*, 20 November 1875.

on the Mississippi River and dubbed the "shoestring district"—was Lynch's district. Although most of the voters were still Republican, there was little hope, even on Lynch's part, that he could win in 1876. His opponent was General James R. Chalmers of Fort Pillow fame, a likely candidate to keep black Republicans in their place![19] During the campaign Lynch experienced numerous incidents of hostility, which he relates at length in his *Reminiscences.* When it was over, the Democrats claimed a majority of more than four thousand votes. Charging fraud, Lynch sought to contest the election in the House of Representatives. His attorney, T. Hewett of Natchez, served notice on General Chalmers to that effect. When Chalmers indicated that he had not received such a notice, Hewett requested him to waive the "want of notice and let the contest proceed." Chalmers declined, insisting that the contest was "prompted by partisan motives and only intended to stimulate and prolong a political assault on the State of Mississippi through him."[20] In the circumstances the Democratic-dominated House Committee on Elections, of which John R. Harris of Virginia was chairman, would not even take up the case for consideration.

Lynch would have another chance to even the score with General Chalmers. In 1880 he announced that he was again a candidate for Congress. The leading paper in his district greeted the announcement with the following rebuff: "Unless we read the times incorrectly she [Adams County] will not only give a majority to [the Democrats] but will also give John such a 'setting down' that he will abandon politics entirely."[21] Lynch was not easily rebuffed. For more than two months he traveled throughout his district organizing Garfield-Arthur-Lynch

19. During the Reconstruction, "black Republican" was an opprobrious term used by conservatives to describe Republicans who supported equal rights for Negroes.

20. *Hinds County Gazette,* 31 January 1877.

21. Natchez *Daily Democrat and Courier,* 12 September 1880.

Clubs and delivering speeches wherever he could find an audience. One hostile paper said that his canvass had been "tame and spiritless, and his speeches received without applause by his meagre audiences."[22] Another, however, no less hostile, reported that every meeting of the local Lynch club was "larger than the preceding one."[23] A Jackson paper recognized the formidable campaign by Lynch when it observed that Chalmers was making a "gallant fight against heavy odds."[24]

Lynch was not surprised to discover that the district, with the election machinery in the hands of the Democrats, gave Chalmers a majority of 1,468. In Warren County alone more than two thousand Lynch votes were thrown out, and several hundred were thrown out in Adams County. It was estimated that of the 5,358 votes declared illegal, some 4,641 were for Lynch and 717 were for Chalmers.[25] During the campaign Lynch had served notice that if he was defeated it would be by fraud and that he would contest the election. On 21 December, he served notice that he would contest the election. In part, the notice said,

> Gen. James R. Chalmers: Please take notice that I intend to contest your pretended election on the second day of this present month as member from the sixth congressional district of Mississippi to the Forty-Seventh Congress of the United States, and to maintain and prove before that body that I was, and you are not, elected as representative to that Congress from said district; and I hereby specify to you the following named frauds and violations of the law of the land and of the purity of elections which I charge were committed on the day of said election, or with ballots cast on that day in the election for Congressman, by our Democratic friends and supporters with your connivance, and in your interest and behalf as Democratic candidate for Congress in that election.

22. Greenville *Times*, quoted in the Natchez *Daily Democrat and Courier*, 24 September, 1880.

23. Natchez *Daily Democrat and Courier*, 30 September 1880.

24. Jackson *Weekly Clarion*, 20 October 1880.

25. *Hinds County Gazette*, 8 December 1880.

Lynch made specific charges of fraud in Adams, Issaquena, Bolivar, Jefferson, Claiborne, Washington, Coahoma, and Warren counties.[26]

Then followed the long, dreary contest before the Committee on Elections, about which Lynch tells, in great detail, in his *Reminiscences*. Meanwhile, the people of the sixth district, who were without effective representation for a year, followed the developments in Washington with great interest. If Lynch had been pessimistic about the outcome of the election itself, some Mississippi Democrats were pessimistic about the outcome before the Committee on Elections. They were especially critical of the young Republicans in the House who made much of "rifled ballot boxes, stifled justice, the shot gun plan, etc." Such comments forced the main points at issue into the background, one paper complained.[27] On 27 April 1882, the House of Representatives, by a vote of 125 to 83, adopted a resolution declaring that Lynch was entitled to the seat. Lynch, escorted by William H. Calkins of Indiana, then went to the bar of the House, where the Speaker administered the oath of office.[28]

If Lynch felt vindicated by the decision of the House to seat him, he also felt obliged to seek reelection to that seat a few months hence. General Chalmers, however, was so disillusioned by what he regarded as the unseemly control of the state Democratic party by United States Senator L. Q. C. Lamar that he announced he would withdraw from the party, become an independent, and support the Republican administration of President Chester A. Arthur.[29] In September the Republican convention at Magnolia conferred the congressional nomination on Lynch, who promised a hard fight to retain his seat.[30] As his opponent the Democrats nominated Judge Henry

26. Natchez *Daily Democrat and Courier*, 21 December 1880.

27. Natchez *Daily Democrat and Courier*, 29 April 1882.

28. Ibid., 30 April 1882.

29. Ibid., 13 May 1882.

30. Natchez *Daily Democrat*, 2 September 1882.

S. Van Eaton, "a strong man, an excellent lawyer, [and] a forceful debater."[31]

During the campaign the newspaper attacks on Lynch were especially harsh. When he said that he did not favor an early or active campaign, a Natchez editor refused to believe him. "Mr. Lynch," he said, "is a cunning politician, and it will do the Democratic Party no harm if a close watch is kept upon him, notwithstanding his quiet professions. He knows very well that still hunting is sometimes better than the most noisy drive."[32] When Lynch visited Ellisville and, instead of speaking, inspected the registration rolls, the same editor pointed to this as an example of "still hunting."[33] The *Ellisville Eagle* said that Lynch's visit was not very productive, since he "found no material to become as clay in the hand of the potter. He said and did enough to give his little game dead away, and to put us on our guard."[34]

Lynch was not merely "still hunting." He spoke throughout the Sixth District during the campaign. At Williamsburg, the judge of the Covington County circuit court adjourned the afternoon session of the court, and Lynch spoke for more than two hours.[35] In Natchez, he spoke to a "tolerably fair audience" on 4 November. He assured his listeners that as a Republican he could do more for them in Washington than a Democrat could.[36] If the Adams County voters believed Lynch, there were others who did not. He carried his home county by a comfortable majority, but he lost the election by some 800 votes. Complimenting Judge Van Eaton for conducting

31. Raymond *Gazette,* 1 November 1882.

32. Natchez *Daily Democrat,* 26 September 1882.

33. Ibid., 3 October 1882.

34. Quoted in the Natchez *Daily Democrat,* 3 October 1882.

35. Natchez *Daily Democrat,* 3 November 1882.

36. Ibid., 5 November 1882.

a fair and honest campaign and thanking him for his courtesies, Lynch announced that he would not contest the election.[37]

The loss of his seat in Congress did not lead to Lynch's retirement from politics. He had been the chairman of the Republican State Executive Committee since 1881, and he would continue to serve in that capacity until 1892. He had been a delegate to the Republican National Convention in 1872 and would be a delegate to four subsequent conventions—in 1884, 1888, 1892, and 1900. At the 1884 convention he received the highest recognition he would ever receive as a party man, even if the circumstances that brought the honor resulted from a factional dispute.

The two principal contenders for the Republican nomination in 1884 were President Chester A. Arthur and James G. Blaine. The followers of Blaine were supporting Powell Clayton of Arkansas for temporary chairman. The Arthur supporters were willing to concede that choice but were prepared to challenge the Blaine forces at some other point. Then, young Henry Cabot Lodge and Theodore Roosevelt, who were supporting Arthur, learned that Clayton hoped to receive a cabinet post in return for delivering the votes of Texas and Arkansas to Blaine. They were outraged, and they decided to oppose Clayton's becoming the temporary chairman.[38]

The two young easterners worked throughout the night to garner support for an opposing candidate. When Clayton's name was presented, Lodge got the floor and said that he wanted to make a nomination. He assured the convention that he did not wish to introduce a personal contest or to make a test vote as to strength of candidates. He merely wanted to make a nomination for temporary chairman

37. Ibid., 17 November 1882.

38. John A. Garraty, *Henry Cabot Lodge: A Biography* (New York, 1953), p. 78.

> which shall have the best possible effect in strengthening the party throught the country. . . . I therefore have the honor to move, as it is certainly most desirable that we should recognize, as you have done, Mr. Chairman, the Republicans of the South—I therefore desire to present the name of a gentleman well known throughout the South for his conspicuous parliamentary ability, for his courage and his character. I move you, Mr. Chairman, to substitute the name of the Hon. John R. Lynch of Mississippi.

The motion was promptly seconded by C. A. Simpson of Mississippi and Silas P. Dutcher of New York.[39] There ensued a lengthy debate with many speeches from both sides. Then, the roll of the states was called, and Lynch was elected by a vote of 424 to 384.[40]

Because Lynch was not aware of the possibility of becoming the temporary chairman until the convention opened, he had not prepared a keynote address. Upon taking the chair, he spoke briefly of the importance of unity in the convention and of supporting the nominees, "whoever they may be." In condemning the Democrats for their fraud and intimidation in elections he concluded,

> I am satisfied that the people of this country are too loyal ever to allow a man to be inaugurated President of the United States, whose title to the position may be brought forth by fraud, and whose garments may be saturated with the innocent blood of hundreds of his countrymen. I am satisfied that the American people will ratify our action.[41]

It was the first time that a Negro American had delivered the keynote address before a major national political convention. There would not be another such occasion until 1968.

39. *Proceedings of the Eighth Republican National Convention Held at Chicago, Illinois, June 3, 4, 5, and 6, 1884* (Washington, D.C., 1884), p. 6.

40. *Proceedings of the Eighth Republican National Convention*, pp. 22–23.

41. Ibid., p. 23.

As a politician, Lynch had few peers in Mississippi or elsewhere. He was a loyal Republican, but he was also loyal to his own supporters within the party. He was a formidable and resourceful foe both within the Republican party and outside it. Much of the appraisal of him by a Mississippi newspaper in 1881 was accurate:

> He made and unmade men, organized and disorganized rings and cliques, and directed and controlled legislatures like a very autocrat. He is yet a man of power and authority—yet a shining light in the Republican camp.[42]

II

From Lynch's retirement from Congress in 1883 to his death in 1939 he was engaged in a variety of activities of both a public and private nature. His strong partisanship prompted him to decline a position offered him in 1885 by the Democratic president, Grover Cleveland. He did, however, accept an appointment by President Harrison as Fourth Auditor of the Treasury, a position which he held from 1889 to 1893. We know almost nothing of the manner in which Lynch conducted that office or if, indeed, he was happy in his position in the bureaucracy. He continued his political activities, however; and one gets the impression that politics continued to be of greater interest to him than the position of Fourth Auditor of the Treasury.

Meanwhile, Lynch had become very active in the plantation and city real estate market in Adams County. He purchased his first parcel of land in Natchez in January 1869 when he was but twenty-one years of age. Before the end of the year he had purchased another parcel of land in Natchez.[43] That was merely the beginning. Between 1870 and 1898 he purchased eleven tracts of land in Natchez, ranging from one to four lots, and

42. *Hinds County Gazette*, 19 October 1881.

43. Indirect Index to Land Conveyances, Adams County, Mississippi, from 1789, bk. PP, pp. 298.

four plantations in Adams County.[44] The property in Natchez was clustered in three areas, each on the outskirts of the city. Several of his lots were on Homochitto Street, in the southwestern part of Natchez. He also had several parcels on Saint Catherine Street, in East Natchez, and several along Pine Ridge Road, in the northeastern part of the city.

None of his plantations was actually on the Mississippi River. Ingleside, which he purchased in 1885 and sold in 1893, was the smallest rural tract, with 84 acres.[45] It was located just south of the city. Providence, a few miles south of Ingleside, was purchased in 1875 and sold in 1898. It contained 189 acres at the time of the purchase, but Lynch purchased some adjoining acreage, so that at the time he sold it there were 221 acres in Providence.[46] In 1891 Lynch purchased 90 acres of the Saragossa plantation, presumably with a view to acquiring all of it later. He had not done so by the time he sold it in 1894.[47] His largest plantation was Grove, the farthest from Natchez, six miles from the city on the southwest side. In 1884 Lynch purchased a part of the plantation, amounting to 694 acres. Two years later he purchased the remainder, 840 acres "more or less."[48] He did not part with Grove until 1905, perhaps the

44. Ibid., bk. QQ, p. 226; SS, pp. 435, 558; VV, p. 657; WW, p. 355; YY, pp. 36, 329, 569; ZZ, pp. 372, 638; 3-A, pp. 469, 757; 3-B, pp. 432, 547, 549, 679, 761; 3-C, pp. 580, 589, 661; 3-D, 260; 3-G, p. 495; 3-O, p. 657; and 3-R, p. 215.

45. Indirect Index to Land Conveyances, Adams County, Mississippi, from 1789, bk. ZZ, p. 372; and Land Deed Records, in the Office of the Chancery Clerk of Adams County, Mississippi, bk. 3-K, p. 348.

46. Index to Land Conveyances, Adams County, bk. UU, p. 444; YY, p. 36; 3-B, pp. 547, 549, 679, 761; and Land Deed Records, in the Office of the Chancery Clerk of Adams County, bk. 3-P, p. 723.

47. Index to Land Conveyances, Adams County, bk. 3-G, p. 495; and Land Deed Records, in the Office of the Chancery Clerk of Adams County, bk. 3-K, p. 371.

48. Index to Land Conveyances, Adams County, bk. YY, p. 569; and 3-A, p. 469.

last piece of property that he had in Mississippi.[49] Lynch's brother, William, was involved in some of the transactions and perhaps served as his attorney and business manager.[50]

Lynch's financial resources must have been considerable, for he was in a position to pay cash in full, $700 for his first piece of property and $775 cash for his second. The same can be said for his next two purchases, in 1870 and 1873, and his purchase of a part of the Grove plantation in 1884. By that time, however, he was also selling property and was doubtless shifting his capital to the transaction that seemed the most attractive. From the 1890s on, Lynch was selling more than he was purchasing. He made his final real estate purchases in Mississippi in 1887. Beginning in 1889, he was selling property: lots in Natchez that year, Ingleside in 1893, and more Natchez property in 1894 and succeeding years.[51] By 1902 he had disposed of all his property in Natchez; and by 1905, when he sold Grove, he had no more plantations in Adams County. Apparently Lynch did well in the real estate business. Only his involvement in other activities, perhaps, could lure him away from dealing in land and houses.

It was in the early 1890s that Lynch began to study law.[52] In 1896, he passed the Mississippi bar on the second attempt. Shortly thereafter, he became a partner in the law firm of Robert H. Terrell in Washington. Terrell had been a clerk in Lynch's office when Lynch was Fourth Auditor of the Treasury, and Lynch had developed a high regard for the young man. Lynch continued to practice law in Mississippi and the District of Columbia until he went into the army in 1898.

49. Land Deed Records, in the Office of the Chancery Clerk of Adams County, bk. 4-P, p. 19.

50. In several of the transactions William Lynch is the grantor, the "agent and attorney" for John R. Lynch, or the plantation lessor.

51. All the references for these transactions have been listed above.

52. Lynch discusses his legal career in his *Reminiscences*. See below, pp. 369, 502.

Surely it was not a strong interest in military life or a deep sense of patriotism that lured Lynch into the United States Army during the Spanish-American War. It was, rather, a high regard for President William McKinley, whom he had known during his years in Congress, and a keen sense of party responsibility when the president asked him to serve. To his surprise, he was immensely pleased with the life of an army officer and, since he was at loose ends, he found it a source of fulfillment. His marriage to Ella Somerville in 1884, by whom he had one daughter, had ended with a divorce in 1900. There was at least no family reason why he should not accept the commission in the regular army that was offered to him in 1901.

As paymaster, Lynch had the opportunity to travel to many parts of the world. He went to Haiti and to other islands in the Caribbean. For a time he was stationed at San Francisco, where he witnessed the earthquake and fire in 1906. He journeyed to the Philippines and visited other faraway places. Everywhere he showed that zest for life and that healthy curiosity about people and places that had characterized his early years. It was during these travels that he met Mrs. Cora Williamson, whom he married in 1911, the year he retired from the army.

In the following year Lynch and his wife moved to Chicago, where he entered into the practice of law and engaged in real estate business. In 1915 they purchased a home at 4028 Grand Boulevard (later South Parkway and still later Dr. Martin Luther King, Jr., Drive) where they lived for the remainder of their lives. In Chicago Lynch lived a rather quiet life. He was not active in politics, and the records do not reveal a very active law practice or real estate business.[53] He saw clients in the late afternoon and evenings. Most of his business dealt with real estate transactions. He took great care in explaining to his clients the meaning of all the statements in the legal documents;

53. One must assume that Lynch conducted all his business from his residence address, since he is not listed for any other address in *Sullivan's Chicago Law Directory*. Chicago, 1934–35.

and he made certain that their income was adequate to make the payments on the property they were purchasing.[54]

When Oscar DePriest was nominated for Congress in 1928, Lynch, referred to as a "patent expert," was asked to comment on his years in Congress and on what would be required of a Negro in Congress in the twentieth century. "We need a man," he said, "who will have the courage to attack not only his political opponents, but those within his own party who fail to fight unfair legislation directed toward people of color who helped to elect them. He should use every effort to force the hand of the man who says he is our friend while seeking support, but maneuvers just the opposite way when vital issues come up."[55] Doubtless the requirements he set up for DePriest were requirements that Lynch felt he had set up for himself some forty-five years earlier.

III

While Lynch's principal lifelong interests were centered in politics, business, and military affairs, he participated in the discussion of the general problem of the position of Negro Americans in the life of their country. To be sure, he frequently spoke on the subject during his years in Congress, but he also played a part with his fellow blacks as they searched for solutions to the critical problems they faced. As early as 1879 he participated in the National Conference of Colored Men held in Nashville. It was an important gathering to consider the implications of Negro migration. Among those in attendance were William H. Councill of Alabama, John W. Cromwell of Washington, Norris Wright Cuney of Texas, Richard R. Wright of Georgia, and William Still of Pennsylvania. Lynch presided over the meeting and may have had something to do

54. William L. Dawson to John Hope Franklin, Tuskegee Institute, Alabama, 19 February 1968. Dawson was a member of the Lynch household for several years.

55. Chicago *Defender*, 12 May 1928.

with writing the address which commended Negroes for leaving their communities, viewing it as "evidence of healthy growth in manly independence."[56]

Several years later Lynch discussed the problem of Negro labor in an article entitled, "Should Colored Men Join Labor Organizations?" He enthusiastically endorsed the proposition that Negroes should join a labor organization if it did not seek to accomplish its objectives "through a resort to lawlessness and violence. They should maintain their reputation of being a law-abiding and law-observing people, except so far as may be necessary for the protection of themselves and their families." Lynch believed that organizations were indeed the best way for laborers to secure the rights to which they were entitled without violating the law. He urged Negro parents to educate their sons and daughters who planned to enter the industrial field so that they could not be denied membership in labor organizations—which he did not seem to trust—because they lacked the training. "There ought not to be any discrimination in the interest of, or against, any class of persons on account of race, color or religion," he concluded.[57]

Lynch believed that the history of Negroes in American life had a direct and important bearing on their current and future status. He was an avid reader and, although he did not mention specific titles of books, he doubtless read many of the works that impugned the ability and integrity of Negroes during Reconstruction. He stated in 1913 that "in nearly everything that has been written about Reconstruction during the last quarter of a century," the claim had been set forth that

56. *Proceedings of the National Conference of Colored Men of the United States, held in the State Capitol at Nashville, Tenn., May 6–9, 1879,* quoted in Herbert Aptheker, ed., *A Documentary History of the Negro People in the United States* (New York, 1951), pp. 723–24.

57. John R. Lynch, "Should Colored Men Join Labor Organizations?" *A.M.E. Church Review,* 3–4 (October 1886): 165–67. For his role in promoting business cooperation in the effort to solve problems of unemployment, see August Meier, *Negro Thought in America, 1880–1915* (Ann Arbor, 1963), p. 138.

the enfranchisement of black men had been a mistake, that the Reconstruction governments in the South were a failure, and that the Fifteenth Amendment was premature and unwise.

The contemporary interpretations of the Reconstruction era greatly distressed Lynch, and in 1913 he published a book entitled *The Facts of Reconstruction* to "present the other side." His primary object, he said, was "to bring to public notice those things that were commendable and meritorious, to prevent the publication of which seems to have been the primary purpose of nearly all who have thus far written upon that important subject." He insisted, however, that his work contained no extravagant or exaggerated statements and there had been no effort to "conceal, excuse, or justify any act that was questionable or wrong."[58] Lynch's work is the most extensive account of the post–Civil War years written by a Negro participant. Since virtually all of it is included in his *Reminiscences*, there is no need to review it here.

Lynch's efforts to write Reconstruction history had little or no immediate impact on the historical profession. The view that James W. Garner had set forth in 1901 in his *Reconstruction in Mississippi* and that Lynch was seeking to refute was widely accepted. And although Lynch's volume went through three printings in two years, his *Facts* did not find its way into the histories that were written in the two decades following its appearance.[59] It received none of the attention that was lavished on Thomas Dixon's *Birth of a Nation*, which was filmed two years after *Facts* appeared, or Claude Bowers's *The Tragic Era*, which appeared in 1929. The film and Bowers's popular, journalistic version of Reconstruction merely made even more acceptable the interpretation that Lynch was attacking.

58. John R. Lynch, *The Facts of Reconstruction* (Boston, 1913), p. 11.

59. Lynch said that he had received hundreds of letters complimenting him on his work. He does not indicate that any of them came from historians. John R. Lynch, *Some Historical Errors of James Ford Rhodes* (Boston, 1922), p. xiii.

In 1906 James Ford Rhodes published the volume of his *History of the United States* for the period of the Reconstruction. Apparently, however, Lynch did not see it until after he had written his *Facts of Reconstruction.* It was called to his attention by George A. Myers, the Negro owner of Cleveland's Hollenden Hotel barbershop, who was friendly with Rhodes. While glancing over one of the volumes in 1916, Lynch came across chapters containing information of what happened in Mississippi during Reconstruction. "I detected so many statements and representations which, to my knowledge, were absolutely groundless that I decided to read carefully the entire work . . . and I regret to say that, so far as the Reconstruction period is concerned, the history is not only inaccurate and unreliable, but is the most one-sided, biased, partisan, and prejudiced historical work I have ever read."[60]

In 1914 Myers had sent Rhodes a copy of Lynch's *Facts of Reconstruction.* Rhodes acknowledged that what Lynch wrote "concerning the Convention of 1884 is correct, only I think Mr. Hanna was a bit more emphatic in his talk with Major Lynch than he represents. Mr. Hanna told me about this immediately upon his return from Chicago."[61] After reading the Rhodes volume, Lynch wrote to Myers who, serving as the intermediary, gave Rhodes Lynch's opinion of his book. Rhodes replied that it did not surprise him that Lynch thought him "inaccurate unjust and unfair, for he was a severely partisan actor at the time while I, an earnest seeker after truth, am trying to hold a judicial balance and to tell the story without fear, favor or prejudice." Apparently Myers offered to arrange for the two men to meet, to which Rhodes replied, "Please do not make any arangement for me to see Mr. Lynch before next

60. Ibid., p. xvii.

61. Rhodes to Myers, Boston, 29 March 1914, in John A. Garraty, ed., *The Barber and the Historian: The Correspondence of George A. Myers and James Ford Rhodes, 1910–1923* (Columbus, 1956), pp. 29–30.

autumn or winter as I shall not be well enough to enter upon a discussion of the matter." Then he added, somewhat sardonically, "Why does not Mr. Lynch write a magazine article and show up my mistakes and inaccuracies and injustice?"[62]

The suggestion was a good one, which Lynch promptly followed. When he had completed the article, he sent it to Myers to pass on to Rhodes so that he could prepare a rejoinder if he cared to. The businessman-historian declined to read it, saying, "It is my rule never to indulge in controversies; such indulgence is a rock on which some historians have split. But I always correct errors of fact. When Mr. Lynch's article is printed, I shall be glad to read it and I will thank you or him to send it to me."[63]

Lynch submitted his piece to the *American Historical Review* and to the *American Political Science Review*, both of which rejected it. Then he submitted it to the *Journal of Negro History*, which accepted it but divided it in half. Consequently, two articles appeared in the *Journal of Negro History*, one in 1917 and one in 1918.[64] When the first article appeared, Myers dutifully sent a copy to Rhodes. Myers was evidently quite proud of the case that Lynch had made, for he said, "I have to say that Mr. Lynch, the past-master of the 'Queen's English' that he is, uses it unsparingly in expressing his diametrical views in such a manner as to carry conviction to those who have not read your History and therefore not conversant with the other side. . . . As I once said to you, I think one of your mistakes was made in not seeing and talking with the

62. Rhodes to Myers, Boston, 5 April 1917, in ibid., pp. 42–43.

63. Rhodes to Myers, Boston, 5 April 1917, in ibid., p. 64.

64. John R. Lynch, "Some Historical Errors of James Ford Rhodes," *Journal of Negro History*, 2 (October 1917): 345–68; and "More About the Historical Errors of James Ford Rhodes," *Journal of Negro History*, 3 (April 1918):139–57.

prominent Negro participants that I could have put you in touch with."[65]

Rhodes was obviously touched by the Lynch article, which he not only gave a "thorough investigation and sifting," but also gave to an "expert," who prepared a rejoinder for the perusal of Myers and Lynch. Myers apparently took some delight in telling Rhodes that everything was not on his side. "The thought occurs to me," he said, "that perhaps Mr. Lynch's statements may be right after all when compared with some of the authority that you quote, which was written while flushed with victory and as a natural sequence painted the other fellow and his methods a little blacker than either was. However I am satisfied that with your usual fairness, that after reading Mr. Lynch's rejoinder and you find anything new or of merit, that you will use the same in your new edition."[66]

In 1922 Lynch brought out in a small volume the two articles critical of Rhodes, together with the comments by the "expert" selected by Rhodes and a rejoinder by Lynch. This gave Lynch an opportunity to seek further consideration for the points he had made in his *Facts of Reconstruction.* He acknowledged that the Reconstruction governments made mistakes, not because Negroes had the vote, as Rhodes suggested, but because of the refusal of the federal government to support law and order in the South and because the problems were so overwhelming that they taxed the intellectual and financial resources of the South beyond its capacity. He also argued against the tired canard that Negroes dominated the Reconstruction governments and that they were incompetent. He pointed out that they dominated no Reconstruction state government and that, on balance, the Negro officeholders, always in the minority, were as honest and as efficient as the

65. Myers to Rhodes, Cleveland, 21 November 1917, in Garraty, ed., *The Barber and the Historian,* pp. 73–74.

66. Myers to Rhodes, Cleveland, 8 January 1918, in ibid., p. 78.

whites. "I do not hesitate to assert," he said, "that the Southern reconstructed governments were the best governments those states ever had before or have ever had since, statements and allegations made by Mr. Rhodes and some other historical writers to the contrary notwithstanding."[67]

Claude Bowers followed the tradition of the historians to which Lynch took exception, and when his *Tragic Era* appeared in 1929, it is not surprising that Lynch would attack it. In a long communication to the *Journal of Negro History*, Lynch said that a more accurate title would have been *The Tragic Error*. He called it intensely partisan and written primarily to reflect credit on the Democratic party. In one place Bowers said that, with the election of Alcorn as governor, Mississippi passed into the hands of the "carpetbaggers and blacks." Lynch said the statement was "not only false, but it is ridiculous and absurd." He then gave the figures to show that the carpetbaggers and Negroes did not dominate the government under Alcorn. When Bowers claimed that in Mississippi all the Democratic candidates for Congress in 1875 were elected, Lynch had merely to remind his readers that in that election the Democratic candidate, Roderick Seal, was defeated by the Republican candidate, John R. Lynch.

Lynch differed with Bowers's assertion that the Democratic victory of 1875 relieved the government of Mississippi of bad government and dishonest officials. "Mr. Bowers failed, intentionally, no doubt, to record the fact that when the insurrectionists took charge of the government every dollar of public money had been faithfully and honestly accounted for. [There was] no defalcation or misappropriation of any kind on the part of any official upon his retirement from office . . . [but] shortly after the assumption of the reins of government by the revolutionist treasurer [William L.] Hemingway was discov-

67. Lynch, *Historical Errors of James Ford Rhodes*, p. 87.

ered to be a defaulter to the amount of three hundred and fifteen thousand, six hundred and twelve dollars and nineteen cents."[68] Thus, in his eighty-third year John Roy Lynch continued to fight the battle of the Reconstruction era.

It was in the 1930s that Lynch began to write *Reminiscences of an Active Life*. He was no doubt stimulated by the "errors" of Rhodes and Bowers to state the case for his "side" of Reconstruction one last time. He also appreciated the fact that he had, indeed, led an active and unusual life; it was something worth sharing with others. In his spare time, at his home on Grand Boulevard in Chicago, Lynch would get out his records as well as a copy of *The Facts of Reconstruction*. He would then dictate his *Reminiscences* to his niece, Mabel Carr, who lived with the Lynches. William Dawson of Tuskegee Institute, who was studying music in Chicago and living in the Lynch household, said it was remarkable to see this man of slight build, well beyond eighty-five but still erect, dictating to his niece. His energy seemed boundless, and at times he would dictate for hours and provide all the punctuation as he went. Then he would have his niece read to him what he had dictated in order to make certain that he had actually said what he had intended to say.[69]

Most of *The Facts of Reconstruction* can be found in *Reminiscences of an Active Life*. The first six chapters, dealing with Lynch's early life, do not appear in *Facts*. From that point on, whenever Lynch felt that some phase of the Reconstruction era had not been adequately handled in the earlier work, he would write new chapters. This was especially the case in matters regarding local politics and personal affairs, since *The*

68. John R. Lynch, "The Tragic Era," *Journal of Negro History*, 16 (January 1931):103–20.

69. William L. Dawson to John Hope Franklin, Tuskegee Institute, Alabama, 19 February 1968.

Facts of Reconstruction deal primarily with national politics and Mississippi's involvement in the national picture. Consequently, the later work contains some of the most detailed and fascinating accounts of local political activities to be found for the Reconstruction era. Following the post-Reconstruction years, most of the writing in the *Reminiscences* is new. Thus, few of the last ten chapters and none of the last five chapters of this work appear in *Facts*. In all, there are twenty-seven chapters in the later work that are not in the earlier work.

Even where he used his earlier work, Lynch did not reproduce it slavishly in his *Reminiscences*. At times he would combine the material from two chapters in *Facts* and use it in one chapter of *Reminiscences*. In using material from the earlier work he did not hesitate to improve the style or clarify the meaning or make his point more forcefully. When he incorporated the first chapter of *Facts* into the later work, for example, he reworked several pages. Nor did he hesitate to omit material that he had used earlier. Apparently by 1937 he did not think that the final three hundred words of *Facts*, in which he praised the Republican party, were any longer appropriate; and he omitted them altogether.

Since *The Facts of Reconstruction* was largely autobiographical, Lynch properly put his earlier work to good use in *Reminiscences of an Active Life*. He was wise, however, in revising the text wherever necessary in order to reflect better perspective as well as an improved writing style. Most important, of course, is the great body of new material which not only extends the story at both ends but provides a rather full-length self-portrait of a very busy man in a most eventful period of American history.

Shortly after Lynch completed his *Reminiscences* his health began to decline. On 2 November 1939 he died in his Chicago home at the age of ninety-two. On the preceding evening he had been leafing through the manuscript of his *Reminiscences*.[70]

70. Chicago *Defender*, 4 November 1939.

Funeral services were held at Saint Thomas Episcopal Church on 4 November; and he was buried with military rites at Arlington Cemetery in Washington on 6 November.[71] The *New York Times* referred to him as "one of the most fluent and forceful speakers in politics in the seventies and eighties."[72] The *Chicago Tribune* called him "the grand old man of Chicago's Negro citizenry."[73]

JOHN HOPE FRANKLIN

71. Chicago *Defender*, 11 November 1939.
72. *New York Times*, 3 November 1939.
73. *Chicago Tribune*, 3 November 1939.

ACKNOWLEDGMENTS

Some years after the death of Mrs. Lynch in 1948, her sister, Mrs. Margaret Stewart, observed to Professor William L. Dawson, the long-time friend of Lynch, that something should be done with the manuscript of *Reminiscences*. He agreed and promised to do what he could to get the manuscript published. Later, Professor Dawson showed the manuscript to the present editor, who indicated that the manuscript was, indeed, worthy of publication. The editor is deeply grateful to Professor Dawson for bringing the manuscript to his attention and for providing intimate and valuable details regarding "the Major," as Dawson called him. He is also grateful to Mrs. Stewart for permission to publish the manuscript. Mrs. Marjorie Hawkins typed the first draft of the manuscript and Miss Margaret Fitzsimmons prepared the final copy, for which the editor is most grateful. Finally, a word of gratitude goes to Loren Schweninger, the editor's research assistant, who has been most helpful in the preparation of the editorial notes and in many other ways.

JOHN HOPE FRANKLIN

The Autobiography of
JOHN ROY LYNCH

John Roy Lynch

Preface

THE AUTHOR OF THIS WORK WAS BORN AND RAISED UPON Southern soil and is therefore imbued with some of the ideas, habits, customs, and traditions that are peculiar to the people of that section, both white and colored. He can therefore look back upon some of them with pardonable pride and satisfaction; some of them from the author's viewpoint of what should constitute a proper standard of living he cannot sanction and approve.

Involuntary servitude to which the colored people were subjected in antebellum days is, in the author's opinion, totally out of harmony with modern Christian civilization; its termination, therefore, in accordance with the advancing tide of civilization was only a question of time. Then there are some other habits and customs which do not merit, but deserve to be condemned by those who are believers in, and advocates of, a strict adherence to correct principles of modern civilization.

In antebellum days—and the same is largely true today—Southern society among the whites was divided into three separate, distinct, and to some extent antagonistic groups. The first group was composed of the large land and slave owners. That group constituted what was known and designated as Southern aristocracy. The second group was composed of professional and business men, such, for instance, as lawyers, doctors, dentists, and merchants; the third group was composed of wage earners. This group also included those designated as "poor white trash."[1]

The first group, though numerically the weakest of the three, was in all other respects the strongest and ruling class. They represented the wealth and the intelligence of that section. Their word was law. They were infallible, could do no wrong, and made no mistakes. They appropriated to themselves the most important and distinguished official positions such as cabinet ministers, foreign representatives, superior court judges, and governors of the states. Inferior offices they allowed to be held by members of the second group. There was very little of what may be called racial friction, because the blacks were under the direction, supervision, and [control] of the aristocrats. What friction existed was more economic than racial, growing out of the fact that slave labor was somewhat antagonistic to free labor, the slave workers being regarded as competitors with the white wage earners. Since the slave laborers were black and the wage earners were white, it had the appearance of racial antagonism.

The so-called race issue at the South has been largely exaggerated. This is due to the fact that it has been made a party question, as pointed out in one of the chapters of this work. After the reelection of Grant in 1872 all opposition, even on

1. The author seemed not to be aware of the fact that most of the slaveholders held only a small number of slaves. Of the 384,000 owners of slaves in 1860, some 338,000, or 88 percent, held fewer than twenty slaves. Indeed, 200,000 owners had five slaves or fewer.

the part of Southern Democrats, to the civil and political rights of the colored American was practically abandoned. But after the sweeping Democratic victories of 1874 the race question was then made the dominant issue which not only prevented influential Southern white men from coming into the Republican party but also made opposition to the participation of colored men in politics the dominant issue. This mythical race question has therefore ever since been the chief political asset of the Democratic party of that section. But it has nearly run its course and the day is not far distant when it will cease to be a political issue, and therefore what is now known as the solid South, which is the outgrowth of an illegal suppression of the popular will in that section, will be a thing of the past.

The tendencies are now all in that direction. When that time comes, as it surely will, in the near future, an appeal to race prejudice as a stepping-stone to official preferment will no longer serve that purpose. Instead of being a stepping-stone to success, it will be the reverse. It will then be seen that the so-called race issue was never based upon actual facts, but as long as the public could be made to believe that the success of one party meant the ascendancy of the white race, and the success of the other meant the ascendancy of the black race, popular sentiment tolerated the introduction of questionable methods to prevent the ascendancy of blacks over whites when in point of fact there has never been any serious apprehension along those lines. The fact will then be clearly demonstrated that there is very little if any real antagonism between the two races, even at the South.

Aside from politics the relations between the two races, even at the South, has been, and will continue to be, friendly and amicable. This has been and is still being demonstrated in a very substantial way. One of the unwritten laws of the South is that a white man's private and domestic life must never be made a subject of public discussion, nor of newspaper notoriety. Whenever that law is violated the violator jeopardizes his own life, and the one who thus takes the law in his own hands stands acquitted before the bar of public opinion. Hence a white man has nothing to lose even if he sees fit to live in concubinage with a colored woman. He is neither socially ostracized nor politically proscribed, because society draws the line only at the marriage altar. As long as the white husband is not united in marriage according to the law to the mother of his colored children he has nothing to fear.

In some sections of the South, it has been and in a large measure still is, a difficult matter for a white woman to get a husband and for a colored man to get a wife. Why? The answer is because the white man appropriates to himself the women of both races—white women for wives when needed—and for this purpose the supply is always greater than the demand, and since he cannot legally marry a colored woman, his relations with her must be one of concubinage, and for this purpose the supply is never equal to the demand. The public, however, has been largely misled with reference to these unions. The public has been made to believe that they are illicit and immoral; this is true in only a few of such cases. From a moral and religious standpoint most of them are just as pure and as moral as if the husband and wife had been united in marriage in accordance with the form prescribed by law. The husband has no other wife and the wife has no other husband, each being faithful, loyal, and true to the other. They not only live happily and contentedly together, but suitable provision is usually made by the white husband and father for the care and custody of his family after his decease. They not only see that their children are educated but they are frequently sent abroad for that purpose. And in many instances they are sent outside of the state to get suitable educational advantages—Oberlin College in Ohio being frequently used for that purpose. They not only supported their families during the lifetime of the husband and father, but made suitable provisions by will or deed for their sustenance and support after the death of the husband and father. It can be said to the credit of the Southern judiciary, as pointed out in one of the chapters of this work, that such instruments have always been sustained when attacked by the white relatives of the deceased. The result is that many of the most valuable cotton plantations at the South today are owned by colored offspring of white fathers.

The author therefore hopes that this work will be carefully read and digested by the intelligent and thoughtful American citizen, since what is herein related is based upon the author's own personal knowledge, contact, and experience and is not a commentary upon what has been written by others.

The reader cannot fail to note from what is set forth in this work that the acuteness of the so-called race issue is due to the fact that it has been injected into and made a political issue. This is being eradicated, slowly but surely. The author is of the opinion that a large majority of the colored Americans will affiliate in national elections with the Republican party when that party will again assume the championship of human rights regardless of race or color and will no longer sanction or tolerate the unwise and fatal blunder instituted under President Taft's administration. The eradication, however, of the race issue from party politics will ultimately result in the material division of the vote of the colored Americans as well as other groups of which our citizenship is composed. It is already a noticeable fact, in view of the changes above referred to, that the complexion of the colored American is no longer indicative of the party affiliation. That is as it should be.

1

His Father's Keeping

John Roy Lynch, third son of Patrick Lynch and Catherine White, was born on Tacony plantation, Concordia Parish, state of Louisiana, on 10 September 1847. Patrick Lynch was a native of Dublin, Ireland. He came to this country with his parents when he was very young. They made their home near Zanesville, in the state of Ohio, where some members of the family are still believed to be living. In company with an older brother, Edward, he went, when quite a young man, to the South, where he soon found employment as plantation manager for a wealthy planter who at that time was the owner of Tacony plantation, Concordia Parish, Louisiana, which was situated about three miles from the town of Vidalia, Louisiana, Vidalia being on the west side of the Mississippi River opposite Natchez, Mississippi.

Edward Lynch continued as far south as New Orleans,

where he made his home, having secured employment in an important capacity with one of the business firms of that city.

It was on Tacony plantation that Patrick Lynch first met Catherine White, who was destined to be his wife and the honored mother of his children. Catherine was a typical Southern beauty. She was young, handsome, attractive, and a most magnificent specimen of physical development. She was the daughter of Robert and Elizabeth White, of the state of Virginia, from which state she was brought when but a girl and sold to the wealthy planter, the owner of Tacony plantation. Her mother, Elizabeth, was evidently the daughter of a white parent on one side, and full-blooded African on the other, while her father, Robert, was unquestionably the son of a white parent on one side and mixed blood on the other. While Catherine, therefore, was identified with the colored or African race, she had enough of the blood of both races in her person to give her a beautiful, bright olive complexion which made her a commanding and attractive figure in any company.

That Patrick Lynch soon found himself a victim to her commanding presence, her charming and captivating beauty, her perfect form and winning ways, was neither strange nor unusual. In fact, his case was only one of thousands of like cases in that part of the country. She, in his opinion, honored him, in consenting to bear his name and to become the honored mother of his children.

It was not only his determination to sustain this relation to her, and that too to the exclusion of any others, but he also determined to be openly responsible for and bravely bear whatever consequences might result therefrom. He was not only willing and anxious that she should be his wife, but when his wishes and desires in that respect had been made an accomplished fact, he gave every evidence, openly and publicly, of being delighted.

He was a good liver and liberal entertainer. He frequently entertained his friends and social companions, and on each of such occasions his wife was the center of attraction. She, however, was not only identified with the colored race, but she was also a slave. She was the property of the owner of Tacony plantation. But, after she became the wife of Patrick Lynch, he decided that she should no longer be a slave.[1] But under the laws of the state, she, as well as her children, had to be the property of some white person; otherwise they could not remain in the state. All colored people, including those known to be or claimed as free, had to have, in form at least, some white person or persons to stand for them or be responsible for them in the capacity of owner.[2] It was ascertained that the only thing Lynch could do was to become, if possible, the owner by purchase, of his own family. With that end in view he opened negotiations with his employer, which finally resulted in the title to Catherine and her children passing to Patrick Lynch as their owner. Shortly after this, however, Tacony plantation passed into the hands of another owner in the person of Alfred V. Davis. Lynch was not retained as manager of the property. The cash paid by him in the purchase of his family had so depleted his means that he could not make immediate provisions for them elsewhere. He succeeded, however, in making arrangements with Davis to have them remain on Tacony until he could place them elsewhere. He then went to New Orleans to live with his brother Edward, bending his efforts to secure employment in some other place. This was in the early part of 1849.

But he had been in New Orleans only a short time before he was taken down with a fatal illness. While on his deathbed his chief concern was about his family. He informed his brother

1. Slaves could not enter into a contract, of course; and consequently Patrick Lynch and Catherine White were never married under the laws of the state of Louisiana.

2. While free Negroes were not required to have a white person vouch for them in the capacity of an owner, they had many difficulties. See Joe Gray Taylor, *Negro Slavery in Louisiana* (Baton Rouge, 1963), pp. 153–67.

that he could not afford to die until he had seen his wife once more in life and had made suitable provisions for her and her children. He stated that he had a true and loyal friend in the person of William G. Deal, who was the business manager of a plantation near Tacony. By his direction his brother wrote Deal that "Pat," though a very sick man, would be there on or about a certain day therein named. He also wrote Catherine informing her when and where to meet her husband. Against the advice of his brother and his physician, Lynch was placed on board a Mississippi River steamer and carried back to Concordia Parish and was conveyed to the home of his friend Deal. Promptly at the appointed time his loyal and faithful wife was at his bedside. She soon saw that the end was near. While he was very weak, he was able to talk and to give intelligent directions with reference to his affairs. He suggested that the children be sent to his parents in Ohio, who would take care of them and give them an education. But this did not meet with the approval of their mother. She could not bear the idea of being separated from her children, to whom she was so much devoted, unless it were done under circumstances that she was powerless to prevent.

In deference to her wishes her husband yielded that point. Only one other thing remained to be done and that was to get some friend, whose name should be substituted for his, in legal form at least, as their owner. This was agreed upon, and Deal, the true and devoted friend, was selected as the one to whom the transfer should be made. Deal was then brought into the conference and informed of what had been agreed upon and asked if he would assume the trust. He consented to do so. He assured his friend upon his deathbed that he would faithfully carry out the trust. He fully understood that the transfer to him was only a matter of legal form to comply with the law of the state in order that they might remain there. He would see to it that they were not neglected in any way, but on the contrary they would have in him a friend and protector. He would make the necessary arrangements, he said, by which Catherine would be so placed that she could work for and support herself and the children, which she was both able and willing to do. The necessary papers were then drawn up, signed, sealed, and delivered, the result of which was that the legal title to Catherine and her children, with the knowledge, sanction, and approval of Catherine, passed from Lynch to Deal. Lynch was then ready to die. He had done all for his family that it was possible for him to do. Catherine was more than pleased with what had been done. She had implicit confidence in her husband's friend Deal. She believed that he would faithfully live up to and honestly carry out and redeem the pledge made on the deathbed of his friend Lynch. Lynch lingered only a few days longer, and on the nineteenth day of April 1849, he breathed his last. His spirit ascended to the God that gave it while his body was ready to be consigned to mother earth. "Peace to his sacred ashes."

By Deal's direction, Catherine returned to Tacony plantation to remain there until further notice; not only weeks, but a month so passed without receiving any information from Deal with reference to the future of herself and children. While she was yet hopeful, she began to feel suspicious. She was apprehensive that something had happened or would happen that would not be satisfactory to her. Yet it was difficult for her to believe that her husband's true, devoted, and loyal friend, in the person of W. G. Deal, would prove false to the sacred trust which he had assumed under the circumstances and conditions related in the preceding paragraphs. Still, his long silence produced a painful apprehension which became so intense that she decided to pay Deal a personal visit. He lived only about seven miles from Tacony. To make the journey on foot was the only available way for her to reach him. So she started on the journey at an early hour in the morning, her purpose being to reach his residence about breakfast hour, or before he left his home in the discharge of his daily duty.

When she made her appearance, he professed to be not only surprised but somewhat irritated. "What has happened to cause you to come here?" he asked. "Your long silence," was the reply. Then, in a calm and deliberate tone he assured her that there was not the slightest ground for apprehension on her part. "I have seen Mr. Davis," he said, "and have made satisfactory arrangements with him under which you and your children are to remain where you now are for an indefinite period. This arrangement ought to be entirely satisfactory to you. You have nothing whatever to complain of or to be dissatisfied about. You not only have a good home that costs you nothing, but the food for yourself and children costs you nothing. This I found to be the very best arrangement it was possible for me to make, for the present at least. Go back there and make yourself satisfied. You are pleasantly and comfortably situated and surrounded by friends, and associates of long standing. Then, bear the fact in mind that I am your friend and protector. The fact that you have not seen nor heard from me since the death of 'Pat' is no evidence that you are being neglected. The sacred promise made by me to my dear and good friend 'Pat' when he was on his deathbed in that room across the hall and when you were sitting by his side with his hand in yours, shall be faithfully observed and religiously carried out. I feel that in this matter my honor is at stake. Be assured, my good friend, that this sacred trust cannot and will not be broken. Return to Tacony. Be of good cheer. Do not allow yourself to feel that there is now or can be in the future any ground for apprehension, suspicion, or doubt. I am your friend. Confide in Him and all will be well with you."[3]

While he thus spoke Catherine was so deeply impressed that she could not refrain from shedding tears. He made a deep and most profound impression upon her. She was glad she made

3. Throughout his autobiography Lynch recreates conversations such as the one between Catherine Lynch and William G. Deal. It is his method of attempting to make the situation as real as possible.

the journey, for his strong words and eloquent language had not only dispelled her fears and destroyed her apprehensions, but had given her renewed hope, faith, and encouragement. She returned to Tacony with a heart that was light and filled with joy, satisfaction, and relief. She believed all she had to do was to be patient and all would be well with her. How could she feel or believe otherwise after listening to the strong and encouraging words that had fallen from the lips of Deal?

In the course of a few weeks, Davis paid Tacony a personal visit. While there he sent for Catherine and requested that she bring her two children with her, which was done. He questioned her closely with reference to age and health, but gave no intimation about his purpose in doing so. He took each of the children in his lap for the purpose apparently of making an examination to his own satisfaction. After talking generally and pleasantly with Catherine for a short while, Davis took his departure, remarking to Catherine that he would see her again in the course of a few weeks. While this interview had, for a short while, a disquieting effect upon Catherine's mind, she would not allow herself to believe that anything was in contemplation that was not in harmony with Deal's pledge, promises, and declarations, although he had not communicated with her directly nor indirectly.

2

Into Bondage Again

In about three weeks Davis paid Tacony plantation another visit. Again he sent for Catherine, but this time she was not requested to bring her children. After talking with her pleasantly for a while, Davis broke the news to her that she and her children had been purchased by him and that they were now his property. "Great God," she exclaimed, "can that be possible?" "Yes," said Davis, "the purchase was consummated a few days ago." Catherine was completely prostrated, and broke down. After she had gained sufficient self-composure, the conversation was resumed. Davis expressed great surprise and disappointment that the news had such a depressing effect upon her. "Do you believe," he asked, "that I am such a cruel and inhuman person that you would rather belong to some one else? If so I shall endeavor to find some other person to whom you can be transferred. I do not think that I have the reputation of being cruel to my slaves, for which reason I thought you would be pleased to know that you and your children had been purchased by me. That such is not the case is a great disappointment to me."

Catherine then gave him a complete history of the case. After hearing her story, Davis remarked that it was no longer a surprise to him that she had broken down when he informed her of what had been done. "But your story," he said, "does not harmonize with that given me by Deal. He informed me that Lynch was in his debt and that you and your children had been transferred to him in payment of the obligation. The bill of sale from Lynch to Deal was drawn up in due legal form and properly witnessed. The transfer from Deal to me was free from any conditions whatever except a verbal understanding or agreement that you and your children should not, if practicable, be separated, and that you should not be sold or transferred to any one that would be likely to subject you to harsh or cruel treatment. To those conditions I did not hesitate to agree, and I shall see that they are faithfully carried out. Since I have heard your story I shall do even a better part than that by you. Neither you nor your children shall ever be subjected to the hardships incident to the life of a slave. I can see that you are considerably above the average of the ordinary slave, and your children of course will not be suited to that sort of a life, and they shall not be subjected to it. I am, as you see, a young man. I am soon to be married to one of the daughters of Frank J. Surgent, a wealthy cotton planter and slave owner of Adams County, Mississippi.[1] Our wedding trip will include a tour of Europe. We shall be gone, probably, more than a year. I shall make arrangements to have you and your children live at Natchez, Mississippi, during my absence. But you shall be allowed to hire your own time, that is, work for different people for whatever you see fit to charge or can get, and pay my

1. Alfred Vidal Davis, the son of Samuel Davis, married Miss Surgent in 1850. *Biographical and Historical Memoirs of Mississippi* (Chicago, 1891), 1:625.

agent fifty cents a day for seven days in the week, the difference between that and what you may make to be your own. In this way you can easily make enough to support yourself and your children, for my information is that you are a very fine cook. One can, as such, command a good salary. Upon my return I shall have you and your children live with me and my family—you to be one of our housemaids and your oldest boy, William, to be a dining-room servant, and the other boy, John, I shall take for my own valet. In other words, you and your children shall share in the comforts and conveniences of my own home. Neither you nor they shall ever feel or experience the hardships of plantation life. But you and your children shall enjoy the privileges and have the liberties that are unknown to the ordinary slave.

"The wonderful and remarkable story of your life, to which I have just listened with much interest, has made a deep and lasting impression upon me. If I had known before this sale took place what I know now, the probabilities are the sale would not have been consummated. If, in this transaction, wrong and injustice have been done you, or any one is guilty of treachery and bad faith, I hope you will not think that I have been a party to them, for I positively assure you that I was entirely ignorant of the facts and circumstances you have just made known to me. I assure you that you have my sympathy and friendship, and I shall do all in my power to make your future as free from sadness and sorrow as I possibly can. I shall not fail to do what I can to lessen, and, if possible, destroy the effect of this serious disappointment to which you have been subjected and of which you are a victim."

The encouraging words that fell from the lips of her new master gave Catherine a great deal of consolation and satisfaction. She accepted the situation with calmness and resignation. There was nothing else for her to do. She recognized the fact that she was powerless and helpless, but she considered herself fortunate in being at the mercy of such a just, fair, and humane man as she had every reason to believe Davis to be. To the everlasting credit of Davis, he lived up to, and faithfully carried out, every pledge and promise he made.

In this connection it may not be inappropriate to call attention to the fact that the reader may not understand the conditions which made it possible for a white man and a colored woman to publicly live together as husband and wife and raise a family of children of whom both parents were proud. Many persons labor under the erroneous impression that such unions were the exception rather than the rule and that they were simply the result of the clandestine and temporary gratification of the propensities. The truth is that in the case of the great majority of such unions, the contracting parties were actuated by the same high-toned motives and considerations by which those were actuated who belonged to the same race and that those who were not thus actuated were exceptions to the rule. As a rule the contracting parties were as faithful, loyal, and devoted to each other and to their children as they could or would have been had both been of the same race and blood. Then again, such unions were not only tolerated by public sentiment, but they had the same effect, legally, as unions between two persons of the colored or African race.

The fact must not be overlooked that, under the municipal or local law, or *lex loci,* there could be no such thing as a legal marriage between two persons of the colored or African race or between a white and colored person. Such unions were recognized and accepted as common-law marriages, although under the common law a marriage is a civil contract entered into between two persons capable of making contracts. Under the municipal law colored people could not legally become parties to a valid contract, marriage contracts not excepted, because in law they were not persons capable of making contracts. They had neither civil nor political rights. They had no voice in making or administering the laws under which they lived. They could not vote, own property, serve on juries, or testify in courts of justice. In fact they were civil and political outcasts, being on a par with animals and other personal property. In whatever states or localities they were found, they were there by sufferance and not by law—by tolerance and not by legal prerogative. So strictly were these rules adhered to and enforced, that those known as free colored people were not excepted. It was necessary for such people to have some responsible white person or persons to stand for them and be responsible in the capacity of master for their presence. While in most cases this was a mere matter of form, yet the form was a legal requirement that could not be dispensed with. It will thus be seen that under the local or municipal law there could be no legal marriages or legitimate offspring in any case where both or either party to the contract was identified with the colored or African race.[2] To remedy this state of affairs after the War of the Rebellion, as far as it was possible to do so, the Mississippi Constitutional Convention of 1869, the Reconstruction convention, inserted the following clause.[3]

> All persons who have not been married but are living together, cohabiting as husband and wife, shall be taken and held for all purposes in law as married, and their children whether born before or after the ratification of this constitution shall be legitimate.

The primary purpose of the above clause was to legalize what was known as slave marriages and to legitimize their children. The fact was soon developed, however, that it not only accomplished the purpose for which it was primarily intended, but that it also included those cases where one party was white and the other colored. In consequence of that fact, the clause was omitted by the convention that framed the constitution of 1890, in which body the Democratic party had a large major-

2. Lynch is in error. Free Negroes, despite the numerous proscriptions under which they lived, could enter into contracts, including the contract of marriage, in any of the slave states.

3. The constitutional convention to which Lynch refers met in January 1868, not 1869.

ity. But the omission could not operate retroactively. Hence, what had been accomplished under the constitution of 1869 could not be undone. It is a fact well known, by Southern people at least, that in nearly all cases in which white men were and are heads of colored families, they are not only faithful, loyal, and devoted to their families, giving them the protection and support that is due from husband and father, but they usually take the necessary steps to see that the family cannot, after his death, be deprived of whatever wealth he may have accumulated during his lifetime. In consequence of this fact some of the finest and most valuable property in every Southern state today is owned by persons of African descent who are the offspring of white fathers. It frequently happens that the property is conveyed by deed during the lifetime of the husband and father. But, whether it be done by deed or will, it can be said to the credit of the judiciary of the South, that validity of such documents are usually sustained when attacked by interested parties, as is frequently done by white relatives of the deceased. To those who are familiar with the fact, it is not at all strange to find a number of colored people in every Southern state who are not only in comfortable circumstances, but some of them are what may be called wealthy.

3

The War Came

BOTH MR. AND MRS. DAVIS HAD THE REPUTATION OF BEING kind to their slaves. For slave owners, they were reasonable, fair, and considerate. Their house servants were very much attached to them. I was a particular favorite of both Mr. and Mrs. Davis. Mrs. Davis was a devout member of the Protestant Episcopal church. It was under her tutelage and influence that I became attached to that church. I was one of a class that was to be confirmed and baptized by Bishop [William Mercer] Green on the occasion of his next visit to Natchez, which was to be made the latter part of 1861. But the war broke out in the meantime, the blockade preventing the bishop from reaching Natchez. During and for a long time after the war, I seldom attended services at an Episcopal church, but attended services quite regularly at the colored churches, which were Methodist and Baptist, there being no colored Episcopal church at Natchez.

Chapter Three

Since slavery had been abolished and I had reached a more mature age, I did not take kindly to the idea of occupying a prescribed seat in a white church. Hence I did not become connected with the church of my youth and choice until late in life. But the seed that was planted by Mrs. Davis had taken deep root and could never be eradicated or destroyed. She also organized a Sunday School class composed exclusively of colored boys. I was a member of the class and was usually at its head. No member of the class was suspected of being able to read. She gave us lessons from the catechism of the church which we were required to study, commit, and recite the following Sunday from memory. She also read interesting passages from the Bible and short stories from the lives of persons whose names figure in Bible history. One of the questions in the catechism and the answer to the same did not impress me favorably. It occurred to me that neither the question nor the answer had any business being in that book. The question was in these words: "What is the duty of a servant to his mistress and master?" The answer was, "To serve them heartily, with a good will and not with eye service." The teacher took particular pains to explain what those words meant. "An eye servant" she said, "is one that will shirk his duty every chance he can get and will not work unless an eye is kept on him. A good servant is one that will render honest and faithful service without being watched. This is what is meant by the words 'not with eye service.' " Of course we accepted the explanation with apparent satisfaction.

She also taught us to sing a number of hymns. A verse in one of them was in these words: "To serve the present age, my calling to fulfill. Oh may it all my powers engage to do my master's will." The impression the teacher endeavored to make upon our youthful minds was that the master referred to was our earthly master, in the person of her husband, Mr. Davis. Usually when this hymn was being sung, Davis would put in an appearance and join in the singing, his purpose being, of course, to illustrate in a practical way the fact of the explanation which had just been given by his wife, the teacher. While we took, of course, an entirely different view of the matter, we did not deem it safe or advisable to give expression to our opinions about it. While I was an especial favorite of both Mr. and Mrs. Davis, this seemed to be particularly true of Mrs. Davis. She would seldom, if ever, go shopping or visiting without having me occupy a seat on the carriage by the side of the driver to open and close gates on the road, and open and close the carriage door for her to get in and out. She would often have me come to her bed chamber during the day, especially when the weather was warm, and sit for hours at a time by her side and fan her and hand her ice water when thirsty. She was very fond of me and would speak of me in terms of commendation and praise when talking with friends and servants. And yet, in a way that was both harmless and innocent on my part, I incurred her ill will and displeasure and thus turned a good and true friend into a strong and bitter enemy, which came near costing me my life.

It was my duty, among others, to brush the flies from the table during meal hours. Davis, who was of a mirthful nature, would frequently bring me into the conversation at the dinner table, for the reason, no doubt, that he enjoyed what he considered my cute and intelligent answers to his questions. On one occasion Mrs. Davis stated that some of the servants had complained of not getting enough to eat. She remarked that she knew of her own personal knowledge that there was no justifiable grounds for such complaints because she gave out the food herself and therefore knew that what was thus given out was ample. Davis gave me a wink of the eye and asked: "Roy how is it with you, do you get enough to eat?" My prompt reply was in these words: "I get a plenty, such as it is, but I could eat as much more of anything that is better." Davis enjoyed this very much and laughed heartily, but his wife was very much incensed. She rebuked me sharply for what she called my insolence and threatened to get even with me in some way.

I took advantage of the first opportunity that presented itself shortly after dinner to approach her and begged her not to be displeased with me on account of the unfortunate remark that I made at the dinner table. I assured her that I was sorry I made it; that no insolence or disrespect was intended and that I would endeavor to be on my guard in the future and would not allow myself to make any remark to which she could take any exception. She relented without hesitation and as a result thereof we were as good friends thereafter as we had been in the past. But a few months later Davis again made the mistake of bringing me into the conversation at the dinner table. On this occasion the topic of conversation was "lying." Mrs. Davis remarked that she could never have any respect for a liar. No one, in her opinion, was ever justified or excused for telling a lie. In this connection she took pleasure in referring to a recent conversation she had with her sister, Mrs. Shields, who was not only a woman who was considerably advanced in years, but was the mother of a large family, some of whom were grown. In that conversation referred to, Mrs. Shields had informed her that she had never told a lie in her life.

Davis, who evidently accepted this statement with some grain of allowance, decided to bring me into the conversation. Looking me squarely in the face he quickly asked: "Roy, what do you think of that statement?" Without giving the matter serious thought I replied, "I think she told one when she said that." Of course, Davis enjoyed that very much and laughed heartily, but Mrs. Davis was so enraged and so indignant that she ordered me to leave the room immediately, remarking that she never wanted to see me or have me come about her again. But Davis, who was responsible for what had taken place, made an objection and, in consequence thereof, I was allowed to remain in the dining room until dinner was over.

Shortly after dinner I made an effort to approach her, as on the other occasion, to explain and apologize for what I had said, but the effort this time was fruitless. She not only repulsed me, but said she did not care to see me or hear anything I had to say. She therefore ordered me to leave her presence and never approach her again. She then gave positive orders that I be sent immediately to Tacony plantation and be subjected to hard plantation labor, but Davis interfered and revoked the order. Consequently I remained at Dunleith until the time came for Davis to go to the front as captain of a company of Confederate soldiers which he had raised.[1] But the only condition upon which I could remain was that I could no longer be present in the dining room during meal hours, or have anything to do with, or say to, Mrs. Davis, one way or the other. In other words, I was to keep out of her sight and away from her presence.

After Davis's company had been ordered to join the Confederate forces then operating in Virginia, Mrs. Davis decided to go with her husband. It thus became necessary for nearly all of the servants to be sent to the plantation, it being necessary for only a few to remain to take care of the property. Davis insisted that my mother and her children should be among those to remain, but Mrs. Davis drew the line on me. She insisted that I be among those to be sent to the plantation. She claimed that I was bad, mischievous, and dangerous and that, nothwithstanding my youth, if I were allowed to remain I might get bad notions and ideas in the heads of the other servants. She was so persistent and insistent that Davis at the last moment reluctantly consented and for the first time in my life I was separated from my mother and subjected to the hard and cruel fate of a plantation laborer. This was in 1862. There had just been a disastrous overflow in that part of Louisiana in

1. Alfred V. Davis was Captain of the Natchez Rifles which was a part of the Fourth Louisiana Battalion Provisional Army. *The War of the Rebellion Official Records of the Union and Confederate Armies* (Washington, 1898), ser. 1, 53: 741–42.

consequence of which that section was very unhealthy. Shortly after I was put to work I was taken with a severe attack of the swamp fever, which very nearly resulted in death, and from the effects of which I did not fully recover for more than a year.

Davis, however, did not remain very long at the front. After an absence of a few months, he and his wife returned to Dunleith. I was not among those that went back from the plantation, but remained there until the occupation of Natchez by the Union forces in July 1863. The return of Davis after such a short absence was a great surprise and disappointment to many of his friends and neighbors. But that service, brief as it was, had no doubt given him all the experience he wanted in that line. He had resigned his commission and the resignation had been accepted. He could not be forced into the service, because the Confederate Congress had passed a law exempting from military service all slave owners who owned over twenty slaves. It was said by some of his friends that his resignation was due to friction and unpleasant relations with some of his superior officers. Whether or not there was any foundation for this report the public was never informed.

After the occupation of Natchez by the Union forces I decided to make an effort to get to my mother. But getting across the Mississippi River was the serious problem that was before me. I had, of course, no money, but I had made an effort to raise some chickens. In that line I had not been very successful, for when I got ready to leave the plantation, I could claim ownership of but one chicken and that one was almost too young to command a fair price. But I took my chance and made a start for Vidalia, the little town situated on the west side of the Mississippi River opposite Natchez. When I reached Vidalia I saw for the first time a live Yankee soldier. I approached him and inquired if he wanted to buy a chicken. "What is it worth?" he asked. "Whatever you choose to give," I replied. "Very well," he said, "I will give you a dime for it." The bargain was closed and I was immediately possessed of my first piece of Yankee money, which was a ten-cent paper bill, of which, however, I had possession only a short while, for I was not long in finding the owner of a small boat, to whom I gave the ten cents to take me across the river.

When I landed on the Mississippi side of the river I was a happy lad once more. I walked to Dunleith with the expectation of meeting my mother there, but in this I was disappointed. I soon found out that she and all the other servants had left. My heart almost melted when I saw Mrs. Davis in the kitchen endeavoring to prepare something for herself, husband, and children to eat. I said nothing to her but the meeting between Davis and myself was both cordial and friendly. He said he was glad to see me and have an opportunity to talk with me because he wanted to say to me that he never regretted anything more in his life than when he yielded to his wife and her determination to have inflicted upon me what he knew was a gross wrong and a grave injustice. He referred with much feeling to the promise he had made to my mother and stated that this cruel and unjust treatment to which I had been subjected was the only instance in which he felt that he had allowed that promise to be violated. And, what made him feel it more keenly, was a knowledge of the fact that he himself was the innocent instrument through whom the injustice had been done. He said he believed my mother appreciated his kindness towards her and her children and, but for this one act in my case, he believed she would have remained with him for a while at least, during the period of his sadness, sorrow, distress, and financial disaster.

As he thus spoke, I could see that he was not only deeply affected, but his emotions were an unmistakable indication of the deep mental strain under which he was laboring, while the visible moisture of the eyes revealed the sadness and sorrow of a broken heart. A few days prior to that time he was not only in opulent circumstances, with money, property, and many slaves at his service, but he was a strong and fortunate factor politically and otherwise in the community in which he lived. His word was law and his personal presence commanded attention, reverence, and respect. Now he found himself without power, without prestige, without slaves, and almost without means. It was a sad and pitiful picture. Even my own presence brought forcibly to his mind the humiliation to which he was then subjected, for I was no longer obliged to address him or refer to him as "master," but merely as Captain or Mr. Davis. Still, my heart went out with some degree of sympathy for him.

Before we separated he requested me to say to my mother that he still had and would continue to have a friendly interest in her and that he desired very much to have her come and see him. Then, with a cordial shake of the hand and an expression of good wishes on the part of each for the other, we separated. I then went to Natchez, and after spending several hours in search of my mother, I finally succeeded in locating her. When we met the union was, of course, cordial and affectionate. I informed her of my interview with Davis and delivered the message he sent her. She said she regretted very much that she could not see her way clear to remain at Dunleith, because she was much attached to Davis, who had always treated her kindly, but that she could never forgive his wife for her cruel and inhuman treatment of me. That, she said, was the reason she had left, as soon as it was possible for her to get away. All of the other servants, it appears, had left for substantially the same reason—dislike of Mrs. Davis. Hence Davis was the unfortunate victim of the unpopularity of his wife with their former house servants.

4

Confederate Looting

BEFORE SEEKING PERMANENT EMPLOYMENT, I DECIDED TO make a brief visit to Tacony plantation, the place of my birth, where I had many good and true friends and where I had some pleasant remembrances in spite of the hardships to which I had been subjected while there.

During the time that I had worked on the plantation, I lived under the roof of "Aunt Julia Ann" and her husband "Uncle Dump," who were good and kind to me and took an especial interest in me. The cabin in which they lived was situated at the lower end of the quarters. Each cabin consisted of two rooms, with a chimney in the center, thus giving each room a fireplace. Aunt Julia Ann's family occupied one room in the last cabin situated at the extreme southern end of the quarters. This room, in point of fact, was occupied by two families, for Uncle Dump had a married son who also lived in the same room. Uncle Dump's bed was in one corner of the room, his son's bed was in another, and I slept on a cot in another corner. I was practically a member of this happy and contented family where I lived for a period of more than fifteen months.

When I returned to Tacony to pay a brief visit, I went, of course, to the cabin of Uncle Dump and Aunt Julia Ann. The son and his wife had left, but Uncle Dump and Aunt Julia Ann were still there. They were glad to see me and insisted that I remain with them at least a week. I agreed to stay three days, which I afterwards had occasion to regret, for on the night of the third day the battle of Vidalia took place. Vidalia is the little town situated on the Mississippi River opposite Natchez. During the night we were aroused by the booming of cannon, the firing of guns, and the noise of horses passing in double-quick time. We soon found out that a battle was being fought. The main body of the Confederate army was between Vidalia and Tacony. The Confederates had approached under cover of night and made a desperate attack upon the Union forces that were in possession of Vidalia. The battle continued for several hours when the Confederates were forced to retreat.

But while the fighting was going on, a part of the Confederate troops were engaged in looting the quarters of Tacony plantation. The wagons were being loaded with everything that could be found, including the wearing apparel of the laborers on the place. The young and able-bodied men and woman were being handcuffed and tied to the wagons, the purpose being to take them off as captives. Fortunately they commenced at the upper or northern end of the quarters and worked towards the lower or southern end, taking in each cabin as it was reached in its order. Aunt Julia Ann and I were the only persons in our cabin.

Just before they reached our cabin an idea occurred to me which I thought might work. I suggested to Aunt Julia Ann that she get in her bed. She at first protested but I insisted and she finally did as I had suggested. When our cabin was reached, I was sitting inside, the door being about half opened. When they reached the cabin one man threw the door open and with an oath commanded me to come outside immediately; at the same time he commanded several of his men to go inside and bring out whatever was found that would be worth taking. I got up and started toward the door, but remarked as I did so in a low tone of voice that they must be very careful about what they might carry away because a woman was confined to her bed with a very severe case of the smallpox. This was sufficient. It worked like a charm. There was not the slightest disposition to make an investigation to test the accuracy of my statement. They took it for granted that this statement was true and acted accordingly. They not only left the quarters as soon as they could and as rapidly as their teams could carry them, but they released the people they had handcuffed and tied to their wagons, and with guns pointed towards them, commanded them to unload the wagons as rapidly as possible.

Inside of ten minutes not one was to be seen in the quarters. Some of them must have communicated with the main body of the retreating army, because we could see that the retreating troops took particular pains not to come within several miles of Tacony. Of course Aunt Julia Ann did not have the smallpox. In fact she was in the enjoyment of good health. But I felt then and feel now that, under the circumstances, the occasion justified the deception.

Late in the day, after the smoke of the battle cleared away, I left Tacony en route to Vidalia and Natchez. In about a mile from Vidalia I could see marked evidences of the engagement, in the form of dead mules and horses, bullet holes in the fences and bridges, and devastation in the cotton and corn fields, but I saw no dead bodies. I had to give a good account of myself before I could cross the picket line just outside the town of Vidalia, but before dark I was happy to find myself once more in the two little rooms occupied by my mother at Natchez. My appearance was a great relief to my mother who was seriously apprehensive that I had either been killed or carried away into captivity by the Confederates.

5

Looking for Employment

THE PROBLEM OF MAKING A LIVING WAS THE ONE THAT WAS before me. I was without means and without an education. The only capital I possessed was youth, health, and a determination to win the race of life. My mother occupied two small rooms in a frame building in Market Street, which building had been converted into flats. Several other families occupied apartments in the same building. My brother had secured employment at army headquarters, as an attendant upon General W. Q. Gresham, the general in command of the Union troops there at that time. As the result of an effort covering about ten days, I finally succeeded in securing employment as a dining-room waiter in a private boarding house at a monthly salary of five dollars. This was a small salary, but I felt that I had to do something to assist my mother in her efforts to make ends meet. Rent, which was unreasonably high at that time, had to be paid promptly at the end of each month, otherwise we would be without a place to lay our heads. My mother was an excellent cook and in that capacity she frequently earned a good sum of money in the course of a month, but the employment was not continuous and permanent, hence the income from that source was uncertain and doubtful. It was absolutely necessary, therefore, that my brother and I should do something to assist in meeting the expense of the home.

My work at the boarding house was not at all satisfactory to me, hence I decided to remain there but one month; when I was paid off at the end of the first month I received four dollars instead of five, one dollar having been deducted, as I was then informed, because one or two knives and forks had disappeared, for which it was alleged I was responsible. After thinking the matter over I came to the conclusion that I was fortunate in that an amount equal to the whole month's salary had not been thus detained. I next found employment as a cook for a company of the Forty-ninth Illinois Volunteers Regiment of Infantry. No fixed sum as a salary was agreed upon. I remained there until the regiment was ordered away, which covered a period of about six weeks. When the regiment was about to leave and while bidding good-bye to the men for whom I had faithfully worked, I was made the happy recipient of the snug sum of two dollars as compensation in full for the services I had rendered. Of this I did not complain and found no fault, because I felt that I had rendered some service to a few of those who had contributed something to the salvation of the Union and the abolition of slavery.

I next found employment in the same line with a small detachment at army headquarters where I remained about three weeks, at the end of which time I was paid five dollars. Before leaving them I had secured employment as pantryman on the government transport *Altamont*, at a stipulated monthly salary of twenty-five dollars. The *Altamont*, it was thought, would remain in the Natchez harbor until the cessation of hostilities. In point of fact, it remained there until shortly after the assassination of President Lincoln. I shall never forget the distressing scenes that took place on the vessel when the news of that terrible tragedy was received. Our hearts were broken, our heads were bowed in grief, and every eye was moistened with the tear of sadness and sorrow. We all felt that the country's greatest statesman had been stricken down at the hands of a cowardly assassin and that his taking off had produced a grave and perplexing situation, the outcome of which no one could foretell or conjecture.

While Vice-President Andrew Johnson was known to be a strong Union man, he was also a Southern man, and it was feared that his sympathies and inclinations would be largely with his own section and people. Subsequent events proved that these fears were not without foundation. When the *Altamont* left Natchez, I had been on board her several months, but my salary, I am pleased to say, had been promptly paid at the end of each month. But since it was about the middle of the month when the boat left Natchez and I had decided to remain at Natchez, I was not paid, of course, for the fractional part of that month. I was informed by the captain that if I would remain until the boat reached its destination I would get every dollar that was due me, but I decided that it would probably be better for me to lose that small amount than to go so far away from home, relatives and friends; hence, I remained at Natchez. I regretted very much to sever my relations with the officers and crew, because they had been pleasant and agreeable. This was especially true of the captain, Charles D. Drake, who was a Massachusetts man, and who was one of the most accomplished and polished gentlemen it had ever been my good fortune to meet. Next to the Captain, the man that stood highest in my estimation was the clerk, Charles D. Devlin of New York. But my relations with all of the officers and crew were so pleasant that the hour of final separation was one of sadness and regret.

6

In the Photography Business

CHIEFLY THROUGH THE EFFORTS OF DR. PATRICK H. MCGRAW, who was an intimate friend of my father, I soon secured employment in the photographic establishment of Hughes and Lakin, whose business was carried on in one of the buildings owned by Dr. McGraw. I was employed merely as a messenger boy at a salary of ten dollars per month. While I faithfully discharged the duties for which I was employed, I took advantage of every opportunity to make myself familiar with every detail of the business of photography. Hughes and Lakin did their own operating, that is, made their own negatives, while an employee in the person of Robert H. Wood served as printer. I rendered such valuable assistance to Wood that I was prepared, after a period of about three months, to take his place as printer while he was promoted to take the place of one of the proprietors as an operator—that is, he was assigned to work in the operating room so that it would not be necessary for both of the proprietors to be at work at the same time.

Shortly after I had been promoted to take the place of Wood as printer, my salary was increased to fifteen dollars per month, since my work in that line gave entire satisfaction. But I was ambitious not only to be a good printer but an operator as well. In fact I was so much in love with the business of photography that I was anxious and determined to master it with the view of devoting my future life to it if necessary. It was not only pleasing to my taste, but I had confidence enough in myself to believe that I could soon make myself thorough and proficient in the knowledge of it. With the assistance of Wood, who proved to be a good and loyal friend, I soon became familiar with every detail of the operating room. I made such rapid progress in mastering the business that my proficiency in that line having been brought to the attention of N. H. Black, proprietor of another photographic establishment, I was made the recipient of an offer to work for him at a salary of twenty-five dollars per month with the promise of an increase if satisfactory services were rendered. I accepted the offer and accordingly, in the early part of 1866, I commenced work for N. H. Black as printer, another and higher-priced employee being in charge of the operating room.

Black, in the meantime, had become interested in the cotton-planting business, which occupied nearly all of his time. Raw cotton at that time was very high. Black had already made a large sum of money through speculating in the staple, in consequence of which he was so much encouraged that he decided to engage in the business of producing it. The result was that his photographic business received very little of his personal attention. Photography was a flourishing and thriving business during wartimes, but at this particular period, 1866, it began to fall off. In fact the falling off was so marked that the proprietor soon found that it was necessary to make a material reduction in expenses to prevent the establishment from running behind. He therefore decided to dispense with the services of his high-salaried operator, and he placed me in full charge of the establishment both as operator and printer at a salary of thirty-five dollars per month.

Accordingly, in the summer of 1866 the whole business was turned over to me, my receipt having been given to the proprietor for the property which was based upon a careful inventory of everything in the establishment. The proprietor, whose business as a cotton planter made it necessary for him to spend the most of his time in the country, came to the city only about once a week, sometimes once in a month. At the end of every month the books were balanced and a written statement was made, giving a detailed account of every transaction during the month, upon which a settlement was made when desired or called for by the proprietor. I was, therefore, not only operator and printer, but bookkeeper and cashier as well. In fact, I was the sole manager of the business and the only employee in the establishment. I was not only the judge of what goods and chemicals were needed to carry on the business but gave orders for the same in the name of the proprietor, paid the bills for the same when presented, as well as all other bills including my own salary and the rent, keeping a careful and accurate account of every thing and every transaction, and faithfully accounting for every dollar that passed through my hands. I frequently had from one to three hundred dollars to turn over to the proprietor as the net profits of the business for the preceding month. At no time and during no one month did the business fail to produce a net profit after all expenses had been paid.

This employment proved to be the opportunity of my life. It marked the beginning of a somewhat eventful career. As soon as I commenced work for Black, I decided to renew my efforts to acquire an education, which had been neglected during the preceding five years. But since I was obliged to be at my place of business every day, it was not possible for me to attend any other than a night school. Such a school was then being conducted by several teachers from the North. I decided to attend this school and was assigned to a class that was in charge of Mr. and Mrs. Charles M. Bingham of New York, both of whom seemed to take an especial interest in me. The school continued for about four months from the time I commenced.[1] At the end of that time I could compose and write a pretty good letter. Composition, grammar, and spelling might have been very imperfect; still it was a letter that could be read and understood. But my occupation happened to be favorable for private study. I had my books at my place of business. It frequently happened that I had time enough to devote two and, some days, as many as three hours to private study during the course of the day. Among the books that I carefully read and studied was one on parliamentary law, which I found to be of great advantage to me in after life. I also kept myself posted on the current events of the day by reading newspapers and magazines. I was especially interested in the proceedings of Congress, for it was just about that time that the bitter fight was going on between Congress and President Johnson.

I also received, in an indirect way, some valuable assistance from the white public school. My place of business was in Main Street. The white public school was across the alley in the rear of this building. I could easily hear the recitations that were going on in the school across the way. I would sometimes sit in the back room for hours and listen with close attention to what was going on in the school across the alley. I could clearly and distinctly hear the questions asked by the teacher and the responses given by the class or individual pupil. In fact, I was sometimes so much absorbed that I would imagine, for the time being, that I was a member of the class and was eager to answer

1. By May 1866, because of the bitter opposition of the whites, it was virtually impossible for Northern teachers to conduct schools for freedmen in Mississippi. "Windows were smashed, schools destroyed, and teachers threatened." Henry L. Swint, *The Northern Teacher in the South, 1862–1870* (Nashville, 1941), pp. 122–23.

some of the questions. I could also see and read the problems in arithmetic that were on the blackboard that was directly in front of where I was sitting. The knowledge and information thus obtained proved to be of great assistance to me.

I remained in charge of this important business until I was appointed to the first civil office ever held by a colored man in Mississippi (except member of the Constitutional Convention of 1868), namely, that of justice of the peace, to which I was appointed in April 1869 by General Adelbert Ames, then military governor of the state.[2] Black, the proprietor of the photographic establishment, hated to give me up. In fact, he found it impossible to find another to take my place. Hence, he closed out the business and retired.

2. Governor Ames took great pride in this appointment. He told the people of Natchez that he was pleased to have had "some agency" in the changes that had taken place in the status of Negroes in general, especially since there was "not a single colored man in office" when he became governor in 1868. "Mr. John R. Lynch, a fellow townsman of yours, I appointed Justice of the Peace. Protest after protest came from members of the Democratic Party, who now profess to be your friends, against that opportunity, with no reason except the fact that he was colored." From the "Diary of Blanche Butler Ames," quoting from a speech by Adelbert Ames, Natchez, 20 November 1870. *Chronicles from the Nineteenth Century: Family Letters of Blanche Butler Ames and Adelbert Ames* (Clinton, Mass., 1957), 2:219–20.

7

A Constitution for Mississippi

Eighteen sixty-six was an eventful year in the history of the country. A bitter war was then going on between Congress and President Andrew Johnson over the question of the reconstruction of the states lately in rebellion against the national government. The president had inaugurated a policy of his own which proved to be very unpopular at the North. He had pardoned nearly all of the leaders in the rebellion through the medium of amnesty proclamations. He appointed a provisional governor in each rebel state, under whose direction legislatures, state officers, and members of Congress had been chosen and United States senators had been elected by the legislators of the different states in accordance with the president's plan of reconstruction. To make restoration to the Union

This and several subsequent chapters of the autobiography, down to the end of chapter 44, contain some material that is similar or identical to Lynch's *Facts of Reconstruction*. For a discussion of the textual similarities and differences, see the editor's introduction, pp. xxxvii–xxxviii.

full and complete nothing remained to be done but to have the senators and representatives that had been chosen admitted to their seats.

These different [state] legislatures in the meantime had enacted laws which virtually reinslaved those that had been emancipated in their respective states. For this, the North would not stand. Sentiment in that section demanded not only justice and fair treatment for the newly emancipated race, but that their emancipation should be thorough and complete, not merely theoretical and in name only. The fact was recognized and appreciated that the colored people had been loyal to the Union and faithful to the flag of their country and that they had rendered valuable assistance in putting down the rebellion. From a standpoint of gratitude, if not justice, the sentiment of the North at that time insisted upon fair play for the colored people of the South. But the president would not yield to what was generally believed to be the dominant sentiment of the North on the question of reconstruction. He insisted that the leaders of the Republican party in Congress did not represent the true sentiment of the country. He determined, therefore, to boldly antagonize the leaders in Congress and to join issue with them and submit their differences to the bar of public opinion at the approaching congressional elections.

The issue was thus joined and the people were called upon to render judgment in the election of members of Congress in the fall of 1866. The president, with the solid support of the Democrats and a small minority of the Republicans, made a brave and gallant fight, but the result was a crushing defeat for him, and a national repudiation of his plan of reconstruction. Still, the president refused to yield. He continued the fight with Congress which finally resulted in his impeachment by the House of Representatives for high crimes and misdemeanors in office and of his trial by the Senate, sitting as a high court for that purpose. When the vote was finally taken, the president was saved from conviction and removal from office by the narrow margin of one vote—a sufficient number of Republican senators having voted with the Democrats to prevent conviction.

It was believed by many at the time that at least some of the Republican senators that voted for acquittal did so chiefly on account of their antipathy to the man that would succeed to the presidency in the event of the conviction of the president. Senator Benjamin Wade of Ohio, president pro tem of the Senate, as the law then stood, would have succeeded to the presidency in the event of a vacancy in that office from any cause. Senator Wade was an able man, but there were others who were more brilliant. He was a strong party man. He had no patience with those who claimed to be Republicans and yet refused to abide by the decision of a majority of their party organization unless the decision should be what they wanted. In short, he was an organization Republican—what has since been characterized by some as a machine man. The very sort of an active and aggressive man that would be likely to make for himself enemies in his own organization—men who were afraid of his great power and influence and jealous of him as a political rival. That some of his senatorial Republican associates would feel that the best service they could render their country would be to do all in their power to prevent such a man from being elected to the presidency was, perhaps, perfectly natural, for while they knew that he was a strong and able man, they also knew that according to his convictions of party duty and party obligations, he firmly believed that he who served his party best served his country best. In giving expression to his views and convictions, as he usually did with force and vigor, he was not always considerate of the wishes and feelings of those with whom he did not agree. That he would have given the country an able administration is the concurrent opinion of those who knew him best.

While President Johnson was retained in office, he was practically shorn of the greater part of the power and patronage that attaches to the office. This was done through the passage of a bill over the president's veto, known as the Tenure of Office Act. The constitutionality of this act, which greatly curtailed the power of the president to make removals from office, was seriously questioned at the time, but it was passed as a political necessity—to meet an unusual and unexpected emergency which seemed to threaten the peace and tranquillity of the country and to practically nullify the fruits of the victory which had been won on the field of battle. The law was repealed or materially modified as soon as President Johnson retired from office. The president also vetoed all the reconstruction bills that passed Congress, but they were promptly passed over his veto. The acts conferred suffrage on the colored man in the states that were to be reconstructed. The Johnson plan of reconstruction, which had been rejected by the country, had clearly demonstrated that there could be no halfway measures. If the colored men were not enfranchised, then the Johnson plan might as well be accepted and acquiesced in.

The Republican or Union white men at the South were not sufficient in number to make their power or influence felt. The necessities of the situation, therefore, left no alternative but the enfranchisement of the blacks. It was ascertained and acknowledged that to make possible the reconstruction of the states lately in rebellion, upon the plan which had met with the emphatic approval of the North, the enfranchisement of the blacks in the states to be reconstructed was an absolute necessity.

The first election held in Mississippi under the Reconstruction Acts took place in 1867, when delegates to a constitutional convention were elected to frame a new constitution. The Democrats decided to adopt what they declared to be a policy of "masterly inactivity"—that is, to refrain from taking any part in the election and allowing the same to go by default. The result was that the Republicans had a large majority of the delegates, only a few counties having elected Democratic delegates.[1] The only reason that there were any Democrats in the convention at all was that the party was not unanimous in the adoption of, and adherence to, the policy of "masterly inactivity." The Democratic party in a few counties in the state rejected the advice and repudiated the action of the state convention of their party on this point. The result was that a few very able men were elected to the convention as Democrats—such men, for instance, as John W. C. Watson and William M. Compton of Marshall County, and William L. Hemingway of Carroll, who was elected state treasurer by the Democrats in 1875, to whom a more extended reference will be made in a subsequent chapter.

The result of the election made it clear that if the Democratic organization in the state had adopted the course that was pursued by the members of that party in the counties by which action of their state convention was repudiated, the Democrats would have had at least a large and influential minority of the delegates and this would have resulted in the framing of a constitution that would have been much more acceptable to the members of that party than the one that was finally agreed upon by the majority members of that body. But the Democratic party in the state was then governed and controlled by the radical element, which took the position that no respectable white Democrat could afford to participate or take part in an election in which colored men were allowed to vote. To do so, they held, would not only be humiliating and wounding to the pride of the white men, but the contamination would be unwise, if not dangerous. Besides, they were firm in the belief and honest in the conviction that the country would ultimately re-

1. Those with Democratic leanings were more numerous than Lynch implies. Of the eighty-four whites in the convention of one hundred delegates, sixty-seven were native Southerners. Of these, two were listed as Democrats, eight "Conservatives," one "Anti-Radical," two "opposed to Radicals of any kind," one "Union," two "Union Conservatives," one "Constitution and Laws of the United States," two "Henry Clay Whigs," four "Old Whigs," and two "none." Vernon L. Wharton, *The Negro in Mississippi, 1865–1890* (Chapel Hill, 1947), pp. 146–47.

pudiate the congressional plan of reconstruction and that in the meantime it would be both safe and wise for them to give expression to their objection to it and abhorrence of it, by pursuing a course of "masterly inactivity." The liberal and conservative element in the party was so bitterly opposed to this course that, in spite of the action of the state convention several counties, as has been already stated, bolted the action of the convention and took part in the election.

Of the Republican membership of the Constitutional Convention, a large majority were white men, many of them being natives of the state, and a number of others, though born elsewhere, had been residents of the state for many years preceding the war of the rebellion. My own county, Adams (Natchez), in which the colored voters were largely in the majority and which was entitled to three delegates in the convention, elected two white men, E. J. Costello and Fred Parsons, and one colored man, H. P. Jacobs, a Baptist preacher.[2] This was about the proportion of white and colored men that were elected as Republicans throughout the state. This was a very great disappointment to the dominating element of the Democratic party who had hoped and expected, through their policy of "masterly inactivity" and intimidation of white men, that the convention would be composed almost exclusively of illiterate and inexperienced colored men.

Although a minor at that time, I took an active part in the local politics of my county.[3] A Republican club had been organized at Natchez of which I was an active member, and which had weekly meetings. I was frequently called upon to address the club. When the state constitution was submitted

2. Henry P. Jacobs, who learned to read and write while a slave, wrote his own pass in 1856 and escaped from Alabama to the North. He took his wife, three children, and brother-in-law with him. After a sojourn in Canada and Michigan, he went to Natchez, Mississippi, during the war and organized Baptist associations in the western part of the state. Wharton, *Negro in Mississippi*, pp. 148–49.

3. Lynch was twenty years old in 1867.

to a popular vote for ratification or rejection, I took an active part in the county campaign in advocacy of its ratification. In this election the Democratic party pursued a course that was just the opposite of that pursued by them in the election of delegates to the Constitutional Convention. They decided that it was no longer unwise and dangerous for white men to take part in an election in which colored men were allowed to participate. This was due largely to the fact that the work of the convention had been far different from and much better than they had anticipated.

The newly framed constitution was, as a whole, such an excellent document that, in all probability, it would have been ratified without serious opposition but for the fact that there was an unfortunate, unwise, and unnecessary clause in it which practically disfranchised those who had held office under the Constitution and laws of the United States or of the state and who had taken an oath to support and defend the Constitution of the United States and had afterwards supported the cause of the Confederacy. This clause caused very bitter and intense opposition to the ratification of the constitution. When the election was over it was found that the constitution had been rejected by a small majority. This result could not be accepted as an indication of the strength of the two parties in the state, for it was a well-known fact that the Republican party had a clear majority of about thirty thousand. There were several causes that contributed to the rejection of the newly framed constitution notwithstanding the large Republican majority in the state which was believed to be safe, sure, and reliable. Among them being the following:

First, in consequence of the bitterness with which the ratification of the constitution was fought on account of the clause referred to, intimidating measures were adopted in several counties in which there was a large colored vote, resulting in a loss of several thousand votes for the constitution.

Second, there were several thousand Republicans, white and

colored, but chiefly colored, who were opposed to the offensive and objectionable clause, believing the same to be unjust, unnecessary, and unwise. Hence many of that class voluntarily voted against ratification, while many others of the same refused to vote either way.

Third, there were thousands of others, the writer being one of that number, who favored ratification because the constitution as a whole was a most excellent document and because its ratification would facilitate the readmission of the state into the Union, after which the one objectionable clause could, and no doubt would, be stricken out by means of a constitutional amendment. All of those of this class favored and advocated ratification for the reasons stated, yet their known attitude towards the clause referred to proved to be a contributory cause of the rejection of the constitution.

The reader of these words may not understand why there was any colored men, especially at that time and in that section, who would have any sympathy for the white men who would have been the victims of the clause in the new constitution, had the same been ratified. But if the reader will closely follow what will be written by this writer in subsequent chapters of this work, he will find that the reasons will be given in full, clear, and unmistakable language why there was, and is, a bond of sympathy between the masses of the two races at the South, which the institution of slavery with all its horrors could not destroy, the Rebellion could not wipe out, Reconstruction could not efface, and subsequent events have not changed. The writer is aware of the fact that thousands of intelligent people are now laboring under the impression that there exists at the South a bitter feeling of racial antipathy between the two races and that this had produced a dangerous and difficult problem for the country to solve. That some things have occurred that would justify such a conclusion, especially by those who are not students upon this subject, will not be denied. But it is a fact nevertheless, which the writer hopes and believes he will be able to make clear to his readers, that those who thus believe have an erroneous conception of the situation as it existed then and as it exists now.

After the rejection of the constitution, no further effort was made to have the state readmitted into the Union until after the presidential and congressional elections of that year—1868. The Democratic party throughout the country was solid in its support of President Andrew Johnson and was bitter in its opposition to and denunciation of the congressional plan of reconstruction. For president and vice-president, respectively, the Democrats nominated ex-Governor Horatio Seymour of New York and General Frank P. Blair of Missouri upon a platform which declared the Reconstruction Acts of Congress to be unconstitutional, revolutionary, and void. The Republicans nominated for president and vice-president, respectively, General U. S. Grant of Illinois and Speaker Schuyler Colfax of Indiana upon a platform which strongly supported and endorsed the congressional plan of reconstruction.

On this issue the two parties went before the people for a decision. The Republicans were successful but not by such a decisive majority as they had in the congressional elections of 1866. In fact, if all the Southern states that took part in that election had gone Democratic, the hero of Appomattox would have been defeated. It was the Southern states that gave Republican majorities through the votes of their colored men that saved that important national election for the Republican party. To the very great surprise of the Republican leaders the party lost the important and pivotal state of New York. The immense popularity and prestige of General Grant as a brilliant and successful Union general, it was confidently believed, would save every doubtful state for the Republicans. But this expectation was not realized. The result, it is needless to say, was a keen and bitter disappointment, for no effort had been spared to bring to the attention of the voters the strong points in General Grant. A vote against Grant, it was strongly contended, was virtually a vote against the Union. It was the eloquent Frederick Douglass, who electrified many audiences in the campaign, who made the notable declaration that while Washington gave us a country, it was Grant who had saved us a country. And yet, the savior of our country failed in that election to save to the Republican party the most important state in the Union. But notwithstanding the loss of New York, the Republicans not only elected the president and vice-president, but also had a safe majority in both branches of Congress.

One of the first acts of Congress after the presidential election of 1868 was one authorizing the president to resubmit Mississippi's rejected constitution to a popular vote. The same act authorized the president to submit to a separate vote such clause or clauses of said constitution as in his judgment might be particularly objectionable or obnoxious to any considerable number of the people of the state. It was not and could not be denied that the constitution as a whole was a most admirable document. The Democrats had no serious objections to the ratification of it if the clause disfranchising most of their leaders were eliminated. When it became known that this clause would be submitted to a separate vote and that the Republican organization would not insist upon its retention, no serious opposition to the ratification of the constitution was anticipated and none was made.

The time fixed for holding the election was November 1869. In the meantime, the state was to be under military control. General Adelbert Ames was made military governor, with power to fill by appointment every civil office in the state. Shortly after General Ames took charge as military governor, the Republican club at Natchez agreed upon a slate to be submitted to the military governor for his favorable consideration, the names upon said slate being the choice of the Republican organization of the county for county and city officials. Among the names thus agreed upon was that of the Reverend H. P. Jacobs for justice of the peace. It was then decided to send a member of the club to Jackson, the state capital, to present the slate to the governor in person and to answer questions that might be asked or give any information that might be desired about any of the persons whose names appeared on the slate. It fell to my lot to be chosen for that purpose, the necessary funds being raised by the club to pay my expenses to Jackson and return. I accepted the mission contingent upon the necessary leave of absence being granted by my employer to enable me to make the trip.

Natchez, at that time, was not connected with Jackson by railroad. The only way to reach Jackson from Natchez at that time, other than over land, was by steamer from Natchez to Vicksburg or New Orleans and by rail from Vicksburg or New Orleans to Jackson. The trip, therefore, would necessarily consume the greater part of a whole week. My employer not only granted me the leave of absence for that purpose, but stated that he would remain in the city and carry on the business during my absence. He was what was known as a Northern man, having come there after the occupation of the place by the federal troops. While he took no part in politics, I was satisfied that his sympathies were with the Republicans. I then proceeded on my mission.

When I arrived at the building occupied by the governor and sent up my card, I had to wait only a few minutes before I was admitted to his office. The governor received me cordially and treated me with marked courtesy and the most respectful consideration. He gave close attention while I presented as forcibly as I could the merits and qualifications of the different persons whose names appeared on the slate that I placed in his hands. When I concluded my remarks, the governor's only reply was that he would give the matter his early and careful consideration.

When the appointments were announced a few weeks later, the names of very few of those on the slate that I had presented were among them. My own name had been substituted for Jacobs for the office of justice of the peace. To me this was a source of much embarrassment. I not only had no ambition in that direction, but was not aware that my name was under consideration or had been suggested or thought of for that or any other office. Besides, I was apprehensive that Jacobs and some of his friends might suspect and accuse me of having been false to the trust that had been reposed in me, at least so far as the office of justice of the peace was concerned. I was strongly inclined to the opinion at first that the only way in which I could disabuse their minds of that erroneous impression was to decline the appointment. But I found out upon inquiry that in no event would Jacobs receive the appointment. I was also reliably informed that I had not been recommended or suggested by any one, but that the governor's action was the result of the favorable impression I had made upon him when I presented the slate referred to. For this, of course, I was in no way responsible. In fact, the impression that my brief talk made upon the governor with reference to my own fitness and qualifications was just what the club hoped I would be able to accomplish with reference to the slate as a whole. That it so happened that I was the personal beneficiary of the favorable impression that my brief talk made upon the governor may have been in one respect fortunate, but it was one for which neither the governor nor the one by whom the favorable impression was made could be justly censured. After consulting with a few personal friends and local party leaders, I decided to accept the appointment, although in consequence of my youth and inexperience I had serious doubts of my ability to discharge the duties of the office which, at that time, was one of considerable importance.

Then the bond question loomed up, which was one of the greatest obstacles in my way, although the amount was only two thousand dollars. How and in what way to give that bond was the grave and important problem I had to solve. It was the first time in the history of the state that a colored man had been commissioned to fill such an office. No one was eligible as a bondsman who was not an owner of real estate. There were very few colored men at that time who were thus eligible, and it was out of the question to expect any white property owner to sign the bond of a colored man at that time. But there were two colored men who were willing to sign the bond for one thousand dollars each who were found by the authorities to be qualified and eligible for that purpose. They were William McCary and David Singleton.[4] The bond having been duly made according to law, I took the oath of office and entered upon the discharge of my duties as a justice of the peace in April 1869, which position I held until the thirty-first of December of the same year when I resigned to accept a seat in the lower branch of the state legislature to which I had been elected the preceding November. When I entered upon the discharge of my duties as a justice of the peace, the only comment that was made by the local Democratic paper of the town was in these words, "We are now beginning to reap the ravishing fruits of reconstruction."

4. William McCary was a Natchez free Negro whose father conducted a successful barber shop for whites and served as a private tutor for free Negro children. McCary, himself quite literate, was a property owner and taxpayer. One can assume that Singleton was also a property owner. John R. Lynch, *Some Historical Errors of James Ford Rhodes* (Boston, 1922), pp. 17–18. See also, Edwin Adams Davis and William Ransom Hogan, *The Barber of Natchez* (Baton Rouge, 1954), pp. 243–46.

8

Justice of the Peace

As a justice of the peace I had a number of peculiar experiences. The appointment, in the first place, was looked upon by many as an experiment, which was largely true. In consequence of my youth and inexperience, I had, at first, serious doubts of my own ability to discharge the duties of the office creditably and acceptably, but I accepted the position with a determination to fill it, if possible, with credit to myself and satisfaction to the public. With that end in view, I took advantage of every spare moment to read and study, not only the manual, but the code and statutes defining the duties of justice of the peace. I had been in the office only a few days when, to my agreeable surprise, I was made the recipient of a justice manual, which was sent to me by the widow of a gentleman who had at one time occupied the same position. This good and kind lady not only sent me the book, but she wrote me a note in which she congratulated me upon my appointment and expressed the hope that I would find the book to be of some service to me and that my administration of the office would be such that the white people of the county would have no occasion to regret that I had been appointed to the position. I was thus so favorably impressed that I was made to feel that I was not without friends and well-wishers among the white people of the community.

Another evidence of goodwill and friendship on the part of the white people of the community was the tendering by a white man, who had had considerable experience in that line, of his assistance and services for a nominal consideration and for a limited period, which I gladly accepted. This gentleman remained with me for about ten days, during which time he drew up the affidavits and prepared all other papers and documents that I was called upon or required to prepare and issue in the discharge of the duties of the position. Without his valuable assistance I would have been at first somewhat embarrassed and of course placed at a considerable disadvantage. He remained with me until I had become sufficiently familiar with all forms to be able to prepare all of them myself without assistance or suggestions from anyone else.

The duties of the office I soon found out to be much more important than I at first supposed they were. A justice of the peace at that time had original jurisdiction in all civil cases where the amount in controversy did not exceed three hundred dollars. In criminal cases he had jurisdiction concurrent with the county court in all cases below the grade of felony, and in felonious and capital cases he could sit as a committing magistrate, examine the witnesses, and decide whether or not the testimony was sufficient to bind the accused over to the next grand jury, with or without bail, to fix the amount and accept or reject such bondsmen as might be offered. If, in his opinion, the testimony was not sufficient to justify holding the accused over to the next grand jury, or if, in his opinion, the testimony established the fact that the act was committed in self-defense or from any other reason was justifiable, he could discharge the accused from further custody. While his decision was not final and therefore not a bar to further action by a higher court, it had, nevertheless, an important bearing upon any subsequent action that might be taken.

To have a young and inexperienced colored man placed in charge of such an important office was looked upon by many, even of his warmest personal friends, with serious misgivings. But after several months had passed these misgivings had entirely disappeared. I soon found out that many of both races had an erroneous and exaggerated idea about the office. While some of the whites looked upon it with an apprehension that the facts did not warrant, some of the blacks on the other hand magnified it far beyond its importance. Some of them were determined to take advantage of the smallest and most unimportant offense to "come to law." To them this was something that was entirely new, and they were anxious to avail themselves of such a glorious privilege. And then, some of them believed that because a colored man was in charge of the office they would have a better standing in court than they otherwise would. It did not require very much time for me to take in the situation and decide upon a course of action that would avoid and prevent friction.

Frequent complaints were made to me by colored servants alleging maltreatment by the white employer. In nearly every case the complaining party was the female cook or housemaid, while the party complained of was the white female head of the house. Instead of issuing a warrant for the arrest of the accused in all such cases, I would write a note to the male head of the house, who was usually engaged in business in the city, informing him of what had been alleged and suggesting that he take the necessary steps to prevent further action in the case. This note I would sometimes send by the complaining party, and other times by the office constable. In every case it had the desired effect. The matter was always adjusted in a way satisfactory to all concerned. These men would either write me or thank me in person when they would meet me on the street for the courtesy and consideration thus shown. It was principally for that reason that they regretted to have me retire from the office.

There was one case, however, in which the complaining party was the colored female cook and the party complained of was the male head of the family. The personal appearance of the complaining party gave evidence of the fact that her statements were not wholly groundless. In that case the warrant was issued and the defendant was brought before the court, tried, and convicted. But since it was the first offense the fine imposed was very light—five dollars and costs, which the defendant promptly paid. About ten days later the defendant was again brought before the court, the complaining party being the same as in the first case. This time he had committed an assault and battery in a more aggravated form than on the first occasion. When the charge was read to him and he was asked to state whether or not he was guilty as charged, he put his head close to mine and asked in a low tone of voice how much the fine would be if he should plead guilty as charged. The answer was that the court could enter into no agreement with him about the case—that he was either guilty or not guilty. If he should plead not guilty we would proceed to trial. If he should plead guilty the court would then determine what the fine should be. "Well," he said, "I guess I will run risk. I am guilty." "Very well," said the court. "Since this is the second offense a fine of ten dollars is imposed and in default of payment the defendant will be confined in the county jail for a period of five days." "Do what?" he exclaimed. "Ten dollars and costs? Then I withdraw the plea. I am not guilty ten dollars worth. Do you want to take all of my money?" He was informed that the court had rendered its decision and that he must govern himself accordingly. With much reluctance and after much protesting, he paid the fine and costs and departed.

It was the last time I had him before me while I remained in charge of the office.

Another case of some significance that came before me was that of a white man that I knew unfavorably and well. He had cursed, abused, and threatened the life of an innocent and inoffensive old colored man on account of a misunderstanding over a small business transaction. Upon the complaint of the colored man, a warrant was issued for the arrest of the party against whom the complaint was made. When he was brought before the court and the charges had been read to him and he was asked whether or not he was guilty as charged, he seemed to be somewhat surprised. "Why," he remarked, "do you mean to tell me that it is a crime for a white man to curse a nigger?" "Yes," the court replied. "It is as much a crime for a white man to curse a Negro as it is for a Negro to curse a white man." "Well!" he exclaimed, "that's news to me. You certainly must be mistaken. If there is such a law I have never heard of it." The court then handed him the code and told him where he could find the section bearing upon the point at issue and requested him to read it for himself, which he did.

When he had finished, he exclaimed in a somewhat subdued tone: "Well I'll be damned." The court then admonished him that if that remark should be repeated he would be committed to the county jail for contempt of court. He quickly apologized and assured the court that no disrespect was intended. He said he could not deny having used the language set forth in the affidavit, but he hoped the court would not be severe because he did not know and did not believe that in using that language he was violating any law. Since it was his first offense he was let off with a fine of five dollars and costs which he promptly paid. It was the first and only time that he was brought before me.

I was frequently called on to perform the rites of matrimony. In the performance of that duty I used the Episcopal prayer book, and following the forms therein prescribed, I usually also delivered a brief lecture to the contracting parties before performing the ceremony, so as to impress them with the importance and sacredness of the relation upon which they were about to enter. On one occasion a couple came before me who impressed me very much. In point of intelligence and personal appearance they were considerably above the average. The bride was particularly attractive and the bridegroom was by no means homely. On that occasion and with that couple I endeavored to make the lecture and the ceremony much more impressive than usual. When the ceremony was over and they had received my congratulations and best wishes for their future happiness, the couple left, apparently happy and very much delighted. In about ten days from that time the bride, very much to my surprise, made her appearance in my office and informed me that her husband had not lived up to the promises made by him when they were united in marriage. She gave me the particulars wherein he had been faithless. When she had concluded her statement I told her to return to her home, which was about ten miles in the country, and tell her husband that I wanted both of them to appear at my office at 9:00 that next morning without fail.

Of course, I had no idea that he would come, but, to my surprise, I found both of them sitting on the steps of my office when I arrived there the next morning. I immediately invited them in, and addressing the young man I asked, "What is this I hear about you?" He arose and began to make an explanatory statement, but I concluded to hear from the bride first. Her statement and recitals were clear and to the point and she seemed to be prepared to substantiate every allegation she made. When she had finished the bridegroom was then called on to make his statement in reply. He frankly confessed that he was guilty of every charge made against him by his wife and threw himself upon the mercy of the court. He faithfully promised that if the court would let him off this time and give him one more chance his wife would never again have occasion to complain of him. The court informed him that his request would be granted but remarked: "Should it become necessary for you to be brought here again, no mercy will be shown, but you will suffer the full penalty of the law." He thanked the court very much for its consideration and mercy, and gave positive assurance that his wife would never again have occasion to complain of him.

They left my office, both laboring under the impression, no doubt, that I had the power and authority to sentence the young man to serve a term in the penitentiary upon the verbal complaint of his wife that he had not lived up to his marriage vows. Of course, I could do nothing of the sort, but it was a case in which I thought it was best for all concerned to let them labor under that impression. A few weeks later I met the bride on the street and asked her how she and her husband were getting along. "Splendidly," she replied. "He is now acting all right. I now have no cause to complain of him and I am of the opinion that I shall have none in the future."

1869: State Elections and Reorganization

EIGHTEEN SIXTY-NINE WAS AN IMPORTANT YEAR IN THE POlitical history of the state. The new constitution which was rejected in 1868 was to be resubmitted to a popular vote in November. At the same time state officers, members of the legislature, congressmen, district and county officers were to be elected. Since the objectionable clauses in the constitution were to be submitted to a separate vote and since it was understood that both parties would favor their rejection, there was no serious opposition to the ratification of the constitution as thus amended. But a hard and stubborn fight was to be made for control of state government.

General James L. Alcorn, who had been a general in the Confederate army and who had recently openly and publicly identified himself with the Republican party, was nominated by the Republicans for the office of governor. Of the other six men who were associated with him on the state ticket, only one, the Reverend James Lynch, an able and eloquent minister of the Methodist church, was a colored man.[1] He was the candidate for secretary of state. He was a man of fine ability, splendidly educated, and one of the most powerful and convincing orators the Republicans had upon the stump in that campaign. He was known and recognized as such an able and brilliant speaker that his services were in great demand from the beginning to the end of the campaign. No Democratic orator, however able, was anxious to meet him in joint debate. He died suddenly in the latter part of 1872.[2] His death was a great loss to the state and to the Republican party and especially to the colored race.

Of the other five candidates on the ticket, two, the candidates for state treasurer and attorney general, were, like General Alcorn, Southern white men. The candidate for state treasurer, Hon. W. H. Vasser, was a strong and successful businessman who lived in the northern part of the state, while the candidate for attorney general was an able and brilliant member of the bar, who lived in the southern part of the state in the person of Hon. Joshua S. Morris. The other three candidates for lieutenant governor, for state auditor, and for state superintendent of education, were Northern men who had settled in the state after the war, called by the Democrats "carpetbaggers." But they were admitted to be clean and good men who had lived in the state long enough to become fully identified with its industrial and business interests.

R. C. Powers, the candidate for lieutenant governor, and H. Musgrove, the candidate for Auditor of Public Accounts, were successful cotton planters in Noxubee and Clarke counties, respectively, while H. R. Pease, the candidate for state

1. James D. Lynch was an able and highly educated Pennsylvania free Negro who went to Mississippi in 1868 to take charge of the activities of the Methodist Episcopal church in the state. Wharton, *Negro in Mississippi*, p. 154.

2. He died in February 1875, not 1872. Wharton, *Negro in Mississippi*, p. 155.

superintendent of education, had been identified with educational work ever since he came to the state.[3] It could not be denied that it was a strong and able ticket—one that Democrats would find it very difficult to defeat. In their desperation the Democrats nominated as their candidate for the office of governor a brother-in-law of President Grant in the person of Judge Lewis Dent, with the hope that the president would throw the weight of his influence and the active support of his administration on the side of his relative, as against the candidate of his own party, especially in view of the fact that Dent had been nominated, not as a Democrat, but as an Independent Republican, his candidacy simply having been endorsed by the Democratic organization. But in this they were disappointed. If the president gave any indication of a preference it was in favor of the Republican ticket. General Ames, for instance, was the military governor of the state, holding that position at the pleasure of the president. Ames was outspoken in his support of the Republican ticket. In fact, he briefly addressed the State Republican Convention that nominated General Alcorn for the governorship, in which he declared "you have my sympathy, and shall have my support."

This declaration was received by the convention with great applause, for it was known that those words carried great weight. They not only meant that the Republican party would have, in that campaign, the active and aggressive support of the military governor, which was very important and would be worth thousands of votes to the party, but they also indicated the attitude of the national administration. The campaign was

3. Powers, a graduate of the University of Michigan, was from Youngstown, Ohio (*Biographical and Historical Memoirs of Mississippi*, 2:612–13). Musgrove was an ex-Union soldier from Illinois (James W. Garner, *Reconstruction in Mississippi* [New York, 1901], p. 243). Pease, an ex-captain in the Union army, went to Mississippi in 1867 from his native Connecticut and served as superintendent of the Freedmen's Bureau Schools before becoming active in state politics (Swint, *Northern Teacher in the South*, pp. 127–28 and George Bentley, *A History of the Freedmen's Bureau* [Philadelphia, 1955], pp. 174, 192).

aggressive from beginning to end. Judge Dent was at a great disadvantage, since his candidacy had failed to bring to his support the influence of the national administration, that being the chief, if not the sole, purpose for which he was nominated. In spite of that fact, he made a game and gallant fight, but the election resulted in a sweeping Republican victory. That party not only elected the state ticket by a majority of about thirty thousand, but also had a large majority in both branches of the state legislature.

The new administration had an important and difficult task before it. A state government had to be organized from top to bottom. A new judiciary had to be inaugurated, consisting of three justices of the state supreme court, fifteen judges of the circuit court, and twenty chancery court judges, all of whom had to be appointed by the governor, by and with the advice and consent of the [state] senate. In addition to this, a new public school system had to be organized and established. There was not a public school building anywhere in the state except in a few of the larger towns, and they, with possibly a few exceptions, were greatly in need of repair. To erect the necessary schoolhouses and to reconstruct and repair those already in existence so as to afford educational facilities for both races was by no means an easy task. It necessitated a very large outlay of cash in the beginning which resulted in a material increase in the rate of taxation for the time being, but the constitution called for the establishment of the system and, of course, the work had to be done. It was not only done, but it was done creditably and as economically as circumstances and conditions at that time made possible. That system, though slightly changed, still stands as a creditable monument to the work of the first Republican state administration that was organized in the state of Mississippi under the Reconstruction Acts of Congress.

It was also necessary to reorganize, reconstruct, and in many instances, rebuild some of the penal, charitable, and other public institutions of the state. A new code of laws also had to be adopted to take the place of the old one, and thus wipe out the black laws that had been passed by what was known as the Johnson legislature. Also it was necessary to change the statutes of the state to harmonize with the new order of things. This was no easy task, especially in view of the fact that a heavy increase in the rate of taxation was thus made necessary. That this great and important work was splendidly, creditably, and economically done, no fair-minded person who is familiar with the facts will question or dispute.

That the state never had before, and has never had since, a finer judiciary than that which was organized under the administration of Governor Alcorn and continued under the administration of Governor Ames, is an indisputable and incontrovertible fact. The judges of the supreme court were E. G. Peyton, H. F. Simrall and J. Tarbell, who, as lawyers, had no superiors in the state. They had the respect and confidence of the bar and people of the state without regard to race or politics. Judge Peyton was the chief justice, Simrall and Tarbell being the associate justices. The first two were old residents of the state, while Mr. Justice Tarbell was what the Democrats would call a "carpetbagger," but that he was an able lawyer and a man and judge of unimpeachable integrity, no one doubted or questioned. During the second administration of President Grant, he held the important position of Second Comptroller of the United States Treasury. The circuit court bench was graced with such able and brilliant lawyers as Jason Niles, G. C. Chandler, George F. Brown, J. A. Orr, John W. Vance, Robert Leachman, B. B. Boone, Orlando Davis, James M. Smiley, Uriah Millsaps, William M. Hancock, E. S. Fisher, C. C. Shackleford, W. B. Cunningham, W. D. Bradford and A. Alderson. Judges Brown and Cunningham were the only ones in the above list who were not old residents of the state. After leaving the bench Judge Chandler served for several years as United States attorney. Judge Niles served one term as a member of Congress, having been elected as a Republican in 1875. His son, Henry Clay Niles, was United States district judge for the state, having been appointed to that important position by President Harrison. He was strongly recommended by many members of the bench and bar of the state by whom he was well and favorably known. The very able and creditable way in which he discharged the duties of the position has more than demonstrated the wisdom of the selection.

The chancery courts as organized by Governor Alcorn and continued by Governor Ames were composed of men no less able and brilliant than those who composed the bench of the circuit courts. They were J. C. Lyon, E. P. Harmon, E. G. Peyton, Jr., J. M. Ellis, G. S. McMillan, Samuel Young, W. G. Henderson, Edwin Hill, T. R. Gowan, J. F. Simmons, Wesley Drane, D. W. Walker, DeWitte Stearns, D. P. Coffee, E. W. Cabiness, A. E. Reynolds, Thomas Christian, Austin Pollard, J. J. Hooker, O. H. Whitfield, E. Stafford, W. A. Drennan, Thomas Walton, E. H. Osgood, C. A. Sullivan, Hiram Cassidy, Jr., W. B. Peyton, J. D. Barton, J. J. Dennis, W. D. Frazee, P. P. Bailey, L. C. Abbott, H. W. Warren, R. Boyd, R. B. Stone, William Brack, J. N. Campbell, H. R. Ware and J. B. Deason. The above members compose those who were appointed both by Governors Alcorn and Ames. A majority of those originally appointed by Governor Alcorn were reappointed by Governor Ames. Of the forty persons appointed as judges of the chancery court under the administration of Alcorn and Ames, not more than about seven were not to "the manor born." The administration of James L. Alcorn as governor of the state of Mississippi is one of the best with which that unfortunate state has ever been blessed. A more extended reference to the subsequent administrations of Governor Ames will be made in a following chapter.

10

Electing a Legislature

ALTHOUGH IT WAS NOT INTIMATED OR CHARGED THAT MY APpointment to, and acceptance of, the office of justice of the peace was the result of bad faith on my part, still the appointment resulted in creating, for the time being, two factions in the Republican party in the county. One was known as the Lynch faction and the other the Jacobs faction.

When the constitution was submitted to a popular vote in November 1869, it was provided that there should be elected at the same time all officers provided for, or created by, the constitution, and [that they] were to be chosen by popular vote, including members of the legislature. The county of Adams—Natchez—was entitled to one member of the state senate and three members of the house of representatives. Jacobs was a candidate for the Republican nomination for state senator. For that position the Lynch faction refused to support him, but it had no objection to his nomination for member of the

House. Since Jacobs persisted in his candidacy for state senator the Lynch faction brought out an opposing candidate in the person of a Baptist minister by the name of J. M. P. Williams. The contest between them was interesting and exciting, though not bitter, and turned out to be very close.

The convention was to be composed of thirty-three delegates, seventeen being necessary to nominate. The result at the primary election of delegates to the convention was so close and doubtful that it was impossible to tell which one, if either, had a majority, since there were several delegates about whose attitude and preference there was some doubt—who refused to commit themselves either way. In the organization of the convention the Williams men gained the first advantage, one of their number having been made the temporary, and afterwards, permanent chairman. But this was not important since there were no contests for seats; consequently the presiding officer would have no occasion to render a decision that could have any bearing upon the composition of the body over which he presided.

Both sides agreed that the nomination for state senator should be made first and that the vote should be by ballot, the ballots to be received and counted by two tellers, one to be selected by each side. When the result of the first ballot was announced, Jacobs had sixteen, Williams sixteen, and a third party had one. Several ballots were taken with the same result, when with consent of both sides a recess was taken until 3 in the afternoon. The one delegate that refused to vote for either Jacobs or Williams made no effort to conceal his identity. On the contrary, he was outspoken in his determination and decision that he would not at any time or under any circumstances vote for either. Strange to say this man was also a colored Baptist preacher, in the person of the Reverend Noah Buchanan, from the Washington district. Members from both sides approached him, but their efforts and pleadings were all in vain. Nothing could move him or change him. He stated that he had given the matter his careful attention and serious consideration and, as a result thereof, he had come to the conclusion that neither Jacobs nor Williams was a fit and suitable man to represent the important county of Adams in the state senate. Hence neither could get his vote. At the afternoon session several ballots were taken with the same result, when an adjournment was taken until 9 the next morning.

Soon after the adjournment each side went into caucus. At the Jacobs meeting it was decided to stick to their man to the very last. At the Williams meeting Hon. H. C. Griffin, white leader of the Williams men, suggested the name of Reverend H. R. Revels as a compromise candidate. Revels was comparatively new in the community. He had recently been stationed at Natchez as Pastor in charge of the A.M.E. church. So far as was known he had never voted, had never attended a political meeting, and of course had never made a political speech. But he was a colored man and therefore presumed to be a Republican. Then, he was believed to be a man of ability and considerably above the average in point of intelligence—just the man, it was thought, that Reverend Noah Buchanan would be willing to vote for.[1]

After considerable discussion, it was agreed that a committee should be appointed to wait on, and consult, first Mr. Williams to find out if he would be willing to withdraw in favor of Revels should his friends and supporters deem such a step necessary and wise. If Williams was willing the committee was next to call on Revels to find out if he would consent to the use of his name. If Revels was willing the committee should next call on Reverend Buchanan to find out whether or not he

1. Revels, a North Carolina free Negro, was a graduate of Knox College. Before the war he was active in the ministry of the Methodist Episcopal church and later the African Methodist Episcopal church. During the war he taught in a school in Saint Louis and assisted the provost marshal at Vicksburg in managing the affairs of the freedmen. William J. Simmons, *Men of Mark, Eminent, Progressive and Rising* (Cleveland, 1887), pp. 948–50.

would vote for Revels. This committee was to report to the caucus at 8 the next morning.

At the appointed time the committee was ready to start. The report was that Williams had stated that he was in the hands of his friends and that he would acquiesce in, and abide by, the decision they might find it necessary to make. Revels, the report stated, was taken very much by surprise. He had no idea that his name would ever be thought of or mentioned in connection with that or any other office. He asked to be allowed until 7 in the morning to consider the matter and talk it over with his wife. At 7 he notified the chairman of the committee that he would accept the nomination if tendered. Buchanan had informed the committee that he had heard of Revels, but did not know him personally. He too had asked to be allowed until 7 in the morning before giving a positive answer, so as to enable him to make the necessary inquiries to find out whether or not Revels was a fit and suitable man for the position. At 7 he informed the chairman of the committee that if the name of Williams should be withdrawn in favor of Revels he would cast his vote for Revels. The caucus then decided by a unanimous vote that upon the assembling of the convention at 9 that morning Mr. Griffin should withdraw the name of Williams from before the convention as a candidate for state senator, but that no other name should be placed in nomination. Every member of the caucus, however, was committed to vote for Revels. This decision was to be communicated to no one outside of the caucus except Mr. Buchanan, who was to be privately informed of it by the chairman of the committee, to whom he had communicated his own decision.

As soon as the convention was called to order Mr. Griffin was recognized by the chair. He stated that he had been requested and authorized to withdraw the name of Reverend J. M. P. Williams from before the convention as a candidate for the state senate. This announcement was received by the Jacobs men with great applause. The withdrawal of the name of Williams without placing any other in nomination they accepted as evidence that further opposition to the nomination of their candidate had been abandoned and that his nomination was now a foregone conclusion. But they were not allowed to labor under that impression very long. The roll call was immediately ordered by the chair and the tellers took their places.

When the roll was finished and the ballots had been counted and tabulated the result was seventeen for Revels and sixteen for Jacobs. The announcement was received by the Williams men with great applause. The result was a victory for them because it was their sixteen votes with the vote of Reverend Noah Buchanan that had nominated Revels. The Jacobs men accepted their defeat gracefully. The motion to make the nomination unanimous was made by their leader and was adopted without a dissenting vote. In anticipation of his nomination Revels was present as one of the interested spectators in the audience. He was called upon for a brief address which he delivered with telling effect. He made a most favorable impression. The Reverend Noah Buchanan was then satisfied that he had made no mistake in voting for Revels. Jacobs was then nominated for member of the house of representatives without opposition, his associates being John R. Lynch and Captain O. C. French, a white Republican. The ticket, as completed, was elected by a majority of from fifteen hundred to two thousand, a Republican nomination in Adams County at that time being equivalent to an election.

When the legislature convened at Jackson the first Monday in January 1870, it was suggested to Lieutenant Governor Powers, presiding officer of the senate, that he invite the Reverend Dr. Revels to open the senate with a prayer. The suggestion was favorably acted upon. That prayer made Revels a United States senator. He made a deep and profound impression upon all who heard him. It was one of the most impressive and eloquent prayers that had ever been delivered in the senate chamber. It impressed those who heard it that Revels was not only a man of great natural ability, but that he was also a man of superior attainments.

The duty devolved upon that legislature to fill three vacancies in the United States Senate. One, a fractional term of about one year, the remainder of the six year term of which Jefferson Davis had been elected before the breaking out of the war of the rebellion. One, a fractional term of about five years and the other the full term of six years, beginning with the expiration of the fractional term of one year. The colored members of the legislature constituted a very small minority not only of the total membership of the body, but also of the Republican members. Of the 33 members of which the senate was composed, 4 of them were colored men: H. R. Revels of Adams, Charles Colwell [*sic*] of Hinds, Robert Gleed of Lowndes, and T. W. Stringer of Warren.[2]

Of the 107 members of which the House was composed, about 30 of them were colored men. It will thus be seen that out of 140 members of which the two houses were composed only about 34 of them were colored men. But the colored members insisted that of the three United States senators to be elected one should be a colored man. The white Republicans were willing that the colored man be given the fractional term of one year, since it was understood that Governor Alcorn was to be elected to the full term of six years and that Governor Ames was to be elected to the fractional term of five years.

2. There were actually five Negro members of the senate. Lynch omitted the name of William Gray, a young Baptist minister from Greenville. Charles Caldwell of Hinds County had been a slave before the war and was trained as a blacksmith and was a member of the Constitutional Convention of 1868. Herbert Aptheker, "Mississippi Reconstruction and the Negro Leader, Charles Caldwell," in *To Be Free: Studies in American Negro History* (New York, 1948), pp. 163, 170–71. Gleed had been a slave until the close of the war. He had a fair education and was an excellent speaker who lectured to Negroes on educational and agricultural matters. Stringer, a former resident of Ohio, went to Mississippi as a minister in the African Methodist Episcopal church. At the convention of 1868 he was one of the most influential members. Wharton, *Negro in Mississippi*, pp. 173, 148–49.

In this connection it may not be out of place to say that ever since the organization of the Republican party in Mississippi, the white Republicans of that state, unlike some in a few of the other Southern states, have never attempted to draw the color line against their colored friends and allies.[3] In this way they proved themselves to be genuine and not sham Republicans. They have shown that they are Republicans from principle and conviction and not for plunder and spoils. They have never failed to recognize the fact that the fundamental principle and doctrine of the Republican party, the one that gave the party its strongest claim upon the confidence and support of the public, is its advocacy of equal civil and political rights and manhood suffrage. If that party should ever reach the point or come to the conclusion that this principle and doctrine should be abandoned, that moment it will merit, and I am sure will receive, the condemnation and repudiation of the public.

It was not, therefore, a surprise to any one when the white Republican members of the Mississippi legislature gave expression to their entire willingness to vote for a suitable colored man to represent in part the state of Mississippi in the highest and most dignified legislative tribunal in the world. The next step was to find the man. The name of the Reverend James Lynch was first suggested. That he was a fit and suitable man for the position could not be denied. But he had just been elected secretary of state for a term of four years. His election to the Senate, therefore, would create a vacancy in the office to which he had just been elected, which would have necessitated the holding of another state election, which all were anxious to avoid. For that reason his name was not seriously considered for the senatorship.

The next name suggested was that of Reverend H. R. Revels.

3. The white Republicans of Mississippi were unwilling, however, to consider a Negro senatorial candidate for more than the fractional term of one year, while reserving for white Republicans the full term of six years and the fractional term of five years.

Those who were so fortunate as to have heard his able, eloquent, and impressive prayer that was delivered on the opening day of the Senate were outspoken in their advocacy of his selection. The white Republicans assured the colored members that if they would unite upon Revels, they were satisfied that he would receive the vote of every white Republican member of the legislature. Governor Alcorn also gave the movement his cordial and active support, thus assuring for Revels the support of the state administration. The colored members then held an informal conference at which it was unanimously decided to present the name of the Reverend H. R. Revels to the Republican legislative caucus for the United States Senate to fill the fractional term of one year. The choice was ratified by the caucus without serious opposition. In the joint legislative session every Republican member, white and colored, voted for the three Republican caucus nominees for United States senators, Alcorn, Ames, and Revels, with one exception, Senator William M. Hancock of Lauderdale who stated, in explanation of his vote against Revels, that, as a lawyer, he did not believe that a colored man was eligible to a seat in the United States Senate. But Judge Hancock seems to have been the only lawyer in the legislature and outside of it, as far as could be learned, who entertained that opinion.

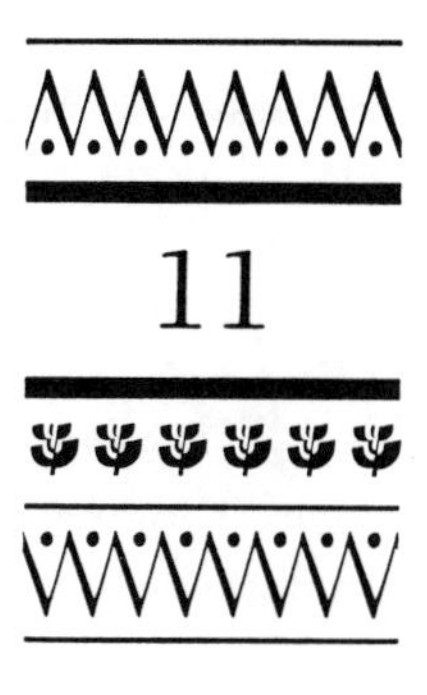

Financing State Reconstruction

In addition to the election of three United States senators this legislature had some very important work before it as has been already stated in a previous chapter. A new public school system had to be inaugurated and put into operation, thus necessitating the construction of schoolhouses throughout the state, some of them, especially in the towns and villages, to be quite large and of course expensive. All of the other public buildings and institutions in the state had to be repaired, some of them rebuilt, all of them having been neglected and some of them destroyed during the progress of the late war. In addition to this, the entire state government in all of its branches had to be reconstructed and so reorganized as to place the same in perfect harmony with the new order of things.

To accomplish these things money was required. There was none in the treasury. There was no cash available even to pay the ordinary expenses of the state government. The government had to be carried on, therefore, on a credit basis—that is, by the issuing of notes or warrants based upon the faith or credit of the state. These were issued at par to the creditors of the state in satisfaction or liquidation of the obligations. These in turn were disposed of to banks and brokers at a discount, by whom they were held until there was cash in the treasury with which to redeem them, which usually covered a period of from three to six months, sometimes longer. To raise the necessary money to put the new machinery in successful operation one of two things had to be done—either materially increase the rate of taxation or issue interest bearing bonds to be placed upon the market, thus adding to the bonded debt of the state. Although the fact was subsequently developed that a small increase in the bonded debt of the state could not very well be avoided, the plan finally agreed upon at that time as the result of careful consideration was to materially increase the rate of taxation. This proved to be so unpopular that it came near losing the legislature to the Republicans at the election of 1871.[1]

Although it was known and explained to the people that this increase was temporary and that the rate would be reduced as soon as some of the schoolhouses had been built and some of the public institutions had been repaired, this was not satisfactory to those by whom these taxes had to be paid. They insisted that some other plan ought to have been adopted, especially at that time. The war had just come to a close, leaving most of the people in an impoverished condition. What was true of the public institutions of the state was equally true of the private property of those who were property owners at that time. Their property, during the war, had been neglected, and what had not been destroyed was in a state of dilapidation and decay. This was especially true of those who had been the owners of large landed estates and of many slaves: many of

1. Lynch doubtless intended to say Democrats, not Republicans; but see *Facts of Reconstruction*, p. 49.

those, people who had been the acknowledged representatives of the wealth, the intelligence, the culture, the refinement, and the aristocracy of the South. In fact, the ruling class in church, in society, and in the state, who made and molded public opinion, who controlled the pulpit and the press and shaped the destiny of the state. Who made and enforced the laws, or at least such laws as they desired to have enforced, and who represented and spoke for the state not only in the state legislature, but in both branches of the national legislature at Washington. Many of these proud men, gallant fathers, cultured mothers and wives, and refined and polished daughters found themselves in a situation and in a condition that was pitiable in the extreme.

It was not only a difficult matter for them to adjust themselves to the new order of things and to the radically changed conditions, but no longer having slaves upon whom they could depend for everything to raise the necessary money to prevent the decay, the dissipation and the ultimate loss or destruction of their large landed estates was the serious and difficult problem they had before them. To have the rate of taxation increased upon this property, especially at that particular time, was to them a very serious matter, which could not have any other effect than to intensify their bitterness and hostility towards the party in control of the state government. But since Governor Alcorn under whose administration, and in accordance with whose recommendation this increase had been made, was a typical representative of this particular class, it was believed and hoped that he would have sufficient influence with the people of his own class to stem the tide of bitterness and resentment and to calm their fears and apprehensions.

That the Republicans retained control of the legislature as a result of the elections of 1871, though by a small majority in the lower house, is conclusive evidence that the governor's efforts in that direction were not wholly in vain. The argument made by the taxpayers, however, was plausible, and it may be conceded that upon the whole they were about right. It, no doubt, would have been much easier upon the taxpayers and therefore a wiser course to have increased at that time the interest-bearing debt of the state rather than increase the tax rate, but the latter course had been adopted and could not then be changed.

Governor Alcorn also recommended, which was favorably considered by the legislature, that there be created and supported by the state a college for the higher education of the colored boys and young men of the state. The bill for that purpose was drawn and promptly passed by the legislature, and in honor of the one by whom its creation was recommended it was named "Alcorn College." The institution was one that was very much needed. The presidency thereof being an honorable and dignified position, with a fair and reasonable salary attached, the governor, who had the appointing power, decided to tender the position to Senator H. R. Revels upon the expiration of his term in the Senate. I had the honor of being named as one of the first trustees of this important institution. After a careful inspection and examination by the governor, the trustees, and Senator Revels of many points which had been suggested for the location of the institution, Oakland College, which was located near the town of Rodney, in the county of Claiborne, was finally selected and purchased, and Alcorn College was then established, with Senator Revels in charge as its first president.[2]

As an evidence of the necessity for such an institution, it will not be out of place to call attention to the fact that when the writer was first elected to Congress in 1872, there was not one young colored man in the state that could pass the necessary

2. Oakland College had been founded in 1830 by the Presbyterians of Mississippi. "During the war its doors were closed, its endowment lost, and under the pressure of debt and a hopeless future the synod sold the property to the state as the site of Alcorn A. and M. College." Dunbar Rowland, *History of Mississippi: The Heart of the South* (Chicago, 1925), 2:498–99.

examination for a clerkship in any one of the departments at Washington. Four years later the supply was greater than the demand, nearly all of the applicants being graduates of Alcorn College. At this writing the institution is still being maintained and supported by the state, although on a reduced appropriation, and on a plan that is somewhat different from that which was inaugurated at its beginning and maintained while the Republicans were in control of the state government. One of the reasons, no doubt, why it is supported by a Democratic state administration is that the state might otherwise forfeit and lose the aid it now receives from the national government for the support of agricultural institutions. But aside from this there are very many liberal, fairminded, and influential Democrats in the state who are strongly in favor of having the state provide for the liberal education of both races.

The knowledge I had acquired of parliamentary law did not only enable me to take a leading part in the deliberations of the legislature, but it resulted in my election as Speaker of the house of representatives that was elected in 1871. Shortly after the adjournment of the first session of the legislature, the Speaker of the House, Hon. F. E. Franklin of Yazoo County died. When the legislature reassembled the first Monday in January 1871, Hon. H. W. Warren of Leake County was made Speaker of the House. In addition to the vacancy from Yazoo, created by the death of Speaker Franklin, one had also occurred from the county of Lowndes which was one of the safe and sure Republican counties. Through apathy, indifference, and over-confidence, the Democratic candidate, Dr. Landrum, was elected to fill this vacancy.

It was a strange and novel sight to see a Democratic member of the legislature from the rock-ribbed Republican county of Lowndes. It was no doubt a source of considerable embarrassment to Dr. Landrum himself, for he was looked upon by all as a marvel and a curiosity. When he got up to deliver his maiden speech, which was a few days after he had been sworn in, he was visibly and perceptibly affected, for every eye was firmly and intently fixed upon him. Everyone seemed to think that the man that could be elected to a seat in the legislature from Lowndes County as a Democrat must be endowed with some strange and hidden power, through the exercise of which he could direct the movements and control the actions of those who might be brought in contact with him or subjected to his hypnotic influence; hence the anxiety and curiosity to hear the maiden speech of this strange and remarkable man.

The voice of a Democrat upon the floor of the House from the county of Lowndes was so strange, so sudden, so unexpected and so remarkable that it was difficult for many to bring themselves to a realization of the fact that such a thing had actually happened and that it was a living reality. To the curious the speech was a disappointment, although it was a plain, calm, conservative, and convincing statement of his position upon public questions. He also related, to the great amusement of those who heard him, some of his experiences while he was engaged in canvassing the county. But the speech revealed the fact that, after all, he was nothing more than an ordinary man. No one was impressed from any word or sentence that had fallen from his lips that there was anything about him that was strange, impressive, or unusual and that his election, after all, was purely accidental, for it was no more surprising than was the election of a colored Republican, Hon. J. M. Wilson, to the same legislature the year before, from the reliable Democratic county of Marion.

There was not much to be done at the second session of the legislature, outside of passing the annual appropriation bills; hence the session was a short one. Although Governor Alcorn's term as a United States senator commenced on 4 March 1871, he did not vacate the office of governor until the meeting of Congress the first Monday in the following December. A new legislature and all county officers were to be elected in November of that year. It was to be the first important election since the inauguration of the Alcorn administration. The governor decided to remain where he could answer officially and otherwise all charges and accusations that might be made against, and criticisms upon, his administration and his official acts.

The Republican majority in the state senate was so large that the holdover senators made it well nigh impossible for the Democrats to secure a majority of that body, but the principal fight was to be made for control of the House. As already stated, the heavy increase in the rate of taxation proved to be very unpopular and this gave the Democrats a decided advantage. They made a strong and bitter fight to gain control of the House and nearly succeeded.

When every county had been heard from, it was found that out of the 115 members of which the House was composed, the Republicans had elected 66 and the Democrats 49. Of the 66 who had been elected as Republicans, two, Messrs. Armstead and Streeter, had been elected from Carroll County on an Independent ticket. They classed themselves, politically, as Independent or Alcorn Republicans. Carroll was the only close and doubtful county in the state that the Democrats had failed to carry. The Independent ticket in that county, which was supported by an influential faction of Democrats, was brought out with the understanding and agreement that it would receive the support of the Republican organization. This support was given, but a pledge that the candidates for the legislature, if elected, should not enter the Democratic caucus or vote for the candidates thereof in the organization of the House, was required. These conditions were accepted, which resulted in the ticket being supported by the Republicans and the Independent ticket being elected.

All the other close and doubtful counties went Democratic which resulted in the defeat of some of the strongest and most influential men in the Republican party, including Speaker Warren of Leake, Lucas and Boyd of Attala, Underwood of Chickasaw, Avery of Tallahatchie, and many others. Notwithstanding these reverses the Republicans sent a number of very able men to the House, among them being French of Adams, Howe and Pyles of Panola, Fisher of Hinds, Chandler and Davis of Noxubee, Huggins of Monroe, Stone and Spelman of Madison, Barrett of Amite, Sullivan and Gayles of Bolivar, Everett and Dixon of Yazoo, Griggs and Houston of Issaquina and many others. In point of experience and ability this legislature was the equal of its immediate predecessor.

12

Speaker of the House Lynch

THE ELECTION BEING OVER AND A REPUBLICAN MAJORITY IN both branches of the legislature being assured, Governor Alcorn was then prepared to vacate the office of governor, turn over the administration of state affairs to Lieutenant Governor Powers and proceed to Washington to be present at the opening session of Congress on the first Monday in December to assume his duties as a United States senator.

The legislature was to meet the first Monday in the following January—1872. As soon as the fact was made known that the Republicans would control the organization of the House, the speakership of that body began to be agitated. If Speaker Warren had been reelected he would have received the Republican caucus nomination without opposition. But his defeat made it necessary for a new man to be brought forward for that position. A movement was immediately put on foot to make me the Speaker of the House.

Chapter Twelve

Upon a careful examination of the returns it was found that of the 115 members of which the House was composed, there were 77 whites and 38 colored. Of the 77 whites, 49 were elected as Democrats and 28 as Republicans. Of course the 38 colored men were Republicans. It will thus be seen that while in the composition of the Republican caucus there were 10 more colored than white members, yet of the total membership of the House there were 39 more white than colored members. But in the organization of the House the contest was not between white and colored, but between Democrats and Republicans. No one had been elected, at least on the Republican side, because he was a white man or because he was a colored man, but because he was a Republican. After a preliminary canvass the fact was developed that I was not only the choice of the colored members for Speaker of the House, but of a large majority of the white Republican members as well. They believed and voted in accordance with that belief, both in the party caucus and in the House, that I was the best equipped man for that responsible position. This fact had been demonstrated to their satisfaction during the two sessions of the preceding legislature.

The nomination of me by the House Republican caucus for Speaker was a foregone conclusion several weeks before the convening of the legislature. With a full membership in attendance, 58 votes would be necessary to perfect the organization. When the Republican caucus convened, 60 members were present and took part in the deliberations thereof. Four of the Republicans-elect had not at that time arrived at the seat of government. The 2 Independents from Carroll refused to attend the caucus, but this did not necessarily mean that they would not vote for the candidates thereof in the organization of the House. But since we had 60, 2 more than was necessary to elect, we believed that the organization would be easily perfected the next day, regardless of the action of the members from Carroll.

In this we were sadly disappointed. The result of the first vote for Speaker of the House was as follows:

Lynch, Republican caucus nominee	55
Street, Democratic caucus nominee	47
Chandler, Independent Republican	7
Armstead, Independent Republican	1
Howe, Regular Republican	1
Necessary to elect	58

Judge Chandler of Noxubee, who had been elected as a regular Republican, with four other white Republicans, all of whom attended and took part in the caucus the night before, refused to vote for the nominee of the caucus for Speaker, but voted instead for Chandler. It will be seen that the vote for Street, the Democratic caucus nominee, was 2 less than the party's strength, thus showing that 2 Democrats must have also voted for Chandler. It will also be seen that if every vote that was not received by me had been given to Chandler or any other one person, he would have received the required number and would have been elected.

The Democrats stood ready to give their solid vote to any one of the Independents, whenever it could be shown that their votes would result in an election. But it so happened that Chandler and Armstead both were ambitious to be Speaker and neither would give way for the other, which, of course, made the election of either impossible. The one vote cast for Howe was, no doubt, Mr. Armstead's vote, while the one vote for Armstead was no doubt cast by his colleague. In the nomination of Hon. H. M. Street, the Democrats selected their strongest man and the best parliamentarian on their side of the House. The refusal of the so-called Independents to vote for the Republican caucus nominee for Speaker produced a deadlock which continued for a period of several days. At no time could any one of the regular Republicans be induced under any circumstances to vote for any one of the Independents. They would much rather have the House organized by Democrats than that party treachery should be thus rewarded.

While the deadlock was in progress, Senators Alcorn and Ames suddenly made their appearance upon the scene of action. They had made the trip from Washington to use their influence to break the deadlock and bring about an organization of the House by the Republican party. But Senator Alcorn was one that could render the most effective service in that direction, since the bolters were men who professed to be followers of his and loyal to his political interests and leadership.

As soon as the senator arrived, he held a conference with the bolters and Messrs. Armstead and Streeter, the two Independents from Carroll. In addressing those who had been elected as Republicans and who had attended and participated in the caucus of the party, the senator did not mince his words. He told them in plain words that they were in honor bound to support the caucus nominees of their party or resign their seats and thus allow their constituents to elect others that would do so. With reference to the Independents from Carroll, the situation was slightly different. They had been elected as Independents under conditions which did not obligate them to enter the Republican caucus or support the candidates thereof. They had pledged themselves not to support the Democratic caucus candidates nor aid that party in the organization of the House.

Up to that time they had not made a move nor given a vote that could be construed into a violation of the pledge or agreement upon which they had been elected, but they had publicly declared on several occasions that they had been elected as Independents, or Alcorn Republicans. In other words, they had been elected as friends and supporters of the Alcorn administration and that type of Republicanism for which he stood, and of which he was the representative. If this were true, then they should not hesitate to take the advice of the man to support whose administration they had been elected. He informed them that if they meant what they said the best way for them to prove it was to vote for the Republican caucus nominees for officers of the House, because he was the recognized leader of the party in the state, and that the issue involved in the elections was an endorsement or repudiation of his administration as governor. Republican success, under such circumstances, meant an endorsement of his administration, while Republican defeat would mean its repudiation. The most effective way, then, in which they could make good their ante-election pledges and promises was to vote for the candidates of the Republican caucus for officers of the House.

The two Carroll County Independents informed the senator that he had correctly outlined their position and their attitude and that it was their purpose and their determination to give a loyal and effective support, so far as the same was in their power, to the policies and principles for which he stood and of which he was the accredited representative, but that they were apprehensive that they could not successfully defend their action and explain their votes to the satisfaction of their constituents if they were to vote for a colored man for Speaker of the House.

"But," said the senator, "could you have been elected without the votes of colored men? If you now vote against a colored man who is in every way a fit and capable man for the position, simply because he is a colored man, could you expect those men to support you in the future?"

The senator reminded them of the fact that they had received many more colored than white votes and that, in his opinion, very few of the white men who had supported them would find fault with them for voting for a capable and intelligent man to preside over the deliberations of the House.

"Can you then," the senator asked, "afford to offend the great mass of the colored men that supported you, in order to please an insignificant, small number of narrow-minded whites?"

The senator assured them that he was satisfied they had nothing to fear as a result of their action in voting to make me

Speaker of the House. He knew me favorably and well, and therefore did not hesitate to assure them that if they contributed to my election they would have no occasion to regret having done so. The conference then came to a close with the understanding that all present would vote the next day for the Republican caucus nominees for officers of the House, which was done. The result of the ballot the following day was as follows:

Lynch, Republican caucus nominee	63
Chandler, Independent Republican	49
Necessary to elect	57

It will be seen that Judge Chandler received the solid Democratic vote, while I received the vote of every Republican present and voting, including Chandler and the two Independents from Carroll, three Republicans still being absent and not paired.

By substantially the same vote, ex-Speaker Warren of Leake County was elected chief clerk and ex-Representative Hill of Marshall County was elected sergeant at arms. The legislature was then organized and was ready to proceed to business.

At the conclusion of the session the House not only adopted a resolution thanking me for, and complimenting me upon, the able and impartial manner in which I had presided over its deliberations, but I was presented with a fine gold watch and chain, purchased with money that had been contributed by members of both parties and a few outside friends, as a token of their esteem and appreciation of me as a presiding officer.[1] On the outside case of the watch these words were engraved: "Presented to Hon. J. R. Lynch, Speaker of the House of Representatives, by the members of the legislature, April 19, 1873."

1. In a letter to his wife, Adelbert Ames reported the ceremony at which Speaker Lynch was presented the watch: "Appropriate speeches were made by two of the colored members. . . . Mr. Lynch made a very pretty speech in reply." Adelbert Ames to Blanche Butler Ames, 19 April 1873, in *Chronicles from the Nineteenth Century*, p. 448.

That watch I still have and will keep as a sacred family heirloom.

A good deal of work was to be done by this legislature. The seats of a number of Democrats were contested, but the decision in a number of cases was in favor of the sitting members. The changes, however, were sufficient to materially increase the Republican majority.

Among the important bills to be passed was one to divide the different counties of the state into six congressional districts. The apportionment of representatives in Congress, according to the apportionment act which had just passed, increased the number of representatives from Mississippi from five to six. Republican leaders in both branches of the legislature decided that the duty of drawing up a bill apportioning the state into congressional districts should devolve upon the Speaker of the House, with the understanding that the party organization would support the bill framed by him.

I accepted the responsibility and immediately proceeded with the work of drafting a bill for that purpose. Two plans had been discussed, both of which had strong supporters and advocates. One plan was to so apportion the state as to make all of the districts Republican, but in doing so the majority in at least two of them would be quite small. The other plan was to so apportion the state as to make five districts safely and reliably Republican and concede one to the Democrats. I had not taken a decided stand for or against either plan. That, perhaps, was one reason why the advocates of both plans agreed to refer the matter to me for a final decision.

The Democrats heard of what had been done. One of them, Hon. F. M. Goar of Lee County, called to see and talk with me about it. He expressed the hope that in drawing up the bill one District would be conceded to the Democrats.

"If this is done," he said, "I assume that the group of counties located in the northeast of the state will be the Democratic district. In that event we will send a very strong and able man to Congress in the person of Hon. L. Q. C. Lamar."

I informed him that from what I had heard of Mr. Lamar I had every reason to believe that if sent to Congress he would reflect credit upon himself, his party, and his state. I promised to give his suggestion earnest and, perhaps, favorable consideration. After going over the matter carefully I came to the conclusion that the better and safer plan was to make five safe and sure Republican districts and concede one to the Democrats. Another reason for this decision was that in so doing the state could be more fairly apportioned. The counties could be easily made contiguous and the population in each district could be made as nearly equal as possible. The apportionment could not have been so fairly and equitably made if the other plan had been adopted.

After the bill had been completed, it was submitted to a joint caucus of the Republican members of the two houses and, after a brief explanation by me of its provisions, it was accepted and approved by the unanimous vote of the caucus. When it was brought before the House, a majority of the Democratic members, under the leadership of Messrs. Street, Roane, and McIntosh, fought it very bitterly. They contended that the Democrats should have at least two of the six congressmen and that an apportionment could have been, and should have been, made with that end in view. The truth was that several of those who made such a stubborn fight against the bill had congressional aspirations themselves, and of course they did not fail to see that, as drawn, the bill did not hold out flattering hopes for the gratification of that ambition. But it was all that Mr. Goar and a few others that he had taken into his confidence expected, or had any right to expect. In fact, the one Democratic district, which was constructed in accordance with their wishes, was just about what they wanted. While they voted against the bill merely to be in accord with their party associates, they insisted that there should be no filibustering or dilatory methods adopted to secure its defeat. After a hard and desperate fight and several days of exciting debate the bill was finally passed by a strict party vote. A few days later it passed the senate without amendment, was signed by the governor, and became a law.

As had been predicted by Mr. Goar, Hon. L. Q. C. Lamar was nominated by the Democrats for Congress in the first district, which was the Democratic district. The Republicans nominated against him a very strong and able man in the person of Hon. R. W. Flournoy, who had served with Mr. Lamar as a member of the Secession Convention of 1861. He made an aggressive and brilliant canvass of the district, but the election of Mr. Lamar was a foregone conclusion since the Democratic majority in the district was very large.

13

1872: Election to Congress

EIGHTEEN SEVENTY-TWO WAS AN IMPORTANT YEAR IN THE political history of the state and nation. It was the year of the presidential and congressional elections. President Grant was a candidate for renomination. A strong opposition to him, however, had developed in the ranks of the Republicans. This opposition was under the able and aggressive leadership of such strong and influential men as Horace Greeley of New York, Charles Sumner of Massachusetts, Carl Schurz and B. Gratz Brown of Missouri, and many others. The rupture between the president and Senator Charles Sumner grew out of the movement to bring about the annexation of Santo Domingo, which was strongly supported by the president and bitterly opposed by Senator Sumner, who was at that time chairman of the Senate Committee on Foreign Relations. In this fight the administration had the support of a large majority of the Republican senators, which resulted in having Senator Sumner deposed from the chairmanship of the important Committee on Foreign Relations and the selection of Senator Cameron of Pennsylvania to succeed him.[1] This step increased the bitterness growing out of differences in the party upon this matter. Public sentiment in the party throughout the country, however, was on the side of the administration. This sentiment was so strong even in Senator Sumner's own state of Massachusetts that it resulted in the passage of a resolution by the state legislature censuring the senator for his attitude towards, and opposition to, the national administration of his own party. But this resolution was rescinded at a subsequent session of the legislature. This, however, was not an indication of a change of sentiment among the Republicans of that state, but it was evidence of the very high esteem in which this great and grand man was held by the people of his state and which was so strong that they were willing to overlook and forgive what in their opinion was nothing more than a mistaken judgment on his part.

The opposition within the party to the national administration took tangible shape which resulted in the call for an Independent-Republican convention at Cincinnati, which nominated Horace Greeley of New York for president and B. Gratz Brown of Missouri for vice-president. An understanding had evidently been reached by which the Democrats would endorse and support this ticket instead of nominating and supporting one of their own. This was the course that was adopted by the National Democratic Convention which was subsequently held at Baltimore. The Republican convention was held at Philadelphia in June and renominated President Grant without opposition, but substituted Senator Henry Wilson of Massachusetts for ex-Speaker Colfax of Indiana for vice-president. The issue was thus joined between the two parties, but it soon developed that the result would be determined more upon the

1. Undoubtedly, Sumner's hostility to any lenient treatment of Britain in the Civil War claims against that country was also a factor in his removal as chairman of the Senate Committee on Foreign Relations.

personality of the opposing candidates than upon the issues of the campaign. It looked for a while as if the contest would not only be an animated and exciting one, but that the result of the election would be close and doubtful.

This was the first national election that Mississippi was to take part in since the readmission of the state into the Union. The National Republican Convention at Philadelphia that year was the first one to which I had been elected as a delegate. The delegation from my state conferred upon me the distinguished honor of making me a member of the Committee on Platform and Resolutions. The chairman of that committee made me a member of the subcommitee that prepared the platform.[2]

Immediately upon my return to the state, the contest for the Republican nomination for Congress in the Sixth District was opened. My friends had decided that this was the time for me to go to Congress. The sitting member, Hon. L. W. Perce, was a strong and able man and had made a creditable and satisfactory representative. He was a candidate for renomination. He and I not only lived in the same county, Adams, but in the same town, Natchez. The district was composed of the sixteen counties situated in the extreme southern end of the state, extending from the Mississippi River on the west to the Alabama line on the east. Adams County not only had the largest population of any county in the district, but it also had the largest Republican majority. It was conceded by all that an Adams County man should be nominated, and, since the two opposing candidates lived in that county, the one that would win the primary therein would receive the nomination.

This made Adams County the battleground of the campaign for the nomination. While the contest was warm and exciting, it was free from bitterness. Every white Republican in the county, with two or three exceptions, supported Colonel Perce,

2. The minutes show only that Lynch was a member of the Committee on Resolutions and on the "roll of delegates and alternates." He made no speeches that were reported. *Presidential Election 1872: Proceedings of the National Union Republican Convention* (Washington, 1872), pp. 9, 33.

and he also had many friends and supporters among the colored Republicans. Colonel Perce's campaign was ably conducted under the leadership of Postmaster E. J. Costello, who received valuable assistance from such influential men as H. C. Griffin, Charles Walden, William Cannon, John Maine, and others. While my interests were in charge of three of the strongest and most popular colored men in the county, in the persons of William McCary, Robert H. Wood and Robert W. Fitzhugh.[3] The county convention, which was to elect the delegates to the district convention, was to be composed of thirty-three delegates, apportioned among the different voting precincts upon the basis of the Republican votes polled in each at the last preceding election. The fairness of the apportionment was conceded by both sides.

After a warm and exciting campaign, extending over a period of about one month, the primaries in the different voting precincts were held which resulted in a sweeping victory for the Lynch ticket, which enabled that faction to send a solid delegation to the congressional district convention. This made John R. Lynch the nominee of the party for Congress in that district, without further serious opposition. The Perce men gracefully acquiesced in the decision and gave the ticket their loyal support. The district convention was held at Brookhaven in August. I reached the constitutional age of eligibility in September and was elected in November of the same year.

The Democrats nominated a very able and popular man in the person of Judge Hiram Cassidy of Franklin County. Both candidates made a thorough canvass of the district, joint debates having been held at several important points. Of the sixteen counties of which the district was composed, only four,

3. Wood was one of the most influential citizens of Natchez. In 1870 he was elected mayor of Natchez. Later he was its postmaster and, still later, the sheriff of Adams County. Lynch, *Historical Errors of James Ford Rhodes*, p. 18. Fitzhugh, a free Negro before the war, was a minister in the Methodist Episcopal church and a member of the convention of 1868. Wharton, *Negro in Mississippi*, p. 147.

Adams, Claiborne, Jefferson, and Wilkinson were safely and reliably Republican, while four others, Copiah, Lincoln, Pike, and Amite, were close and doubtful. The other eight counties were reliably Democratic, but the normal Republican majority in the four Republican counties was believed to be large enough to overcome the Democratic majority in the other twelve counties, assuming that the Democrats would carry all of them, which, however, they did not do.

When the returns were all in, the result was not only a Republican majority of more than five thousand, but the same party had carried nearly every one of the doubtful counties. The Republicans also elected the congressmen from every district in the state, except one, the first, in which the Democrats elected their candidate, in the person of Hon. L. Q. C. Lamar, over Colonel R. W. Flournoy, an able and eloquent man, who made the race on the Republican ticket. The delegation was composed of the following members: First District: L. Q. C. Lamar, D.; Second District: Albert R. Howe, R.; Third District: Henry W. Barry, R.; Fourth District: Jason Niles, R.; Fifth District: George C. McKee, R.; Sixth District: John R. Lynch, R. The Republican electoral ticket also carried the state by a majority of about thirty thousand. The returns from the country at large indicated that only about five states had been carried by the combination of Democrats and Independent Republicans. The regular Republicans not only carried the presidential election, but the same party had a very large majority in both houses of Congress.

The next important local election to be held before the end of that year was the municipal election at Natchez, which was to take place in December. Robert H. Wood, who had been one of the leaders for Lynch in the campaign for Congress, was mayor of Natchez and was a candidate for renomination and election. His renomination was a foregone conclusion. While the Republican majority in the county was large, in the city it was small. While Wood's renomination was assured, his reelection was impossible if the Perce men should vote against him or even fail to vote for him. Their opposition to him had been threatened, in retaliation for his opposition to the renomination of Perce, but it had not been openly declared. I came to the conclusion that Postmaster Costello held the key to the situation. His term as postmaster would expire the following April. He desired very much to be reappointed. Although he had strongly opposed my nomination for Congress, he had loyally supported the ticket after the nomination had been made. There was no reason, therefore, why I could not consistently support him for reappointment. I therefore approached him and urged him to take an active part in the municipal campaign in behalf of the Republican ticket for which he would merit and would receive my support for reappointment to the postmastership, let the result of the election be what it may.

He was very much gratified with my promised support of him upon such easy and agreeable terms and conditions. He had never, he said, bolted the nomination of his party and could not be induced to do so now. I could, therefore, depend upon his cooperation, influence, and support in behalf of the Republican municipal ticket and that he would take an active part in the campaign in behalf of that ticket. This made the outlook much more encouraging than it otherwise would have been. When Wood was renominated by the regular-Republican convention, some of the Perce men, as had been expected, bolted the nomination and put out an Independent ticket with H. C. Griffin at its head for mayor. There had evidently been an understanding with the Democrats to the effect that the Independent ticket receive the support of their party, for when the Democratic convention was held later, it endorsed the Griffin Independent ticket instead of nominating one of its own.

This made the outlook for Republican success somewhat doubtful, but it was hoped and believed that with the loyal, active, and aggressive support of Postmaster Costello, who had been the leader of the Perce forces in the fight for the congressional nomination, Republican success was not only possible but more than probable. But it was noticed and occasioned unfavorable comment that, even in the heat of the campaign, Costello could not be induced to make any speeches or even attend a Republican meeting or a meeting of any kind. His time was always otherwise occupied, but he gave positive assurances that his most effective work would be done during the last ten days of the campaign. He was making his plans and arranging his business affairs so as to enable him to do this. This last promise he faithfully kept, but instead of coming out in support of Wood and the Republican ticket, he came out in support of Griffin and the Independent ticket, thus violating and repudiating his agreement or understanding with me. This surprised me very much. I could not understand it or account for it. I could not believe that his action was patriotic and unselfish. I knew the man was not built that way and I also knew that he was very anxious to succeed himself as postmaster. His action, however, made sure the defeat of Wood and his associates, and the election of Griffin and the other Independent candidates.

The secret of Costello's action was made public, or became known, shortly after the election. Senator Ames had made Natchez his home. It had been the custom, it was claimed, for the national administration to allow each senator in harmony with the administration to control the appointment of the postmaster, or name the postmaster of the town in which the senator lived. Some of the Griffin supporters claimed to have been in correspondence with Senator Ames and that a letter had been received from the senator in which he had promised to favor the reappointment of Costello without regard to my wishes in the matter. In other words, that the member of Congress from the district would be entirely ignored in that particular case and that Costello would be reappointed upon the recommendation of Senator Ames alone. Costello seemed to have been convinced that such a letter had been written, although he had not seen it, and such a pledge had been made through a third party, and that the congressman from the district would have no voice whatever in making that appointment.

Being satisfied and convinced that I was powerless to harm him, Costello felt that he could safely break his agreement with me; hence he opposed and secured the defeat of the regular Republican ticket in the municipal election. As soon as the alleged correspondence with Senator Ames was brought to my notice, I wrote to both Senators Ames and Alcorn in which I insisted upon my right as the member of Congress from that district to name the successor to Costello as postmaster at Natchez. Both senators replied, conceding me this right and promising to support the candidate of my choice, whoever he might be. I then requested Wood, the defeated candidate for mayor, to draw up an application for postmaster, which was done. This application was, at the proper and opportune time, forwarded to Senator Ames with my endorsement and with the request that he place the same on file at the Post Office Department with his own and Senator Alcorn's endorsement. I wrote a separate letter to Senator Alcorn, requesting his cooperation with Senator Ames in the support of Wood. Wood's application was endorsed by both senators, and in the course of time the appointment was duly made. It was not publicly known that Wood's name was sent to the Senate for confirmation. As soon as the appointment was announced, Costello took the first train to Washington, but the trip was made in vain. The nomination was promptly confirmed and, upon the expiration of Costello's term, Wood took charge of the office, the duties of which he discharged in a creditable and satisfactory manner for several years, when he voluntarily gave it up to assume the duties of the important office of sheriff and Tax Collector of the county to which he had been elected.

14

Visit to Saint Louis

In 1873 a movement was put on foot to have the national capital moved from Washington, D.C., to Saint Louis, Missouri.[1] With this in view, a convention was held at Saint Louis in the summer of that year to which the congressmen-elect from the South and West were cordially invited. I decided to accept the invitation but found out after I arrived there that I had made a mistake in doing so. Elaborate preparations had been made to entertain the delegates and visitors, the congressmen from the various states having been assigned to quarters at the different hotels in the city. Publication had been made in the daily papers of the assignments, so that every mem-

1. The movement to transfer the capital to Saint Louis was launched in 1869, when the citizens of Saint Louis called a "Capital Removal Convention" which met in October of that year. The agitation continued in subsequent years. Floyd Shoemaker, editor, *Missouri, Day by Day* (Jefferson City, 1943), 2:269–70.

ber would know where he was assigned, even if he should be missed by a member of the reception committee.

The train on which I was a passenger arrived there about three o'clock in the morning. No member of the reception committee was present, but having seen in the papers of the day before that the Mississippi delegation had been located at the Planters House I took a seat in the "bus" from that hotel with the expectation of being assigned a room there. When I made my appearance at the office and handed the clerk the invitation I had received from the chairman of the reception committee, informing him at the same time that I had been located at that house, he informed me in such a polite way that the assignment had been changed and the Mississippi delegation had been assigned to the Saint Nicholas Hotel that I did not for one moment question the accuracy of the statement. But, when I appeared at the office of the Saint Nicholas I was politely informed that the Mississippi delegation had been located at the Planters House. When I informed the clerk that I was just from that hotel and that I was informed while there that the location of the Mississippi delegation had been changed from the Planters House to the Saint Nicholas Hotel, he smiled and stated that he had no notice of such a change.

I then realized for the first time the actual situation. Fortunately I had left my valise each time in the bus, requesting the driver to wait until it was sent for. When I returned to the bus from the office of the Saint Nicholas and informed the driver that I had to go elsewhere, he exhibited impatience, stating that he could not be driving me all over the city, especially at that hour in the morning. I was very much puzzled. I had never been to Saint Louis before. I knew no one there and of course did not know where to go. Like the son of men about whom we read in the Bible, I had no where to lay my head. I had been informed that the next train for the South would not leave before eight o'clock at night. I did not like the idea of sitting in the waiting room at the station fifteen or sixteen hours. I therefore requested the driver to take me to the Southern Hotel. That hotel had the reputation of being the finest and most aristocratic in the city.

When I arrived there I took my valise out of the bus and dismissed the driver. I then went to the office and asked for the proprietor. I was informed that he was in bed and could not be seen at that hour in the morning. "But," I replied, "it is absolutely essential that I see him and that too without delay. The business is very important and I must see him." The office boy was then sent up to the room of the proprietor and I was requested to take a seat until he made his appearance. After I had waited about one-half hour he appeared. When he approached me, I presented him the invitation card I had received from the reception committee. After reading it, he gave me a cordial shake of the hand, said he was very glad to see me, at the same time introducing himself to me, his name being Warner. I then related to him the unpleasant and embarrassing experiences that I had had since I arrived in the city about three o'clock that morning. "Now," I said, "I do not want to be the occasion of the slightest embarrassment to you. Therefore the request I shall make of you will not, I am sure, give you any. That request is that you allow me to check my valise at the check room at the hotel and allow me to occupy a seat in the gentlemen's reception room from time to time during the day until a short while before the departure of the next train going south, at which time I shall shake the dust of Saint Louis from my feet never to return again."

"Oh, no," he replied, "that will never do. You are here by invitation as a guest of the city of Saint Louis, and you must be looked after and appropriately attended to as such. Your case is one which must have escaped the attention of the reception committee, which committee should have two or more representatives to meet every incoming train. Some of the members of that committee will no doubt be here in the course of a few hours. I am sure they will insist upon your remaining to attend the convention and they will, of course, see that satisfactory arrangements are made for your accommodation while you are here. To provide for you in the meantime is the problem which seems to have fallen, unexpectedly, to my lot. What am I to do? I can not turn you away from my hotel after you have given me the reason why you are not at the one to which you were assigned, and yet how can I entertain you here? This, you know, is a Southern city. I am afraid if you are allowed to stop here, some, if not the greater part of my guests, will leave. In addition to this, most of my employees are Irish. You know something about their attitude towards people of your race. If, therefore, I should allow you to stop here, I very much fear they will strike and thus involve me in a great deal of trouble. But if, in view of what I have told you, you will be reasonable and meet me halfway, I will take care of you, will assign you to a room which you can occupy until the reception committee shall have made other arrangements, upon condition that you allow your meals to be served in your rooms."

I confess that Mr. Warner impressed me favorably; from the way in which he spoke I believe he was both honest and sincere. I therefore assented to the condition without the slightest hesitation. I informed him at the same time that although a colored man, I was of Irish descent, a knowledge of which fact might lessen to some extent the embarrassment growing out of the fact that the most of his employees were of that race. With this he seemed to be considerably amused but assured me that he would select one of his best Irish waiters whose services would be at my disposal. He then went to the office and had me assigned to one of the best and most commodious rooms in the hotel. I gave instructions at the office that I must not be disturbed before 9. It was then about 5 or a little after.

Shortly after 9 several members of the reception committee called. They regretted very much the inconveniences to which I had been subjected and insisted that I remain there during the three days session of the convention which would commence that day. They further stated that they had seen the proprietor of the hotel and had confirmed the arrangements already made in my case, the same to cover a period of three days or during the sitting of the convention. This was satisfactory and I decided to remain.

The next morning the newspapers had a full account of the whole affair, attention being called to the fact that I was the first colored man that had ever been allowed to be a guest at any one of the first-class hotels of that city. On the whole, the newspaper comments were both favorable and friendly. When the time came for me to leave, I gave my Irish attendant, who had been faithful, polite, and attentive, a tip of one dollar, for which he was very grateful and expressed his regrets that I could not remain longer, as it gave him pleasure to attend to my wants.

Of course I could not think of leaving without seeing Mr. Warner once more in person and thanking him for his kindness, courtesy, and consideration. He expressed himself as being very much pleased with the way in which the affair was managed and assured me that if I should ever come to Saint Louis again I would not be denied accommodation at the Southern Hotel if he were connected with it, especially if I should see him in person, or communicate with him in advance. But I have never had occasion to act upon his suggestion and the probabilities now are that I never shall. I must say that my stay there did not favorably impress me with the idea that Saint Louis was a desirable place for the national capital. I left, therefore, with my mind made up that if a proposition for that purpose should be brought before Congress while I was a member of that body, my vote would be cast in the negative. Other members must have been impressed the same way, since the proposition was never brought before Congress for action.

1873: Mississippi Senatorial Elections

Eighteen seventy-three was a year in which an important election was to be held in Mississippi. State, district, and county officers and members of the legislature were to be elected. The tenure of office for the state and county officers was four years. Eighteen seventy-three, therefore, was the year in which the successors of those that were elected in 1869 had to be elected. The legislature to be elected that year would elect the successor of Senator Ames as United States senator. Senator Ames was a candidate to succeed himself. For some unaccountable reason there had been a falling out between Senator Alcorn and himself, for which reason Senator Alcorn decided to use his influence to prevent the reelection of Senator Ames. This meant that there would be a bitter factional fight in the party because both senators were popular with the rank and file of the party.

The fact was soon developed, however, that the people

favored the return of Senator Ames to the Senate. This did not necessarily mean opposition or unfriendliness to Senator Alcorn. It simply meant that both were to be treated fairly and justly and that each was to stand upon his own record and merits regardless of their personal differences.

If Senator Alcorn had been in Senator Ames's place, the probabilities are that the sentiment of the party would have been just as strongly in his favor as it was at that time in favor of Ames. But on this occasion Senator Alcorn made the mistake of making opposition to Senator Ames the test of loyalty to himself. In this he was not supported even by many of his warmest personal and political friends. In consequence of the bitter fight that was to be made by Senator Alcorn to prevent the return of Senator Ames to the Senate, many of Senator Ames's friends advised him to become a candidate for the office of governor. In that way it was believed he could command the situation and thus make sure his election to succeed himself as senator; otherwise it might be doubtful.

But this involved the retirement of Governor Powers, who was a candidate to succeed himself. Second, the candidate for lieutenant governor would have to be selected with great care, since if that program were carried out he would be in point of fact the governor of the state for practically the whole term.

After going over the situation very carefully with his friends and supporters, Senator Ames decided to be a candidate for governor, public announcement of which was duly made. This announcement seemed to have increased the intensity of Senator Alcorn's opposition to Senator Ames, who did not hesitate to declare that in the event of Ames's nomination for governor by the regular party convention, he would bolt the action of the convention and make the race for governor himself as an Independent candidate. But this declaration made no impression upon the friends and supporters of Ames and evidently had very little effect upon the rank and file of the party, for the fact became apparent shortly after the announcement of the candidacy of Ames that his nomination was a foregone conclusion. In fact, Senator Ames had such a strong hold upon the rank and file of the party throughout the state that when the convention met there was practically no opposition to his nomination. The friends and supporters of Governor Powers realized early in the campaign the hopelessness of the situation so far as he was concerned and therefore made no serious effort in his behalf.

But what gave the Ames's managers more concern than anything else was the selection of a suitable man for lieutenant governor. Many of the colored delegates insisted that three of the seven men to be nominated should be members of that race. The positions they insisted upon were lieutenant governor, secretary of state, and superintendent of education. Since the colored men had been particularly loyal and faithful to Senator Ames, it was not deemed wise to ignore their demands.

But, was there a colored man possessing the necessary qualifications to be placed in charge of the executive department of the state? Yes. After going over the field very carefully it was decided that there was just one possessing the necessary qualifications—B. K. Bruce of Bolivar County.[1] He, it was decided, was just the man for the place, and to him the nomination was to be tendered. A committee was appointed to wait on Mr. Bruce and inform him of the action of the conference and urge him to consent to the use of his name. But Mr. Bruce positively declined. He could not be induced under any circumstances to change his mind. He was fixed in his determination not to allow his name to be used for the office of lieutenant governor and from that determination he could not be moved.

1. Blanche Kelso Bruce, a Virginia free Negro, attended Oberlin College before the war. In 1868, after a teaching career, he became a planter in Floreyville, Mississippi. He held many state offices before going to the United States Senate in 1874: sergeant at arms in the state senate, assessor and sheriff of Bolivar County, and member of the Board of Levee Commissioners. *Dictionary of American Biography* (New York, 1958), vol. 2, pt. 1, pp. 180–81.

Mr. Bruce's unexpected attitude and action necessitated a radical change in the entire program. It had been agreed that the lieutenant governorship should go to a colored man, but since Bruce's declination, the Ames managers were obliged to take one of two men—H. C. Carter or A. K. Davis. Davis was the more acceptable of the two, but neither, it was thought, was a fit and suitable man to be placed at the head of the executive department of the state. After again going over the field and canvassing the situation very carefully, it was decided that Ames would not be a candidate to succeed himself as United States senator, but that he would be a candidate to succeed Senator Alcorn. This decision, in all probability, would not have been made if Alcorn had been willing to abide by the decision of the convention. But since he announced his determination to bolt the nomination of his party for governor and run as an Independent candidate, it was decided that he had forfeited any claim he otherwise would have had upon the party to succeed himself in the Senate.

Senator Alcorn's term would expire on 4 March 1877. His successor would be elected by the legislature that would be chosen in November 1875. If Ames should be elected to the governorship, his successor in that office would be elected in November 1877. In the event of his election to the Senate to succeed Senator Alcorn, his term as Senator would commence on 4 March 1877, yet he could remain in the office of governor until the meeting of Congress the following December, thus practically serving out the full term as governor.

With that plan mapped out and agreed upon and the party leaders committed to its support, Davis was allowed to be nominated for the office of lieutenant governor.[2] Two other colored men were also placed upon the state ticket—James Hill

2. Alexander K. Davis moved in 1869 from Tennessee to Mississippi, where he became a lawyer and was elected to the state senate from Noxubee County. Lerone Bennett, Jr., *Black Power, U.S.A.: The Human Side of Reconstruction, 1867–1877* (Chicago, 1967), p. 226.

for secretary of state and T. W. Cardozo for state superintendent of education.[3] While Davis had made quite a creditable record as a member of the legislature, it could not be said that his name added strength to the ticket. Hill, on the other hand, was active, aggressive, and considerably above the average colored man in point of intelligence at that time. His nomination was favorably received, because it was generally believed that if elected he would discharge the duties of the office in a way that would reflect credit upon himself and give satisfaction to the public. In point of education and experience Cardozo was known and admitted to be entirely capable of filling the office of superintendent of education, but he was not well known outside of his own county—Warren. In fact, his nomination was largely a concession to that strong Republican county for representation on the state ticket.

The three white men nominated, besides the candidate for governor, were W. H. Gibbs, for Auditor of Public Accounts, George E. Harris, for attorney general, and George H. Holland, for state treasurer. Gibbs had been a member of the Constitutional Convention of 1868 and subsequently a member of the state senate. Holland had served as a member of the legislature from Oktibbeha County. Harris had been a member of Congress from the Second, or Holly Springs, District, having been defeated for the nomination in 1872 by A. R. Howe of Panola County. While the ticket as a whole was not a weak one, its principal strength was in its head, the candidate for governor.

Shortly after the adjournment of the convention, Senator Alcorn had another convention called, which nominated a

3. Hill was born a slave on a plantation near Holly Springs, Mississippi. Without formal training, he nevertheless learned much from his owner's children. He went to the state legislature in 1871 and soon became very influential in Republican councils. Cardozo, a New Yorker, settled in Vicksburg after the war. As an important figure in Warren County politics, he was in a position to bid successfully for a high state office. Wharton, *Negro in Mississippi*, pp. 163, 164.

ticket composed exclusively of Republicans, with himself at its head for governor. The Democrats, at their convention, endorsed the Alcorn ticket. While it would seem that this action on the part of the Democrats ought to have increased Alcorn's chances of success, it appears to have been a contributory cause of his defeat. Thousands of Republicans who were in sympathy with the movement and would have otherwise voted the Alcorn ticket refused to do so, for the reason that if it had been elected, the Democrats could have, and no doubt would have, claimed it as a victory for their party. On the other hand, both tickets being composed exclusively of Republicans, thousands of Democrats refused to vote for either, while some of them voted the Ames ticket. At any rate, the election resulted in the success of the Ames ticket by a majority of more than twenty thousand. The regular Republicans also had a large majority in both branches of the legislature.

As soon as the election was over and the result was known, the candidacy of B. K. Bruce for United States senator to succeed Senator Ames was announced. Ames's term as governor was to commence the first Monday in January 1874. His term as Senator would expire on 4 March 1875. Upon assuming the duties of governor, therefore, he had to tender his resignation as a senator, thus devolving upon the incoming legislature the election of a senator to serve out the unexpired term as well as for the full term of six years. Bruce's candidacy was for the full term.

The secret of Mr. Bruce's positive refusal to allow his name to be used for the lieutenant governorship, which would have resulted in making him governor, was revealed. He had the senatorship in mind at the time, but of course no allusion to that fact was made. As between the senatorship and the governorship he chose the former, which proved to be a wise decision in view of subsequent events. It was soon developed that he was the choice of a large majority of the Republican members of the legislature, white as well as colored. His nomination by the party caucus, therefore, was a foregone conclusion. Before the legislature met, it had been practically settled that Mr. Bruce should be sent to the Senate for the long term and ex-Superintendent of Education H. R. Pease should be elected to serve out the unexpired term of Governor-elect Ames.

This slate was approved by the joint legislative caucus without a hitch, and the candidates thus nominated were duly elected by the legislature, not only by the solid Republican vote of that body, but one member of the state senate, Hiram Cassidy, Jr., who had been elected as a Democrat, voted for Mr. Bruce.

As an evidence of Senator Alcorn's keen disappointment and chagrin over the outcome of his fight with Governor Ames, when Senator Bruce made his appearance to be sworn in as senator, it was presumed that Senator Alcorn, in accordance with the uniform custom on such occasions, would escort his colleague to the president's desk to be sworn in. This Senator Alcorn refused to do. When Mr. Bruce's name was called, Senator Alcorn did not move, but remained in his seat, apparently giving his attention to his private correspondence. Mr. Bruce, somewhat nervous and slightly excited, started to the president's desk unattended. Senator Roscoe Conkling of New York, who was sitting nearby, immediately rose and extended his arm to Mr. Bruce and escorted him to the president's desk and stood by his side until the oath had been administered, and then tendered his hearty congratulations, in which all the other Republican senators, except Senator Alcorn, subsequently joined.

This gracious act on the part of the New York senator made for him a life-long friend and admirer in the person of Senator Bruce. This friendship was so strong that Senator Bruce named his first and only son Roscoe Conkling in honor of the able, distinguished, and gallant senator from New York.

Senator Alcorn's action in this matter was the occasion of considerable unfavorable criticism and comment, some of his critics going so far as to intimate that his action was due to the fact that Mr. Bruce was a colored man. But from my knowledge of the man and the circumstances connected with the case, I am satisfied that this was not true. His antipathy to Mr. Bruce grew out of the fact that Mr. Bruce opposed him and supported Ames in the fight for governor in 1873. So far as I have been able to learn, I am the only one of the senator's friends and admirers who opposed his course in that contest that he ever forgave. He no doubt felt that I was under less personal obligations to him than many others who pursued the same course that I did, since he had never rendered me any effective personal or political service, except when he brought the Independent members of the House in line for me in the contest for Speaker of that body in 1872 and, even then, his action was not so much an act of personal friendship for me as it was in the interest of the party of which he was at that time the recognized head, and to secure an endorsement of his own administration as governor.

In Mr. Bruce's case he took an entirely different view of the matter. He believed that he had been the making of Mr. Bruce. Mr. Bruce came to the state in 1869 and took an active part in the campaign of that year. When the legislature was organized he was elected sergeant at arms of the state senate. When the legislature adjourned, Governor Alcorn sent him to Bolivar County with a commission in his pocket as county assessor. He discharged the duties of that office in such a creditable and satisfactory manner that he was elected in 1871 sheriff and Tax Collector of that important and wealthy county, the most responsible and lucrative office in the gift of the people of the county. He was holding that office when elected to the United States Senate. Senator Alcorn felt, therefore, that in taking sides against him and in favor of Ames in 1873, Mr. Bruce was guilty of gross ingratitude. This accounted for his action in refusing to escort Mr. Bruce to the president's desk to be sworn in as a senator. In this, however, he did Mr. Bruce a grave injustice.

To my personal knowledge, gratitude was one of Mr. Bruce's principal characteristics.

If Senator Alcorn had been a candidate from the start for the Republican nomination for governor, Mr. Bruce, I am sure, would have supported him even against Senator Ames. But it was known that the senator had no ambition to be governor. His sole purpose was to defeat Senator Ames, at any cost, and that too on account of matters that were purely personal and therefore had no connection with party or political affairs. Mr. Bruce, like very many other friends and admirers of the senator, simply refused to follow him in open rebellion against his own party. I am satisfied, however, that Mr. Bruce's race identity did not influence the action of Senator Alcorn in the slightest degree. As further evidence of that fact, his position and action in the Pinchback case may be mentioned. He spoke and voted for the admission of Mr. Pinchback to a seat in the Senate when such a staunch Republican as Senator Edmunds of Vermont opposed and voted against admission. In spite of Senator Alcorn's political defeat and humiliation in his own state, he remained true and loyal to the national Republican party to the end of his senatorial term, which terminated with the beginning of the Hayes administration. Up to that time he had strong hopes for the future of the Republican party at the South.

16

Governors Alcorn and Ames

THE ADMINISTRATIONS OF GOVERNORS ALCORN AND AMES, THE two Republican governors, products of Reconstruction, both having been elected chiefly by the votes of colored men, were among the best with which that state was ever blessed, the generally accepted impression to the contrary notwithstanding. Alcorn was elected in 1869 to serve a term of four years. Ames was elected to the succeeding term in 1873. Alcorn was one of the old citizens of the state and was therefore thoroughly identified with its business, industrial, and social interests. He had been one of the large and wealthy land and slave owners and therefore belonged to that small but select and influential class known as Southern aristocrats. He had taken an active and prominent part in public matters since his early manhood. Before the War of the Rebellion he had served several terms as a member of the legislature. He represented his county, Coahoma, in the Secession Convention of 1861. He was bitterly opposed to secession and fought it bravely, but when he found himself in a hopeless minority, he gracefully acquiesced in the decision of the majority and signed the ordinance of secession. He also joined the Confederate army and took an active part in raising troops for the same. He was made brigadier general and had command of the Confederate forces in Mississippi for a good while, but, since the president of the Confederacy did not seem to be particularly partial to him, he was not allowed to see very much field service.[1]

When the war was over, he took an active part in the work of rehabilitation and reconstruction. He strongly supported the Andrew Johnson plan of reconstruction, and, by the legislature that was elected under that plan, he was chosen one of the United States senators, but was not admitted to the seat to which he had been elected. When the Johnson plan of reconstruction was repudiated and rejected by the voters of the Northern states and what was known as the congressional plan of reconstruction was endorsed and approved, Alcorn decided that further opposition to that plan was useless and unwise and therefore publicly advised acquiescence in, and acceptance of, the same. His advice having been rejected by the Democrats, nothing remained for him to do but to join the Republican party which he did in the early part of 1869.

Since he was known to be a strong, able, and influential man, one who possessed the respect and confidence of the white people of the state, regardless of party differences, he was tendered the Republican nomination for the governorship at the election that was to be held the latter part of that year. He accepted the nomination and was duly elected. He discharged the duties of the office in an able, creditable, and satisfactory manner. The only point upon which the administration was

1. For an account of Alcorn's career before Reconstruction see Lillian A. Pereyra, *James Lusk Alcorn, Persistent Whig* (Baton Rouge, 1966).

at all subject to unfavorable criticism was the high rate of taxation to which the people were subjected for the support of the state government, but the reader will see that, at that particular time, this could hardly have been avoided. In his message to the legislature in January 1910, Governor E. F. Noel accurately stated the principle by which an administration is necessarily governed in raising revenue to carry on the government. This is the same principle that governed the Alcorn administration when it took charge of the state government in 1870. Governor Noel, in the message referred to, said: "The amount of assessment determines the tax burden of each individual, corporation, town and county. The legislature or local authorities could settle the amount necessary to be provided for their respective treasuries. If all property be assessed at the same rate, whether full or ten percent of its value, the payment of each owner would be unaffected, the higher the assessment the lower the levy; and the lower the assessment the higher the levy. Our state revenue is mainly derived from a six mill ad valorem tax."

When the Alcorn administration took charge of the state government, the war had just come to a close.[2] Everything was in a prostrate condition. There had been great depreciation in the value of real and personal property. The public institutions that had not been destroyed were in a dilapidated condition. It was not only necessary to rebuild many, but to repair those that had not been destroyed. A new public school system was, for the first time, to be put in operation. For that purpose schoolhouses had to be erected throughout the state. Money had to be raised for these purposes in addition to what was necessary to meet the current demands. There were only two ways in which the money could be raised—to borrow it or raise it by taxation. The credit of the state was not very good.

2. Alcorn took office as governor on 10 March 1870, five years after the close of the war.

The rate of interest for borrowed money was high. To materially increase the bonded debt of the state was not deemed wise, yet some had to be raised in that way. To raise the balance, a higher rate of taxation had to be imposed since the assessed valuation of the taxable property was so low. The figures showing the assessed valuation of the taxable property in the state and the receipts and disbursements prior to 1875 are not available, but taking the figures for that year, the reader can form a pretty accurate idea of what the situation must have been prior to that time. In 1875 the assessed valuation of real and personal property subject to taxation in the state was $119,313,834. The receipts from all sources that year amounted to $1,801,129.12. The disbursements for the same year were $1,430,192.83.

Now let us see what the situation was after the Ames administration had been in power about two years, or half of the term for which it had been elected. According to a very carefully prepared statement that was made and published by an expert accountant in the state treasurer's office in the latter part of 1875, the ad valorem rate of taxes for general purposes had been reduced from seven to four mills, and yet the amount paid into the treasury was not only enough to meet all demands upon the state, but to make a material reduction in the bonded debt. The following is taken from that statement.

> An examination of the report of the State Treasurer, of the first of January, 1874, at which time the administration of Governor Ames commenced, exhibits the fact that the indebtedness of the state at that date, exclusive of the amounts to the credit of the Chickasaw and common school funds, balance of current funds on hand, and warrants in the Treasury belonging to the state, was $1,765,554.33. The amount of the tax of the previous year remaining uncollected on January first, 1874, and afterward collected, $944,261.51, should be deducted from the above amount, which will show the actual indebtedness of the state at that date to be $821,292.82. A further examination of the report of

the same officer for January first, 1875, shows the indebtedness, after deducting amounts to the credit of the Chickasaw and common school funds, balance of current funds on hand and warrants in the Treasury belonging to the state to be $1,707,-056.24. Then deducting the amount of the tax of the previous year remaining uncollected January first, 1875, and afterwards collected, $998,628.11, the result shows the actual indebtedness on January first, 1875, to be $708,428.13.

The forthcoming annual report of the State Treasurer for January first, 1876, will show the indebtedness of the state, exclusive of the amounts to the credit of the Chickasaw and common school funds, the balance of current funds on hand, and warrants in the Treasury belonging to the state, to be $980,-138.33. Then, by proceeding again as above, and deducting the amount of the tax of the previous year, uncollected on January first, 1876, and now being rapidly paid into the Treasury, at a low estimate, $460,000.00, we have as an actual indebtedness of the state on January first 1876, $520,138.33. Thus it will be seen that the actual indebtedness of the state is but little over half million dollars, and that during the two years of Governor Ames' administration the state debt has been reduced from $821,292.82, on January first, 1874, to $520,138.33, on January first, 1876, or a reduction of more than three hundred thousand dollars in two years—upwards of one third of the state debt wiped out in that time. Not only has the debt been reduced as above, but the rate of taxation for general purposes has been reduced from seven mills in 1873 to four mills in 1875.

Notwithstanding the fact that the rate of taxation under the administration of Governor Ames had been reduced, as shown above, from seven mills in 1873 to four mills in 1875, the amount paid into the state treasury was substantially the same as that paid in prior years, which was due to the great appreciation to the value of taxable property. Then again, a material reduction in the rate of taxation was made possible because the public institutions had all been rebuilt and repaired and a sufficient number of school buildings had been erected, thus doing away with the necessity for a special levy for such purposes.

From this showing it would seem as if it were reasonable to assume that if such an administration like the one then in power could have been retained a few years longer there would not only have been a still further reduction in the rate of taxation, but that the payable debt of the state would have been entirely wiped out. Instead of this we find the situation to be about as follows.

First, shortly after the first reform state treasurer had been in charge of that office, it was developed that he was a defaulter to the amount of $315,612.19. Second, notwithstanding the immense increase in the value of taxable property from year to year, it appears from the official records that the rate of ad valorem tax for general purposes has been increased from four to six mills. Third, there has been a very heavy increase in what is known as the specific or privilege taxes—that is, a specific sum or amount that business and professional persons must pay for the privilege of doing business or practising their professions in the state. Fourth, the amounts now collected and paid out for the support of the state government are more than double what they were a few years ago or ought to be now, thus showing extravagance if not recklessness in the administration of the affairs of the state, which is the natural result of a condition by which the existence of but one political party is tolerated. Fifth, notwithstanding the immense increase in the value of taxable property and the enormous sums paid into the state treasury each year, there has been a material increase in the bonded debt of the state. In fact, it has been necessary at different times to borrow money with which to pay the current expenses of the state government.

The statistics for three years, 1907, 1908, and 1909, would seem to substantiate the conclusions arrived at, as stated above. The value of the taxable property of the state in 1907 was $373,584,960.00. Receipts from all sources that year were $3,-391,127.15. Disbursements of the same period were $3,370,343.-

29. Excess of disbursements over receipts was $339,218.14. In 1908 the value of taxable property was $383,823,739.00. Receipts from all sources that year were $3,338,398.98. Disbursements, same period, were $3,351,119.46. Excess of disbursement over receipts was $12,720.48. In 1909, the value of taxable property was $393,297,173.00. Receipts from all sources were $3,-303,965.65. Disbursements, same period, were $3,315,201.00. Excess of disbursements over receipts was $11,237.83. On the first day of January 1907, what is called the payable debt of the state was reported to be $1,253,029.07. On the first day of January 1876, it was $520,138.33; the increase, $732,890.74.

The Colored Vote: Mississippi

It is claimed that in states, districts, and counties in which the colored people are in the majority, the suppression of the colored vote is necessary to prevent "Negro domination"—to prevent the ascendancy of the blacks over the whites in the administration of the state and local governments. This claim is based upon the assumption that in all such states, districts, and counties, if the black vote were not suppressed, black men would be supported and elected to the office because they are black, and white men would be opposed and defeated because they are white.

Taking Mississippi for purposes of illustration, it will be seen that there has never been the slightest ground for such an apprehension. No colored man in that state ever occupied or aspired to a judicial position above that of justice of the peace and very few aspired to, or occupied, even that position. Of 7 state offices only 1, secretary of state, was filled by a colored man until 1873, when colored men were elected to 3 of the 7—lieutenant governor, secretary of state, and state superintendent of education. Of the 2 United States senators and 7 members of the lower house of Congress, not more than 1 colored man occupied a seat in each house at the same time. Of the 35 members of the state senate and 115 members of the House, which composed the total membership of the state legislature prior to 1874, there were never more than about 7 colored men in the senate and 40 in the lower house. Of the 97 members that composed the Constitutional Convention of 1868 but 17 were colored men. The composition of the lower house of the state legislature that was elected in 1871 was as follows: total membership, 115; republicans, 66; democrats, 49; colored members, 38; white members, 77; white majority, 39.

Of the sixty-six Republicans there were thirty-eight colored and twenty-eight whites. There was a slight increase in the colored membership as a result of the election of 1873, but the colored man never at any time had control of the state government or any branch of department thereof, or even that of any county or municipality. Out of seventy-two counties in the state at that time electing on an average, twenty-eight officers to a county, it is safe to assert that not over five out of one hundred of such officers were colored men. The state, district, county, and municipal governments were not only in control of white men but white men who were to the manor born, or who were known as old citizens of the state—those who had lived in the state many years before the War of the Rebellion. There was, therefore, never a time when that class of white man known as carpetbaggers ever had absolute control of the state government, or any district, county, or municipality or any branch or department thereof. There was never, therefore, any ground for the alleged apprehension of "Negro domination" as a result of a free, fair, and honest election in any one of the Southern or reconstructed states.

But this brings us to a consideration of the question as to what is meant by "Negro domination." The answer that the average reader would give to that question would be that it means the actual, physical domination of the blacks over the whites. But according to a high Democratic authority, that would be an incorrect answer. The definition given by that authority, I have every reason to believe, is the correct one—the generally accepted one. The authority referred to is the late associate justice of the supreme court of the state of Mississippi, H. H. Chalmers, who, in an article published in the *North American Review* about March 1881, explained and defined what is meant or understood by the term "Negro domination."[1]

According to his definition, to constitute "Negro domination" it does not necessarily follow that Negroes must be elected to office, but that in all elections in which white men may be divided, if the Negro vote should be sufficiently decisive in determining the result, the white man or men that would be elected through the aid of Negro votes would represent "Negro domination." In other words, we would have "Negro domination" whenever the will of a majority of the whites would be defeated through the votes of colored men. If this is the correct definition of that term, and it is no doubt the generally accepted one, then the friends and advocates of manhood suffrage will not deny that we have had in the past and may have in the future "Negro domination" nationally as well as locally.

If this is the correct definition, then we are liable to have "Negro domination" not only in states, districts, and counties where the blacks are in the majority, but in states, districts, and counties where they are few in number. If this is the correct definition of "Negro domination" to prevent which the Negro vote should be suppressed, then the suppression of that vote is

1. H. H. Chalmers, "The Effects of Negro Suffrage," *The North American Review* (March 1881), pp. 239–49.

not only necessary in states, districts, and counties in which the blacks are in the majority, but in every state, district, and county in the Union; for it will not be denied that the primary purpose of the ballot, whether the voter be white or colored, male or female, is to make his or her vote decisive and potential. If, then, the vote of a colored man, or the vote of a white man, determines the result of an election in which he participates, then the very purpose for which he was given the right or privilege will have been accomplished whether the result, as we understand it, be wise or unwise.

In this connection it cannot and will not be denied that the colored vote has been decisive and potential in very many important national as well as local and state elections. In the presidential election of 1868, for instance, General Grant, the Republican candidate, lost the important and pivotal state of New York, which would have resulted in his defeat if the Southern states that took part in that election had all voted against him. That they did not do so was due to the votes of the colored men in those states. Grant's first administration, therefore, represented "Negro domination." Again, in 1876, Hayes was declared elected president by a majority of one vote in the electoral college. This was made possible by the result of the election in the states of Louisiana, South Carolina, and Florida about which there was much doubt and considerable dispute and over which there was a bitter controversy. But for the colored vote in those states there would have been no doubt, no dispute, and no controversy. The defeat of Mr. Hayes would have been an undisputed and an uncontested fact. The Hayes administration, therefore, represented "Negro domination."

Again, in 1880 General Garfield, the Republican candidate for president, carried the state of New York by a plurality of about 20,000, without which he could not have been elected. It will not be denied by those who are well informed that if the colored men who voted for him in that state at that time had voted against him, he would have lost the state and with it, the presidency. The Garfield-Arthur administration, therefore, represented "Negro domination." Again in 1884, Mr. Cleveland, the Democratic candidate for president, carried the close and doubtful but very important state of New York by the narrow margin of 1,147, the plurality which resulted in his election. It cannot and will not be denied that even at that early date the number of colored men that voted for Mr. Cleveland was far in excess of the plurality by which he carried the state. Mr. Cleveland's first administration, therefore, represented "Negro domination." Mr. Cleveland did not hesitate to admit and appreciate the fact that colored men contributed largely to his success; hence, he did not fail to give that element of his party appropriate and satisfactory official recognition. Again, in 1888, General Harrison, the Republican presidential candidate, carried the state of New York by a plurality of about 20,000, which resulted in his election, which he would have lost but for the votes of the colored men in that state. Harrison's administration, therefore, represented "Negro domination."

The same is true of important elections in a number of states, districts, and counties in which the colored vote proved to be potential and decisive. But enough has been written to show the absurdity of the claim that the suppression of the colored vote is necessary to prevent "Negro domination." So far as the state of Mississippi is concerned, in spite of the favorable conditions as shown above, the legitimate state government, the one that represented the honestly expressed will of a majority of the voters of the state, was, in the fall of 1875, overthrown through the medium of a sanguinary revolution. The state government was virtually seized and taken possession of *vie et armis*. Why was this? What was the excuse for it? What was the motive, the incentive that caused it? It was not in the interest of good, efficient, and capable government, for that we already had. It was not on account of dishonesty, maladministration, and misappropriation of public funds, for every dollar of the public funds had been faithfully accounted for. It was not on account of high taxes, for it has been shown that while the tax rate was quite high during the Alcorn administration, it had been reduced under the Ames administration to a point considerably less than it is now, or has been for a number of years. It was not to prevent "Negro domination" and to make sure the ascendancy of the whites in the administration of the state and local governments, for that was then the recognized and established order of things, from which there was no apprehension of a departure. Then what was the cause of this sudden and unexpected uprising? There must have been a strange if not justifiable reason for it. What was it? That question will be answered in a subsequent chapter.

18

The Colored Vote: The South

In the last preceding chapter it was stated that the reason for the sanguinary revolution which resulted in the overthrow of the Republican state government in the state of Mississippi in 1875 would be given in a subsequent chapter. What was true of Mississippi at that time was largely true of the other reconstructed states where similar results subsequently followed. When the War of the Rebellion came to an end, it was believed by some and apprehended by others that serious and radical changes in the previous order of things would necessarily follow.

But when what was known as the Johnson plan of reconstruction was disclosed, it was soon made plain that if that plan should be accepted by the country no material change would follow, for the reason, chiefly, that the abolition of slavery would have been only in name. While physical slavery would have been abolished, yet a sort of feudal or peonage system would have been established in its place, the effect of which would have been practically the same as the system which had been abolished. The former slaves would have been held in a state of servitude through the medium of labor contracts which they would have been obliged to sign, or have signed for them, from which they and their children, and perhaps their children's children, could never have been released. This would have left the order of things practically unchanged. The large land owners would still be the masters of the situation, the power being still possessed by them to perpetuate their own potential influence and maintain their own political supremacy.

But it was the rejection of the Johnson plan of reconstruction that upset these plans and destroyed these calculations. The Johnson plan was not only rejected, but what was known as the congressional plan of reconstruction, by which suffrage was conferred upon the colored men in all the states that were to be reconstructed, was accepted by the people of the North as the permanent policy of the government and thus made the basis of reconstruction and readmission of those states into the Union.

Of course, this meant a change in the established order of things that was both serious and radical. It meant the destruction of the power and influence of the Southern aristocracy. It meant not only the physical emancipation of the blacks, but the political emancipation of the poor whites as well. It meant the destruction, in a large measure, of the social, political, and industrial distinctions that had been maintained among the whites under the old order of things. But was this to be the settled policy of the government? Was it a fact that the incorporation of the blacks into the body politic of the country was to be the settled policy of the government, or was it an experiment and a temporary expedient?

These were doubtful and debatable questions, pending the settlement of which, matters could not be expected to take a definite shape. With the incorporation of the blacks into the body politic of the country, which would have the effect of destroying the ability of the aristocracy to maintain their political supremacy, and which would have the effect of bringing about the political emancipation of the whites of the middle and lower classes, a desperate struggle between the antagonistic elements of the whites for political supremacy was inevitable and unavoidable. But the uncertainty growing out of the possibility of the rejection by the country of the congressional plan of reconstruction was what held matters in temporary abeyance. President Johnson was confident, or pretended to be, that as soon as the people of the North had an opportunity to pass judgment upon the issues involved, the result would be the acceptance of his plan and the rejection of the one proposed by Congress.

While the Republicans were successful in 1868, not only electing the president and vice-president and a safe majority in both branches of Congress, yet the closeness of the results had the effect of preventing the abandonment of the hope on the part of the supporters of the Johnson administration that the administration plan of reconstruction would ultimately be adopted and accepted as the basis of reconstruction. Hence bitter and continued opposition to the congressional plan of reconstruction was declared by the ruling class of the South to be the policy of that section. While the Republicans were again successful in the congressional election of 1870, the advocates of the Johnson plan did not abandon hope of the ultimate success and acceptance by the country of that plan until after the presidential and congressional elections of 1872.[1]

Since the result of the election was so large and so decisive and since every branch of the government was then in the hands of the Republicans, further opposition to the congressional plan of reconstruction was for the first time completely abandoned. The fact was then recognized that this was the set-

1. There follows a discussion of the campaign and election of 1872 that is virtually identical to the discussion in the previous chapter.

tled and accepted policy of the government and that further opposition to it was useless. A few of the Southern whites, General Alcorn being one of the number, had accepted the result of the presidential and congressional elections of 1868 as conclusive as to the policy of the country with reference to reconstruction, but those who thought and acted along those lines at that time were exceptions to the general rule. After the presidential and congressional elections of 1872 all doubt upon that subject was entirely removed. The Southern whites were now confronted with a problem that was both grave and momentous. But the gravity of the situation was chiefly based upon the possibility, if not probability, of a reversal of what had been the established order of things, especially those of a political nature.

The inevitable conflict between the antagonistic elements of which Southern society was composed could no longer be postponed or deferred. The colored vote was the important factor which now had to be considered and taken into account. It was conceded that whatever element or faction could secure the favor and win the support of the colored vote would be the dominant and controlling one in the state. It is true that between 1868 and 1872 when the great majority of Southern whites maintained a policy of "masterly inactivity," the colored voters were obliged to utilize such material among the whites as was available; but it is a well-known fact that much of the material thus utilized was from necessity and not from choice, and that whenever and wherever an acceptable and reputable white man would place himself in a position where his services could be utilized was gladly taken up and loyally supported by the colored voters.

After 1872 the necessity for supporting undesirable material by the colored voters no longer existed. They not only had the opportunity of supporting Southern whites for all the important positions in the state, but of selecting the best and most desirable among them. Whether the poor whites or the aristocrats of former days were to be placed in control of the affairs of the state was a question which the colored voters alone could settle and determine. That the colored man's preference should be the aristocrat of the past was perfectly natural, since the relations between them had been friendly, cordial, and amicable even during the days of slavery. Between the blacks and the poor whites the feeling had been just the other way. This, however, was due not so much to race antipathy as to jealousy and envy on the part of the poor whites, growing out of the cordial and friendly relations between the aristocrats and their slaves, and because the slaves were, in a large measure, their competitors in the industrial market. When the partiality for the former aristocrats on the part of the colored man became generally known, these former aristocrats began to come into the Republican party in large numbers.

They were led by such men as Alcorn, in Mississippi, Longstreet, in Georgia, Moseby in Virginia, and such ex-governors as Orr of South Carolina, Brown of Georgia, and Parsons of Alabama. Between 1872 and 1875, the accessions to the Republican ranks were so large that it is safe to assume and assert that from twenty-five to thirty percent of the white men of the Southern states were identified with the Republican party. This was not only true as to numbers, but those who thus acted were among the best and most substantial men of that section. Among that number in the state of Mississippi were J. L. Alcorn, J. A. Orr, J. B. Deason, R. W. Flournoy and Orlando Davis. In addition to these there were thousands of others, many of them among the most prominent men of the state. The names of only a few will here be mentioned, merely as examples. In that number was Judge Hiram Cassidy, who ran against me as the candidate of the Democratic party for Congress from the Sixth District in 1872. He was one of the most brilliant and successful members of the bar in southern Mississippi. Captain Thomas W. Bunt of Jefferson County was a member of one of the oldest, best, and most influential families at the South. The family connections were not, however, confined to the South; George Hunt Pendleton of Ohio, for instance, who was the Democratic candidate for vice-president of the United States on the ticket with McClellan in 1864, and who was later one of the United States senators from Ohio, was a member of the same family.

While the colored men held the key to the situation, the white men knew that the colored men had no desire to rule or dominate even the Republican party. All the colored men wanted and demanded was a voice in the government under which they lived and to the support of which they contributed, and a small but fair and reasonable proportion of the positions that were at the disposal of the voters of the state and of the administration.

While the colored men did not look with favor upon a political alliance with the poor whites, it must be admitted that, with very few exceptions, that class of whites did not seek and did not seem to desire such an alliance. For this there were several well-defined reasons. In the first place, while the primary object of importing slaves into that section was to secure labor for the cultivation of cotton, the slave was soon found to be an apt pupil in other lines of industry. In addition to having his immense plantations cultivated with slave labor, the slave owner soon learned that he could utilize the same kind of labor as carpenters, painters, plasterers, bricklayers, blacksmiths, and in all other fields of industrial occupation and usefulness. The whites who depended upon their labor for a living along these lines had their field of opportunity thus very much curtailed. Although the slaves were not responsible for this condition, the fact that they were there and thus utilized created a feeling of bitterness and antipathy on the part of the laboring whites which could not be easily removed and wiped out.

In the second place, the whites of that class were not at that time as ambitious politically as were the aristocrats. They had been held in political subjection so long that it required some time for them to realize that there had been a change. At that time they, with a few exceptions, were less efficient, less capable and knew less about matters of state and governmental administration than the ex-slaves. It was a rare thing, therefore, to find one of that class at that time that had any political ambition or manifested any desire for political distinction or official recognition. As a rule the whites that came into and took charge of the leadership of the Republican party between 1872 and 1875 were therefore members and representatives of the most substantial families of the land.

After the presidential election of 1872, none could be found who questioned the wisdom or practicability of the congressional plan of reconstruction or looked for its overthrow, change, or modification. After that election the situation was accepted and acquiesced in by everyone in perfect good faith. No one could be found in any party of either race who was bold or reckless enough to express the opinion that the congressional plan of reconstruction was a mistake or that Negro suffrage was a failure. On the contrary, it was admitted by all and denied by none that the wisdom of both had been fully tested and clearly vindicated. It will not be denied even now by those who will take the time to make a careful examination of the situation that no other plan could have been devised or adopted that could or would have saved the country the fruits of the victory that had been won on the field of battle. The adoption of any other plan would have resulted in the accomplishment of nothing but the mere physical abolition of slavery and a denial of the right of a state to withdraw from the Union. These would have been more abstract propositions with no authority vested in the national government for their enforcement. The war for the Union would have been practically a failure. The South would have gained and secured substantially everything for which it contended, except the establishment of an independent government. The black man, therefore, was the savior of his country not only on the field of battle, but after the smoke of battle had cleared away.

Notwithstanding the general acceptance of this plan after the presidential election of 1872, we find that, in the fall of 1874, there was a complete and radical change in the situation. It was sudden and unexpected. It came, as it were, in the twinkling of an eye. It was like a clap of thunder from a clear sky. It was the state and congressional elections of that year.

In the elections of 1872 nearly every state in the Union went Republican. In the state and congressional elections of 1874 the result was the reverse of what it was two years before–nearly every state going Democratic. Democrats were surprised and Republicans were dumbfounded. Such a result had not been expected, looked for, predicted, or anticipated by anyone. Even the state of Massachusetts, the birthplace of abolitionism–the cradle of American liberty–elected a Democratic governor. The Democrats had a majority in the national House of Representatives that was about equal to that which the Republicans elected two years before. Such veteran Republican leaders in the United States Senate as Chandler of Michigan, Windom of Minnesota, and Carpenter of Wisconsin were retired from the Senate. When the returns were all in it was developed that the Democrats did not have a clear majority joint-ballot in the Michigan legislature, but the margin between the two parties was so close that a few men who had been elected as Independent Republicans had the balance of power. These Independents were opposed to the reelection of Senator Chandler. That the Democrats should be anxious for the retirement of such an able, active, aggressive, and influential Republican leader as Chandler was to be expected. That party, therefore, joined with the Independents in the vote for senator which resulted in the election of a harmless old gentleman by the name of Christianson. What was true of Michigan was also found to be true of Minnesota, which resulted in the retirement of that strong and able leader in the person of Senator William Windom and the election of a new and unknown man by the name of McMillan.

What was true of Michigan and Minnesota was also found to be true of Wisconsin. The same sort of a combination was made which resulted in the retirement of the able and brilliant Matt Carpenter and the election of a new man who was not then known outside of the boundaries of his state, by the name of Cameron. Cameron proved to be an able man, a useful senator, a good Republican, and an improvement in some respects upon his predecessor, but his election was a defeat of the Republican organization in the state, which, of course, was the objective point with the Democrats.

It was the state and congressional elections of 1874 which proved to be the death of the Republican party at the South. The party at that section might have survived even such a crushing blow as this but for subsequent unfortunate events to which allusion has been made in a previous chapter and which will be touched upon in some that are to follow. Under these conditions its survival was impossible. If the state and congressional elections of 1874 had been a repetition of those of 1872, or if they had resulted in a Republican victory at all, Republican success in the presidential election of 1876 would have been a reasonably assured fact. By that time the party at the South would have included in its membership from forty to fifty percent of the white men of their respective states, and as a result thereof, it would have been strong enough to stand on its own feet and maintain its own independent existence regardless of reverses which the parent organization might have sustained in other sections. But at that time the party in that section was in its infancy. It was young, weak, and comparatively helpless. It still needed the fostering care and protecting hand of the paternal source of its existence.

When the smoke of the political battle that was fought in the early part of November 1874 had cleared away, it was found that this strong, vigorous, and healthy parent had been carried from the battlefield seriously wounded and unable to administer to the wants of its Southern offspring. The offspring was not strong enough to stand alone. The result was that its demise soon followed because it had been deprived of that nourishment, that sustenance, and that support which were essential to its existence and which could come only from the parent which had been seriously, if not fatally, wounded upon the field of battle. After the presidential election of 1872 Southern white men were not only coming into the Republican party in large numbers, but the liberal and progressive element of the Democracy was in the ascendancy in that organization. That element, therefore, shaped the policy and declared the principles for which their organization stood. This meant the acceptance of, and acquiescence in, what was regarded as the settled policy of the national government, by all political parties. In proof of this assertion, a quotation from a political editorial which appeared about that time in the Jackson, Mississippi, *Clarion*, the organ of the Democratic party, will not be out of place. In speaking of the colored people and their attitude towards the whites, that able and influential paper said, "While they [the colored people] have been naturally tenacious of their newly acquired privileges, their general conduct will bear them witness that they have shown consideration for the feelings of the whites. The race line in politics would never have been drawn if opposition had not been made to their enjoyment of equal privileges in the government and under the laws after they were emancipated."

In other words, the colored people had manifested no disposition to rule or dominate the whites, and that the only color line which had existed grew out of the unwise policy which had previously been pursued by the Democratic party in its efforts to prevent the enjoyment by the newly emancipated race of the rights and privileges to which they were entitled under the Constitution and laws of the country. But after the state and congressional elections of 1874 the situation was materially changed. The liberal and conservative element of the Democracy was relegated to the rear and the radical element came to the front and assumed charge. Subsequent to 1872 and prior to 1875 race proscription and social ostracism had been completely abandoned. A Southern white man could become a Republican without being socially ostracised. Such a man was no longer looked upon as a traitor to his section, an enemy to his people, or false to his race. He no longer forfeited the respect, confidence, goodwill, and favorable opinion of his friends and neighbors.

Bulldozing, criminal assaults, and lynchings were seldom heard of. On the contrary, cordial, friendly, and amicable relations between all classes and parties and both races prevailed everywhere. Fraud, violence, and intimidation at elections were neither suspected nor charged by anyone, for everyone knew that no occasion existed for such things. But after the state and congressional elections of 1874, there was a complete change of front. The new order of things was then set aside and the abandoned methods of a few years back were reviewed, reinaugurated, and readopted.

It is no doubt true that very few men at the North who voted the Republican ticket in 1872 and the Democratic ticket in 1874 were influenced in changing their votes by anything connected with reconstruction. There were other questions at issue, no doubt, that influenced their action. There had been in 1873, for instance, a disastrous financial panic. Then there were other things and acts connected with the national administration which met with popular disfavor. These were the reasons, no doubt, that influenced thousands of Republicans in voting the Democratic ticket at that time, merely as an indication of their dissatisfaction with the national administration.[2]

2. Lynch's acceptance of the view that Southerners who voted with the Republicans had accepted congressional reconstruction seems naïve. After all, various Southern states had been going Democratic since 1869, long before the panic of 1873. The path to domination was through the Repub-

Let their motives and reasons be what they may, the effect was the same as if they had intended their votes to be accepted and construed as an endorsement of the platform declarations of the National Democratic Convention of 1868, at least so far as reconstruction was concerned. Democrats claimed, and Republicans could not deny, that so far as the South was concerned, this was the effect of the congressional elections of 1874. Desertions from the Republican ranks at the South, in consequence thereof, became more rapid than had been the accessions between 1872 and 1875. Thousands who had not taken an open stand, but who were suspected of being inclined to the Republican party, denied that there had ever been any justifiable ground for such suspicions. Many who had taken an open stand on that side returned to the fold of the Democracy in sackcloth and ashes and upon bended knees, pleading for mercy, forgiveness, and for charitable forbearance. They had seen a new light; and they were ready to confess that they had made a grave mistake, but since their motives were good and their intentions were honest, they hoped that they would not be rashly treated nor harshly judged.

The prospects for the gratification and realization of the ambition that white men in that section might have had had been completely changed. The conviction became a settled fact that the Democratic party was the only channel through which it would be possible in the future for anyone to secure political distinction or receive official recognition—hence the return to the ranks of that party of thousands of white men who had left it. All of them were eventually received, but some were kept on the anxious seat and held as probationers for a long time. It was soon developed that what was left of the once promising and flourishing Republican party at the South was the true, faithful, loyal, and sincere colored men, who remained Repub-

---

lican party. Since they owed no loyalty to the party, they shifted at the first opportunity, as many did in 1874.

licans from necessity as well as from choice, and a few white men who were Republicans from principle and conviction and who were willing to incur the odium, run the risks, take the chances, and pay the penalty that every white Republican must then pay who had the courage of his convictions.

This was a sad and serious disappointment to the colored men who were just about to realize the hope and expectation of a permanent political combination and union between themselves and the better element of the whites, which would have resulted in good, honest, capable, and efficient local government and in the establishment and maintenance of peace, goodwill, friendly, cordial, and amicable relations between the two races. But this hope, politically at least, had now been destroyed and these expectations had been shattered and scattered to the four winds. For the colored men the outlook was dark and anything but encouraging. Many of the parting scenes that took place between the colored men and the whites who decided to return to the fold of the Democracy were both affecting and pathetic in the extreme.

The writer cannot resist the temptation to bring to the notice of the reader one of those scenes of which he had personal knowledge. Colonel James Lusk had been a prominent, conspicuous, and influential representative of the Southern aristocracy of the antebellum days. He enjoyed the respect and confidence of the people of the community in which he lived. This was especially true of the colored people. He, like thousands of others of his class, had identified himself with the Republican party. There was a Republican club in that community, of which Sam Henry, a colored man who was well and favorably known, was president. When it was rumored, and before it could be verified, that Colonel Lusk had decided to cast his fortunes with the Republican party, Henry appointed a committee of three to call on him and extend him a cordial invitation to appear before the club at its next meeting and deliver an address. The invitation was accepted. As soon as the colonel entered the door of the club escorted by the committee, every man in the house immediately arose and all joined in giving three cheers and hearty welcome to the gallant statesman and brave ex-Confederate soldier who had honored them with his distinguished presence on that occasion. He delivered a splendid speech, in which he informed his hearers that he had decided to cast his lot with the Republican party. It was the first public announcement of that fact that had been made. Of course he was honored, idolized, and lionized by the colored people wherever he was known.

After the congressional elections of 1874, Colonel Lusk decided that he would return to the ranks of the Democracy. Before making public announcement of that fact he decided to send for his faithful, loyal friend, Sam Henry, to come to see him at his private residence. He had something of importance to communicate to him. Promptly at the appointed time, Henry made his appearance. He did not know for what he was wanted, but he had a well-founded suspicion, based upon the changed conditions which were apparent in every direction; hence, a nervous apprehension could be easily detected in his countenance. Colonel Lusk commenced by reminding Henry of the fact that it was before the club of which he was president and upon his invitation that he, Lusk, had made public announcement of his intention to act in the future with the Republican party. Now that he had decided to renounce any further allegiance to that party, he thought that his faithful friend and loyal supporter, Sam Henry, should be the first to whom that announcement should be made. When this was done Henry was visibly affected and completely broke down.

"Oh no, Colonel!" he declared. "I beg of you do not leave us. You are our chief, if not sole dependence; you are our Moses. If you leave us, hundreds of others, in our immediate neighborhood, will be sure to follow your lead. We will thus be left without solid and substantial friends. I admit that with you, party affiliation is optional. With me it is not. You can be either a Republican or a Democrat and be honored and supported by the party to which you belong. With me it is different. I must remain a Republican whether I want to or not. While it is impossible for me to be a Democrat, it is not impossible for you to be a Republican. We need you. We need your prestige, your power, your influence, and your name. I pray you, therefore, not to leave us. For if you and those who will follow your lead will leave us now, we will be made to feel that we are without a country, without a home, without friends, and without a hope for the future. Oh no, Colonel! I beg of you, I plead with you, don't go, but stay with us, lead us and guide us as you have so faithfully done during the last few years."

Henry's remarks made a deep and profound impression upon Colonel Lusk. He informed Henry that no step he could take was more painful to him than this. He assured Henry that this act on his part was from necessity and not from choice. "The statement you have made, Henry, that party affiliations with me is optional, is presumed to be true, but in point of fact, it is not. No white man can live in the South in the future and act with any other than the Democratic party unless he is willing and prepared to live a life of social isolation and remain in political oblivion. While I am somewhat advanced in years, I am not so old as to be devoid of political ambition. Besides, I have two grown sons. There is, no doubt, a bright, brilliant, and successful future before them, if they are Democrats, otherwise not. If I remain in the Republican party, which can hereafter exist at the South only in name, I will thereby retard, if not mar, and possibly destroy, their future prospects. Then, you must remember that a man's first duty is to his family. My daughters are the pride of my home. I cannot afford to have them suffer the humiliating consequences of the social ostracism to which they may be subjected if I remain in the Republican party.

"The die is cast. I must yield to the inevitable and surrender my convictions upon the altar of my family's good, the outgrowth of circumstances and conditions which I am powerless to prevent and cannot control. Henceforth, I must act with the Democratic party or make myself a martyr, and I do not feel that there is enough at stake to justify me in making such a fearful sacrifice as that. It is, therefore, with deep sorrow and sincere regret, Henry, that I am constrained to leave you politically, but I find that I am confronted with a condition, not a theory. I am compelled to choose between you on one side and my family and personal interests on the other. That I have decided to sacrifice you and yours upon the altar of my family's good, is a decision for which you should neither blame nor censure me. If I could see my way clear to pursue a different course, it would be done, but my decision is based upon a careful and thoughtful consideration and must stand."

Of course a stubborn and bitter fight was now on, between the antagonistic and conflicting elements among the whites for the supremacy in, and control of, the Democratic organization. It was to be a desperate struggle between the former aristocrats on one side and what was known as the poor whites on the other. While the aristocrats had always been the weaker in point of numbers, they had always been the stronger in point of wealth, intelligence, ability, skill, and experience. As a result of their wide experience, able and skillful management, the aristocrats were successful in the preliminary struggles, as illustrated in the persons of Stephens, Gordon, Brown, and Hill of Georgia, Daniels and Lee of Virginia, Hampton and Butler of South Carolina, Lamar and Walthall of Mississippi, and Garland of Arkansas; but in the course of time and in the natural order of things, the poor whites were bound to win. All that was needed was a few years tutelage and a few daring and unscrupulous leaders to play upon their ignorance and magnify their vanity—to bring them to a realization and knowledge of the fact that their former political masters were now completely at their mercy and subject to their will.

That the poor whites of the antebellum period in most of

the late slaveholding reconstructed states are now the masters of the political situation in said states is a fact that will not be questioned, disputed, or denied by anyone who is well informed or who is familiar with the facts. The aristocracy of the ante-bellum days and their descendants in such states are as completely under the political control and domination of the poor whites of the antebellum period as those whites were under them at that time. And yet the reader must not assume that the election returns from the states referred to indicate the actual or even relative strength of the opposing and antagonistic elements and factions. They simply indicate that the poor whites of the past and their descendants are now the masters and leaders, and that the masters and leaders of the past are now the submissive followers.

In the ranks, therefore, of those who are now the recognized leaders is found some of the very best blood of the land—the descendants of the finest, best, most cultivated and refined families of their respective states. But as a rule they are there, not from choice, but from necessity—not because they are in harmony with, or because they approve of, what is being done and the methods that are being employed and pursued, but on account of circumstances and conditions which they can neither control or prevent. They would not hesitate to raise the arm of revolt if they had any hope or believed that ultimate success would be the result thereof. But as matters now stand, they can detect no ray of hope and can see no avenue of escape.

Hence, nothing remains for them to do but to hold the chain of political oppression and subjugation, while their former political subservients rivet and fasten the same around their unwilling necks. They find they can do nothing but sink their pride, their manhood, and their self-respect upon the altar of political necessity. They see, feel, and fully realize the hopelessness of their condition and the helplessness of their situation. They see, know, and acknowledge that in the line of political distinction and official recognition they can get nothing that their former political subservients are not willing for them to have. With a hope of getting a few crumbs that may fall from the official table, they make very wry faces and pretend to be satisfied and pleased with what is being done and the way in which it is done. They are looked upon with suspicion and their loyalty to the new order of things is a constant source of speculation, conjecture, and doubt. But, for reasons of political expediency, a few crumbs are allowed occasionally to go to someone of that class, which is gratefully acknowledged and thankfully received, upon the theory that some little consideration is better than none at all, especially in their present helpless and dependent condition. But even these small crumbs are confined to those who are most pronounced and outspoken in their declaration and protestations of loyalty, devotion, and subservient submission to the new order of things.[3]

3. This is a simplistic analysis of developments in the post-Reconstruction South. That the "former aristocrats" were not so helpless as Lynch suggests and that their stake in the New South was substantial and important have been treated by several students of the period. See, for example, C. Vann Woodward, *Origins of the New South, 1877–1913* (Baton Rouge, 1951).

1874: *Diminishing Republican Power*

THE FORTY-THIRD CONGRESS, THE ONE THAT WAS ELECTED IN 1872, met in regular session the first Monday in December 1873. I was thus brought in official contact with many of the most prominent men of the country of both parties. . . .[1] Mr. Blaine was speaker of the House and Hon. Edward McPherson of Pennsylvania was elected chief clerk. I was made a member of the Committee on Mines and Mining, of which Judge Lowe of Kansas was chairman.

The Mississippi Constitution, having been ratified in 1869, an odd year of the calendar, caused the regular elections for state, district, and county officers to occur on the odd years of the calendar, while the national election occurred on the even years of the calendar, thus necessitating the holding of an elec-

1. At this point Lynch lists the prominent Republican and Democratic members of the House.

tion in the state every year. No election was to be held in 1874, therefore, except to choose members of Congress and to fill a few vacancies. The regular election for county officers and members of the legislature would be held in 1875. Since the regular session of the Forty-fourth Congress would not convene before December 1875, to avoid the trouble and expense incident to holding an election in 1874, the legislature passed a bill postponing the elections of members of Congress until November 1875. There being some doubt about the legality of this legislature, Congress passed a bill legalizing the act of the legislature. Consequently no election was held in the state in 1874 except to fill a few vacancies that had occurred in the legislature and in some of the districts and counties.

One of the vacancies to be filled was that of state senator created by the resignation of Senator Hiram Cassidy, Jr. Senator Cassidy, who was elected in 1873 as a Democrat and who had voted for Mr. Bruce, the Republican caucus nominee for United States senator, had, in the meantime, publicly identified himself with the Republican party, thus following in the footsteps of his able and illustrious father, Judge Hiram Cassidy, Sr., who gave his active support to the Republican candidate for governor in 1873. Governor Ames had appointed Senator Cassidy a judge of the chancery court, to accept which it was necessary for him to resign his seat as a member of the state senate. A special election was held in November 1874 to fill that vacancy. The Democrats nominated a strong and able man in the person of Judge R. H. Thompson, of Brookhaven, Lincoln County. The Republicans nominated a still stronger and abler man in the person of Hon. J. F. Sessions of the same town and county. He had served several terms in the legislature as a Democrat from Franklin County, but had that year identified himself with the Republican party. He was Chancellor Cassidy's partner.

Since the counties comprising that senatorial district constituted a part of the district I then represented in Congress, I took an active part in the support of the candidacy of Sessions. Although a Democrat was elected from that district in 1873 in the person of Hiram Cassidy, Jr., Sessions was elected in 1874 as a Republican by a handsome majority. A vacancy had also occurred in the legislature from Franklin County, to fill which the Republicans nominated Hon. William P. Cassidy, brother of Chancellor C. Cassidy, but the Democratic majority in the county was too large for one even so popular as William P. Cassidy to overcome; hence, he was defeated by a small majority.

From a Republican point of view Mississippi, as was true of the other reconstructed states, up to 1875 was all that could be expected and desired and no doubt would have remained so for many years but for the unexpected results of the state and congressional elections of 1874. While, it is true, as stated and explained in a previous chapter, that Grant carried nearly every state in the Union for president in 1872, the state and congressional elections throughout the country two years later went just the other way and by majorities just as decisive as those given the Republicans two years before.

Notwithstanding the severe and crushing defeat sustained by the Republicans at that time, it was claimed by some, believed by others, and predicted by many, that, by the time the election for president in 1876 would roll around, it would be found that the Republicans had regained substantially all they had lost in 1874, but these hopes, predictions, and expectations were not realized. The presidential election of 1876 turned out to be so close and doubtful that neither party could claim a substantial victory. While it is true that Hayes, the Republican candidate for president, was finally declared elected according to the form of law, yet the terms and conditions upon which he was allowed to be peaceably inaugurated were such as to complete the extinction and annihilation of the Republican party at the

South. The price that the Hayes managers stipulated to pay and did pay for the peaceable inauguration of Hayes was that the South was to be turned over to the Democrats and that the administration was not to enforce the Constitution and the laws of the land in that section against the expressed will of the Democrats thereof. In other words so far as the South was concerned, the Constitution was not to follow the flag.[2]

In the Forty-third Congress, which was elected in 1872 and which would expire by limitation on 4 March 1875, the Republicans had a large majority in both houses. In the House of Representatives of the Forty-fourth Congress, which was elected in 1874, the Democratic majority was about as large as was the Republican majority in the House of the Forty-third Congress. The Republicans still retained control of the Senate but by a greatly reduced majority.

During the short session of the Forty-third Congress, important legislation was contemplated by the Republican leaders. Alabama was one of the states which the Democrats were charged with having carried in 1874 by resorting to methods which were believed to be questionable and illegal. An investigation was ordered by the House. A committee was appointed to make the investigation, of which General Albright of Pennsylvania was chairman. This committee was authorized to report by bill or otherwise. After a thorough investigation, the chairman was directed and instructed by the vote of every Republican member of the committee, which constituted a majority thereof, to report and recommend the passage of what was called a Federal Elections Bill. This bill was carefully drawn. It followed, substantially, the same lines as a previous temporary measure under the provisions of which what was

2. For the most recent discussion of the several factors that determined the outcome of the disputed election of 1876, see C. Vann Woodward, *Reunion and Reaction: The Compromise of 1877 and the End of Reconstruction* (Boston, 1951).

known as the Ku Klux Klan had been crushed out and order and fair elections had been restored in North Carolina.

It is safe to say that this bill would have passed both houses and become a law, but for the unexpected opposition of Speaker Blaine. Mr. Blaine was not only opposed to the bill, but his opposition was so intense that he felt it his duty to leave the Speaker's chair and come on the floor for the purpose of leading the opposition to its passage. This, of course, was fatal to the passage of the measure. After a desperate struggle of a few days, in which the Speaker was found to be in opposition to a large majority of his party associates, which revealed the fact that the party was hopelessly divided, the leaders in the House abandoned the effort to bring the measure to a vote.

Mr. Blaine's motives in taking this strange and unexpected position in open opposition to the great majority of his party associates has always been open to speculation and conjecture. His personal and political enemies charged that it was due to jealousy of President Grant. Mr. Blaine was a pronounced candidate for the Republican presidential nomination the following year. It was a well-known fact that President Grant was not favorable to Mr. Blaine's nomination, but was in sympathy with the movement to have Senator Roscoe Conkling of New York, Mr. Blaine's bitterest political enemy, nominated. Mr. Blaine was afraid, his enemies asserted, that if the Federal Elections Bill had become a law under the provisions of which great additional power would have been conferred upon the president, that power would be used to defeat his nomination for the presidency in 1876—hence his opposition to the bill. Whatever his motives were, his opposition to and defeat of that measure no doubt resulted in his failure to realize the ambition of his life—the presidency of the United States. But for the stand he took on that occasion, he no doubt would have received enough support in the national convention from the South to secure him the nomination, and had he been nominated at that time, the probabilities are that he would have been elected. But his opposition to that bill practically solidified the Southern delegates in that convention against him, and as a result thereof, he was defeated for the nomination, although he was the choice of a majority of the delegates from the North.

Even when he received the nomination in 1884, it was developed that he could not have been nominated then if the Southern delegates had been as solidly against him at that time as they were in 1876. By that time, however, the Southern Republicans had somewhat relented in their opposition to him, and as a result thereof he received sufficient support from that section to give him the nomination. But he was defeated at the polls because the South was solid against him, a condition which was made possible by his own action in defeating the Federal Elections Bill in 1875. In consequence of his action in that matter, he was severely criticized and censured by Republicans generally and Southern Republicans especially.

Although I was not favorable to his nomination for the presidency at any time, my relations with Mr. Blaine had been so cordial and friendly that I felt at liberty to approach him and ask him, for my own satisfaction and information, for an explanation of his action in opposing and defeating the Federal Elections Bill. I therefore approached him just before the final adjournment of the Forty-third Congress and informed him that I desired to have a few minutes private audience with him whenever it would be convenient for him to see me. He requested me to come to the Speaker's room immediately after the adjournment of the House that afternoon.

When I entered he was alone. I took a seat, at his request, only a few feet from him. I informed him of the great disappointment and intense dissatisfaction which his action had caused in defeating what was not only regarded as a party measure, but which was believed by Republicans generally and Southern Republicans especially to be of vital importance from a party point of view, to say nothing of its equity and justice. I remarked that for him to array himself in opposition to the great majority of his own party associates and throw the weight of his great power and influence against such an important party measure as the Federal Elections Bill was believed to be, he must have had some motive, some reason, and some justifiable grounds of which the public was ignorant, but about which I believed it was fair to himself and just to his own friends and party associates that at least some of them be informed and enlightened.

"As a Southern Republican member of the House and one that is not hostile or particularly unfriendly to you, I feel that I have a right to make this request of you."

At first he gave me a look of surprise and for several seconds he remained silent. Then straightening himself up in his chair he said, "I am glad, Mr. Lynch, you have made this request of me, since I am satisfied you are not actuated by any unfriendly motive in doing so. I shall, therefore, give a frank and candid answer to your question. In my judgment," he said, "if that bill had become a law, the defeat of the Republican party throughout the country would have been a foregone conclusion. We could not have saved the South even if the bill had passed, but its passage would have lost us the North. I could not have carried my own state, Maine, if that bill had passed. In my opinion it was better to lose the South and save the North than to try through such legislation to save the South and thus lose both North and South. I believed that if we saved the North we could then look after and take care of the South. If the Southern Democrats are foolish enough to bring about a solid South, the result will be a solid North against a solid South; in which case the Republicans would have nothing to fear. You now have my reasons, frankly and candidly given, for the action taken by me on the occasion referred to with which I hope you are satisfied."

I thanked Mr. Blaine cordially for giving me the desired information in explanation of his remarkable action in that important matter. "I feel better satisfied with reference to your action upon that occasion. While I do not and cannot agree with you in your conclusions and believe your reasoning to be unsound and fallacious, still I cannot help but give you credit for having been actuated by no other motive than to do what you honestly believed was for the best interest of the country and the Republican party."

1875: Gloomy Prospects for Reelection

When I returned to my home after the adjournment of Congress in March 1875, the political clouds were dark. The outlook, politically, was discouraging. The prospect of Republican success was not at all bright. There had been a marked change in the situation from every point of view. Democrats were bold, outspoken, defiant, and determined. In addition to these unfavorable indications, I noticed that I was not received and greeted by them with the same warmth and cordiality as on previous occasions. With a few exceptions, they were cold and indifferent in their attitude and manner. This treatment was so radically different from that to which I had been accustomed that I could not help but feel it keenly. I knew it was indicative of a change in the political situation which meant that I had before me the fight of my life.

My advocacy and support of the Federal Elections Bill, commonly called the "Force Bill" was occasionally given as the reason for this change, but I knew this was not the true reason. In fact, that bill would hardly have been thought of or referred to but for the fact that Mr. Blaine, the Republican Speaker of the House, had attracted national attention to it through his action in vacating the chair and coming on the floor of the House to lead the opposition to its passage. This act on the part of the statesman from Maine made him, in the opinion of many Southern Democrats, the greatest man that our country had ever produced, George Washington, the father of the Republic, not excepted. They were loud in their thanks for the valuable service he had thus rendered them, and as evidence of their gratitude to him, they declared it to be their determination to show their appreciation of this valuable service in a substantial manner whenever the opportunity presented itself for it to be done.

No man in the country was stronger, or more popular, than the statesman from Maine, until his name came before them as a candidate for president of the United States on a Republican ticket. A sudden transformation then took place. It was then discovered, to their great surprise and disappointment, that he was such an unsafe and dangerous man that no greater calamity could happen to the country than his elevation to the presidency. Nothing, therefore, must be left undone to bring about his defeat.

I was well aware of the fact at the time that it was the result of the state and congressional elections at the North in 1874 that had convinced Southern Democrats that Republican ascendancy in the national government would soon be a thing of the past—that the Democrats would be successful in the presidential and congressional elections of 1876 and that that party would no doubt remain in power for at least a quarter of a century. It was this, and not the unsuccessful effort to pass a Federal Elections Bill that produced the marked change that was noticeable on every hand. Every indication seemed to point to a confirmation of the impression that Democratic national success was practically an assured fact.

There had been a disastrous financial panic in 1873 which was no doubt largely responsible for the political upheaval in 1874, but that was lost sight of in accounting for that result. In fact, they made no effort to explain it or account for it except in their own way. The Democrats had carried the country, the reasons for which they construed to suit themselves. The construction they placed upon it was that it was a national condemnation and repudiation of the congressional plan of reconstruction and they intended to govern themselves accordingly.

The election in Mississippi in 1875 was for members of Congress, members of the legislature, and county officers, and also a state treasurer to serve out the unexpired term of Treasurer Holland, deceased. My own renomination for Congress from the Sixth, or Natchez, District was a foregone conclusion, since I had no opposition in my own party, but I realized the painful fact that a nomination this time was not equivalent to an election. Still, I felt that it was my duty to make the fight, let the result be what it may.

If congressmen had been elected in 1874, the state would have returned five Republicans and one Democrat as was done in 1872. But in 1875 the prospect was not so bright and the indications were not so favorable. The Democrats nominated for treasurer Hon. William L. Hemingway of Carroll County. He was an able man and had been quite prominent as a party leader in his section of the state. The defiant attitude assumed, the aggressive position taken, and the bold declaration contained in the platform upon which he was nominated were accepted by the Republicans as notice that the Democrats intended to carry the election—"peaceably" and "fairly"—but of course to carry it just the same.

The Republicans nominated Hon. George M. Buchanan of Marshall County upon a platform which strongly endorsed the national and state administrations. Mr. Buchanan was a strong and popular man. He had been a brave and gallant Confederate soldier. He had been for several years sheriff and Tax Collector of his county. He was known, therefore, to be especially fitted for the office of state treasurer. As sheriff and Tax Collector of Marshall County, one of the wealthiest counties in the state, he had handled and disbursed many thousands of dollars, every dollar of which had been faithfully accounted for. His honesty, integrity, ability, fitness, and capacity no one questioned, but everyone unhesitatingly admitted.

The administration of Governor Ames was one of the best the state had ever had. The judiciary was quite equal to that which had been appointed by Governor Alcorn. The public revenues had been promptly collected and honestly accounted for. There had not only been no increase in the rate of taxation, but, on the contrary, there had been a material reduction. Notwithstanding these things, the Democrats, with the radical element in charge of the party machinery, determined to seize possession of the state government *vie et armis*, not because it was at all necessary for any reason or from any point of view, but simply because conditions at that time seemed to indicate that it could be safely and easily done.

After the nominations had all been made, the campaign was opened in dead earnest. Nearly all Democratic clubs in the state were converted into armed military companies. Funds with which to purchase arms were believed to have been contributed by the national Democratic organization. Nearly every Republican meeting was attended by one or more of those clubs or companies, the members of which were distinguished by red shirts indicative of blood, the attendance being for the purpose, of course, of keeping the peace and preserving order. To enable the Democrats to carry the state, a Republican majority of between twenty and thirty thousand had to be overcome. This could be done only by the adoption and enforcement of questionable methods. It was a case in which the end justified the means and the means had to be supplied.

The Republican vote consisted of about ninety-five percent of the colored men and about twenty-five percent of the white men. The other seventy-five percent of the whites, or most of them, formerly constituted a part of the flower of the Confederate army. They were not only tried and experienced soldiers, but they were fully armed and equipped for the work before them. Some of the colored Republicans had been Union soldiers, but they were neither organized nor armed. In such a contest, therefore, they and their white allies were entirely at the mercy of their political adversaries.

Governor Ames soon took in the situation. He saw he could not depend upon the white members of the state militia to obey his orders and support him in his efforts to uphold the majesty of the law and to protect the law-abiding citizens in the enjoyment of life, liberty, and property. To use the colored members of the militia for such a purpose would be adding fuel to the flames. Nothing, therefore, remained for him to do but to call on the national administration for military aid in his efforts to crush out domestic violence and enforce the laws of the state, which was done, but which, for reasons that will be given in a subsequent chapter, was not granted.

When the polls closed on the day of election, the Democrats, of course, had carried the state by a large majority, the same party having secured a heavy majority in both branches of the legislature. Of the six members of Congress, I was the only one of the regular Republican candidates that pulled through and that by a greatly reduced majority. In the Second, or Holly Springs, District, G. Wiley Wells ran as an Independent Republican against A. R. Howe, the sitting member and regular Republican candidate for reelection. The Democrats supported Wells, who was elected.

The delegation therefore consisted of four Democrats, one Republican, and one Independent Republican. While the delegation would have consisted of five straight Republicans and one Democrat had the election been held in 1874; still, since the Democrats had such a large majority in the House, the political complexion of the Mississippi delegation was not important. My election, it was afterwards developed, was due in all probability to a miscalculation on the part of some of the Democratic managers. Their purpose was to have a solid delegation, counting Wells as one of that number, since his election would be due to the support of that party.

But in my district the plan miscarried. In one of the counties there were two conflicting reports as to what the Democratic majority was. According to one report it was 250. According to the other it was 500. The report giving 250 was no doubt the correct one, but the other no doubt would have been accepted had it been believed at the time to be necessary to insure the election of the Democratic candidate. To overcome the majority in that district was more difficult than that of any of the others. While their candidate, Colonel Roderick Seal, was a popular man, yet it was well known that I would poll a solid Republican vote, or such of it as would be allowed to vote, and some Democratic votes in addition. Fortunately for me, there was a split in the party in my own county, Adams, for county officers, which resulted in bringing out a very heavy vote. This split also made the count very slow, covering a period of several days. My name was on both tickets. The election took place on Tuesday, but the count was not finished until the following Friday evening. Hence the result for member of Congress in that county could not be definitely ascertained until that time.

The Democratic managers at the state capital were anxious to know as soon as possible what the Republican majority in Adams County would be for congressman; hence, on Wednesday evening the editor of the local Democratic paper received a telegram from the Secretary of the Democratic state committee, requesting to be informed, immediately, about what the

Republican majority would be in Adams County for congressman. The editor read the telegram to me and asked what, in my opinion, would be my majority in the county. My reply was that I did not think it would exceed 1200. In that opinion he concurred, hence his reply was in these words: "Lynch's majority in Adams will not exceed 1200."

Upon receipt of this telegram the majority of 250 instead of 500 was deemed sufficient from the county heretofore referred to. If the Republican majority in Adams would not exceed 1200, the success of the Democratic congressional candidate by a small but safe majority was assured on the face of the returns. Since Adams was the last county to be reported, no change could thereafter be made. When the count was finally finished in Adams, it was found that I had a majority of over 1800. This gave me a majority in the district of a little over 200 on the face of the returns.

The disappointment and chagrin on the part of the Democratic managers can better be imagined than described. But the agreeable surprise to the Republicans was at least equal to the disappointment and chagrin on the part of the Democrats. The defeated Democratic candidate threatened to make a contest for the seat on the ground of violence and fraud, but this was so ridiculous and absurd that the managers and leaders of his own party would not allow him to carry the threat into execution.

1875: Conversation with the President

SHORTLY AFTER I REACHED WASHINGTON, THE LATTER PART OF November 1875, I called on the president to pay my respects and to see him on business. The president had recently issued a Civil Service order which some of the federal officeholders evidently misunderstood.[1] Postmaster Purcell of Summit, an important town in my district, was one of that number. He was supposed to be Republican, having been appointed as such. But he not only refused to take any part in the campaign of 1875, he also declined to contribute a dollar to meet the legitimate expenses of the same. The President's Civil Service order was his excuse. According to his construction of that order, federal officeholders must not only take no part in political or party campaigns but they must make no contributions

1. This apparently refers to "Further Rules for Promoting the Efficiency of the Civil Service of the United States," issued by President Grant, 5 August 1873. James D. Richardson, *Messages and Papers of the Presidents* (New York, 1897), 9:4184–89.

for political purposes. He not only said nothing and did nothing in the interest of his party in that campaign, but it was believed by some that he did not even vote the Republican ticket.

After paying my respects to the president, I brought this case to his attention. I informed him that I very much desired to have Postmaster Purcell removed and a good Republican appointed in his stead.

"What is the matter with him?" the president asked. "Is he not a good postmaster?"

"Yes," I replied, "there is nothing to be said against him so far as I know, with reference to his administration of the office. What I have against him is solely on account of politics. He may be, and no doubt is, a good, capable, and efficient postmaster, but politically he is worthless. From a party point of view he is no good. In my opinion there ought to be a man in that office who will not only discharge the duties of the same in a creditable and satisfactory manner, but who will also be of some service to the party and the administration under which he serves. In the place of the present postmaster of the town of Summit, we have one whose name I now present and ask for your favorable consideration. We had, as you know, a bitter and desperate struggle. It was the very time that we stood sadly in need of every man and every vote. We lost the county that Summit is in, by a small majority. If an active and aggressive man, such as the one whose name I now place before you, had been postmaster at Summit, the result in that county might have been different. I therefore earnestly recommend that Purcell be removed and that Mr. Garland be appointed to succeed him."

The president replied, "You have given good and sufficient reason for a change. Leave with me the name of the man you desire to have appointed and his name will be sent to the Senate as soon as Congress meets." I thanked the president cordially and assured him that he would have no occasion to regret making the change. In explanation of his Civil Service order, the president remarked that quite a number of officeholders had seemed to misunderstand it, although it was plainly worded and, as he thought, not difficult to understand. There had never been any serious complaints growing out of active participation in political campaigns on the part of officeholders, and that it was not, and never had been, the purpose of the administration, by executive order or otherwise, to limit or restrict any American citizen in the discharge and exercise of his duties as such, simply because he happened to be an officeholder, provided in so doing he did not neglect his official duties. But there had been serious complaints from many parts of the country about the use and abuse of federal patronage in efforts to manipulate party conventions and to dictate and control party nominations. To break up and, if possible, to destroy this evil was the primary purpose of the Civil Service order referred to.

I informed the president that his explanation of the order was in harmony with my own construction and interpretation of it. That is why I made the recommendation for a change in the postmastership at Summit. The change was promptly made. But I informed the president that there was another matter about which I desired to talk with him briefly, and that was the recent election in Mississippi. After calling his attention to the sanguinary struggle through which we had passed and the great disadvantages under which we labored, I reminded him of the fact that when the governor saw that we could not put down, without the assistance of the national administration, what was practically an insurrection against the state government, he made application for that assistance in the manner and form prescribed by the Constitution, with the confident hope and belief that it would be forthcoming. But in this we were, for some reason, sadly and seriously disappointed and greatly surprised. The reason for this action, or rather nonaction, is still an unexplained mystery to us. For my own satisfaction and information I should be pleased to have the president enlighten me on the subject.

The president said he was glad I asked him the question. He said he would take pleasure in giving me a frank and candid answer. He said he had sent Governor Ames's requisition to the War Department with his approval and with instructions to have the necessary assistance furnished without delay. He had also given instructions to the attorney general to use the marshals and the machinery of the federal judiciary as far as possible or practicable in cooperation with the War Department in an effort to maintain order and in bringing about a condition which would insure a peaceable and fair election.

But before the orders were put into execution, a committee of prominent Republicans from Ohio called on him. Ohio was then an October state. That is, her elections took place in October instead of November. An important election was then pending in that state. This committee, the president stated, protested against having the requisition of Governor Ames honored. The committee, the president said, informed him in a most emphatic way that if the requisition of Governor Ames were honored, the Democrats would not only carry Mississippi, which would be lost to the Republicans in any event, but the Democratic success in Ohio would, in that event, be an assured fact. If the requisition were not honored, it would make no change in the result in Mississippi but Ohio would be saved to the Republicans. The president stated that with great reluctance he had yielded, against his own judgment and sense of official duty, to the arguments and requests of this committee and thereupon directed the withdrawal of the orders which had been given the secretary of war and the attorney general in that matter. This statement, I confess, surprised me very much.

"Can it be possible," I said, "that there is such a prevailing sentiment in any state at the North, East, or West, as renders it necessary for a Republican president to virtually give his sanction to what is equivalent to a suspension of the Constitution and the laws of the land to insure Republican success in such a state? I cannot believe this to be true, the opinion of the Republican committee from Ohio to the contrary notwithstanding. What surprises me more, Mr. President, is that you yielded and granted this remarkable request. That is not like you. It is the first time I have ever known you to show the white feather. Instead of granting the request of that committee, you should have rebuked them and told them that it is your duty as chief magistrate of the country to enforce the Constitution and laws of the land and to protect the American citizens in the exercise and enjoyment of their rights, let the consequences be what they may, and that if in doing this Ohio would be lost to the Republicans, it ought to be lost—in other words, no victory is worth having if it is to be brought about upon such conditions as those—if it is to be purchased at such a fearful cost as was paid in this case."

"Yes!" said the president, "I admit that you are right. I should not have yielded. I believed at the time that I was making a grave mistake. But the way in which it was presented, it was duty on one side and party obligation on the other. Between the two, I hesitated, but finally yielded to what was believed to be party obligation. If a mistake was made, it was one of the head and not of the heart. That my heart was right and my intentions good, no one who knows me will question. If I had believed that any effort on my part would have saved Mississippi I would have made it, even if I had been convinced that it would have resulted in the loss of Ohio to the Republicans. But I was satisfied then, as I am now, that Mississippi could not have been saved to the party in any event, and I wanted to avoid the responsibility of the loss of Ohio in addition. This was the turning point in that case.[2]

2. President Grant said nothing to Lynch regarding the efforts of Mississippi's Senator H. R. Pease to persuade the president *not* to send troops to Mississippi. A member of the anti-Ames faction of the Republican party, Pease apparently convinced the President that the citizens could maintain order and that the sending of federal troops would be "a positive injury to the state." Garner, *Reconstruction in Mississippi*, p. 391.

Chapter Twenty-one

"But while on this subject," said the president, "let us look more closely into the significance of this situation. I am very much concerned about the future of our country. When the war came to an end it was thought that four things had been brought about and effectually accomplished as a result thereof. They were: first, that slavery had been forever abolished; second, that the indissolubility of the federal union had been permanently established and universally recognized and acquiesced in by all; third, that the absolute and independent sovereignty of the several states was a thing of the past; fourth, that a national sovereignty had been at last created and established, resulting in sufficient power being vested in the general government, not only to guarantee to every state in the Union a republican form of government, but to protect, when necessary, the citizen's enjoyment of the rights and privileges to which he is entitled under the Constitution and laws of his country. In other words, that there had been created a national citizenship as distinguished from state citizenship resulting in a paramount allegiance to the United States, the general government, having ample power to protect its own citizens against domestic and personal violence whenever the state in which he may live should fail, refuse, or neglect to do so. In other words, so far as citizens of the United States are concerned, the states in the future would only act as agents of the general government in protecting the citizens of the United States in the enjoyment of life, liberty, and property.

"This has been my conception of the duties of the president, and until recently I have pursued that course. But there seems to be a number of leading and influential men in the Republican party who take a different view of these matters. These men have used and are still using their power and influence, not to strengthen, but to cripple the president and thus prevent him from enforcing the Constitution and laws along these lines. They have not only used and are using their power and influence to prevent and defeat wise and necessary legislation for these purposes, but they have contributed and are contributing, through the medium of public meetings and newspaper and magazine articles, to the creation of a public sentiment hostile to the policy of the administration. Whatever their motives may be, future mischief of a very serious nature is bound to be the result.

"It requires no prophet to foresee that the national government will soon be at a great disadvantage, and the results of the War of the Rebellion will have been, in a large measure, lost. In other words, that the first two of the four propositions above stated will represent all that will have been accomplished as a result of the war, and even they, for the lack of power in the general government for their enforcement, will be largely of a negative character. What you have just passed through in the state of Mississippi is only the beginning of what is sure to follow. I do not wish to create unnecessary alarm, or to be looked upon as a prophet of evil, but it is impossible for me to close my eyes in the face of things that are as plain to me as the noonday sun."

It is needless to say that I was deeply and profoundly interested in, and completely carried away with, the president's eloquent and prophetic language which subsequent events have more than fully verified.

Eighteen seventy-six was the year of the presidential election. The Republicans had carried the country in 1872 by such a decisive majority that it indicated a continuation of Republican ascendancy in the national government for many years. But the severe reverses sustained by that party at the polls two years later completely changed this situation and outlook. Democrats confidently expected and Republicans seriously apprehended that the presidential election of 1876 would result in a substantial Democratic victory. Mr. Blaine was the leading candidate for the Republican presidential nomination, but he had strong and bitter opposition in the ranks of his own party.

That opposition came chiefly from friends and supporters of Senator Conkling at the North and from Southern Republicans generally. The opposition of the Conkling men to Mr. Blaine was largely personal, while Southern Republicans were opposed to him on account of his opposition to, and defeat of, the Federal Elections Bill. The great majority of Southern Republicans supported Senator Oliver P. Morton of Indiana.

After the national convention had been organized, it looked for a while as if Mr. Blaine's nomination was a foregone conclusion. Hon. Edward McPherson of Pennsylvania, a strong Blaine man, had been made president of the convention. In placing Mr. Blaine's name in nomination, Hon. Robert G. Ingersoll of Illinois made such an able, eloquent, and effective speech that he came very near, it was thought by many, to carrying the convention by storm and thus securing the nomination of the statesman from Maine. But the opposition to Mr. Blaine was too well organized to allow the convention to be stampeded even by the power and eloquence of an Ingersoll. It was this speech that gave Mr. Ingersoll his national fame and brought him to the front as a public speaker and lecturer. It was the most eloquent and impressive speech that was delivered during the sitting of the convention. After a bitter struggle of many hours and a number of fruitless ballots, the convention finally nominated Governor R. B. Hayes of Ohio as a compromise candidate. This result was brought about through a union of the combined opposition to Mr. Blaine. Hon. William A. Wheeler of New York was nominated for vice-president and the work of the convention was over.

The Democrats nominated ex-Governor Samuel J. Tilden of New York for president and Thomas A. Hendricks of Indiana for vice-president, upon a platform which pledged and promised many radical reforms in the administration of the government. This ticket was made with the hope and expectation that it would be successful in the doubtful and debatable states of New York, New Jersey, Indiana, and Connecticut, which, with the solid South, would constitute a majority of the electoral college, even if all the other states should go Republican, which was not anticipated.

That the prospect of Democratic success was exceedingly bright and the probability of a Republican victory extremely dark was generally conceded. The South was counted upon to be solid in its support of the Democratic ticket, for the methods that had been successfully inaugurated in Mississippi the year before to overcome a Republican majority of more than twenty thousand were to be introduced and adopted in all the other states in that section in which conditions were practically the same.

To insure success, therefore, it was only necessary for the Democrats to concentrate their efforts upon the four doubtful states outside of the solid South. Up to a certain point the plan worked admirably well. Every indication seemed to point to its successful consummation. As had been anticipated, the Democrats were successful in the four doubtful Northern states, and they also carried, on the face of the returns, every Southern state, just as had been planned and calculated, the Mississippi methods having been adopted in such of them as had Republican majorities to overcome. Since through those methods they had succeeded in overcoming a large Republican majority in Mississippi, there was no reason why the same methods should not produce like results in South Carolina, Louisiana, and Florida. In fact, it was looked upon as a reflection upon the bravery and party loyalty of the Democracy of those states if they could not do what had been done under like conditions in Mississippi. Hence those states *had* to be carried, "peaceably" and "fairly," of course, but they must be carried just the same. Failure to carry them was out of the question, because too much was involved. According to the plans and calculations that had been carefully made, no Southern state could be lost. While it might be possible to win without all of them, still it was not believed to be safe to run any such risk or take any such chance. If they should happen to carry a state that was not included in the combination, so much the better, but no one in the combination must be allowed to fail.

Everything seemed to work admirably well. That it was a plan by which elections could be easily carried with or without votes had been clearly demonstrated. On the face of the returns, therefore, the majorities were brought forth, just as had been ordered and directed. But it seems that such methods had been anticipated by the Republican state governments in South Carolina, Louisiana, and Florida, and that suitable steps had been taken to prevent their successful consummation through the medium of state returning boards. When the returning boards had rejected and thrown out many of the majorities that had been returned from some of the counties and parishes, the result was changed and the Republican candidates for presidential electors were officially declared elected. This gave the Republican candidates for president and vice-president a majority of one vote in the electoral college.

It has, of course, been alleged by many and believed by some that the actions of those returning boards defeated the will of the people as expressed at the polls, thus bringing about the seating in the presidential chair of the man that had been fairly and honestly defeated. And yet no one who is familiar with the facts and who is honest enough to admit them will deny that, but for the inauguration in South Carolina, Florida, and Louisiana of the Mississippi methods, those three states would have been as safely and reliably Republican at that time and in that election as were the states of Pennsylvania and Vermont. The plans of the Democratic managers had been defeated. It was hard for them to lose a victory they felt and believed, many of them honestly, that they had won, notwithstanding the extraneous methods that had been employed to bring about such results.

22

1875: Democratic Victory

Although as a result of the sanguinary revolution in 1875 there was no hope or prospect of future Republican success in Mississippi, the Republican leaders in that state did not abandon their efforts to bring about and reestablish friendly relations between Senator Alcorn and Governor Ames. With that end in view, both were made delegates to the National Republican Convention of 1876 from the state at large. But this failed to accomplish the purpose desired. When the newly-elected legislature met the first Monday in January 1876, the fact was developed that the Lamar faction was slightly in the ascendancy in the Democratic party. This, of course, resulted in the election of Mr. Lamar to the United States Senate to succeed Senator Alcorn whose term would expire on 4 March 1877.

One of the first bills passed by the legislature was one changing the boundaries of the congressional districts of the state.

The apportionment was so arranged as to make five Democratic districts and one Republican. It was found to be a very difficult matter to make an apportionment by which the Democrats would be sure of success in five districts, but it was believed and finally decided that since the newly invented Mississippi plan was to be continued, in part at least, they could safely rely upon having five of the six districts return Democrats to Congress. The Republican district took in every county on the Mississippi River, the entire length of the state. On account of its length and shape it was called the "shoestring district." The Republican majority therein was about thirty thousand. That party had not only a majority in every county in the district, but also in nearly every voting precinct or subdivision of each county. It was evidently the intention of the legislature that this district be conceded to the Republicans, the other five to be represented by Democrats.

Mr. Lamar and his friends evidently believed that this was not only fair and reasonable, the Republican legislature having done the same thing for the Democrats when the situation was reversed, but that as a matter of party politics it was the wise and prudent thing to do. But while Mr. Lamar's friends were in the ascendancy in the legislature at that time, they could not at all times control Democratic conventions. Just then the Democrats, not only in Mississippi but throughout the country, were much elated over the prospect of national Democratic success, which made it extremely difficult for the conservatives to hold the radicals in check and keep them within reasonable bounds. When the Democratic state convention met that year, the radicals were found to be in control of the party organization. The result was the election of a state committee, which, in accordance with the expressed will of the majority, decided to take everything in sight, the "shoestring district" included.

General James R. Chalmers, of Fort Pillow fame, was agreed upon to make the fight in the "shoestring district." They realized the fact that, to overcome the Republican majority in that district, it was necessary to have a leader who had neither conscience nor scruples and who would inaugurate, encourage, and countenance and approve any and all methods and schemes that would be found to be necessary to accomplish the desired purpose, however questionable, despicable, vicious, or criminal they might be, the shedding of innocent blood not excepted. Chalmers had demonstrated at the Fort Pillow massacre that he was the man for the occasion, hence he was selected.[1] Mr. Lamar and his friends felt and believed that this was a grave political blunder but, under the circumstances, all they could do was to hold their peace and wait for future developments.

The radicals were in control of the party organization and therefore declared the party policy, which the conservatives could not afford to openly antagonize. The radicals held that conditions at that time did not make it necessary for them to concede anything to the Republicans or show them any consideration whatever. The Democrats not only had complete control of the state government, but were reasonably sure of success at the approaching presidential and congressional elections. They were, therefore, masters of the situation. Their acts, however questionable, would not and could not be made a subject of inquiry or investigation by anyone, because the party to which they belonged and which would be the beneficiary of their acts and deeds would control the machinery through which such an inquiry or investigation would be made, if at all. They therefore had nothing to fear. On the contrary they felt, and not without reason, that every restraint had been removed and that they were at liberty to do whatever was believed to be necessary to accomplish the purpose desired. Why, then,

1. The Joint Committee on the Conduct and Expenditures of the War heard testimony that General Chalmers, among other things, ordered a Confederate soldier to put down a Negro child and shoot him, "which was done." U.S., Congress, House, *House Reports*, 38th Cong., 1st sess., 1864, no. 65, p. 5.

show favors or grant concessions? The fact that the Republicans had a large majority in the "shoestring district" made no material difference. What was true of that district was equally true of the state. That is, the Republican majority in the state was nearly, if not quite, as large as it was in that district, and yet they had captured the state.

Since that had been done, why not, through the same methods, complete the work and take everything? "No," they declared, "we concede nothing. We want and must have everything in sight, the 'shoestring district' included; hence Chalmers *must* be returned elected. He is just as much entitled to a seat in Congress as any of the others, because it is impossible to so apportion the state into congressional districts as to make five Democratic districts out of six without resorting to extraneous methods to secure their election. The same methods that we shall be obliged to adopt in the 'shoestring district' will have to be adopted in the other five, the only difference being that in the 'shoestring district' we shall have to supply them upon a larger scale, since we shall have a much larger majority to overcome, but the methods will be the same. Then why not take all?"

The conservatives could not deny that the radicals had reason and logic on their side as matters than stood, but in applying them, they were, in the opinion of the conservatives, making a grave political mistake. The conservatives not only admit the truth of every assertion. The concessions advocated and advised by the conservatives were believed by them to be expedient, judicious, and wise from a party standpoint. The "shoestring district" was the one in which I lived. In the formation of that district the members of the legislature no doubt believed that I would be the candidate of the Republicans since I was at that time a member of Congress. Although the fact was developed before the nomination was made that the Democrats had decided to carry the district at any cost, I felt it was my duty to make the fight for the Republicans if they desired to have me do so.

It was the opinion of the party leaders that I was the strongest and most available man in the district to make the race; hence I had no opposition for the Republican nomination. When the district convention met at Vicksburg, my name was placed in nomination in a very able and eloquent speech delivered by Captain Thomas W. Hunt, a brave and gallant ex-Confederate soldier. I made an active and aggressive canvass of the district, which covered a period of more than two months, although at several points I did this at a very great personal risk. This was especially true at Friar's Point, Port Gibson, Fayette, and Woodville.

At Friar's Point, which was said to be the home of Chalmers, it came to my knowledge that an organized plan had been perfected to create a disturbance at the meeting that I was to address, which would result in breaking it up with possible bloodshed and rioting, which I am sure was true, for I could not fail to see unmistakable evidences of it when walking the streets of the town. It so happened that Friar's Point was also the home of Senator Alcorn who, when this was brought to his notice, took the necessary steps to prevent it and succeeded in doing so. To make sure his plans should not miscarry, the senator not only attended the meeting, but acted as its presiding officer. The result was a peaceable and orderly meeting which I addressed without serious interference or interruption.

At the other places I was fortunate enough to have personal friends among the Democrats who used their influence to preserve the public peace and maintain order, in which they were successful, at least to the extent of preventing riotous outbreaks, but they could not at every point prevent the breaking up of the meeting. At Fayette, for instance, the armed Democratic club took possession of the place where the meeting was to be held, the Republicans standing in the rear. When I ascended the platform and attempted to speak, my voice was drowned by the noise, yells, and groans of the crowd. After a fruitless effort of about an hour in this direction, the attempt to deliver an address was abandoned. This, however, was harmless and innocent amusement, in comparison with the riot and bloodshed which had been contemplated and which no doubt would have been carried out but for the admonition and advice of wiser heads.

Before the campaign was over, I could see just what was contemplated being done. It was not possible to inaugurate violence enough to prevent the polling of a Republican majority in the district. In any event, the decision had been made that Chalmers must be returned elected. What they might fail to accomplish through intimidation and violence must be accomplished in some other way, and it was done. Of the votes polled, there was a Republican majority of about 10,000. According to the *official* returns, however, there was a Democratic majority of 4,600. This was only one of a large number of instances that contributed to Mr. Tilden's immense popular majority for president. While Mr. Tilden did not reach the presidency, the Democrats had a large majority in the House of Representatives. I contested the pretended election of Chalmers but the House Committee on Elections, of which John R. Harris of Virginia was Chairman, would not even take up the case for consideration. It was a case that could not bear the light of day. The best thing to do with it, therefore, was to suppress it and thus allow nothing to be said about it or done with it in the House.

Because the Democrats carried the election in Mississippi in 1875, they did not thereby secure control of the state government. That election was for members of the legislature, members of Congress, and state treasurer, to fill the vacancy created by the death of Treasurer Holland. All the other state officers were Republicans. But the Democrats could not afford to wait until Governor Ames's term expired. They were determined to get immediate control of the state government. There was only one way in which this could be done and that was by impeachment.

This course they decided to take. It could not be truthfully denied that Governor Ames was a clean, pure, and honest man. He had given the state an excellent administration. The state judiciary had been kept up to the high standard established by Governor Alcorn. Every dollar of the public money had been collected and honestly accounted for. The state was in a flourishing and prosperous condition. The rate of taxation had been greatly reduced and there was every prospect of a still further reduction before the end of his administration. But these facts made no difference with those who were flushed and elated over a victory they had so easily won. They wanted the offices and were determined to have them, and that too, without very much delay. Hence, impeachment proceedings were immediately instituted against the governor and lieutenant governor, not in the interest of reform, of good government, or low taxes, but simply and solely to get possession of the state government.

The weakness of the case against the governor was shown when it was developed that the strongest charge against him was that he had entered into an alleged corrupt bargain with State Senator Cassidy, resulting in Cassidy's appointment as one of the judges of the chancery court. Cassidy had been elected a member of the state senate as a Democrat. Nothwithstanding that fact he voted for Mr. Bruce, the Republican caucus nominee, for United States senator and subsequently publicly identified himself with the Republican party. Later, his brother, William P. Cassidy, and his law partner, Hon. J. F. Sessions, did likewise. In 1874 Sessions was elected to the state senate as a Republican to serve out the unexpired term of his law partner, Cassidy, who had resigned his seat in the senate upon his appointment as a judge of the chancery court.

Cassidy was a brilliant young man and an able lawyer. That the governor should have selected him for an important judicial position was both wise and proper. It was one of his best and most creditable appointments and was generally commended as such when it was made. The fact that he had been elected to the state senate as a Democrat and shortly thereafter joined the Republican party was made the basis of the charge that his change of party affiliations was the result of a corrupt bargain between the governor and himself, for which the governor, but not the judge, should be impeached and removed from office. There were a few other vague and unimportant charges, but this one, as weak as it was, was the strongest of the number.

When the articles were presented to the House, it was seen that they were so weak and so groundless that the governor believed it would be an easy matter for him to discredit and disprove them even before that legislature. With that end in view, he employed several of the ablest lawyers in the country to represent him. They came to Jackson and commenced the preparation of the case, but it did not take them long to find out that their case was a hopeless one. They soon found out to their entire satisfaction that it was not to be a judicial, but a political trial and that the jury was already prepared for conviction without regard to the law, the constitution, the evidence, or the facts. Governor Ames was to be convicted, not because he was guilty of any offense, but because he was in the way of complete Democratic control of the state government.

Personally they had nothing against him. It was not the man, but the office they wanted and were determined to have. They knew he had committed no offense, but as matters then stood, being a Republican was an offense which justified removal from office. To punish him otherwise, therefore, for anything he had done or failed to do did not at any time enter into their calculations. The governorship was the prize at stake. In this matter there was no concealment of their purposes and intentions. As soon as the governor's legal advisers found out what the actual situation was, they saw it was useless to continue the fight. Upon their advice, therefore, the governor tendered his resignation, which was promptly accepted. He then left the state never to return again.

If the impeachment proceedings had been instituted in good faith—upon an honest belief that the chief executive had committed offenses which merited punishment—the resignation would not have been accepted. The fact that it was accepted and that too without hesitation or question, was equivalent to a confession that the purpose of the proceedings was to get possession of the office. Short work was made of the lieutenant governor's case and State Senator John M. Stone, the Democratic president pro tem of the state senate, was duly sworn in and installed as the acting governor of the state.[2] Thus culminated and terminated a long series of questionable acts and deeds the conception and inauguration of which had no other purpose and object than to secure the ascendancy of one political party over another in the administration of the government of the state.

The sanguinary revolution in the state in 1875 was claimed to be in the interest of good administration and honest government—to wrest the state from the control of dishonest men, Negroes, carpetbaggers, and scalawags and place it in control of intelligent, pure, and honest white men. With that end in view, George M. Buchanan, a brave and gallant ex-Confederate soldier was, through questionable and indefensible methods, defeated for the office of state treasurer, and William L. Heming-

2. Lieutenant Governor A. K. Davis, the Negro Republican, also attempted to resign, but he was not permitted to do so. Garner, *Reconstruction in Mississippi*, p. 404.

way was declared elected. And yet when the change took place, it was found that every dollar of the public money was accounted for. During the whole period of Republican administration, not a dollar had been misappropriated and there had been not a single defalcation, although millions of dollars had been passed through the hands of the fiscal agents of the state and of the different counties.

How was it with the new reform administration? Treasurer Hemingway had been in office only a comparatively short while before the startling information was given out that he was a defaulter to the amount of $315,612.19. William L. Hemingway a defaulter! Can such a thing be possible? Yes, it is an admitted and undisputed fact.

Mr. Hemingway had been quite prominent in the politics of the state. But those who knew the man, and I was one of that number, had every reason to believe that he was an honest and honorable man and that he was the personification of integrity. He was neither a speculator nor a gambler. Even after the defalcation was made known, there was nothing to indicate that the money, or any part thereof, had been appropriated to his own use. Yet the money had mysteriously disappeared. Where was it and who had it? These were questions the people of the state desired to have answered, but they have never been and it is safe to say, they never will be. Hemingway no doubt could answer them, but he has not done so and the probabilities now are that he never will. He evidently believed that to turn state's evidence would be more culpable than the act which he had allowed to be committed.

He might have been forced to make a confession or at least give the prosecution a clue to the real criminal or criminals in the act if the prosecution had been in charge of persons who could not be suspected of being the political beneficiaries of the methods by which it was possible for him to be placed in charge of the office. It was hardly reasonable to expect such men to make much of an effort to secure a confession. In fact, it seems to have been a relief to them to have the accused take the position that he alone was the responsible party and that he was willing to bear all the blame and assume all the consequences that would result from the act. The names, therefore, of those, if any, that were the beneficiaries of this remarkable defalcation will no doubt remain a secret in the bosom of William L. Hemingway and will be buried with him in his grave.

Hemingway was tried, convicted, and sentenced and served a term in the state prison, all of which he calmly endured and bravely submitted to rather than give the name or names of any person or persons as having any connection with, or knowledge of, that unfortunate affair. All the satisfaction that the public can get with reference to it, in addition to the punishment to which Hemingway was subjected, is to indulge in conjectures about it. One conjecture, and the most reasonable and plausible one, is that if Hemingway had made a confession that would have been full and complete, it would have, or might have, involved not only some men who were prominent and influential, but perhaps the Democratic state organization as well. For it was a well-known fact that in 1875 nearly every Democratic club in the state was converted into an armed military company. To fully organize, equip, and arm such a large body of men required an outlay of a large sum of money. The money was evidently furnished by some persons or through some organization. Those who raised the money or caused it to be raised no doubt had an eye on the main chance.

A patriotic desire to have the state redeemed (?) was not with them the controlling or actuating motive. When the redemption (?) of the state was an accomplished fact, they no doubt felt that they were entitled to a share in the fruits of that redemption. Their idea evidently was that the state should be made to pay for its own salvation and redemption; but the only way in which this could be done was to have the people's money in the state treasury appropriated other than by legislative enactment, for that purpose. This, as I have already stated, is only a conjecture, but under the circumstances, it is the most reasonable and plausible one that can be imagined. The case of Treasurer Hemingway is conclusive evidence that in point of efficiency, honesty, and official integrity, the Democratic party had no advantage over the party that was placed in power chiefly through the votes of colored men. What was true of Mississippi in this respect was also true, in a measure at least, of the other reconstructed states.[3]

3. For a discussion of defalcation by "redeemers" in other states, see Woodward, *Origins of the New South*, pp. 66–70.

23

The Disputed Presidency

Although the action of the returning boards in South Carolina, Louisiana, and Florida gave Mr. Hayes a majority of one vote in the electoral college, the Democrats, who were largely in the majority in the national House of Representatives, were evidently not willing to acquiesce in the declared result, claiming that Mr. Tilden had been fairly elected and that he ought to be inaugurated. Hon. Henry Waterson of Kentucky, who was at that time a member of the House, delivered a fiery speech in which he declared that one hundred thousand armed men would march to Washington to see that Mr. Tilden was inaugurated. The situation for a while looked very grave. It seemed as if there would be a dual government, both Hayes and Tilden claiming to be the legally elected president. To prevent this was the problem then before Congress and the American people. Conferences, composed of influential men of both parties, were being frequently held in different parts of the city.

The creation of an electoral commission to pass upon and decide the disputed points involved was finally suggested and accepted by a majority of both parties. The name of the originator of this suggestion has never been made public. It is believed by many that Senator Edmunds of Vermont was the man, since he was the principal champion of the measure in the Senate. Subsequent events appeared to indicate that Hon. William M. Evarts of New York was also an influential party to the scheme, if not the originator of it. At any rate, no one seemed to have been sufficiently proud of it to lay claim to its paternity. It was merely a temporary scheme, intended to tide over an unpleasant, disagreeable, and perhaps dangerous condition which existing remedies did not fully meet. It was equivalent to disposing of the presidency by a game of chance, of luck, for the composition of the proposed commission was, politically, purely a matter of choice.

As finally agreed upon, the measure provided for a commission to be composed of fifteen members—five from the House, five from the Senate, and five justices of the Supreme Court. The Democrats, having a majority in the House, it was agreed they should have three and the Republicans two of the five members of that body. The Republicans, having a majority in the Senate, it was agreed that they should have three and two of the five members of that body should go to the Democrats. Of the five justices of the Supreme Court, two were to be Republicans and two Democrats, the fifth justice to be an Independent, or one who was as near an Independent as could be found on the bench of that Court.

When the bill creating this commission came before the House, I spoke and voted against it, chiefly for two reasons.[1]

1. The speech by Lynch appears in U.S., Congress, House, *Congressional Record*, 44th Cong., 2d sess., 1877, pt. 2:1025–26.

In the first place, I believed it was a bad and dangerous precedent to subject the presidency of the United States to a game or scheme of luck or chance as was contemplated by the bill then under consideration. Either Hayes or Tilden had been elected and the result should be ascertained and declared according to the forms of law. In the second place, I had a suspicion that it was the outgrowth of an understanding or agreement which would result in the abandonment of Southern Republicans by the national administration.

Mr. Lamar, for instance, did not hesitate to declare that it was more important that the South should have local self-government than that the president should be a Democrat. In other words, what Southern Democrats wanted was to be let alone—that the national administration should keep hands off and allow them to manage their own affairs in their own way, even if that way should result in a virtual nullification, in part at least, of the war amendments to the federal Constitution.

I had a suspicion that this concession had been granted upon condition that the Southern Democratic leaders in Congress would consent to the creation of the proposed commission and to the ratification of this decision whatever it might be. To such a bargain I did not care to be even an innocent party. My suspicions were strengthened by the fact that the principal opposition among Democrats to the creation of the commission and the ratification of its decision came from Northern Democrats. Southern Democrats, with a few notable exceptions, not only favored the creation of the commission and the ratification of this decision, but even the fiery Waterson was induced to hold his peace and to give expression to his righteous indignation through the medium of a silent vote. That my suspicions were well founded, subsequent events more than demonstrated. I took the position that Mr. Hayes had been duly and legally elected, at least according to the forms of law and in the matter prescribed by the Constitution and that he should, therefore, be duly inaugurated and inducted into office even if it should be necessary for the then president, Grant, as commander-in-chief of the army and navy, to use the military force of the government for that purpose. I contended that having been thus duly and legally elected, the title to the office should not be subjected to chance or luck and that the incoming president should not be bound by any ante-inauguration pledges, promises, or agreements which, in the opinion of some, would have a tendency to put a cloud upon his title to the office. But the bill was passed and the commission was duly appointed.

At this point the game of chance turned in favor of the Republicans. It was generally understood, if not agreed, that Justice David Davis of Illinois would be the fifth justice to be placed on the commission. He was said to be an Independent—the only member of the Court that could be thus classed politically. But in point of fact he was more a Democrat than an Independent. Had he been made a member of the commission it is more than probable that Mr. Tilden instead of Mr. Hayes would have been made president. The legislature of Illinois was at that time engaged in an effort to elect a United States senator. The legislature was composed of about an equal number of Republicans and Democrats, with three Independents holding the balance of power. The Independents finally presented the name of Justice David Davis as their choice for senator. To make sure of the defeat of a Republican, the Democrats joined the Independents in the support of Justice Davis, which resulted in his election. This took place only a few days before the time appointed for the selection of the commissioners.

As soon as it was announced that Justice Davis had been elected to the Senate, the Republican leaders in Congress insisted that he was no longer eligible to a seat on the electoral commission. This was first strongly combatted by the Democrats, who contended that the justice was only a senator-elect and that he did not cease to be a member of the Court until he tendered his resignation as such, which he was neither required nor expected to do until shortly before the beginning of his term as a senator. But the Republicans pressed their objections so strongly and so forcibly that the Democrats were induced to yield the point and Justice Bradley was selected as the fifth justice. Next to Davis, Bradley came as near to being an Independent as any member of the Court. Although he had been appointed as a Republican by President Grant, as had Justice Davis by President Lincoln, he had rendered several decisions which gave the Democrats hope that he might give the deciding vote in their favor and thus make Mr. Tilden president. In this they were disappointed, for it turned out, to their sorrow, that the substitution of Bradley for Davis made Hayes instead of Tilden president of the United States. It would, perhaps, be unfair to say that the decisions of the commission were rendered regardless of the evidence, the law, and the arguments, yet it so happened that every important point was decided by a strict party vote—eight to seven.

In this connection it will not be out of place to refer to a scene that was created on the Democratic side of the House by Hon. Benjamin Hill of Georgia. Mr. Hill entered the House one afternoon, having just returned from the Supreme Court chamber where the commission was in session. He remarked to one of his colleagues in a low tone of voice that he had just returned from where the sessions of the commission were being held and while there, the important and valuable information had been imparted to him that on a most vital point the Democrats could with absolute certainty depend upon the vote of Mr. Justice Bradley.

"Can that be possible?" exclaimed his excited and highly elated colleague.

"Yes," replied Mr. Hill, "there can be no doubt about it. I know whereof I speak. It came to me through a source that cannot be questioned."

"Then wait until I can call several of our friends," replied his colleague. "I want them to hear the good news at the same time it is heard by me, so that we can rejoice together."

Mr. Hill was soon surrounded by an eager, excited, and interested group of anxious Democratic members. "We are now ready," said his delighted colleague, whose face was covered with a smile of satisfaction and delight, "to hear the good news."

"Well," replied Mr. Hill, whose manner was grave and whose countenance gave every evidence of deep emotion, "whenever a motion to adjourn is made by a Democratic member of the commission, we can safely depend upon the vote of Mr. Justice Bradley being cast in the affirmative."

The heads of the anxious group immediately fell in deep disappointment and despair. But of course they did not fail to see the irony of Mr. Hill's remark. It did transpire that whenever a motion to adjourn was made by a Democratic member of the commission, it was usually carried by a vote of eight to seven, Mr. Justice Bradley voting in the affirmative with the Democrats. But on no other question could they depend on his vote.

The decision was finally rendered in favor of Mr. Hayes by a strict party vote—eight to seven. Strong and bitter opposition was made in the House by quite a number of Northern Democrats, to the approval of the decision, but the majority of Southern Democrats, aided by such Northern Democrats as represented districts having large commercial interests—interests that are at all times willing to pay any price for peace—the decision was accepted and approved, and Mr. Hayes was allowed to be peaceably inaugurated.

The new administration had been in power only a short while before it became apparent to Southern Republicans that they had very little to expect or hope for from this administration. It was generally understood that a Southern man would be made postmaster general in the new cabinet, but it was assumed, of course, at least by those who were not fully informed about the secret deals and bargains that had been made and entered into as a condition precedent to a peaceable inauguration of the new administration, that he would be a Republican.

Senator Alcorn, of my own state, Mississippi, who had just retired from the Senate, had an ambition to occupy that position. I was one to whom that fact was made known, and I did not hesitate to use what little influence I had to have that ambition gratified. I was so earnest and persistent in pressing his claims and merits upon those who were known or believed to be close to the appointing power, that I succeeded at least in finding out definitely and authoritatively the name of the man that had been agreed upon and would be no doubt appointed to that position. Ex-Senator Key, a Democrat from Tennessee, was the man.

When I informed Senator Alcorn of that fact, the manifestation of surprise, disappointment, and disgust with which he received it can better be imagined than described. This was not due so much to the fact that some one other than himself had been selected, but to the fact that the fortunate man was a Southern Democrat. For the first time the senator became convinced that Southern Republicans had been made the subject of barter and trade in the shuffle for the presidency, and that the sacrifice of Southern Republicans was the price that had to be paid for the peaceable inauguration of Mr. Hayes. This, in Senator Alcorn's opinion, meant that [the participation of] the Republican party in the reconstruction in the states of the South was a thing of the past. There was no hope for it in the future.

"It would have been far better," said the senator, "not only for the Republican party at the South, but for the country at large, to have allowed the Democrats to inaugurate Tilden and to have taken charge of the government than to have purchased Republican victory at such a fearful cost. What inducement can a Southern white man now have for becoming a Republican? Under the present state of things he will be hated at home and despised abroad. He will be rejected by his old friends and associates and discountenanced by his new ones. He will incur the odium and merit the displeasure and censure of his former friends, associates, and companions, with no compensating advantages for the sacrifices thus made."

The senator spoke with deep feeling and intense emotion. He could see that his efforts to build up a strong Republican party at the South must necessarily fail under such conditions and that it was useless to make any further efforts in that direction. Under his influence and leadership very many of the best and most influential white men in his state had identified themselves with the Republican party. His efforts in that direction would have continued, in spite of the temporary defeat of the party at the polls, however severe the defeat might have been, if those efforts were appreciated and appropriately recognized by the national leaders of the organization. But when he saw that this was not only not to be done, but that one of those who was known to be fully identified with the political persecution of Southern Republicans was to be thus recognized, thus placing the stamp of approval upon their work by an administration that was supposed to be Republican and therefore opposed to such methods, he realized that it was time for Southern white men who have been acting with the Republican party and those who may have such action in contemplation to stop and seriously consider the situation. It was now in order for each one of them to ask himself the question: "Can I afford to do this?"

The appointment of a Southern Democrat to a seat in the cabinet of a Republican president, especially at that particular time, was a crushing blow to Southern Republicans. It was the straw that broke the camel's back. Senator Alcorn was a fit and suitable man in every way for the office of postmaster general. He had a commanding presence. He was an eloquent speaker and an able debater. He was by nature a leader and not a follower. He took an active part in the politics of his state before and after the War of the Rebellion. After he identified himself with the Republican party, he was ambitious to be chiefly instrumental in building up a strong party in his state and throughout the South which would not only recognize merit in, and accord absolute justice and fair play to, the colored people, but which would include in its membership a large percentage, if not a majority of, the best and most substantial white men of that section.[2]

That he had made splendid progress along those lines cannot be denied. The announced Southern policy of the Hayes administration not only completed the destruction of what had been thus accomplished, but made any further progress in that direction absolutely impossible. But the selection of ex-Senator Key was not the only cabinet appointment which clearly indicated the Southern policy of the administration. There were two others, in the persons of Hon. William M. Evarts and Hon. Carl Schurz. Those men had been prominent and conspicuous in their bitter opposition to the Southern policy of President Grant. Mr. Schurz was one of the leaders in the Greeley movement against President Grant and the Republican party in 1872, while Mr. Evarts was, later, the principal speaker at a public indignation meeting that was held at New York to denounce the Southern policy of the Grant administration.

In fact, John Sherman was the only one of the cabinet ministers that had a positive national standing, and even his brilliant star was somewhat marred on account of the impression that, as one of the Hayes managers, he was a party to, or had guilty knowledge of, the deals and agreements that had been made and entered into as a condition precedent to the peaceable induction

2. It will be recalled, however, that Lynch accused Alcorn of splitting the Mississippi Republican party in his bitter personal feud with Adelbert Ames. See above, pp. 113–21.

of Mr. Hayes into office. It was known, or at any rate believed, that Mr. Sherman's appointment as secretary of the treasury was for the one specific purpose of bringing about the resumption of specie payments. He was the author of the act which fixed the date when specie payments should be resumed. He had the reputation of being one of the ablest financiers the country had produced. That he should be named to carry into effect the act of which he was the author was to be expected. For the reasons above stated it was the one cabinet appointment that met with general approval.

It was soon seen, however, that the cabinet was so constructed as to make it harmonize with the Southern policy of the administration. It was not long before the announcement was officially made in prolix sentences, of which Secretary Evarts was no doubt the author, that the army could not and would not be used to uphold and sustain any state government in an effort to maintain its supremacy and enforce obedience to its mandates. In other words, it was a public announcement of the fact that if there should be an armed revolt in a state against the lawful state government which would be strong enough to seize and take possession of the government, the national administration would refuse to interfere, even though a request for assistance should be made by the chief executive of the state in the manner and form prescribed by the Constitution. I have never believed that this policy, which was meant, of course, for the South, was in harmony with Mr. Hayes's personal convictions, especially in view of his public utterances during the progress of the campaign and immediately after the announcement had been made that he had been defeated. But he no doubt asked himself the question, "What can I do?" This is what he had been bound to do, by his managers, through the medium of an ante-inauguration pledge, and which he felt in honor bound to respect and carry out. Mr. Hayes was not a man of sufficient force of character to disregard and repudiate such a pledge or bargain. Had he been a Napoleon, or even an Andrew Jackson, he would have declared that no man or set of men had any authority to make for him and in his name any ante-inauguration pledge, promise, or bargain by which he would be bound as chief magistrate of the country. On the contrary, he would have openly and publicly declared: "I am either president or I am not. That I am the lawful and legally elected president is a recognized and undisputed fact and, as such, I shall neither recognize nor respect any pledge, promise, or bargain which involves dishonor on my part or acquiescence in the suspension, violation, or evasion of the Constitution or any law made in pursuance thereof. As president of the United States I have taken and subscribed to an oath by which I am bound to uphold, support, and defend the Constitution of my country and to see that the laws are duly executed and enforced. That oath I am determined to respect and honor. I shall not only do all in my power to see that the Constitution and the laws of the land are obeyed and enforced, both in letter and in spirit, but it is also my determination to see that every American citizen is protected in the exercise and enjoyment of his rights, as far as it may be in the power of the president to do so."

Such an declaration, accompanied with an honest effort to carry the same into effect, even if he had been unsuccessful, would have carried the name of Rutherford B. Hayes down in history as one of the greatest and most brilliant statesmen our country has ever produced. But he was not equal to the occasion and therefore failed to take advantage of such a golden opportunity. On the contrary, he decided to live up to and carry out to the very letter, every pledge, promise, agreement, or bargain that had been made in his behalf, which involved the dishonor of his own name and the disgrace of his country.

[Stephen B.] Packard, for governor of Louisiana, and [Daniel H.] Chamberlain, for governor of South Carolina, were voted for at the same time that the Hayes electors were voted for in their respective states. Each polled a much larger vote than the Hayes electors. If, therefore, Mr. Hayes was legally or morally entitled to the electoral votes of those states, without which he could not have been elected, these men were entitled to be recognized and supported as governors of their respective states. But it was a well-known fact that without the support and backing of the national administration at that particular time, they could not maintain and enforce their authority against the organization of the Democratic party. The public announcement of the Southern policy of the national administration put an effectual end to any further efforts on the part of either Packard or Chamberlain. The administration not only deserted and abandoned these two men and the party for which they had so bravely and so gallantly stood, but it allowed the very men whose votes made Mr. Hayes president to be harassed and persecuted for what they had done in that direction. After Packard surrendered to the inevitable, he was tendered and accepted a position in the foreign service. When Chamberlain was forced to abandon the hopeless struggle in South Carolina, he moved to New York and engaged in the practice of law. Politically he affiliated with the Democratic party until his death.

Mr. Blaine had been elected to the United States Senate from Maine, his term beginning on 4 March 1877. The term for which Mr. Lamar had been elected from Mississippi commenced the same time. It was not possible to have a congressional investigation of the Mississippi election of 1875 unless the same should be ordered by the Senate, the Republicans having a small majority in that body. Each house being the sole judge of the elections, returns, and qualifications of its own members, the Senate could, of course, have Mr. Lamar's credentials referred to the committee of privileges and elections with instructions to make an investigation of the methods used and employed to carry the election and to ascertain and report whether or not, in the opinion and judgment of the committee, there had been a legal and valid election in that state, the seat to which Mr. Lamar had been elected to remain vacant, pending the investigation and report by the committee and the disposition of the same by the Senate.

As the result of a number of conferences between Republican senators and representatives, Mississippi Republicans, this course was decided upon as the one to be pursued. But the Senate must have something upon which to base its contemplated action. It could not be expected to take official notice of, or affirmative action based upon, rumors or newspaper reports of what had taken place. It was therefore decided that a memorial should be drawn up and signed by a number of reputable and well-known citizens of the state, making specific allegations with reference to that election and concluding with a request that a thorough investigation be made before the senator chosen by the legislature that was brought into existence by that election be admitted to the Senate.

In support of this contemplated action, there had been a number of precedents, the recent case of Mr. Pinchback of Louisiana being one of them.[3] It fell to my lot to draw up the memorial. It was to be presented to the Senate and championed in that body by Senator Morton of Indiana. The Republican majority in the Senate was small. The Democrats, of course, would bitterly oppose the Morton motion. To make sure of this adoption the affirmative vote of nearly every Republican senator was necessary. At any rate, there could be no serious

3. P. B. S. Pinchback, prominent Louisiana Negro and former lieutenant governor, had been elected to the United States Senate by the legislature in 1873. The election was challenged by P. H. Sheridan, who argued that Pinchback had not been legally elected. After months of debate and postponement, the Senate voted not to seat him. Ella Lonn, *Reconstruction in Louisiana After 1868* (New York, 1918), pp. 308–38.

defection in the Republican ranks; otherwise the Morton proposition would not prevail. That anyone on the Republican side would oppose it was not anticipated, for everyone that had been approached expressed his intention of supporting it. No one of the newly elected senators had been approached. It was not deemed necessary. It was not anticipated that any one of them would do otherwise than support the program that had been agreed upon by the older members and leaders of the Senate. Senator Morton was to submit the memorial and make the motion when the name of Mr. Lamar was called to take the oath of office.

The names of the states were called in alphabetical order, about three being called at a time. Maine was reached before Mississippi, and Mr. Blaine was duly sworn in as a senator from that state. No one expected that he would do otherwise than support the program that had been agreed upon, but contrary to expectations, as soon as Mississippi was called, Mr. Blaine was on his feet demanding recognition. Of course he was recognized by the chair. He made a motion that Mr. Lamar be sworn in prima facie as the senator from Mississippi. His contention was that the credentials being regular and in due form, the senator-elect should be sworn in, and if there should be any questions about the legality of the election, it could be made the subject of a subsequent investigation.

This unexpected and unlooked for action on the part of Mr. Blaine took everyone by surprise, with the exception, possibly, of Mr. Lamar, who was no doubt well aware of what was in contemplation. It produced consternation and caused a panic among the Republican leaders in the Senate. Hurried and excited conferences were being held while the subject was being debated. The seriousness of the situation was recognized and realized. Mr. Blaine's defection meant the defeat of the Morton motion should it be made, and the adoption of the Blaine motion by the solid vote of the Democrats and a small minority of the Republicans. This division in the ranks of the party at the beginning of the Hayes administration had to be avoided and prevented, if possible.

That Mr. Blaine should recede from his position was, of course, out of the question. Nothing, therefore, remained to be done but for Senator Morton to refrain from making his motion, for a hurried canvass of the Senate had revealed the fact that the motion if made and brought to a vote would have been defeated, the effect of which would have been worse than if the motion had not been made. The Blaine motion was, therefore, allowed to go by default, and Mr. Lamar was duly sworn in as a senator from Mississippi. Of course, it was well known at the time, Mr. Blaine among the number, that this ended the controversy and that no subsequent investigation would be made. That Mr. Blaine was sadly and seriously disappointed as a result of his action in this case as well as in his action in defeating the Federal Elections Bill will be made clear in a subsequent chapter.

1880: Garfield, the Compromise Candidate

SINCE THE INDICATIONS WERE THAT THE DEMOCRATS WOULD be successful in the congressional election of 1878, the election in the "shoestring district" that year was allowed to go by default.

In 1880, the year of the presidential election, I decided that I would again measure arms with Chalmers for representative in Congress from that district. It was a pretty well settled fact that there was to be a bitter and perhaps close fight for the Republican presidential nomination that year. There were three prominent candidates in the field for nomination—James G. Blaine, U. S. Grant, and John Sherman. Grant was especially strong with Southern Republicans, while Blaine had very little support in that section. Sherman was well thought of on account of the splendid record he had made as a member of the United States Senate, and in addition to that, he had the influence and support of the national administration of which he was a member, being at that time secretary of the treasury.

In the state of Mississippi, Bruce, Hill, and I, the three leading colored men in that state, had an alliance, offensive and defensive. Bruce was United States senator, which position he had secured largely through the influence and active support of Hill and me, Hill especially, since he was on the ground at the time of the election which enabled him to take personal charge of the campaign in the interest of Mr. Bruce before the legislature.

Hill had been elected secretary of state on the ticket with Ames in 1873, and after the expiration of his term as such, he was, through the influence and support of Bruce and me, made Collector of Internal Revenue for the state of Mississippi. The office of secretary of state, to which he was elected in 1873, was one that the Democrats did not take possession of in 1876. Unlike the governor and lieutenant governor, the removal of the incumbent [secretary of state] was not necessary to put that party in possession of the state government.

I had been and was then a member of the national House of Representatives, which position I was able to retain for a long time with the active assistance and support of Bruce and Hill, Bruce especially. That we three men should work in perfect political union and harmony was both natural and proper, since in doing so we protected our own interests and secured for ourselves and our friends and supporters appropriate official recognition. At nearly every state convention either Bruce or I was made chairman of the convention, with Hill as floor manager.

The state committee was organized and controlled in the same way. Through that thorough and effective organization, I was made chairman of the Republican State Committee from 1881 to 1892 and could have retained it longer had I consented to serve, notwithstanding the dissolution of the combination which took place about that time, as will be shown and explained in a subsequent chapter.

There was a faction in the party that was opposed to the leadership of us three influential colored men, but it was never strong enough to control or organize a state convention as long as the three of us worked in union and harmony. While this union had the effect of keeping the three of us to the front as recognized leaders of the party, it could not be said that it was detrimental to the party organization, for the reason that the organization under our leadership never failed to support the man that the party, as a whole, believed to be the strongest and most available. In other words, while we used the party machinery to prevent our own political extinction and destruction, we never allowed our own ambitions to conflict with what was believed by other influential members of the party to be for the best interest of the organization.

It looked for a while as if the state convention of 1880 would result in a dissolution of this combination, which had so successfully controlled the party organization in the state for many years. Bruce and Hill were supporters of Secretary Sherman for the Republican presidential nomination, while I was favorable to the candidacy of ex-President Grant. That Grant was the choice of a large majority of the Republicans of the state could not be truthfully denied. Mr. Bruce was the Republican United States senator in harmony with the administration. Mr. Hill was an officeholder under that administration, and Secretary Sherman was believed to be the administration candidate for the nomination.

As soon as the fact was developed that Bruce and Hill were for Sherman and that I was for Grant, the faction which had always opposed and fought the leadership of the Bruce-Lynch-Hill combination took up the fight for Grant with the determination to take advantage of Grant's strength and popularity to secure control of the party machinery. It was this that prevented at that time a dissolution of the Bruce-Hill-Lynch combination. The situation with which we were confronted made it necessary for the three of us to come together and in a spirit of concession agree upon a common line of action. Upon the suggestion and at the request of Mr. Bruce, a conference soon took place at which it was agreed that, since it was my purpose to be a candidate for the congressional nomination in the Sixth, or "shoestring," District, I would not be a candidate for delegate to the national convention, but that I should support Bruce and Hill for delegates from the state at large with the understanding that if at any time Sherman's name should be withdrawn and Grant's nomination was believed to be possible, they should support Grant. It was further agreed that I should support the Bruce-Lynch-Hill combination in the fight for the organization of the state convention but was at liberty to use my influence for the election of Grant men as delegates, other than Bruce and Hill.

At the conclusion of this conference I made public announcement of the fact that, since it was my purpose to become a candidate for Congress in the Sixth, or "shoestring," District, I would not be a candidate for delegate to the national convention, but would give my support to Bruce and Hill for two of the four places on the delegation from the state at large, with the understanding that the delegation, if controlled by them, would not be hostile or unfriendly to Grant. I had reasons to know that Mr. Bruce, in consequence of his friendly and cordial relations with Senator Conkling, the national leader of the Grant forces, was not unfriendly to Grant and that he would use his influence to prevent the delegation from going into any combination for the sole purpose of defeating the nomination of Grant. In other words, Grant was, in good faith, his second choice for the nomination.

The fight for the delegation was waged with a good deal of heat and bitterness. The canvass had not progressed very far before it was developed that Grant was much stronger than the faction by which he was being supported. The fight was so bitter and the delegates to the state convention were so evenly divided that the final result was the election of a compromise delegation which was about evenly divided between Grant and Sherman. Bruce and Hill were among those that were elected.

The national convention, which was held at Chicago in June of that year, was one of the most exciting and interesting in the history of the party. It was that convention that abolished what was known as the unit rule. Up to that time the right of a state convention to elect all the delegates to which the state was entitled, district as well as state, and to instruct them, as a body, had never before been questioned or denied. New York, as well as other states, had by action of the state convention instructed the delegates to cast the entire vote of the state for Grant. This was the unit rule. It is a rule which even now is carried out and enforced in national conventions of the Democratic party. It was through the enforcement of this rule that Mr. Cleveland was renominated, when he was so bitterly opposed by a portion of the delegation from his own state, especially the Tammany delegates, which caused General Bragg to make the celebrated declaration that he loved Mr. Cleveland on account of the enemies he had made. Notwithstanding the fact that those delegates were strongly opposed to Mr. Cleveland and protested against having their votes recorded for him, they were so recorded, however, through the application and enforcement of the unit rule. It was the enforcement of this rule upon which Mr. Conkling insisted in the National Republican Convention of 1880. About twenty of the New York district delegates under the leadership of Judge W. H. Robertson refused to be governed by the instructions of the state convention. Their contention was that the state convention had no right to bind by instructions any delegates except the four from the state at large. After a lengthy and heated debate, the convention finally sustained his contention, since which time the unit rule has not been recognized in a National Republican Convention.

This action, no doubt, resulted in the defeat of General Grant for the nomination, for it was a well-known fact that his nomination was possible only through the enforcement of the unit rule. His friends and supporters, however, under the leadership of Senator Conkling, made a strong and desperate fight with the hope that the tide might ultimately turn in their favor, but with the intention, in any event, of preventing, if possible, the nomination of Mr. Blaine. General Grant's name was placed before the convention by Senator Conkling in one of his most eloquent and masterly efforts.

"The man whose name I shall place in nomination," he said, "does not hail from any particular state; he hails from the United States. It is not necessary to nominate a man that can carry Michigan. Any Republican can carry Michigan. You should nominate a man that can carry New York. That man is U. S. Grant."

Mr. Blaine's name was placed in nomination by a delegate from Michigan by the name of [James F.] Joy. His effort did not come up to public expectation. The eloquent speech of Senator [William P.] Frye of Maine, who seconded the nomination, made up in part for the public disappointment in Mr. Joy's effort. The name of Secretary John Sherman was placed before the convention in one of General [James A.] Garfield's most powerful and convincing efforts. It is safe to say that the speech delivered by General Garfield on that occasion made him the nominee of that convention. After drawing an eloquent and vivid picture of the kind of man that should be made president, with the intention of naming John Sherman as the man thus described, he asked in a tone of voice that was pitched in a high key, "Who is that man?" The response came from different parts of the hall, "Garfield."

Garfield, the Compromise Candidate

And sure enough it was Garfield. After a number of fruitless ballots, it became apparent that neither of the three leading candidates could possibly be nominated. Very few, if any, of the Sherman men would go to Blaine, while the Blaine men could not be induced in any considerable numbers to go either to Grant or Sherman. While a number of Sherman men would have supported Grant in preference to Blaine, there were not enough of them, with the Grant men, to constitute a majority. When Garfield's name was suggested as a compromise candidate, he was found to be acceptable to both the Blaine and Sherman men and to some of the Grant men who had abandoned all hope of Grant's nomination. The result was that Garfield was finally made the unanimous choice of the convention for president of the United States. The New York delegation was allowed to name the man for vice-president, which was done in the person of Chester A. Arthur of that state.

Although General Garfield was nominated as a compromise candidate, his election was by no means a foregone conclusion. The Democrats nominated a strong and popular man in the person of General W. S. Hancock, one of the most brilliant and successful generals in the Union army. Associated on the ticket with him was a popular Indiana Democrat named William H. English. It looked for a while as if Democratic success was reasonably certain, especially after the September state and congressional elections in the state of Maine, the result of which was virtually a Democratic victory. What was known as the celebrated Mentor Conference took place. Mentor was the home of General Garfield. The conference consisted of General Garfield, General Grant, and Senator Conkling. Who was instrumental in bringing that conference into existence perhaps will never be known, and what was actually said and done on that occasion will no doubt remain a mystery. But it resulted in bringing the Grant-Conkling wing of the party, which up to that time had been lukewarm and indifferent, into the active and aggressive support of the ticket. Senator Conkling immediately took to the stump and made a brilliant and successful campaign, not only in New York but also in the other close and doubtful states.

The result was Garfield carried New York by a majority of about twenty thousand and was elected. Without New York he would have been defeated, for the South this time was unquestionably solid in its support of the Democratic ticket, at least according to the form of law. It was not necessary to resort to the questionable expediency of an electoral commission to determine the result of that election. It is safe to say that, but for the active support given the ticket in that campaign by General Grant and Senator Conkling, New York would have been lost to the party and Garfield would have been defeated. With the election of Garfield, the national House of Representatives was also Republican. The majority was small but it was large enough to enable the party to organize the House. The Garfield administration started out under very favorable auspices. How it ended will be told in another chapter.

25

1880: The Battle for Reelection

As indicated in a previous chapter, I decided to measure arms with General Chalmers in 1880 for representative in Congress from the Sixth, or "shoestring," District. The fact was soon made plain to me, however, that I had on my hands the fight of my life, not only for the election but for the nomination. There were three candidates for the nomination besides myself—Judge E. Jeffords of Issaquena County, General W. F. Fitzgerald of Warren County, and my personal friend, Captain Thomas W. Hunt of Jefferson County. Captain Hunt was the man that placed my name in nomination for Congress in 1876. Chiefly through my efforts and influence he had been made United States marshal for the southern judicial district of the state, with headquarters at Jackson, the state capital.

To my great surprise I found out that my personal friend and political ally, James Hill, was responsible for the candidacy of Captain Hunt. This meant that the political alliance and combination composed of Bruce, Lynch, and Hill was at last to be dissolved. This made the fight on my part much harder and more doubtful than it otherwise would have been, since it meant a division in the ranks of those upon whom I relied for support. It was at first denied that Hill was responsible for the candidacy of Hunt, but when I made known to Hunt the source of my information, the authenticity of which could not be questioned, he frankly confessed that it was true.

"But," he said, "since giving the matter careful consideration, I have decided not to become a candidate but will give you the benefit of whatever influence and support I can command." For this I thanked him and expressed the hope that he would have no occasion to regret coming to that conclusion. Subsequent developments, however, seemed to indicate that this statement was made to throw me off my guard and to prevent me from making a canvass in that part of the district upon which he chiefly relied for support. For a few days subsequent to this conversation, I took a trip to Greenville, Washington County, to see what could be done in that part of the district in which it was believed Judge Jeffords was especially strong. One of the first men I met after I reached Greenville was A. G. Pearce, a colored man who was believed to be quite popular in that county and who was one of Mr. Hill's subordinates and the one upon whom Hill and Hunt relied for at least a part of the Washington County delegation. My relations with Pearce had been pleasant and friendly. I had every reason to believe, therefore, that I could safely count upon his support as against any other candidate for the nomination, unless his chief, Mr. Hill, had a candidate in the person of someone else, in which case it was to be presumed that he would support the choice of his official chief. When I informed him of what I desired he frankly stated that his first choice was Captain Hunt.

"But," I stated, "Hunt is no longer a candidate. He has withdrawn in my favor."

"When did that happen?" asked Pearce. I informed him of

the time and place. "Well," he replied, "there must be some mistake about it, for I just received a letter from Captain Hunt which I will allow you to read." He then took the letter from his pocket and handed it to me. It was not marked confidential. It was in Captain Hunt's own handwriting. It was written the day after his conversation with me in which he stated that he would not be a candidate but that he would support me. In this letter Pearce was urged to redouble his efforts—that the outlook was brighter than ever and that if his friends and supporters would do their duty he was reasonably sure of the nomination.

I then said to Pearce that I guessed I had misunderstood Captain Hunt, and therefore made myself satisfied with Pearce's promise that he would make me his second choice. But he frankly stated that Judge Jeffords was very strong in that county and that the probabilities were that he would get the delegation. I began to realize what I had before me. Through Bruce, Hill was in absolute control of the federal patronage of the state, except in the Sixth, or "shoestring," District, which had been conceded to me. I saw that the Internal Revenue Office with Hill at its head, and with its immense patronage, would be used to insure my defeat and to bring about the nomination of Hunt. I knew that if Hill could have his own way, the patronage and influence of every office, even in the Sixth District, would be used for the same purpose. In addition to this the United States Census would be taken that year. The state was divided into three census supervisors' districts, one supervisor to be appointed for each district: the appointments to be made by the president, by and with the advice and consent of the Senate. Each supervisor would appoint, subject to the approval of the Superintendent of the Census, all of the enumerators to which his district would be entitled. I knew that if Hill could have his way, this patronage would also be used in the same way for the same purpose.

After giving the matter careful consideration, I decided to

take a trip to Washington to see and confer with Senator Bruce, upon whose recommendation the census supervisors would be appointed. The conference took place the day after I reached Washington, at which I did not hesitate to ask Mr. Bruce whether or not he was for or against me in my fight for Congress. He promptly replied that he was for me and that I should have all the assistance it was in his power to render me. This was the first time I had approached him upon the subject. His answer to my direct question was pleasant news to me, for he was then in a position where his influence was potential and his assistance valuable. I then informed him that the best and most effective way in which he could demonstrate to my satisfaction that he was with me in the fight was to have me appointed supervisor of the census for the census district in which I lived.

"You shall have the appointment," was his immediate reply. "I shall see that your name is sent to the Senate for the position."

Of course Hill had a candidate of his own in the person of Hon. W. H. Gibbs. When Hill heard that I had gone to Washington, he wired Mr. Bruce that he would be there in the course of a few days. But Mr. Bruce had some very important business just at that time that demanded his personal attention at his cotton plantation in Mississippi.

The day that Mr. Hill arrived in Washington, Mr. Bruce reached his Mississippi plantation. Mr. Hill remained in Washington long enough to find out that my name had been selected for census supervisor for the district for which he desired the appointment of Gibbs. This was the beginning of the subsequent severance of political and personal friendly relations between Bruce and Hill about which more will be made in subsequent chapters. My name was sent to the Senate, but at that time the Democrats had a majority in that body. Chalmers was a member of the House. When he saw my name on the list of those sent to the Senate for census supervisor, it was like shaking a red flag in the face of a bull. He immediately became very much excited and considerably alarmed. He knew what it meant. Of all the aspirants for the Republican congressional nomination, it seemed that I was the one he most feared. He therefore made an earnest appeal to the Democratic senators not to allow the nomination to be confirmed unless I should make a pledge that under no circumstances would I allow my name to be used as a candidate for Congress.

Mr. Bruce wired me to come to Washington. I did so, and appeared before the Senate Census Committee, of which Senator Harris of Tennessee was chairman and before which the nominations were pending. Chalmers was also present. Senator Harris informed me that there would be no objection to my confirmation if I would state that I was not a candidate for Congress and that I would not allow my name to be used for the nomination. I replied somewhat facetiously that I was a candidate for Congress in the same sense that the distinguished senator was a candidate for the presidency.

"You will observe," I remarked, "that I recognize the fitness of things in placing your own aspirations a few degrees above those of my own." Of course this answer was not satisfactory, as I knew it would not be, but I did not intend to give any other. My purpose in asking for the appointment was not to use the patronage in my own interest, but to prevent it from being used against me. No one knew better than Chalmers that while the office would be of some advantage to me in an indirect way in the contest for the Republican nomination, a contest in which Democrats were supposed to have no interest, it could not possibly be of any advantage to me at the election. Evidently it was my nomination as his opponent that he was anxious to defeat. Through his earnest efforts and pathetic appeals to the Democratic senators, the nomination was reported adversely and rejected by a strict party vote.

Mr. Hill then renewed his efforts in behalf of his friend Gibbs. Mr. Bruce brought about a conference between Gibbs and myself which resulted in an agreement that my friends should name the census enumerators in my own county and a fair proportion of them in all the other counties in the Sixth District. With this understanding I consented to the appointment of Gibbs, whose nomination was promptly confirmed. Gibbs redeemed his pledge and acted in good faith in the disposition of the patronage at his disposal. No favoritism was shown and no advantage was taken of any one of the candidates for the nomination; consequently there was no complaint in any quarter. As the canvass progressed, the fact became more and more apparent to Hill and Hunt that Hunt would stand no chance whatever of the nomination if he did not maintain friendly relations with me. The Jeffords supporters were the ideal representatives and, since it was known that Hunt was Hill's candidate, if it should come to a choice between Hunt and myself, the Jeffords men would support me. Hence, Hill and Hunt were anxious to have an understanding and make a combination with me.

When this fact was communicated to me through the medium of a third party, I was not inclined to favorably consider it, on account of Hunt's previous action in an effort to mislead me with reference to his own candidacy, but I finally consented to meet them. This conference resulted in an understanding and agreement upon three points, as follows: first, my own county, Adams, with six delegates, should be conceded to me without a fight. Second, Captain Hunt's county, Jefferson, with four delegates, should be conceded to him in the same way. Third, if at any time the fact should be developed that the vote of Lynch and Hunt combined should constitute a majority of the convention, the one having the smaller number should withdraw in favor of the other. I am pleased to say that this understanding was carried out in good faith. Judge Jeffords had no support south of Issaquena County. His strength was confined to the counties north of Warren; Fitzgerald had no support outside of Warren. Warren (Vicksburg) was about in the center of the long narrow district. Of the forty-two delegates of which the convention was composed, eighteen came from south and seventeen from north of Warren County. Warren had a representation of seven. When all the delegates had been elected, it was found that Jeffords had sixteen of the seventeen from the counties north of Warren, one of the candidates on the Lynch slate in Washington County having been elected. Of the eighteen south of Warren, I had fourteen and Hunt four. The seven from Warren were for Fitzgerald. In some mysterious and unaccountable way, one of the four Lynch delegates from Claiborne County betrayed his trust and violated his instructions by voting for Hunt on every ballot as long as Hunt's name remained before the convention. But in view of the understanding and agreement between Hunt and myself, the defection of this delegate made no material difference.

The votes therefore stood as follows: Jeffords, sixteen; Lynch, fourteen; Fitzgerald, seven; Hunt, five. The result was the same on every ballot until eighty-three ballots had been taken. On the eighty-fourth one of the delegates from Warren, J. W. Short, white, voted for me. It was then seen that my votes—fifteen, with Hunt's five—lacked but two of the number required to nominate. The Fitzgerald men then asked for a brief recess to enable them to have a conference, which was granted. At this conference Mr. Short stated that while he was for Fitzgerald, the fact had been unmistakably demonstrated that the nominee of the convention would ultimately be Jeffords or me and that of the two he preferred me. Two others, Edwards and Foreman, colored, took the same position. This practically settled the contest. Immediately upon the reassembling of the convention, the eighty-fifth ballot was proceeded with, which resulted as follows: Lynch, seventeen; Jeffords, sixteen; Hunt, five; Fitzgerald, four. In accordance with the understanding and agreement between Hunt and myself, Hunt's name at this point was withdrawn in my favor, after which the nomination was, on motion of the leader of the Jeffords men, made unanimous. Thus ended one of the most memorable and remarkable conventions in the history of the Republican party in Mississippi.

Shortly after the nomination, I entered upon an active and aggressive canvass of the district. One of the greatest difficulties I encountered was to get the Republican voters to turn out on election day. This was not due to indifference or lack of interest on their part, but on account of the way they had been treated at previous elections. They had turned out in large numbers on such occasions only to find that all sort of tricks and devices, sometimes violence, were resorted to, to prevent them from voting; and if they were allowed to vote, their votes had been counted and returned against the candidates for whom they had voted and for the candidates against whom they had voted. In other words, a Republican vote polled in some counties meant a Democratic vote counted and returned. This, of course, had a very discouraging effect upon the Republican voters.

"What is the use," they would say, "for us to go to the polls when we know that if we are permitted to vote, our votes will simply swell the Democratic majority as officially counted and returned?" This was both logical and true, yet it was useless for anyone to make the race unless his supporters would at least make an effort to elect him, in spite of such adverse conditions. In some counties conditions were better than in others. After going over the situation carefully with my campaign managers and advisers, the plan finally agreed upon was to select the counties, and a certain precinct, Rodney, in which the Republicans could vote and in which there would be a fair and honest count. In other words, a fair and honest election. This proved to be true. It was the only precinct in that county in which the Republicans were advised to turn out and vote. The result was a heavy Republican vote and a large Republican majority, polled, counted, certified, and returned. But the officer that was selected to take the ballot box containing the ballots and tally sheets to the county seat was attacked by a mob on the road, resulting in the destruction of the box with all of its contents. The returns from Rodney, therefore, were not included in the *official* returns of the election in that county. It was the only precinct in which the Republicans made an effort to vote and the only one, of course, that had gone Republican.

In the adjoining county of Claiborne, there were in round numbers fifteen hundred Republican and five hundred Democratic voters. At several previous elections the Democrats had been given the Republican votes and the Republicans the Democratic votes, or what was about equivalent to this. This gave the Democrats instead of the Republicans about a one thousand majority in the county. There was not one precinct in the whole county in which a fair and honest election could be expected and looked for. In that county, therefore, the Republicans were advised to remain away from the polls, which was done. The result was that the Democratic majority was five hundred less than it otherwise would have been.

It may not be out of place to say in this connection that the Democratic managers were entitled to the questionable or doubtful credit, growing out of the fact that they did not count and return for the candidates of their party any votes that were not actually polled. It could not be denied and was not denied that at that election at least, they made an honest return of the votes that were actually polled. Why the Republicans did not turn out and vote as at several previous elections, they did not know and could not understand. It took them by surprise. Had this been anticipated by them, some other plan or scheme might have been adopted to swell the Democratic majority in the county. But they were kept in ignorance of the plans of the Republican managers until it was too late for them to invent any other scheme for the purpose desired.

Nationally the Democrats were more confident of success than they were in 1876. They knew that Tilden would have been elected president that year if all of the votes of what was then the solid South had been counted for him. This time they knew there would be no doubt about the South being solid in its support of the Democratic ticket; at least according to the forms of law. Since, then, Hancock was absolutely sure of getting the votes from the South that Tilden lacked to make him president, it seemed to them as if Hancock's election was a foregone conclusion, with a majority in both branches of Congress in harmony with the administration. There was nothing, therefore, to operate as a restraining influence upon them in any effort they might make or methods they saw fit to adopt to overcome the heavy Republican majority in the Sixth, or "shoestring," District, especially under the leadership of a man like Chalmers who was known to be willing to endorse, approve, and defend any methods however questionable, to have himself returned to a seat in Congress to which he knew he could not be fairly and honestly elected.

I had never failed at any previous election to carry my own county, Adams, but I was informed by a member of the Democratic County Committee that it had been decided to have the county go Democratic at that election. The argument used in the committee, he said, was that it was a reproach and reflection upon the Adams County Democracy for them not to be able to do what had been done and was being done in other Republican counties. The Democrats in a number of other Republican counties had adopted and enforced methods by which large majorities against them had been overcome; why can't the same be done in Adams? I therefore knew from an authentic source, fully a month before the election, what was going to be done in my own county. But I was satisfied that no method could be adopted by which a majority could be manufactured that would be equal to the Democratic vote of the county—about one thousand. So my advice to the Republican voters of the county was to turn out in force and vote or make an effort to do so. This was done.

In the city of Natchez where the two parties were nearly evenly divided, the policy of obstruction and delay was the one adopted. There was supposed to be but one door through which Republicans were allowed to enter, while Democrats were admitted from several different directions. In that way every Democrat was allowed easy access to the polls, while many hundreds of Republicans, after remaining in line nearly all day, were obliged to leave without having had an opportunity to vote. Those who succeeded in gaining admission to the room were challenged and were subjected to a number of unnecessary questions before being allowed to vote. This was simply a part of the plan that had been adopted to overcome the large Republican majority. Many of those who had been denied access to the room left in disgust shortly before the polls closed; but those that remained were invited to a room across the street where their names and residences were written down and their votes received.

The clerk of the circuit court, who was at that time a Republican, and who, under the law, was the custodian of the election machinery, afterwards certified that the names of the persons on those lists were duly qualified voters. This was to be used as evidence in a contest, if necessary. In the county precincts, in every one of which the Republicans were largely in the majority, a different policy, that of fraud in the count and perjury in the returns, was adopted. I attended the election at one of the precincts, Kingston, myself. Two Republican United States supervisors or watchers for each precinct had been appointed. For the purpose of detecting and exposing and, if possible, preventing the fraud that was known to be in contemplation, each Republican voter was requested to hold his ballot in such a way as he approached the ballot box to enable the two supervisors or watchers to distinctly see and read the name of the Republican candidate for Congress, "Lynch," which was the last name printed at the end of the ballot. This was done. In that way the supervisors or watchers kept an accurate tally of the votes polled for the Republican candidate for Congress. There was no obstruction and no delay.

By noon nearly the entire vote of the precinct had been polled. Between twelve and one o'clock the election officers, consisting of two Democrats and one Republican, decided by a vote of two to one to take a recess of an hour for lunch. It was necessary, they said, to satisfy the wants of the inner man, and, incidentally, of course, to give some attention to the ballot box. In fact, to give effect to their plans and purposes, that box stood more in need of being fed than the election officers. When the recess was taken, every Republican present knew then that the precinct had gone Democratic by a large majority. As soon as the recess was announced, I walked into the room and protested against the box being taken away until after the polls had been closed for the day and the ballots counted. But the protest was disregarded. The box was locked and the key was handed to the Republican member, the two Democratic members leaving with the box in their possession. They got into a buggy and rode off to a house about a half a mile away. I knew then just about what the *official* result of that precinct would be.

Of course Kingston was returned as having gone Democratic by a handsome majority, as was true of all the other precincts in the county, and yet the majority in the county as a whole, purchased at such a fearful cost, was only about two hundred. It can be said to the credit of the Adams County Democracy, however, that 1880 was the first and only time that criminal methods had been adopted to carry an election in that county. When the decision was reached, even at that time, to adopt and enforce such methods, it was done against the advice and over the protest of many of the best and most reputable Democrats in the county. While they were as anxious for party success as their more radical associates, they did not believe that the end justified the means, and that a victory purchased upon such conditions was not worth having. Besides, from a local point of view, there was no excuse or justification for the inauguration of questionable methods to carry an election in that county. Notwithstanding the fact that it was a strong Republican county, in the election of county officers party lines had not been drawn for a number of years. Through what was known as the fusion system both parties and races were given a fair and equitable representation in the administration of county affairs.

Adams County was noted for its wealth and prosperity and for the conservatism, intelligence, culture, and refinement of its people. They looked with abhorrence upon criminal, vicious, or questionable methods to carry elections or for any other purpose. They believed in and generally followed the golden rule, Do unto others as you would have them do unto you. Consequently there never was at any time, not even during the intense excitement growing out of, and incident to, the early days of Reconstruction, when party spirit ran high and sectional animosity was extreme, any race antipathy or bitter party strife. On the contrary, there was peace and order throughout the county and friendly, cordial, and amicable relations between both races and all parties. Even in 1880 when questionable methods were, for the first time, allowed to be inaugurated to carry an election, the conservative element was strong enough to prevent the adoption of any plan which involved violence and bloodshed. They said to the radicals, who were at that time under the vicious leadership of General Chalmers, that if they were determined to overcome the Republican majority in the county, it must be done in some other way than by violence.

The methods already described were then inaugurated, but never repeated at any subsequent election. They brought a blush of shame upon the cheeks of every man in the county and consequently a strong determination that never again should such methods be allowed to be inaugurated in that county, and they never were. At the very next national election two years later, there was a free ballot, and a fair count, resulting in the usual large Republican majority. The same was true at each subsequent state and national election until 1890, when a new state constitution was declared adopted, the main purpose of which was to disfranchise the mass of colored voters through an evasion of the Fifteenth Amendment to the federal Constitution, about which more will be said in a subsequent chapter. The writer is pleased to note that one of the two Democratic members of that convention from Adams County, General William T. Martin, refused to attach his signature to that instrument. In this he reflected the sentiments and respected the wishes of the dominant and better element of the people of his county.

General Chalmers had changed his alleged residence from Friars Point to Vicksburg, where he had purchased a controlling interest in the *Commercial* and to which he was an editorial contributor. This paper was the principal rival of the *Herald*, the most popular and influential Democratic paper published in that part of the state. Although it was a strong party paper, the *Herald* insisted at that time upon a fair and honest election, and it had influence enough to bring it about, at least in Warren County. How this was to be done was not made known to Chalmers and his friends and of course they had no suspicion that such a thing was possible. They felt perfectly safe and easy because they had named the County Returning Board, which would appoint the election officers for the different precincts. These officers would be selected by the Chalmers managers, and they of course would be sure to select such men as would bring in, from their respective precincts, just what they would be instructed to bring in. Under these circumstances they felt sure that the county was safe for about a one thousand majority. Why, then, should they concern themselves, or give themselves any uneasiness about Warren County, in which everything was, or would be, cut and dried for the occasion? The result, as they thought, was a foregone conclusion.

But the *Herald* was resourceful. It was not without friends. In fact, it had a number of them. Among them was one John D. Tinney. Tinney was an ex-federal soldier and a brave man. In national politics he was Republican, but in local matters he had acted with the Democrats, because he was not satisfied with local conditions in Warren County under the leadership of those who had been in control of the Republican organization in the county. He was, therefore, strong and popular with the rank and file of the Democrats of the county, including many of those who had the reputation of being bulldozers. He had acted with the Democrats in 1875 and 1876, but he had since been largely instrumental in the election of a Republican as sheriff and Tax Collector of his county. He was at that time the chief deputy sheriff of the county.

In a conversation I had with him he informed me that, with the influence and backing of the *Herald*, he was satisfied he could secure me a fair count in Warren County. He said his sympathies were with me in the fight that I was making and he believed that I was entitled to whatever assistance he could render me. I informed him that he was the very man for whom I was looking. I assured him that all I wanted was a fair and honest election and that if he could do anything to bring that about he was at liberty to proceed.

"Very well," he replied. "I think I shall be able to convince you that I know whereof I speak."

A week or ten days before the election he had perfected an organization consisting of about one hundred men. They were all white men and Democrats. Some of them were bulldozers. The purpose of the organization was to see that there were fair elections and an honest count in Warren County. On election day, a certain number of those men made their appearance at every polling place in the county, especially in the country districts. They were there to see that there was a fair election and an honest count, and their mission was not in vain. One of those men was named Jack Kain. Everybody in Warren County knew Jack Kain. He was made captain of the squad that was sent to one of the worst country precincts in the county—a place where it was thought there might be trouble if the plan to manipulate the ballot box should be interfered with. At the usual time the lunch recess was ordered. That was the time the box was to be fixed, as was then being done in a number of other counties in the district and, as they supposed, in all the other precincts in Warren County. The election officers at no one precinct knew that any effort was being made at any other precinct to prevent the successful execution of the plan that had been agreed upon by the Chalmers managers. Hence the impression at each precinct was that that was the only one in which there might be a failure of the plan.

When the recess was ordered at the precinct where Jack Kain and has associates were present, Kain and his associates made their appearance. They were prepared for whatever might happen. Kain made his mission known, which was that he and his friends were there to see that there was a fair election and an honest count; hence, he must insist that the ballot box remain there until the election was over, the ballots counted, and the result made known. This took the election officers very much by surprise. One of them that knew him personally asked him if he were serious and really meant what he said, to which he not only gave an affirmative answer, but gave it in a tone and manner that could not be misunderstood. The ballot box was not moved. Very much to the surprise and astonishment of those election officers, they found out the next day that what had taken place at their precinct had taken place at every precinct in the county, which resulted in a Republican majority of over two thousand in Warren County and over six hundred on the face of the returns in the district.

Consternation was created in the ranks of the Democracy. Something had to be done to save Chalmers. The discovery was finally made that the tickets used by the Republicans had a printer's dash to separate the different groups of candidates. This innocent and harmless little dash, it was claimed, was a violation of the state law which provided that no ticket should have any distinguishing mark or device by which one ticket could be distinguished from another. The tickets used in the other counties in the districts were not unlike those used in Warren, yet Warren was the only county in which that point was raised. It is safe to say it would not have been raised there if the plans of the Chalmers managers had not miscarried. This little dash was seized upon and made the basis of an appeal to the County Returning Board to reject all the Republican ballots cast in Warren County at that election, which was done, and Chalmers was declared duly elected to Congress and was given the certificate of election. But, fortunately for the disfranchised Republicans of that district, the Republican party had not only elected the president, but had a small but safe majority in the lower house of Congress. I therefore carried the case to the House through the medium of a contest, about which something will be said in a subsequent chapter.

26

The Vicksburg Postmastership

After the presidential and congressional elections, I found that my friend Hill was still on my trail. Senator Bruce was to retire from the Senate the same day that President Hayes would retire from the presidency. Mr. Bruce was an applicant for an appointive office under the incoming administration. While he had been a true and consistent friend of mine, he had not been unfriendly to Mr. Hill. In fact he had been, in a political or party sense, everything to Mr. Hill. While Hill had the credit of being the dispenser of federal patronage throughout the state, except in the Sixth District, those who were in a position to know were aware of the fact that Mr. Bruce was the one through whom this power came. Mr. Bruce never at any time allowed his friendship for Mr. Hill to make him the medium through whom an injustice should be done to me. Besides, he wanted the benefit of my influence and support in his efforts to secure an appointment under the new administration. Consequently, he did not intend to do anything which might have a tendency to lessen my interest in him or friendship for him. He knew that while I had been officially declared defeated for Congress, I had in fact been elected and would be placed upon the same footing by the new administration as other congressmen-elect in harmony with the same.

But Mr. Hill had a few political debts he wanted paid through Mr. Bruce before the end of the Hayes administration. Some of them involved important changes in certain federal positions in the Sixth District, about which I was not to be consulted. That this would be a grave injustice to me was immaterial with Mr. Hill, but not so with Mr. Bruce. Among the political debts referred to was the postmastership at Vicksburg. The term of the postmaster there had expired. In the fight for delegates to the national convention that year Warren County was for Grant. It elected what was supposed to be a solid Grant delegation to the state convention, but Mr. Hill succeeded in getting some of the delegates from that county to support the state in the interest of Secretary Sherman. J. W. Bourne, white, was one of that number. For this Bourne was to be made postmaster at Vicksburg. The appointment was to be made immediately after the adjournment of the national convention, which no doubt would have been done if Secretary Sherman had been nominated for the presidency. But since General Garfield, who was a Sherman man, had been nominated, Mr. Hill thought that the political obligations he had incurred in the interest of Secretary Sherman could be paid just the same. Consequently, he went to Washington upon the adjournment of the national convention to have his friend Bourne appointed postmaster at Vicksburg.

Senator Bruce, who had voted in the national convention for Grant after the name of Secretary Sherman had been withdrawn, was not prepared to act, and, of course, his concurrence was necessary to bring about the change. In conversation with Mr. Bruce before we left the convention city, Chicago, I protested against any changes being made in federal positions in the Sixth, or "shoestring," District until a candidate for Congress in that district had been nominated. In this Mr. Bruce agreed with me and assured me that this course would be pursued by him; hence, Mr. Hill and his friend Bourne were obliged to wait a while longer.

After the candidate for Congress had been nominated in the person of myself, I wrote the senator a letter in which I stated that, since I was a candidate for Congress in that district, it was my desire that no changes be made in any of the federal offices therein without my concurrence and that as matters then stood I preferred that no changes be made until after the election. Mr. Bruce wrote me in reply that my wishes in such matters would be respected and carried out. When, therefore, the postmastership at Vicksburg was brought to the senator's attention by Mr. Hill, the senator informed him that it would be treating the Republican candidate for Congress in that district with marked discourtesy to take the action he suggested without the knowledge and concurrence of that candidate. Consequently, he must decline to act favorably upon the suggestion.

A few days after this interview, I was approached by a friend and supporter of Mr. Bourne to whom I did not hesitate to say that I should make no recommendation for a change in that office until after the election. I called his attention to the fact, in which he professed to concur, that it was not worthwhile to make a change before the election, for the reason that should Hancock, the Democratic candidate for president, be elected, the newly appointed postmaster would have only a few months to serve before he would be obliged to turn the office over to his Democratic successor; hence, the matter should remain in abeyance until after the election. He then wanted to know if I would support Bourne in the event of Mr. Garfield's election, to which I replied that I never cross a bridge until I get to it.

"See me about that," I said, "after the election." Nothing more was said about the Vicksburg postmastership during the campaign.

As soon as the election was over, I wrote Mr. Bruce that since he was shortly to retire from the Senate and would be an applicant for an appointive office under the new administration, I would relieve him of the embarrassment that would result from having him take sides in the contest over the postmastership at Vicksburg. Hence, my suggestion was that the matter be held in further abeyance until after the inauguration of the new administration. "By that time," I said, "you will have retired from the Senate and my term as a member of the House will have virtually commenced. I think I shall then be able to control the appointment without assistance." I further informed him that I should be in attendance at the inauguration and that he could depend upon me to render whatever assistance and whatever influence I might have to secure for him the position he desired under the new administration.

Mr. Bruce was not only grateful for my promised support of himself, but also for the consideration I had shown in reference to the contest over the Vicksburg postmastership. I had already made up my mind to tender the position to John D. Tinney, a man who, so far as the public knew, had taken no part in the campaign, but who, to my personal knowledge, had done more to make my election possible than any other one man in the district, and that too, without any pledge, promise, consideration, or condition whatever. He was not an applicant for any office. No one could have been more surprised than he was when I approached him and asked him if he would accept the postmastership would it be tendered him. He said he would take it under advisement and give me an answer later. I replied that I would be in the city only two days and that I must have definite answer before I left. "Very well," he said, "I shall give you a definite answer tomorrow morning." He did so, informing me of his willingness to accept.

During the same visit to Vicksburg I had, by appointment, a conference with Mr. Bourne and a few of his friends. They desired to have a positive statement from me as soon as possible as to whether or not I would support Bourne for postmaster. I frankly informed them that I would not. While I did not feel at liberty to give them the name of the man I had decided to recommend, or even that I had made any decision at all, I believed it was due to them to say that Bourne would not be my choice. This ended the conference, and Bourne and his friends decided to make the best fight they could with such assistance as they might be able to command. I informed my friend Tinney that he need not make his candidacy public until after the inauguration of the new administration. He should then draw up an application and have it endorsed by Republicans whose names I would send him for that purpose. He was also instructed not to approach any Republican whose name was not on that list. This was done, and consequently the application was endorsed by every Republican who was approached or asked to do so.

While the name of the man I intended to recommend had not been made known even to my intimate friends and supporters, still they knew that Bourne would not be my choice and they also had an intimation as to what was in contemplation. They were satisfied that I would make no mistake in that matter; hence, they were prepared to stand by me in whatever action I might see fit to take. Tinney was also instructed to have another paper drawn up, to be signed by a number of white businessmen and Democrats, including the editor of the *Herald*, commending him as a fit and suitable man for the office. All of these papers, when completed, were to be placed in my hands, and the rest was to be left to me. These directions and instructions were followed.

Shortly after the inauguration, I presented the papers in person to the postmaster general with my own endorsement thereon, and the appointment was promptly made. The announcement that John D. Tinney had been appointed postmaster at Vicksburg was favorably received and commended by the public and the patrons of the office. He made one of the best postmasters the city had ever had.

While at Washington to witness the inauguration, I wrote and placed on file a strong letter in behalf of my friend Bruce, who aspired to be an assistant postmaster general. In addition to this I saw the president in person, by whom I was assured that Mr. Bruce would be appropriately recognized by the administration. He was finally made Register of the Treasury, General Schofield, who then held the office, having been transferred to a seat on the bench of the court of claims. The registership of the treasury for Mr. Bruce, therefore, was President Garfield's own selection.

But before the appointment had been made, I received a telegram from Mr. Bruce urging me to come to Washington immediately on very important business. I supposed it had some connection with matters personal to himself; hence, I took the first train to Washington. When I arrived, Mr. Bruce informed me that he had something of a very startling nature to reveal to me.

"When I sent you the telegram," he said, "I had just received information through a very reliable source, which has since been verified, that the president has decided to remove from office, or in other words refuse to reappoint, both Hill and Hunt. General George C. McKee, the leader of the faction which has always bitterly opposed and fought the faction with which we have acted and by which we have been supported, who served in Congress with General Garfield, has evidently succeeded in making an impression upon the president unfavorable to both Hill and Hunt. My information is that he has succeeded in convincing the president that we can never have a strong and effective party organization in that state as long as it is dominated and the patronage is allowed to be controlled by a man like Hill, and as for Hunt, he is nothing more than a faithful follower of Hill. I know that Hill has not always done the square thing by you, but you are now so situated that you can return good for evil. At any rate you are the only one that can now save Hill. I am powerless to serve him. I am not only a mere private citizen, but an applicant for office myself. I cannot, therefore, take an aggressive stand in this case. You can. If you feel that you cannot do this for Hill, I want you and ask you to do it for me. If you have occasion to question Hill's friendship for you and loyalty to you (and I admit that you have) you have had no occasion to question mine. I therefore appeal to you to make the effort to save Hill."

Mr. Bruce's appeal was impressive. I confess that it touched me. But, in reply I said: "Mr. Bruce, I fear you are asking too much of me. Mr. Hill has done very little to merit but very much to forfeit, in recent years at least, my friendship for him and support of him, and yet I have said and done nothing to harm him. It is true that I have been in the past the beneficiary of some of the power and influence which has been at his disposal, but which came chiefly through instrumentalities for the existence of which you were largely responsible. With a few exceptions whenever he has given me the benefit of his influence and support, it has been due largely to the fact that he was obliged to choose between me and someone representative of the faction that was known to be bitterly opposed not only to his leadership but to the leadership of those who were responsible for the power and influence he possessed.

"The reasons for Hill's indifference or hostility to me are well known to you. They are that I have ideas, opinions, and convictions of my own and that no man, whoever he may be, can think, speak, and act for me. This is contrary to Hill's conception of political or party leadership. This, as you know, has always been the one weak spot in the Bruce-Lynch-Hill combination and the rock upon which I fear it will be destroyed if it has not been already. And yet up to this hour I have not only said and done nothing against him, but have joined you in every effort you have made in his behalf. One reason I have done this is that I have never believed it was possible for him to get what I wanted and that I would never want what it was possible for him to get. In view, however, of the course pursued by him in the campaign just closed, I thought that neither you nor any other friend of his could ask or expect me to do anything more for him than to give him the benefit of my silence. If it be true that he is about to fall, through the efforts of others, is it not asking too much of me to come to his rescue, even as a personal favor to you? No, Mr. Bruce, I fear you are asking too much of me. You have proved to my satisfaction that you are my friend. Any request you may make of me with reference to matters personal to yourself will be cheerfully granted. But the request you now make of me I cannot see my way clear to grant."

"I see your point," said Mr. Bruce, "and, taking your view of the matter, I cannot blame you, but I am sure I can bring about conditions which will be to the mutual interest of all concerned to have you do what I have requested of you in this case. I shall neither ask nor expect you to do it unconditionally. In other words, I will not ask you to come to his rescue and save him, if he can be saved, unless it be done upon such conditions and in such a way as will put him under obligations to you and make him your faithful friend and loyal supporter in the future. If you will allow this effort to be made on my part, I think I can bring about a renewal of the combination consisting of Bruce, Lynch, and Hill, and that too, in such a way as will give you no occasion to question the friendship and loyalty of either party to the combination."

"If you think that can be done," I replied, "you are at liberty to proceed." Mr. Bruce then wired Hill to come to Washington without delay. When he arrived, Mr. Bruce not only gave him the startling information about his own case but also informed him of his interview with me. Mr. Hill was both surprised and shocked. To him such a report was incredible. He could not believe it, for he had been laboring under the impression that the nomination and election of General Garfield, so far at least as he was concerned, was substantially the same as if it had been Secretary Sherman. He insisted, therefore, that he be allowed to find out through sources of his own selection whether or not there was any foundation for the report. It did not take him long to find out that Mr. Bruce had not been misinformed. He was then not only willing but anxious to become a party to any combination that would retain him in the position he then held, that of Collector of Internal Revenue. Mr. Bruce then fixed the time and place for the conference, which resulted in an alliance, offensive and defensive.

It was a reestablishment of the personal and political relations of the three parties to the compact. In other words, new life was given to the Bruce-Lynch-Hill combination which in days gone by had seldom experienced defeat in a party convention whenever a fight was made. An effort was then to be made to save Hill, and if possible, Hunt as well; but Hill in any event.

It was arranged that Mr. Bruce and I should call on the president the next day, but the aggressive fight was to be made by me. Mr. Bruce's presence was merely to let the president see that he was in sympathy with me. When I informed the president that we had called to ask that Mr. Hill be reappointed he seemed somewhat surprised.

Addressing me, the president asked, "Are you for Hill?"

"Yes, sir," I replied.

"Well," said the president, "I have been informed that you were opposed to him. Did he not oppose your nomination for Congress?"

"Yes, sir," I answered, "but I am returning good for evil. His opposition to me was personal rather than political. My support of him now is political rather than personal. Those who took it for granted that I was opposed to reappointment of Mr. Hill and so informed you had no authority from me to do so. Yes, Mr. President, the removal of Mr. Hill, at this time would be in my opinion a political mistake. It would be, from a party standpoint, a blunder which I know you would not care to make, and which I am sure you would not think of making if the facts were brought to your notice. To bring those facts to your notice is why we are here now. Retain Mr. Hill in office and you will make no mistake."

"Well," said the president, "with such a request coming from both Mr. Bruce and yourself I cannot afford to disregard it, but assuming that you were in favor of a change and that Mr. Bruce was at least indifferent, I had decided to make a change. I shall now reconsider that decision so far as Mr. Hill is concerned, but I shall not under any circumstances reappoint Hunt." While expressing deep regret that the president could not see his way clear to reappoint Hunt, we thanked him for the concession he had made in the case of Mr. Hill and then bade him good-bye.

When General George C. McKee heard of this interview he was furious. I met him on the street a day or two later when he remarked: "Lynch, I thought you had some political sense, but I have come to the conclusion that you have none."

"For my action in this matter," I replied, "I have no explanations, excuses, or apologies to make. Whether or not I have made a mistake the future will determine."

27

The Garfield Years

THE GARFIELD ADMINISTRATION STARTED OUT UNDER MOST favorable auspices. Mr. Conkling took an active and leading part in the Senate as a champion and spokesman of the administration. He seemed to have taken it for granted that, although his bitter enemy in the person of Mr. Blaine was secretary of state, his own influence with the administration would be potential. In conversation with his personal friends he insisted that this was a part of the agreement that had been made and entered into at the famous Mentor Conference, about which so much had been said and published. If it were true that Mr. Conkling's control of the federal patronage in New York in the event of Republican success was part of the agreement that was made and entered into at the celebrated Mentor Conference, it transpired that Mr. Blaine had sufficient influence with the president to bring about its repudiation.

It was well known that the president was anxious to avoid a

break with Senator Conkling. Judge W. H. Robertson was a candidate for the collectorship of the Port of New York, whose candidacy was strongly supported by Mr. Blaine. Judge Robertson had been one of the influential leaders of the Blaine movement in New York. It was he who disregarded the action of the state convention in instructing the delegation to cast the vote of the state as a unit for General Grant. In bolting the action of the state convention, Judge Robertson carried about nineteen delegates with him in voting for Mr. Blaine. Mr. Blaine insisted upon the appointment of Judge Robertson to the collectorship of the Port of New York. Senator Conkling would not consent under any circumstances to this appointment. Mr. Blaine, it appears, succeeded in convincing the president that, but for Judge Robertson's action, his, Garfield's, nomination would have been impossible and that, consequently, it would be base ingratitude not to appoint him to the position for which he was an applicant. Mr. Blaine contended that the administration would not only be guilty of ingratitude should it refuse to appoint Judge Robertson, but that it would thereby allow itself to be the medium through which this man was to be punished for his action in making the existence of the administration possible.

"Can you, Mr. President, afford to do such a thing as this?" asked Mr. Blaine.

The president gave this a negative answer. Perhaps it did not occur to Mr. Blaine at that time that while the action of Judge Robertson may have made the nomination of Mr. Garfield possible, the subsequent action of Senator Conkling made his election possible. But, notwithstanding this, the president decided that Judge Robertson should have the office for which he was an applicant.

As previously stated, however, the president was anxious to avoid a break with Senator Conkling. To get the senator to consent to the appointment of Judge Robertson was the task the president had before him. With that end in view the president had invited Mr. Conkling to a private conference, at which he expressed a willingness to allow the New York senator to name every important federal office in New York, other than the collectorship of the Port, if he would consent to the appointment of Judge Robertson to that office. But the only concession Senator Conkling was willing to make was to give his consent to the appointment of Judge Robertson to any position in the foreign service. This was not satisfactory; hence the conference was a failure. The president was thus placed in a very disagreeable dilemma. He was thus forced, very much against his own wishes and inclinations, to take a decided stand in a very unpleasant and disagreeable controversy. He was thus forced to choose between Mr. Blaine, his own secretary of state on one side, and Senator Conkling on the other. To one he felt that he was obligated for his nomination. To the other he believed he was largely indebted for his election.

It was asserted by some who were in a position to know that if the president had taken sides with Mr. Conkling, Mr. Blaine would have immediately tendered his resignation and thus severed his official connection with the administration. While no intimation of this was made known to the president, yet he no doubt believed, in consequence of the deep and intense interest Mr. Blaine had shown in the matter, that such action on his part, in the event of an adverse decision, was more than probable. When the president saw that there was no escape, that he was obliged to take a decided stand one way or the other, he finally decided to sustain the contention of his secretary of state. Consequently, after the fruitless conference between the president and Senator Conkling the name of Judge Robertson was sent to the Senate for Collector of the Port of New York. Senator Conkling, joined by his colleague Senator Platt, at first made an effort to have the nomination rejected, but the other Republican senators were not willing to place themselves in open opposition to the administration. When the fact was developed that the nomination would be confirmed, Senators Conkling and Platt immediately tendered their resignations.

This in my opinion was a grave blunder on their part, as subsequent events more than proved. They had before them the example of Senator Sumner, by which they should have profited. Senator Sumner was greatly humiliated when, through the influence of the administration, he was supplanted by Senator Cameron as chairman of the Senate Committee on Foreign Relations on account of a misunderstanding with President Grant that grew out of the effort on the part of the administration to bring about the annexation of Santo Domingo, to which Senator Sumner was bitterly opposed. Yet he did not resign his seat in the Senate because he was thus, as he felt, unjustly humiliated. He realized and appreciated the fact that while he was commissioned to speak and vote as a senator for his own state, his great power and immense influence were not confined to the boundaries of his own state.

He knew and appreciated the fact that when he spoke and voted as a senator, he did so, not merely as a senator from the state of Massachusetts, but as a senator of the United States. He belonged to no one state, but to the United States. He had, on account of his great intellect, power, influence, and ability, long since ceased to be the spokesman and representative of any particular state or section, but he was a representative of his country—recognized as such throughout the civilized world. Knowing these things to be true of himself, he did not feel that he should deprive the people of his valuable services simply because he was not in harmony with the administration upon some one matter, however important it may be. In this Senator Sumner was unquestionably right. What was true of Senator Sumner at that time was equally true of Senators Conkling and Platt in their misunderstanding with President Garfield about the collectorship of the Port of New York.

Mr. Conkling was one of the greatest men our country had

ever produced. He was a man of great force and power. He was not only an intellectual giant, but he was a man of commanding presence and attractive personality. As a speaker and orator he had few equals and no superiors. As in the case of Senator Sumner he spoke and voted as a senator not merely for his state, but for his country; not for any particular section or locality, but for the United States. He was too great a man and his services were too important and valuable for his country to be deprived of them merely on account of a misunderstanding between the president and himself about federal patronage in New York. He and his colleague should have retained their seats in the Senate and trusted to the judgment of their fellow citizens for a vindication of their course and action in that as in other matters. They not only made a mistake in resigning their seats in the Senate but consummated it when they went before the legislature of their state, which was then in session, and asked for a vindication through the medium of a reelection. This was subjecting their friends to a test to which they were not willing to submit. Their friends in and out of the legislature were faithful, true, and loyal to them, which would have been demonstrated at the proper time and in the right way, had they remained in a position which would have enabled them to do so without serious injury to the party organization. But when they asked, as the price of their loyalty, that the party organization in the state be placed in open opposition to the national administration for no other reason than a misunderstanding about federal patronage in the city of New York, they did not think that the controversy was worth the price they were asked to pay. Hence, the request was denied, resulting in the defeat of Messrs. Conkling and Platt and the election of two administration Republicans, in the persons of Messrs. Warner Miller and E. G. Lapham.

This had the unfortunate effect of eliminating Mr. Conkling from public life, at least so far as active participation in public affairs was concerned. But this was not true of Mr. Platt. He was determined to come to the front again and in this he was successful. At the very next national convention, 1884, he turned up as one of the Blaine delegates from New York and was one of the speakers that seconded Mr. Blaine's nomination. That was something Mr. Conkling never could have been induced to do. He was proud, haughty, and dictatorial. He would never forget a friend nor forgive an enemy. To his friends he was loyal and true. To his enemies he was bitter and unrelenting. For his friends he could not do too much. From his enemies he would ask no quarter and would give none. More than one man of national reputation had been made to feel the power and suffer the consequences resulting from his ill will and displeasure. But for the unfriendliness of Mr. Conkling, Mr. Blaine no doubt would have attained the acme of his ambition in reaching the presidency of the United States. It was Mr. Blaine's misfortune to have made an enemy of the one man who, by a stroke of destiny, was so situated as to make it possible for him to prevent the realization of Mr. Blaine's life ambition. It was due more to Mr. Conkling than to any other man that Mr. Blaine was defeated for the Republican presidential nomination in 1876—the year in which he could have been elected had he been nominated.

Mr. Conkling was too much of a party man to support the Democratic ticket at any time or under any circumstances. Hence, in 1884, when Mr. Blaine was finally nominated for the presidency, Mr. Conkling gave the ticket the benefit of his silence. That silence proved to be fatal, which in all probability would have had the same result in 1880 had he pursued the same course at that time. In consequence of Mr. Conkling's silence and apparent indifference in 1884, Mr. Blaine lost New York, the pivotal state, and was defeated by Mr. Cleveland for the presidency. The falling off in the Republican vote in Mr. Conkling's home county alone caused the loss of the state and the presidency of the United States to the Republican party.

The quarrel between Blaine and Conkling originated when

both of them were members of the House of Representatives. In a controversy that took place between them on the House floor, Mr. Blaine referred to Mr. Conkling as a member from New York with the "turkey gobbler strut." That remark made the two men enemies for life. That remark touched and wounded Mr. Conkling's pride, for which he could never be induced to forgive the one by whom it was made.

As a United States senator he was both felt and feared. No senator ever desired to get into a controversy with him, because he was not only a speaker of great force, power, and eloquence, but as a debater he was keen, cutting, sarcastic, and ironical. Senator Lamar of Mississippi, who as an eloquent orator compared favorably with the best on both sides of the chamber, had the misfortune to get into a controversy on one occasion with the distinguished New York senator. In repelling an accusation the senator from Mississippi had made against him, Mr. Conkling said, "If it were not that this is the United States I would characterize the member from Mississippi as a coward and a prevaricator."

If those words had been uttered by any other senator than Roscoe Conkling, it is more than probable that he would have been severely reprimanded and censured. Not so with Conkling, for no other senator cared to incur his displeasure by becoming the author of such a resolution for that purpose.

Senator John J. Ingalls of Kansas was the only other senator that came near, in after years, to sustaining a similar position. While he was by no means the equal of Conkling, he was both eloquent and sarcastic. For that reason senators were not anxious to get him into a controversy with them. On one occasion it seemed that he came near getting into one with Senator [Charles F.] Manderson of Nebraska. While the senator from Nebraska was delivering a speech, he made a remark to which the senator from Kansas took exception. When the Kansas senator arose, flushed evidently with anger and laboring under intense excitement, to correct what he declared, in words that were more forcible than elegant, to be a misstatement of his position, the senator from Nebraska did not hesitate for a moment to accept the correction, remarking by way of explanation and apology that he had not distinctly heard the remark the senator from Kansas had made and to which he was alluding when interrupted.

"Then," retorted the senator from Kansas, "that is your misfortune."

"I admit," the senator from Nebraska quickly replied, "it is always a misfortune not to hear the senator from Kansas."

The unfortunate controversy between President Garfield and Senator Conkling resulted in a national calamity. The bitterness and ill feeling that grew out of it had the effect of bringing a crank on the scene of action, who, early in July 1881 when the president, in company with Mr. Blaine, was leaving the city of Washington for his summer vacation, awaited the arrival of the distinguished party at the railroad station and fired the fatal shot which a few months later terminated the earthly career of a president who was beloved by his countrymen without regard to party or section.

Whatever may have been the merits connected with, or the real cause of this unfortunate controversy, it resulted in the political death of one and the physical death of the other, thus depriving the country of the valuable services of two of the greatest and most intellectual men that our country had ever produced.

When the president died, I was at my home, Natchez, Mississippi, where a memorial meeting was held in honor of his memory, participated in by both races and both parties. I had the honor of being one of the speakers on that occasion. That part of my remarks which seemed to attract most attention and made the deepest impression was the declaration that it was my good fortune, as a member of the House of Representatives, to sit under the sound of his eloquent voice on a certain memorable occasion when he declared that there could never be a permanent peace and union between the North and the South until the South would admit that, in the controversy that brought on the War of the Rebellion, the North was right and the South was wrong. Notwithstanding that declaration, in which he was unquestionably right, I ventured the opinion that, had he been spared to serve out the term for which he had been elected, those who had voted for him would have been proud of the fact that they had done so, while those who had voted against him would have had no occasion to regret that he had been elected.

Upon the death of President Garfield, Vice-President Arthur, who had been named for that office by Mr. Conkling, became president; but he, too, soon incurred the displeasure of Mr. Conkling. Mr. Conkling had occasion to make a request of the president which the latter could not see his way clear to grant. For this Mr. Conkling never forgave him. The president tried hard afterwards to regain Mr. Conkling's friendship, but in vain. He even went so far, it is said, to tender Mr. Conkling a seat on the bench of the Supreme Court, but that tender was contemptuously declined.

President Arthur aspired to succeed himself as president. As a whole he gave the country a splendid administration for which he merited a renomination and election as his own successor. While there was a strong and well-organized effort to secure for him a renomination, the probabilities are that the attitude of Mr. Conkling towards him contributed largely to his defeat, although the ex-senator took no active part in the contest. But as in the case of Mr. Blaine for the election, his silence no doubt was fatal to Mr. Arthur's renomination.

1881: Republican and Greenback Alliance

IN 1881 THERE WAS TO BE AN ELECTION IN MISSISSIPPI FOR GOVernor and other state officers. What was known as the Greenback, or Populist, party had made some headway in the state, especially in the Second, or Holly Springs, Congressional District.[1] It looked at that time as if that party would cut an important figure in the politics of the state. Believing that the Greenback party was strong enough to secure a fair election and an honest count in localities where it had an organized existence, it was suggested that the Republicans and Greenbackers form a fusion, the two parties to unite in the support of one state ticket. The suggestion was favorably received. But

1. The Greenback party, sometimes in cooperation with the Independent party, was active in Mississippi from 1878 to 1881. The Populist party did not emerge until almost a decade later. Albert D. Kirwan, *Revolt of the Rednecks, Mississippi Politics, 1876–1925* (Lexington, 1951), pp. 8, 12, 93.

it occurred to me that the ticket would be very much stronger if we could find a liberal and conservative Democrat who would be willing to accept the nomination for governor. The man I had in mind at the time was State Senator Benjamin King of Copiah County. I had watched his course as a member of the state senate with keen interest and satisfaction. The impression he made upon my mind was that, although a Democrat, he was conservative, fair-minded and very liberal in his views upon public questions. This impression was strengthened by the speeches he delivered and the votes he gave as a member of the state senate. In consequence of his liberal and conservative views, he was often found speaking and voting against some of the favorite measures of his own party. But this made no difference with him because he was always willing to subordinate party interest to what he believed was for the public good.

In conversation with a number of the leaders of the Republican and Greenback parties I brought these facts to their notice and stated that if Senator King could be induced to consent to head the ticket, the chances of success would be very much better, for his well-known standing as a reputable citizen, his great ability as a lawyer and public speaker, and his standing as an influential Democrat ought to secure for the ticket fair treatment and an honest count in counties it would be necessary for us to carry to win the election, and in which neither the Republicans nor Greenbackers, I apprehended, had sufficient following among the whites to accomplish. The result was I was authorized to approach the senator upon the subject which I did without hesitation and without delay. When I called on him he received me cordially, but was very much surprised when I made known to him the purpose of my call. The fact, however, that he did not immediately repulse me gave me some hope that my mission might not be wholly in vain. I urged him with all the power and eloquence at my command to consent to make the race. I called his attention to the fact that his public record was an open book from which he had nothing to fear. That which made him the most eligible and acceptable man to head the ticket was the splendid reputation he had made as an honest, safe, prudent, conservative, and upright public servant. The fact that he was a Democrat would lose the odium which had been attached to that name, and the honest men of the state, both white and colored, would cheerfully give their support and votes for the perpetuation of that type of Democracy, for after all, it is not the name but the substance for which we are looking.

"As a member of the state senate I recognize the fact that you are a representative of the Democratic party of your senatorial district. If that party can reap and enjoy the fruits of the influence for good that you have so long produced and get the benefit of the splendid work you have so successfully accomplished, then so much the better for that party. But you now have the opportunity to do for the state what you have so well and so creditably done for your district. Hide not your splendid light under a bushel, but let it be set upon a hill that your fellow citizens may see the good work you have done for some and wish to do for others, so that they may be benefited and saved thereby. This is a case where the office seeks the man, not the man the office. The governorship, doubtless, is an office that has no charms for you, and to fill which I am sure you have no ambition. But you owe a duty to your state and to your fellow citizens which you should be willing and ready to discharge, even though it be done at some sacrifice on your part. You are not asked to renounce your party allegiance or change your political affiliations. All that is asked and desired of you is to allow the people of your state, without regard to race or party differences, to avail themselves of the benefit of your ripe experience, sound judgment, and the splendid and satisfactory services which we know you will render, and that too in a way that will add to the honor and glory of the state and the peace, happiness, and prosperity of its citizens. You have been a Democrat in the past. You are not expected to be anything else in the future. The only effect that the acceptance of this nomination by you can possibly have upon your party in the state will be to bring that party up, and place it in harmonious relations with the splendid position which you have so long and so consistently occupied. I sincerely hope, therefore, that you will give this matter your favorable consideration."

The senator listened to my remarks with close attention. I was sure when I had finished that I had made a favorable impression upon him. When I had finished, he asked me to give him a few days to consider it. He said if I would call again in two or three days he would be prepared to give me a definite answer. When I left him, I felt that I had won my case. I was not at all surprised, therefore, when I called on him at the end of the third day to find that he had given the matter favorable consideration. He informed me that the conditions upon which he would make the race were that he should be nominated as an Independent Democrat, his candidacy to be endorsed by a regular delegate convention of both the Republican and Greenback parties, each to ratify the action of the other. I told him that the conditions were entirely satisfactory so far as I was able to speak, which was authoritative in the case of the Republicans, and I had every reason to believe they would be satisfactory to the Greenbackers; but if I found that they could not be complied with in every detail, he would be notified before any publicity was given to what had transpired.

I then reported the result of my mission to a conference composed of Republicans and Greenbackers, which was called for that purpose, and by which the same was approved without a dissenting vote. A state convention of each party was then called, both conventions to meet at Jackson, the state capital, the same day. I was chosen to preside over the deliberations of the Republican convention. Both conventions approved, ratified, and endorsed the candidacy of Hon. Benjamin King for governor. Of the other six places on the ticket it was agreed that each party should have three. The Greenbackers were to have lieutenant governor, Auditor of Public Accounts, and state superintendent of education. The Republicans were given secretary of state, treasurer, and attorney general. The selections made by each convention were duly ratified and approved by the other. The ticket having been completed, both conventions adjourned.

James J. Spelman, who was nominated by the Republicans for secretary of state, was the only colored man on the ticket.[2] Democrats were obliged to admit that it was a strong and able ticket. The Democratic candidate for governor was General Robert Lowry, one of the most brilliant lawyers and speakers in the state. But when it became known that State Senator Benjamin King had consented to run against him he was considerably alarmed and worried. He was an interested spectator during the harmonious proceedings of the Republican State Convention. King immediately commenced an active campaign. He and General Lowry met in joint debate at several important points, at all of which King maintained with marked ability his reputation as an eloquent speaker. Shortly after the nominations had been made, a campaign committee was formed, consisting of a part of the executive committee of each party, with Mr. Hull, a Greenbacker, who was also the editor of a campaign paper, in active management and control. The Demo-

2. James J. Spelman was born in Connecticut in 1841 and attended school in New York. As a journalist he wrote for the *Anglo-African* and *Pine and Palm,* its successor. During the war he recruited Negro soldiers and served as major in a New York battalion known as the "Shaw cadets." In 1868 he went to Mississippi to work for the Freedmen's Bureau. Later he served as justice of the peace and alderman in Canton. In 1870, he was elected to the legislature, where he served for six years. He served on the board of trustees of Alcorn College and was aide-de-camp to the governor with the rank of lieutenant colonel. Simmons, *Men of Mark,* pp. 928–32.

crats were successful, but by a greatly reduced majority.[3] Their success was due largely to the fact that the Greenbackers had practically no organization in any of the black counties, and King could not command a sufficient following among the whites in those counties to secure for the ticket a fair election and an honest count. The Democrats won, therefore, not by the votes but by the official returns from the black belt. But King made a brave and gallant fight of which he was justly proud, and for which, as he afterwards expressed to me, he had no regrets, although his efforts had not been crowned with success, at least according to the official returns.

3. The Democratic candidate, Robert Lowry, polled 47,960 votes, while King received 31,256. Kirwan, *Revolt of the Rednecks*, p. 8.

1882: Party and Election Disputes

THE CONTESTED-ELECTION CASE OF LYNCH AGAINST CHALMERS was finally disposed of by the House of Representatives in the spring of 1882. The Committee on Elections, of which Hon. W. H. Calkins of Indiana was chairman, gave the case a thorough, careful, and patient investigation. I could have established my right to the seat by setting up the rejected votes of Warren County alone, but I decided to expose and show up, as far as possible, the illegal and questionable methods that have been adopted throughout the district to overcome the heavy Republican majority and have a Democrat returned to Congress from that district. For this purpose I secured the legal services of ex-Attorney General [Joshua S.] Morris to manage the case and to conduct the examination of witnesses in the district. To represent me before the committee in Washington I secured the legal services of the law firm of Shellabarger and Wilson and also Gen. Stewart L. Woodford of New York.

CHAPTER TWENTY-NINE

The duty of making a careful examination of the evidence and preparing the briefs in support of my claim to the seat devolved upon Judge Shellabarger. Upon one important point there was a difference of opinion between Judge Shellabarger and myself. In the county of Issaquena I had received a majority in every voting precinct, the returns having been properly made, certified, and returned by the election officers, which certificates, with the tally sheets, poll lists, ballot boxes, and the ballots, had been filed in the office of the circuit court, who under the law, was the custodian of the same. To reduce the Republican majority in that county the County Returning Board, without cause, justification, or complaint, threw out, rejected, and suppressed the returns from every precinct in the county except one. The certificate sent to the secretary of state, giving the result of the election in that county, was in point of fact the vote of but one precinct.

To set up the rejected vote in that county was the task I had before me. To have each voter examined as a witness was both a physical and financial impossibility. After giving the case careful consideration, it was decided that there were only two ways in which it was possible to set up and prove the vote at the rejected precincts. One was to have the clerk of the United States district court, who, under the federal law, was the custodian of the returns made by the United States supervisors, furnish certified copies of the returns made by the United States supervisors from the rejected precincts in that county. This had been done. The other was to have the clerk of the circuit court of that county, who, under the state law, was the custodian of everything pertaining to the elections, furnish certified copies of the returns made by the different precinct officers, including their certificates and tally sheets. This had also been done.

In the brief filed in behalf of the contestee it was contended that all of these certificates were void *ab initio* and that as evidence they were worthless and valueless. With reference to the certificates furnished by the clerk of the circuit court of the county, Judge Shellabarger was disposed to yield the point. In his opinion they could not be received as evidence, but those furnished by the clerk of the United States district court could and would be. His advice, therefore, was to rely wholly upon the certificates furnished by the clerk of the United States district court, and mine to be in support of the validity of those furnished by the clerk of the circuit court of the county. This was done. Each of us also made a legal oral argument before the committee in support of our respective contentions. The result was the committee accepted my contention and rejected Judge Shellabarger's.

It was the brief filed in that case and the legal oral argument made by me in support of it that contributed more largely than any other to my appointment as an auditor in the Treasury Department under the administration of President Harrison. Judge Wilson, who came from Indiana and with whom I had served as a member of Congress and who was Judge Shellabarger's law partner, in a letter addressed to the president in my behalf called attention to the fact that the brief filed by me in that case and the legal argument made in support of it established the fact beyond question that I was legally qualified to discharge in a satisfactory manner the duties of any one of the accounting offices of the Treasury.

Judge T. J. Wharton, one of the judges of the circuit court of my state, also informed me that if I should make application before his court for admission to the bar, he would have me admitted without examination by a committee, his action being based upon the brief filed by me in that case which he had carefully read. When a vote was finally reached in the committee, every Republican member thereof, joined by Mr. Jones of Texas, the Independent member, voted in favor of awarding the seat to me. The Democratic members filed a minority report, but they did not make a strong effort to retain Mr. Chalmers in the seat. In fact, the refusal of the Democrats to make this effort was given by Chalmers subsequently as one of his reasons for leaving the Democratic party. But the Democratic members no doubt felt that Chalmers had done himself much harm and the Democratic party no good in claiming a seat in Congress to which it was well known he had not been elected; hence, they refused to make a strong fight in his behalf.

The case was strongly and ably presented to the House by the chairman and several other members of the committee, and in accordance with the custom and practice in such cases, I was allowed one hour to present the case from my own standpoint and in my own way. In that speech I decided not to touch upon the legal points involved, but to leave them to be presented and argued by members of the committee. I therefore confined my remarks to the facts rather than the law of the case. The contestee paid close and strict attention to my remarks. The sentence that seemed to affect him more than any other was this: "In the official person of the contestee in this case the country is presented with a living monument of rifled ballot boxes, stifled public justice, and a prostituted suffrage." When I had concluded my remarks, I was the recipient of the applause and hearty congratulations of the Republican members. When the vote was taken, every Republican and Independent member voted for the resolution which declared that I had been legally elected and entitled to the seat as a representative in Congress from the Sixth District of Mississippi, while a large number of Democratic members refrained from voting, their action in so doing being intended no doubt to be construed as a silent but effective protest against retaining a man in a seat to which they knew he had not been and could not be fairly elected, but whose conduct and influence had been the occasion of much embarrassment to them as well as injury to the good name of the Democratic party.

As a result of the Lynch-Chalmers contest, the Democratic legislature of Mississippi decided to put an end to such contests in the future by reorganizing the congressional districts. Adams County, in which I lived, was attached to a long string of Democratic counties, the district extending from the Mississippi River to the Alabama line. Of the thirteen counties of which the new district was composed, only two, Adams and Wilkinson, were reliably Republican. Two others, Amite and Pike, were close and doubtful, with the chances in favor of the Democrats, while the other nine were hopelessly Democratic by majorities of from 100 to 1,000 each. The counties of which the district was composed gave a Democratic majority in 1881, on the vote for governor, of 1,850. Since Hon. Benjamin King, the Independent candidate for governor in 1881, was a strong and popular man, the vote of that year seemed to indicate that the district was safely and reliably Democratic.

Since I was already in Congress, the Republicans of the new district insisted that I make the race therein for Congress, which I finally consented to do. The Democrats nominated one of their strongest and best men, in the person of Judge Henry S. Van Eaton of Wilkinson. I was nominated by the unanimous vote of the Republican convention and shortly thereafter I entered upon an active and aggressive canvass of the district. Judge Van Eaton and I met in joint debate at several places. The canvass was entirely free from bitterness and excitement, and I was treated with marked courtesy and respect at every point.

The absolute fairness with which the election was conducted took the Republicans very much by surprise. Had this been anticipated, Republican success would have been an assured fact. But, believing as they did that there would be a repetition of some of the methods of two years before, at least in one if not both of the two Republican counties, a full Republican vote was not polled, as it would have been had it been known or believed that the election would be fair and the count honest. That it was so conducted may have been due to the fact that the district was believed to be reliably Democratic anyway and that questionable methods were not necessary to insure Democratic success. But, let the reasons be what they may, it was a fact that the election was absolutely free and fair and the count honest. In spite of the fact that there was a material falling off in the Republican vote for the reasons above stated, when the returns were all in, it was developed that the Democratic majority had been reduced to six hundred. Judge Van Eaton's own county, Wilkinson, gave a majority against him of more than one thousand, while my own home county, Adams, which was counted against me two years before, gave me a majority of more than thirteen hundred. It could and would have been about two thousand had it been known or believed that there would be a free, fair, and honest election.

In my canvass of the district I had some peculiar and amusing experiences. The counties east of the Pearl River were sparsely populated and quite inaccessible. No railroad at that time passed through any of them except those on the coast between New Orleans and Mobile. To canvass the interior counties it was necessary to make the trip in a buggy, which occupied nearly two weeks, and even then I could speak at not more than two points in any one county. I started from Summit, Pike County, in a four-seated buggy, in which there were three persons, the driver, a traveling companion, and myself. We visited the counties of Marion, Lawrence, Covington, Jones, Perry, and Greene, reaching the railroad again at a point on the Alabama line in the northern end of Greene County.

Since there were very few colored people in those counties I found some difficulty in being accommodated at different points overnight. When we arrived at Williamsburg, the county seat of Covington County, I was agreeably surprised to find that I had no difficulty in securing accommodations at the principal hotel, such as it was. I accidentally met United States

Senator [James Z.] George at that place, who was also on a campaign tour and who was a guest at the same hotel. I remained there about twenty-four hours. I had a splendid meeting, more than half of the audience being white people and Democrats, many of whom, no doubt, being actuated by curiosity in attending the meeting. But they were orderly, respectful, and attentive. At night I attended a religious meeting that was held at the courthouse, composed exclusively of whites. That seemed to have been the camp-meeting season of the year in that part of the state.

My next point was Ellisville, the county seat of Jones County. I arrived there about an hour before dark. I saw a white man standing on the corner of what appeared to be two of the principal streets of the town. I asked him if there was a hotel in town.

"No," he replied, "there is no hotel here, but there are one or two private boarding houses here for white people."

I then asked him if any colored people lived in town. His reply was in the negative.

"No colored people," he said, "live in town, but there is a colored family living about a mile from town near the Augusta Road. The name of the head of the family is Jackson Showers."

I thanked him for the information and directed the driver to proceed. We were in search of the home of Jackson Showers. We had no time to lose, because night would soon overtake us. We had difficulty in finding the house. In fact, we had passed the crossroad which led to his house when, fortunately, we met another white man of whom we inquired for directions to the home of Jackson Showers. He informed us that we had passed the road that would take us to the home of Mr. Showers and that if we would turn back and follow him he would put us in the right road, which we gladly did.

By the time we reached the crossroad that led to the home of Mr. Showers, it was dark, but our guide told us to follow that road, which was nothing more than a cow path through a thick woods, and we would eventually reach the home of Mr. Showers. After we had traveled some little distance, we detected a dim light which created the hope within us that we were at last in sight of the promised land. We were much relieved and greatly pleased when we found out that in this we were not mistaken. It was a loghouse built out in the pine woods, with neither fences nor outhouses. When we drove up to the door a nice-looking woman came out, of whom we inquired if that was the home of Mr. Jackson Showers. She answered in the affirmative, but she informed us that Mr. Showers was not at home.

"He went to town this afternoon," she said, "and has not yet returned."

She was the wife of Mr. Showers. I then introduced myself to her and informed her that it would be necessary for her and her husband to accommodate my traveling companion, the driver, and myself at their home that night. This she said was impossible because they had no accommodations whatever, not even anything in the house to eat.

"You can see," she said, "that we have a house of but one room, with a very small room attached which we use as a kitchen and dining room, and yet our family consists of five persons–husband, wife, and three children. How, then, can we accommodate you and your friends?"

I informed her that I appreciated what she had said but with us it was absolutely necessary to remain there and make ourselves satisfied with such accommodations as she and her husband could give us.

"Very well," she said, "be seated and wait until my husband returns."

She then went to the kitchen to prepare supper. The driver unhitched his horses and tied them to a tree, and we prepared to spend the night at the humble home of Mr. Jackson Showers. Finally, Mr. Showers made his appearance and after a few minutes conference with his wife, he informed us that he had no accommodations whatever, but that if we were willing to put up with what he had, he had no objections to us remaining at his house that night. Of course, we were more than willing. When the announcement was made that supper was ready, we were delighted because we were very hungry. But we were very much disappointed when we found that the supper consisted of cowpeas and cornbread, which had been cooked without salt. It was impossible for me to eat what was put before me. The driver and my friends did a little better, but their hunger was not at all satisfied. I then fully realized that Mr. Showers meant what he said when he informed us that he had no accommodations whatever.

When Mr. Showers saw that the supper was a sad disappointment to us and that we did not enjoy it, he informed us that he had a few chickens but they had gone to roost in the tall pine trees; hence, it would not be possible to get one of them that night unless he could succeed in shooting one. He said he had a shotgun in the house with two loads but he had no additional ammunition. If he could shoot a chicken with one of those loads we would have a fine chicken supper. That was a most delightful prospect. So we built a bonfire near the tree in which he said the chickens were so that he could take a good aim and therefore be sure to bring down a chicken. When all was ready, Mr. Showers fired. We looked with anxious eyes for a chicken to fall, but in this we were doomed to disappointment. The outlook was somewhat discouraging, for we knew we had just one more chance. So we renewed the bonfire and implored Mr. Showers to be more careful and to be sure to take a good and accurate aim so that a chicken would be certain to fall; but in this we were again sadly disappointed.

The only consolation Mr. Showers could give us was that he would get up early the next morning and go to town and purchase some meat so as to enable us to have a good breakfast before we started on the long and tedious ride to Augusta, the county seat of Perry County, that being the next point for which we were destined. We were up the next morning at an early hour. Mr. Showers had gone to town for the meat for breakfast. We tried to wait until he returned, but his stay was so prolonged that we were obliged to give up in hopeless despair. I therefore settled with Mrs. Showers and we then bade her good-bye and thanked her for their kindness and started on our journey without having had anything to eat.

Just then Mr. Showers made his appearance with the meat. It was bacon. But it was then too late for us to wait until his wife could prepare breakfast, because it was a long way from there to Augusta and our team was not a fast one. So Mr. Showers cut off a piece of the meat and put it in the buggy and bade us good-bye. My friends and the driver ate some of the meat and seemed to enjoy it while I subsisted that day on sugar cane, which could be purchased at different points along the road. Mr. Showers had informed me of a place about ten miles out from Augusta, which we would pass en route, at which he was sure we could stop overnight. It was the home of Widow McComb. He said he always stopped there overnight whenever he went to Augusta, which was several times in the course of a year, and notwithstanding the fact they were white people, he was at all times nicely treated. "I am sure," he said, "Widow McComb will accommodate you and your party."

This was encouraging, for I knew we would be obliged to stop at some point overnight en route to Augusta. I was anxious to reach Augusta at an early hour in the day so as to give me time in which to work up a meeting, and thus avoid a repetition of what occurred at Ellisville where no meeting was held at all. We reached the home of Widow McComb about an hour before dark. The house was a nice-looking white-painted building, two stories high. It was a finer-looking building than that section seemed to justify. It was about one hundred yards from the main road, the yard being enclosed with a well-built fence which seemed to have been newly whitewashed. The place and its surroundings indicated wealth, prosperity, and enterprise. As soon as I saw the place, I was somewhat apprehensive that so far as our purposes were concerned, it was an unfavorable indication. A lady and gentleman were sitting on the porch when we drove up to the front gate. When we halted, I inquired if this was the home of Widow McComb. The gentleman answered in the affirmative. I then stated we were en route to Augusta and asked if we could be accommodated there that night.

"Certainly," the gentleman replied.

My traveling companion, who was a shade darker than I, alighted from the buggy first. I then noticed that the gentleman and lady put their heads close together and carried on a brief whispered conversation. I was satisfied that that was an unfavorable sign. The gentleman then came towards the front gate with his hands in his pockets, and when he had gotten within a few feet of us he stated that he was very sorry but that it would not be possible for them to accommodate us there that night because the cook was sick and his sister had gone to the camp meeting. I informed him that it would not be necessary for any meals to be prepared. If he would have the horses fed and cared for and give us a room to ourselves, we would remain in it until the next morning when we would pay our bill and resume our journey.

"Oh well," he replied. "I guess most anybody down here will take you on them terms."

"But," I replied, "if you will not, how can I expect anyone else to do so?"

"I cannot say as to that," he replied. "All I know is that we cannot accommodate you."

"Very well, sir, good-bye."

So we got back in the buggy and I gave directions to the driver to proceed. Just as we had started the gentleman hailed us. Of course we immediately halted.

He asked, "Have you any objections to telling me who you

are?" This question impressed my companion favorably, so he took the liberty of answering the question and informed him that this is the Honorable John R. Lynch, member of Congress from this district and candidate for reelection.

"That," he replied, "is just who I thought it was, go on."

As serious as the situation was this reply brought from us a hearty laugh. After going a few miles further, we came to the village. The postmaster, a man named McDonald, was on the lookout for us. He had received through the mails some of my notices. He hailed us, introduced himself, and said he was pleased to meet me. I replied that I would be pleased at having met him if he could tell me where I could be accommodated that night, because from present indications it looked as if we shall be obliged to camp some point on the road. I also informed him of what had just taken place at the home of Widow McComb. At this he professed to be very much surprised. He said he would accommodate us at his home but for the fact that his people had all gone to camp meeting.

"But," he said, "I will direct you to a place where I know you will be accommodated. It is the home of Mr. Joseph Runnells, who lives just about a mile from here in the direction you are going. Go there and tell him that I sent you there. I know he will take pleasure in accommodating you."

I thanked him and we bade him good-bye and drove on. When we reached Mr. Runnells's home it was, fortunately, after dark. The house was only a few yards from the main road. We distinctly heard several persons talking on the front porch. When we drove up to the front gate I called out and asked if this is the home of Mr. Joseph Runnells. The answer was in the affirmative. I then stated that we were on our way to Augusta and desired to know if we could be accommodated there overnight.

"Oh yes," was the prompt reply. "We can take care of you."

My traveling companion began to feel a little nervous. He insisted that I tell the man that we were colored people, otherwise we might get ourselves in trouble. But I replied that he must be quiet, hold his peace, and leave the matter to me. When Mr. Runnells came to the front gate and shook hands with me he asked if I had any colored people in my party.

"Yes," I said, "I have one besides the driver, but he is a nice young man who knows his place and will give no trouble."

"Very well," he replied, "I thought I would ask you because you know how it is out in this part of the country."

"Yes," I said, "I know all about it but the presence of this young man will cause no embarrassment whatever."

He then had two of his grown sons to take charge of the horses and he invited us to the house. Fortunately the weather was a little warm so I insisted that we occupy seats on the front porch, where the light was quite dim. My companion and the driver took seats at the extreme end of the porch while I took one near the front door and soon became engaged in conversation with Mr. Runnells while his wife was preparing supper. Mr. and Mrs. Runnells were blessed with a large number of children, by whom we were surrounded during the conversation. They appeared to be very much interested in what was being said. I was unusually communicative and endeavored at times to be somewhat eloquent. My main object was to get them worked up to a point where they would be both interested and absorbed. I gave detailed information about the administration of President Grant, the controversy between Blaine, Conkling, and Garfield, and many other points of general interest, for some of which I had to draw largely upon my imagination. Finally Mr. Runnells put the direct question to me.

"Who are you anyway?" I knew then that the crisis had come and that I must face it. My identity could not be concealed very much longer anyway, because the time would soon come when supper would be ready, which of itself would bring the revelation, because I would then be obliged to face the light. So in answer to his question, I stated frankly that my name was Lynch.

"Lynch!" he said, in a somewhat subdued tone of voice. "It occurs to me that I have heard of that name before, but the Lynch of whom I have heard and about whom I have read is a colored man. You are not that man, are you?"

"Yes, I guess I am the Lynch of whom you have heard and about whom you have read."

He then drew his chair close to mine and gave me a square look in the face and then said: "Well, you are not much colored anyway."

This remark gave me much relief. I knew then that our presence until the next morning would at least be tolerated. The conversation was resumed and continued until the announcement was made that supper was ready in the dining room. Mr. Runnells accompanied us to the supper table, where the conversation was continued while we were doing justice to the inner man. A splendid supper was served and Mr. Runnells saw that we were not neglected in any particular. After supper we were invited to seats in the parlor, where the conversation was continued until a late hour. Mrs. Runnells, who was deprived of the opportunity of hearing any part of the conversation on the front porch before supper, because she was in the kitchen, was then an interested listener. We were furnished with good beds and had a splendid night's rest. We were up at an early hour the next morning, feeling fresh and fine. An excellent breakfast was prepared for us, which we very much enjoyed.

When I paid the bill, which was quite reasonable, and bade Mr. Runnells and his interesting family good-bye, after thanking them for their courteous treatment, Mr. Runnells assured me that if I should ever come through that part of the country again I must not fail to come to his home, for he would be pleased to see me and to entertain me at any time. But that was my first and last trip through that section of the state. I left there with a much more favorable impression of the people of that neighborhood than I supposed I would, although it may be that Mr. Runnells would not have accommodated me and my party if my identity had been made known to him in the beginning, especially in view of the fact that he inquired so particularly as to whether or not I had any colored people in my party. But, let the facts be what they may, I certainly had no cause to complain, but many reasons to feel grateful on account of the treatment I received at the home of Mr. Runnells.

We arrived at Augusta at an early hour that day. While there, we stopped at the home of an excellent and prosperous colored family by the name of Holloman, where we remained about two days and where we were splendidly entertained. At that place I had a good meeting, which was held the day after I arrived, the same having been largely attended by both colored and white. There seemed to be more colored people in the neighborhood of Augusta than at any point I had visited while on that trip.

From Augusta we went to Leakesville, the county seat of the adjoining county of Greene. At that place I was also agreeably surprised to find that I had no difficulty in securing accommodations at the hotel, although court was in session and the hotel, on that account, was pretty well filled. We were not only accommodated, but I was given one of the two best rooms in the house, the other being occupied by the judge of the court, whose name was Woods, and whom I found to be a most dignified, courteous, and affable gentleman. I was also assigned to a seat at the table next to one occupied by the judge. The proprietor of the hotel, Mr. John McInnis, took particular pains to make my stay there pleasant and agreeable. My traveling companion and the driver were also suitably and appropriately provided for. I had a splendid meeting there also, the whites having turned out in large numbers to hear me. They paid close and respectful attention to my remarks. Very few colored people lived in that locality. When the judge of the court found out the time I desired to speak, he adjourned his court for about two hours so that the meeting could be held at the courthouse.

He also honored me with his personal presence during the delivery of my address, which occupied about an hour and a half.

This was the last place at which I was to speak on that famous trip. From there I went to a point called State Line in the northern part of the same county, where I took the train going south on the Mobile and Ohio Railroad, which carried me through Mobile to Scranton, in the county of Jackson. Thus ended the most eventful overland trip I had ever taken.

In breaking up the "shoestring" district when the legislature reorganized the congressional districts of the state, there were several districts in which Democratic success was endangered. As thus reorganized, the Second, or Holly Springs, District, was the most uncertain of them all. In that district the Greenback, or Populist, party had made considerable headway. Hon. George M. Buchanan, the most popular and influential Republican leader in that district, was the Republican candidate for Congress in 1880. He was an ex-Confederate soldier, serving at one time under General Chalmers. If any man knew Chalmers well, Buchanan was that man. Chalmers had just lost the seat in Congress from the "shoestring district," which he had held as the representative, champion, and spokesman of the most ultra and radical wing or faction of the Democratic party.

Buchanan conceived the idea that General Chalmers might be induced to run for Congress in the Second District in 1882 as the candidate for the Greenback, or Populist, party, endorsed by the Republicans. The idea at first seemed absurd, but Buchanan evidently knew his man. After the leading Greenbackers had been sounded and it was developed that they would have him nominated as the candidate of their party if he would accept the nomination, the announcement was given out that General Chalmers was to run for Congress in the Second District, as the candidate of the Greenback party endorsed by the Republican organization, against Hon. Van H. Manning, the sitting member from that district and the Democratic candidate for reelection.

The report was promptly denied by many Democrats who assumed and asserted that Chalmers was too good a Democrat to allow his name to be used for any such purpose. But those Democrats tried in vain to get Chalmers to confirm what they had said. On the contrary, they soon found out what others had known all along, that Chalmers was a man that was incapable of being true and loyal to any party or any cause. With him a party was merely a means to an end. He could not be a party man, because his allegiance to the party with which he may be acting would cease as soon as that party could or would no longer serve his purpose and gratify his ambition. With him it was not a matter of principle, for he had none. It was not a matter of convictions, for he was without convictions. His ambition was to be a member of Congress. How he got there and what he was to represent while there were with him minor and secondary matters. He was ready at any and all times to shape his course and fit his politics to suit the conditions. He was willing to speak for any cause and represent any party through which his ambition could be gratified. To change, then, from an extreme and radical Democrat to a Republican Greenbacker was not a difficult thing for Chalmers to do. When Democrats who had faithfully supported him and followed his leadership because they believed he was honest and sincere in what he had said and done expressed their abhorrence at what he was then doing, he merely smiled at their credulity. In fact, he seemed to be surprised that they had believed he was ever serious in anything he had said and done.

He was nominated by the Greenbackers in the Second District as their candidate for Congress, which he promptly accepted. Through the influence of Hon. George M. Buchanan, the nomination was endorsed by the Republican district convention. Chalmers made an active canvass of the district, and although the Democrats induced a colored man by the name of [Ham C.] Carter to run as an Independent Republican, Chalmers was successful by a small but safe majority. Of course, he was counted out and the certificate given to his opponent, Judge Manning, but Chalmers made a contest before the House, proved that he had been fairly and legally elected, and was admitted to the seat. This was a very strange and remarkable case. Here was a man appearing before Congress as a contestant, who had previously served several terms in that body through a fraudulent and violent suppression of the colored vote, but who now asked to be seated by giving effect to the votes of the very class or race of men the suppression of whose votes he had recently been the most radical and conspicuous advocate.

There were many members of the House who would have been pleased if they could have seen their way clear to vote against seating such a man, but his right to the seat had been so clearly established and the case was so plain that nothing remained to be done but to admit him to the seat to which he had been elected—which was promptly done. This was the last official position held by him, although he lived many years longer and made a number of unsuccessful efforts to secure other positions of profit, honor, and distinction.[1]

1. For an account of this election contest see Willie D. Halsell, "James R. Chalmers and 'Mahoneism' in Mississippi," *Journal of Southern History*, 10 (Feb. 1944): 37–58.

30

1884: Presidential Nominations

When the Forty-seventh Congress expired on 4 March 1883, I returned to my home at Natchez, Mississippi. Eighteen eighty-four was the year of the presidential election. Early in the year it was made clear that there was to be a bitter fight for the Republican presidential nomination.

President Arthur was a candidate to succeed himself, but Mr. Blaine, it was conceded, would be the leading candidate before the convention. Senator John Sherman was also a candidate. It was generally believed that Senator [George F.] Edmunds of Vermont would get a majority of the delegates from the New England states. Mr. Blaine was weaker in his own section—New England—than in any other part of the country except the South. The South, however, had somewhat relented in its opposition to him, as previously stated, in consequence of which he had a stronger support from that section than in any other of his previous contests for the nomination, which resulted in his nomination by that convention [in 1884]. That support, it was believed, was due more to a deference to public opinion at the North—the section that must be depended upon to elect the ticket—than love for, or confidence in, Mr. Blaine.

The delegation from my own state, Mississippi, was with one exception solid in its support of President Arthur. The one exception was Hon. H. C. Powers, one of the delegates from the first district who was suspected, but not known, to be a Blaine man when he was elected.

Two active, aggressive, able, and brilliant young men had just entered the field of national politics, both of them having been elected delegates to this convention. Those men were Theodore Roosevelt of New York and H. C. Lodge of Massachusetts. Both were intensely opposed to the nomination of Mr. Blaine. Roosevelt's election as a delegate from New York was in the nature of a national surprise. Mr. Blaine was known or, at any rate, believed to be very strong in that state. The public, therefore, was not prepared for the announcement that Theodore Roosevelt, an anti-Blaine man, had defeated Senator Warner Miller, the able and popular leader of the Blaine forces in that state, for delegate to the national convention from the state at large. The Blaine leaders were brought to a realization of the fact that, in consequence of their unexpected defeat in New York, it was absolutely necessary, to make sure of the nomination of their candidate, that they must retain the support they had among the Southern delegates.

With that end in view, the national committee, in which the Blaine men had a majority, selected a Southern man in the person of Hon. Powell Clayton of Arkansas for temporary chairman of the convention.[1] The anti-Blaine men, under the

1. Clayton, born in Pennsylvania in 1833, moved to Kansas in 1855. After rising to brigadier general in the Union army, he was mustered out and moved to Arkansas, where he bought a cotton plantation near Pine Bluff. In 1868 he was elected governor, and after a stormy four years he went to the United States Senate. See Thomas S. Staples, *Reconstruction in Arkansas, 1862–1874* (New York, 1923).

leadership of Messrs. Roosevelt, Lodge, Hoar, Hanna, George William Curtis, and others, decided to select another Southern man to run against Clayton. For that purpose a conference was held composed of many of the active supporters of Arthur, Sherman, and Edmunds, to select the man to put up against Clayton. I did not attend the conference. Senator Hoar suggested my name and insisted that I was the best-fitted man for the position. After a brief discussion, it was decided unanimously to select me as the choice of the conference for that purpose. A committee was appointed, of which ex-Governor Pinchback of Louisiana was chairman, to wait on me and inform me of what had been done and to insist upon the acceptance by me of the distinguished honor which had thus been conferred upon me. Another committee was appointed, of which Hon. M. A. Hanna of Ohio was chairman, to poll the convention to find out the strength of the movement. This committee subsequently reported that Clayton would be defeated and Lynch elected by a majority of about thirty-five votes.

I had some doubt about the propriety of allowing my name to be thus used, for two reasons. First, I doubted the wisdom of the movement. It had been the uniform custom to allow the national committee to select the temporary chairman of the convention, and I was inclined to the opinion that a departure from that custom might not be a wise step. My second reason was I did not think I could possibly win. My opinion was that a number of delegates that might otherwise vote for me could not be induced to vote in favor of breaking what had been an unbroken custom since the organization of the party.

I did not come to a definite decision until the morning of the day that the convention was to be organized. Just before that body was called to order, I decided to confer with, and act upon the advice of, Major William McKinley and Hon. M. A. Hanna of Ohio. McKinley was for Blaine and Hanna was for Sherman, but my confidence in the two men was such that I believed their advice would not be influenced by their personal preferences for the presidential nomination. I did not know at that time that Mr. Hanna had taken an active part in the deliberations of the conference that resulted in my selection for temporary chairman of the convention. I first consulted Major McKinley. I had served with him in Congress and had become very much attached to him. He frankly stated that, since he was a Blaine man, he would be obliged to vote against me, but this was an opportunity, he said, that comes to a man but once in a lifetime.

"If you decline, the anti-Blaine men will probably put up someone else who would no doubt receive the same votes that you would receive. If it is possible for them to elect anyone, I know of no man I would rather have them thus honor than you. While, therefore, I shall vote against you and hope you will not be elected, simply because I am a Blaine man, and a vote for you means a vote against Blaine, I shall not advise you to decline the use of your name."

I then approached Mr. Hanna, who appeared to be surprised that I hesitated about consenting to the use of my name.

"We have you elected," he said, "by a majority of about thirty-five. You cannot decline the use of your name, for two reasons: first, since we know we have the votes necessary to elect you, should you now decline, the public would never believe otherwise than that you had been improperly influenced. This you cannot afford. In the second place, it would not be treating us fairly. We have selected you in perfect good faith, with the expectation that you would allow your name to be thus used, or if not, you would have declined in ample time to enable us to reconvene and select someone else. To decline now, on the eve of the election, when it is impossible for us to confer and agree upon another man for the position, would be manifestly unfair and unjust to us as well as to your own candidate for the presidential nomination, whose chances may be injuriously affected thereby."

This argument was both impressive and effective. I then and there decided to allow my name to be used. I learned afterwards that it was under the direction and management of Mr. Hanna that the convention had been so carefully and accurately polled. That his poll was entirely correct was demonstrated by the result. This also established the fact that as an organizer Mr. Hanna was master, which was subsequently proved when he managed Mr. McKinley's campaign both for the nomination and election to the presidency in 1896.

When the convention was called to order and the announcement was made that the national committee had selected Hon. Powell Clayton of Arkansas for temporary chairman of the convention, an attractive young man in the Massachusetts delegation was recognized by the chair. He gave his name as H. C. Lodge. He said he rose to place the name of another gentleman in nomination, and, after making a neat and appropriate speech in commendation of his candidate, which evidently created a favorable impression, he named ex-Congressman John R. Lynch of Mississippi, whom he believed to be a more suitable man for the position. The call was then opened. This was an indication of a combination of the field against Blaine. Many speeches were made on both sides, but they were temperate in tone and free from bitterness or acrimony. Among those that spoke in support of my candidacy were Messrs. Theodore Roosevelt and George William Curtis of New York. When the debate was over, the chairman directed that the states be called in alphabetical order, the roll of delegates from each state to be called so as to allow each individual delegate to cast his own vote. When Mississippi was reached, I joined with H. C. Powers, the Blaine member of the delegation, in voting for Clayton. The result was just about what Mr. Hanna said it would be.[2]

2. For an account of the contest over the election of a temporary chairman, see the *Proceedings of the Eighth Republican National Convention Held at Chicago* (Chicago, 1884), pp. 6–10 ff. and John A. Garraty, *Henry Cabot Lodge: A Biography* (New York, 1953), p. 78.

The Blaine men were discouraged and the anti-Blaine men were jubilant. It was claimed by the latter and apprehended by the former that it was indicative of Mr. Blaine's defeat for the nomination. It certainly looked that way, but the result of the election for the temporary chairmanship proved to be misleading. Mr. Hanna's poll was not to find out how many delegates would vote for the nomination of Mr. Blaine, but how many would vote for me for temporary chairman. On that point his poll was substantially accurate. It was assumed that every Blaine man would vote for Mr. Clayton. This is where the mistake was made. It turned out that there were some Blaine men, especially from the South, that voted for me. The result, therefore, was not, as it was hoped it would be, an accurate test of the strength of the Blaine and anti-Blaine forces in the convention.

Since my election had not been anticipated, at least by me, my speech of acceptance was necessarily brief. I presided over the deliberations of the convention the greater part of two days, when Hon. John B. Henderson of Missouri was introduced as the permanent chairman. This is the same Henderson who, as a Republican United States senator from Missouri, voted against the conviction of President Andrew Johnson, who had been impeached by the House of Representatives for high crimes and misdemeanors in office. The Democratic senators needed but seven votes from the Republican side of the chamber to prevent conviction. They succeeded in getting the exact number: Senator Henderson being one of them. He appears to have been the only one of that number that politically survived that act. All the others soon passed into political oblivion, although several of them subsequently identified themselves with the Democratic party. While it may be said that Senator Henderson survived the act, it is true nevertheless that his election as a delegate to the National Republican Convention of 1884 and his selection as the permanent chairman thereof are the only prominent and conspicuous illustrations of that fact.

During the deliberations of the convention, Mr. Bishop, one of the delegates from Massachusetts, introduced a resolution to change the basis of representation in future national conventions of the party. His plan, in substance, was to make the number of Republican votes cast, counted, certified, and returned at the last preceding national election the basis of representation in succeeding national conventions, instead of the representation to which each state is entitled in the Congress of the United States at present. Hon. W. O. Bradley of Kentucky led off in a very able, eloquent, and convincing speech in opposition to the resolution.

The colored delegates from the South selected me to present their side of the question. For that purpose I was recognized by the chair and spoke against the resolution. In the first place, I called attention to the fact that if elections were fair and the official count honest in every state, the probabilities were that there would be no occasion for the proposed change. That the change proposed would result in a material reduction in the representation in future conventions chiefly from Southern states was due to the fact that the greater part of the Republican votes in some of said states were suppressed by violence or nullified by fraud. The effect, then, of the change proposed would be to make such questionable methods the basis of representation in future National Republican Conventions. This, I claimed, the Republican party could not afford to do. At the conclusion of my remarks, the resolution was withdrawn by its author, Mr. Bishop, who came over to my seat and congratulated me upon the way in which I had presented the case, stating at the same time that my speech had convinced him that his proposition was a mistake.[3]

After a hotly contested fight, Mr. Blaine was finally nomi-

3. Lynch's speech is recorded in the *Proceedings of the Eighth Republican National Convention*, pp. 86–87.

nated. Senator John A. Logan of Illinois was named as the candidate for vice-president. It therefore looked as if the time had at last come when the brilliant statesman from Maine would have the acme of his ambition completely realized.

I was honored by the delegation from my own state with being made a member of the national committee and also a member of the committee that was named to wait on Mr. Blaine and notify him officially of his nomination. The notification committee went all the way to Mr. Blaine's home, at Augusta, Maine, to discharge that duty. The ceremony took place in Mr. Blaine's front yard. The weather was fine. The notification speech was delivered by the chairman, Senator [John B.] Henderson, to which Mr. Blaine briefly responded, promising to make a more lengthy reply in the form of a letter of acceptance. At the conclusion of the ceremony, he called me to one side and asked what was the outlook in Mississippi. I informed him that he could easily carry the state by a substantial majority if we could have a fair election and an honest count, but that under the existing order of things, this would not be possible and that the state would be returned against him.

"Oh no," he replied, "you are mistaken about that; Mr. Lamar will see that I get a fair count in Mississippi."

I confess that this remark surprised me very much, in reply to which I said: "Mr. Blaine, you may understand the political situation in Mississippi better than I do, but I know whereof I speak when I say that Mr. Lamar would not if he could and could not if he would secure you a fair count in Mississippi. The state will be returned against you."

"You will find," he said, "that you are mistaken. Mr. Lamar will see that I get a fair count in Mississippi."

Mr. Lamar not only made an aggressive campaign against Mr. Blaine, but it was chiefly through his influence and efforts that the state was returned against Mr. Blaine by a very large majority. And yet no one who knew Mr. Lamar could justly accuse him of being an ingrate. He was essentially a grateful and an appreciative man, which he never failed to demonstrate whenever and wherever it was possible for him to do so. No one knew better than did Mr. Lamar that he was under deep and lasting obligations to Mr. Blaine, but it seems that with all of his wisdom and political sagacity and foresight, Mr. Blaine was unable to distinguish between a personal and a political obligation. Mr. Lamar felt that what Mr. Blaine had done for him was personal, not political, and that if his—Lamar's—party was in any respect the beneficiary thereof, it was merely incidental. At any rate, it was utterly impossible for him to serve Mr. Blaine in a political way. Had he made the effort to do so he not only would have subjected himself to the accusation of party treachery, but it would have resulted in his own political downfall. To ask or expect any ambitious man to make such a sacrifice as this was contrary to human nature.

The truth was Mr. Blaine had been chiefly instrumental in bringing about, or permitting to be brought about, a condition of affairs at the South which made it impossible for any of his Democratic or Republican friends in that section to be of any material service to him at the time he most needed them. And yet he could not see this until it was too late. In spite of this he would have been elected anyway, but for the fact that he lost the pivotal state of New York by a small plurality, about 1,147, the reasons for which have been given in a previous chapter. It is therefore sad but true that this able and brilliant man, like Henry Clay, died without having reached the acme of his ambition—the presidency of the United States.

The Republicans of my district insisted that I make the race for Congress again in 1884, which I decided to do, although I knew it would be useless for me to do so with the expectation, or hope, of being elected. I knew the prospect of success was not as favorable as two years previous. Judge Van Eaton, the Democratic candidate in 1882, was a representative of the better element and would therefore rather be defeated than be declared elected through the enforcement and application of questionable methods. He publicly declared on several occasions that, as anxious as he was to be a member of Congress, he would rather be defeated than have a certificate of election tainted with fraud. In other words, if he could not be fairly and honestly elected, he preferred to be defeated. He therefore insisted upon a fair election and an honest count.

This was not agreeable to many of his party associates. They believed and privately asserted that his position and open declarations on that point not only carried an implied reflection upon his party in connection with previous elections, but that he was taking an unnecessary risk in his own case. Chiefly for these reasons, the judge, though a strong and able man, was denied the courtesy of a nomination for a second term. It had always been the custom to allow a member to serve at least two terms; but this honor was denied Judge Van Eaton, the nomination being given to Hon. T. R. Stockdale of Pike County.

Stockdale was a different type of man. He was in perfect accord with the dominant and controlling sentiment of his party. He felt that he had been nominated to go to Congress peaceably and fairly if possible, but to go in any event. Then again that was the year of the presidential election and the Democrats were as confident of success that year as they were in 1876 and 1880.

For president and vice-president the opposing candidates were Blaine and Logan, Republicans, and Cleveland and Hendricks, Democrats.

Mr. Cleveland had the prestige of having been elected governor of New York by a majority of about one hundred thousand. New York was believed to be the pivotal and decisive state and that its votes would determine the election for president.. That the Republicans, even with such a popular man as Mr. Blaine as their candidate, would be able to overcome the immense majority by which Mr. Cleveland had carried the state for governor, was not believed by any Democrat to be possible.

The Democrats did not take into account any of the local circumstances that contributed to such a remarkable result, but they were well known to Republicans in and out of that state. One of the principal contributory causes was a determination on the part of thousands of Republican voters in that state to resent at the polls national interference with local state affairs.

Judge [Charles J.] Folger, President Arthur's secretary of the treasury, was the Republican candidate against Mr. Cleveland for the governorship when the latter was elected by such an immense majority. It was a well-known fact that Judge Folger could not and would not have been nominated but for the active and aggressive efforts of the national administration and its agents and representatives. The fight for the Republican nomination for governor that year was the beginning of the bitter fight between the Blaine and the Arthur forces in the state for the delegation in 1884. In the nomination of Judge Folger the Blaine men were defeated. To neutralize the prestige which the Arthur men had thus secured, thousands of the Blaine men, and some who were not Blaine men, but who were against the national administration for other reasons, refused to vote for Judge Folger and thus allowed the state to go Democratic by default. In 1884 when Mr. Blaine was the candidate of the Republicans for the presidency, a sufficient number of anti-Blaine men in New York, in a spirit of retaliation, no doubt, pursued the same course and thus allowed the state again to go Democratic by default. The loss which Mr. Blaine sustained in the latter case, therefore, was much greater than that gained by him in the former.

But, let the causes, circumstances, and conditions be what they may, there was not a Democrat in Mississippi in 1884 who did not believe that Mr. Cleveland's election to the presidency was a foregone conclusion. That he would have the support of the solid South there was no doubt. Those states, they believed, were as certain to be returned Democratic as the sun would rise on the morning of the day of the election.

Chapter Thirty

Although I accepted the nomination for Congress, I devoted the greater part of my time, as chairman of the Republican State Committee, to the campaign throughout the state. Mr. Blaine had many warm friends and admirers among the white men and Democrats in the state, some of them being outspoken in their advocacy of his election. In making up the electoral ticket, I made every effort to get some of those men to consent to the use of their names. One of them, Joseph N. Carpenter of my own home town, Natchez, gave his consent to the use of his name. He was one of the solid businessmen of the town. He was not only a large property owner but the principal owner of a local steamboat that was engaged in the trade on the Mississippi River between Natchez and Vicksburg. He was also the principal proprietor of one of the cottonseed mills of the town. In fact, his name was associated with nearly every important enterprise in that community. Socially no family stood higher in any part of the South. His accomplished wife was a Miss Mellon, whose brother, William F. Mellon, was one of the most brilliant members of the bar that the state had ever produced. She had another brother who acquired quite a distinction as a minister of the Gospel.

When the announcement was made public that Joseph N. Carpenter was to be an elector on the Blaine-Republican ticket, intense excitement was immediately created. The Democratic press of the state immediately turned their batteries upon him. Personal friends called upon him in large numbers and urged him to decline. But he had consented to serve and he felt that it was his duty and ought to be his privilege to do so. Besides, he was a sincere Blaine man. To these appeals, therefore, he turned a deaf ear.

But it was not long before he was obliged to yield to the pressure. The fact was soon made plain to him that if he allowed his name to remain on that ticket, the probabilities were that he would be financially ruined. He would soon find that his boat would be without either passengers or freight. His oil mill would probably be obliged to close because there would be no owners of the raw material of whom he could make purchases at any price. Even his children at school would no doubt be subjected to taunts and insults, to say nothing of the social cuts to which his family might be subjected. He was, therefore, brought to a painful realization of the fact that he was confronted with conditions which he had not fully anticipated. He could then see, as he had never seen before, that he had been brought face to face with a condition and not a theory. He was thus obliged to make his choice between accepting those conditions upon the one hand, and the empty and temporary honor of serving as an elector on the Blaine-Republican ticket on the other. His opinion, his manhood, and his self-respect were on one side; his material interests and family obligations were on the other. His mental condition during that period can better be imagined than described. After giving the matter deliberate and thoughtful consideration, if not sleepless nights, he finally decided to yield to the pressure and decline the use of his name. He informed me of his decision through the medium of a private letter which he said he had written with great reluctance and sincere regret. Of course, his declination was accepted by the committee, and the name of Dr. T. J. Jackson of Amite County, an old-line Republican, was selected to fill the vacancy.

It will thus be seen that in pursuing a course which Mr. Blaine thought would place Southern Democrats under obligations to him, he placed a weapon in the hands of his own personal and political enemies by which they were enabled to crush and silence his friends and supporters, for, after all, it is not so much the love of justice and fair play, as it is the fear of punishment, that actuates the average man in obeying the laws and respecting the rights and privileges of others. Mr. Blaine's friends and supporters in the South were the very people who stood most in need of that security and protection which can come only through a thorough and impartial enforcement of laws for the protection of citizens in the exercise and enjoyment of their civil and political rights, as well as those for the protection of life, liberty, and property.

Judge H. F. Simrall, one of the most brilliant lawyers in the state, who came into the Republican party under the leadership of General Alcorn in 1869, and who served as a justice of the supreme court of the state, made an effort to canvass the state for Mr. Blaine, but his former associates, with whom he tried to reason, treated him with such scant courtesy that he soon became discouraged and abandoned the effort.

There were two factions in the Democratic party, Mr. Lamar being the recognized head of one of them. His political enemies had suspected and accused him of being partial to Mr. Blaine. To save himself and his friends from humiliation and defeat in his own party, it was necessary for him to disprove these accusations and dispel those suspicions. With that end in view he made a thorough canvass of the state in the interest of Mr. Cleveland and the Democratic party. The state was returned for Mr. Cleveland by a large majority, for which Mr. Lamar was in a great measure credited. Mr. Blaine finally saw his mistake, which he virtually admitted in the speech delivered by him at his home immediately after the election, but it was then too late to undo the mischief that had been done. It was like locking the stable door after the horse had been stolen. That Mr. Blaine died without having attained the goal of his ambition, was due chiefly to his lack of foresight, poor judgment, political blunders and mistakes, and a lack of that sagacity and acumen which are so essential in a successful party leader.

31

1885: The Failure of J. R. Chalmers

EIGHTEEN EIGHTY-FIVE WAS THE YEAR IN WHICH THE GENERAL election in the state of Mississippi was held for the election of governor and other state officers, district and county officials. The state was hopelessly Democratic. In view of unfavorable political conditions, many Republicans doubted the wisdom of putting a ticket in the field in opposition to the Democratic machine, but after consultation, and since the organization called Greenbackers had made some headway, it was decided to put a ticket in the field if fusion between Republicans and Greenbackers could be agreed upon, which was found to be possible.

General James R. Chalmers, who had publicly identified himself with the Republican party, was willing to accept the Republican nomination for governor, if his nomination would be endorsed by the Greenback party. If a man more acceptable than Chalmers would have been found willing to serve, the name of Chalmers would not have been considered. But since such a man could not be found, we were obliged to accept Chalmers or allow the election to go by default.

The state committee was convened. Prominent members of the party from different sections of the state who were not members of the committee were invited to be present for consultation and advice. After going over the situation fully, carefully, and thoroughly, it was unanimously decided to give Chalmers an opportunity to show what he could do. A state convention was called, with the understanding that Chalmers would be nominated for governor. His name was not only to be placed at the head of the ticket, but he was to be virtually allowed to name his associates on the ticket. In other words, he was to be given a clear field and allowed to have everything his own way so that if he failed, no one but himself would be blamed; and if he won, no one but himself could share with him in the glory, honor, and distinction that would come to him in consequence thereof.

I was urged and consented to remain chairman of the state committee, but my consent was based upon the condition that the active management of the campaign should be placed in charge of a campaign committee to be composed of a small number of persons selected from the membership of the general committee of the party. This was done; hence, there was no evidence of friction or dissatisfaction in any quarter. After the nomination for governor had been made, a committee was appointed to wait upon the nominee and inform him of his nomination and request him to appear before the convention and make a speech of acceptance. The committee soon returned, with the distinguished nominee, who was introduced to the convention. His speech was not well received, on account of its radical and intemperate tone. It was plain to those who heard him that the motive by which he was actuated was one of retaliation and revenge rather than redemption and reform. He was willing to run as the Republican candidate for governor, not because he had been converted to the principles and doctrine of the party, but merely because it gave him an opportunity to utilize that organization as a medium through which he hoped to be able to punish others for refusing to follow wherever he saw fit to lead.

In his intemperate speech of acceptance he was bold, outspoken, and defiant. He notified his former party associates that his acceptance of this nomination was not merely a matter of form. He boldly declared that it was a well-known fact that the Republicans were largely in the majority in the state and that it was his purpose and determination to see that the minority no longer suppressed the will and stifled the voice of the majority. In private conversation he was still more emphatic. He stated that the trouble with the Republican party in the state heretofore had been that it did not have a bold, fearless, and aggressive leader. It now had one in the person of himself. He declared that he not only had the courage of his convictions, but that he had the physical courage to carry the banner of the party into all parts of the state and command a respectful hearing, decent treatment, and a fair and honest election.

As evidence of his determination in this respect, he prepared a long list of places at which he intended to speak, Columbus being the first place named on his list. No Republican meeting had been held and no Republican speech had been delivered in that town since 1875. It was a place where free speech was unknown and where it was believed to be unsafe for anyone, a white man especially, to openly oppose the Democratic machine, locally at least. That was the very place for which Chalmers was looking. He therefore selected Columbus as the place for the opening of his aggressive campaign.

In the meantime, the Democratic press of the state had accepted the challenge he had thrown out in his speech of acceptance. He was made to understand that Democratic leaders and speakers would be ready and prepared to meet him on every point. The papers published at Columbus were especially bitter in their editorial denunciations of him. They declared that the Democracy of that section would tolerate the presence and give respectful and courteous treatment to any man white or colored who was a Republican from principle and conviction, but that Chalmers was not such a man. On the contrary, he was denounced as a traitor to his party, his state, his race, and his country. He was declared to be another Benedict Arnold. For such a man they had nothing but the utmost contempt. For him they could not possibly have any respect.

These assertions, declarations, and threatening intimations Chalmers at first ridiculed, but he was soon brought to a realization of the fact that the situation was serious. What was believed to be authentic and reliable information was brought to him through channels of his own selection, that if he went to Columbus to deliver a Republican speech, he might not be allowed to come away alive. This was a mild way of stating the case. He came to the reluctant conclusion that it was not an idle bluff made by irresponsible parties, but a fixed and settled determination made by those who could and would see that their plans and purposes were carried out. After giving the matter careful consideration, Chalmers decided that he would not attempt to speak at Columbus. As old as he was, he was not then ready to die. The appointment at Columbus was allowed to go by default, which resulted in the bottom dropping out of his whole campaign. He became very much discouraged. His friends throughout the state lost heart and became despondent. The field was soon completely abandoned. Meetings were called off, appointments cancelled, and the election, like the campaign, was allowed to go by default.

Thus ended the brilliant and aggressive campaign which Chalmers declared he intended to make. It was a complete and humiliating failure. He not only did not have the courage of his convictions, if he had any, but he did not have the physical courage to face danger to his person. To his personal friends and admirers, who had built such high hopes upon what they believed would be accomplished through and by him, he was a great disappointment. Democrats claimed, of course, that he was never in danger of personal violence—that the threats were made by irresponsible parties and that if he had gone to Columbus he could have and would have been allowed to speak in perfect safety. Since he did not go, there was no way to disprove those assertions.

After his humiliating defeat for governor, Chalmers retired to private life where he remained until the meeting of the National Republican Convention in Chicago in 1888, when he made another effort to bring himself into public notice. He attended that convention as a spectator, where he made public announcement of the fact that he had decided to fully identify himself with the Republican party nationally and that he wanted an opportunity to publicly proclaim that fact from the platform of the convention. While he was known to be very much conceited, it was hoped that his defeat for the governorship of his state had knocked some of it out of him. But it had not. He was so full of egotism and placed such a high estimate upon his own importance that he thought the mere announcement of the fact that General J. R. Chalmers had decided to cast his lot with the national Republican party would be received with such great satisfaction and delight that the convention would suspend its regular business at any stage of its proceedings to hear him speak. He must have been greatly and keenly disappointed when the convention adjourned without giving him that opportunity.

Notwithstanding this, he decided to support the Republican ticket that year and tendered the national committee his services as a campaign speaker, but the tender was not accepted.

Chapter Thirty-one

When the election was over, resulting in the success of General Harrison for president, Chalmers made an application to be appointed a federal judge, but the application was not favorably considered. He then came to the conclusion that he was not and could not be a Harrison Republican. He was against Harrison because he was not a good Republican. As between a Harrison Republican and a Cleveland Democrat, he was a Cleveland Democrat. He was bitterly opposed to the renomination of Harrison in 1892, and it is believed that he voted for Cleveland at that election, if he voted at all, although the Democrats were not concerned about, nor were they solicitous for, his vote.

After the election of Mr. Cleveland in 1892, nothing more was heard of Chalmers until the meeting of the National Republican Convention at St. Louis in 1896. He was noticed several times among the immense crowds on that occasion, but no one seemed to have time to pay very much attention to him. There was a contest for seats in the convention from the district in which he lived, and it was said that he came there with the expectation of appearing before the committee as an attorney for one of the parties to the contest. If so, the plan was evidently changed after he came there, for he was never called upon to appear in the case.

Shortly thereafter he moved to Memphis, Tennessee, where he opened a small law office in an obscure locality, where, for a few years, he eked out a miserable existence, and shortly thereafter passed away, practically without friends, without means, without a party, without a hope, and virtually without a country. His whole life had been a complete and miserable failure. His only distinction as an officer in the Confederate army was the part he took in the massacre at Fort Pillow. His only achievement was in being the author of methods that were vicious and practices that were criminal, thus becoming the medium through whom odium, shame, and disgrace were brought upon the name of his party and state. He was so constituted that he was incapable of being loyal to a party or true to a friend. Such a man is not only undesirable but dangerous to any community in which he may live, because being fairly well educated and being endowed by nature with a certain amount of oratorical power and ability, he can always be a menace to the peace and good order of the community by working upon the ignorant and arousing the passions and prejudices of the lower, degraded, and vicious elements of society. Such was the unfortunate life of James R. Chalmers.

32

Marriage and Divorce

On 18 December 1884, I was united in marriage at Washington, D.C., by the Reverend F. J. Grimke, to Ella Wickham, daughter of James A. and M. E. Somerville of Mobile, Alabama. James A. Somerville was a member of one of the oldest and most aristocratic families at the South. Members of that family were prominently identified with nearly every important enterprise in that section of the country. James A. Somerville was, before the War of the Rebellion, in opulent circumstances, but as a result of that war he was reduced almost to poverty. His sympathies being with the South in that struggle, whether from conviction or policy, is a question which need not be considered. At any rate, he was induced to invest nearly all of his means in Confederate bonds. This was not only believed at the time to be a safe investment, but it was an unmistakable evidence of his loyalty to the Southern cause. The final result was to him a financial disaster. He was by that time an old man.

Martha Ella, the honored mother of Ella Wickham, was his second wife. He was the father of several grown children by his first marriage. Although he had been financially crushed and that too at a time when he was beginning to feel the infirmities of age, yet he was not crushed in either spirit or energy. On the contrary, as long as his health and strength enabled him to do so, he made every possible effort to regain, in part at least, what he had lost as a result of the war. He took an active part in the reconstruction of his state. In the controversy between the Republican party and President Andrew Johnson, he took sides with the Republicans and in consequence of his activity, succeeded in making himself quite prominent and influential as a leader in the Republican party in his state. He actively supported General Grant in the presidential campaigns of 1868 and 1872. He was appointed to an important office in the state by President Grant, the duties of which he discharged with credit to himself and satisfaction to the administration. But it was not possible for him to regain even a tenth part of the fortune he had lost.

By his second marriage he was the father of a large family of girls, who had to be supported and educated. Fortunately for him, his accomplished wife was a fine dressmaker. To properly raise and educate her daughters she did not hesitate to put her shoulder to the wheel and thus render valuable assistance to her husband, whose devotion and loyalty to his family had been severely tested on many occasions. Husband and wife, father and mother thus put their heads together and determined to bid defiance to reverses and misfortunes of any and all kinds. As a result thereof, the girls not only received a good common and high school education, but some of them succeeded in accumulating valuable property besides.

Ella Wickham, who seems to have been the favorite and pet

of the family, was sent to Salem, Mass., where she graduated from one of the finest educational institutions of that city. Before she left Massachusetts she accepted an offer to become a teacher in one of the colored schools in Washington, D.C. It was there I first met her, in the winter of 1875, and became very much attached to her. Her mother was one of the finest and most accomplished women that ever lived. In her younger days the beauty, the charm, the sweetness, the grace, the culture, modesty, and refinement for which many Southern women are noted, were magnificently and splendidly typified in her. In height she was about 5 feet seven inches, and she weighed about 175 pounds. In physical appearance, therefore, she was as handsome and attractive as her face was beautiful and captivating. She was what was known as a Southern Creole.

There are white and colored Creoles. The white Creoles are a mixture of English, French, and Spanish and, in some cases, Indian. The colored Creoles are of the same mixture with a little African blood added. The complexion very seldom reveals the existence of the African blood. In fact, many of those who are supposed to have none are darker than some who have. Mrs. Somerville was of Spanish origin on the paternal side and French on the maternal side, her grandmother being a native of the island of Martinique. The few drops of English and African blood in her veins came through a union on the paternal side with native Americans upon the soil of Alabama where she was born. While she was believed to be identified with those who were known as colored Creoles, she and others like her were not classed with the native colored population. Under the provisions of the Spanish-American treaty by which Florida was ceded to the United States, she and all others of that class enjoyed certain rights and privileges that were denied to the most favored class of colored Americans.[1]

1. There is no specific mention of the treatment of colored Creoles in the Treaty of 1819 between Spain and the United States. The treaty did

She had just enough African blood in her veins to give her a beautiful and creamy complexion. In fact her physical composition was perfect and absolutely faultless. Her nose was an exact type of the Grecian, while her large hazel eyes were attractive and penetrating. She had beautiful straight black hair, which was a marked indication of the Indian blood that coursed through her veins, while her pure and perfect teeth seemed as if her mouth had been set with precious pearls. Her language was at all times chaste, which was unmistakable evidence of the fact that her girlhood surroundings had been the very best. She was an interesting and entertaining conversationalist, thus showing that she had not only been endowed by nature with good conversational power, but that she was well posted and fully informed upon current events, especially those that would be likely to attract public notice.

She was carefully raised and, while her education had not been seriously neglected, she did not have the advantages of a collegiate course. In style, manner, carriage, and deportment she was both captivating and winning. She dressed with becoming modesty and always in good taste. She was a woman that would grace the parlor and illuminate the home of the very best man that nature could produce, regardless of his race, color, nationality, or religion. The man, therefore, that could win the heart and hand of this beautiful and remarkable young woman was extremely fortunate. And yet, she was only one of a large number of the same class and type. She was one of those at whose feet the proudest and finest aristocrats of antebellum days would kneel in recognition of their accomplishments, beauty, charms, personal appearance, and attractive bearing.

---

provide, however, that the inhabitants of the ceded territories were to be "admitted to the enjoyment of all the privileges, rights, and immunities of the citizens of the United States." *Treaties and Conventions Concluded between the United States of America and Other Powers Since July 4, 1776* (Washington, 1889), pp. 1016–22.

Although James A. Somerville was a man of high standing, socially and otherwise, yet it was admitted that he was a very fortunate man in having won the heart and hand of this attractive young Creole in the person of Martha Ella. It proved to be a happy union. Their children by this marriage were all girls and all intelligent and accomplished, only three of whom at this writing, however, are still living, one of them being the mother of my daughter, the youngest of the three.

The one that is next to the oldest, and in my opinion the flower of the family, is still living the secluded life of a charming old maid, which she will no doubt continue to do the remainder of her days, notwithstanding the fact that her mother, to whom she was so intensely devoted, has passed away. She could have been and no doubt would have been married in her younger days but for her devotion to, and affection for, her mother. Knowing and realizing the helpless condition of her father, financially and otherwise, and the physical infirmities of her mother as an incident of advancing years, she felt and knew that she was her mother's principal support and that it was her duty as well as her pleasure to faithfully discharge that obligation. In her unselfish devotion to her mother, to whom she felt that she was deeply obligated, to say nothing of the natural attachment that is reasonable to presume would exist between mother and daughter, she was more than willing to sacrifice her own future, as bright and as promising as it was, upon the altar of her mother's pleasure and happiness. No man, regardless of his station in life, could have influence enough over her to induce her to change her mind on that point. This is a most commendable, unselfish, and self-sacrificing position, especially for one so handsome, so graceful, and so attractive, and who had so many flattering opportunities to change her name and improve her condition in life. But between duty to her mother on one side and self-interest on the other, she unselfishly chose the former.

Chapter Thirty-two

For many years prior to his death, James A. Somerville had reached that stage of life where he was entirely dependent upon his wife and daughters for support. He was, for many years before he died, physically incapacitated to earn a dollar, and he had not been able since the cessation of hostilities to accumulate anything from which he could derive an income in his old age. He finally passed away at Washington, D.C., in 1894 in the eighty-seventh year of his age. His wife lived until 1907, when she had but three children and two grandchildren to mourn her loss, one of the two grandchildren being my daughter, the other being the same of her oldest daughter.

My marriage to the mother of my daughter proved to be unfortunate, and it was finally dissolved by judicial decree in August 1900 to which, contrary to my religious convictions upon that subject, I was obliged to give my reluctant consent. This was the saddest blow of my eventful life. I was brought up in the faith of the Protestant Episcopal church and was therefore a believer in the indissolubility of the marriage tie. Divorce I believed and still believe to be one of the curses of society, and I have always looked upon it with abhorrence. And yet, I found myself confronted with a situation for the existence of which I was not responsible and which I was unable to avoid and powerless to prevent.

I have always been of a domestic nature. From early manhood, therefore, I looked with anticipatory pleasure, satisfaction, and delight for a full and complete realization of my cherished and commendable ambition along those lines. But the years of my young manhood were so much absorbed in other matters that I did not seek the realization of that ambition until somewhat late in life—after I had passed the age of thirty-five. When, however, I was united in marriage to the woman that became the honored mother of my daughter, my only offspring, my heart was filled with inexpressible joy and intense delight. I looked forward to a bright, beautiful, and delightful married life, but this I am sorry to say was a dream, the practical realization of which covered a period of only about ten years.

Then suddenly there came a complete and radical change. What had been a charming and cheerful home had been transformed into one of darkness, sadness, and gloom. Why was this? What was the cause? The public cannot possibly have very much interest in any answer that might be given to those questions. They must therefore remain to be buried with those who were a party to them. Nothing, however, transpired which could be construed into a serious reflection upon the character of anyone connected with the affair. The mother of my daughter was a bright, intelligent, and in many respects a most charming and delightful woman. When, therefore, I look back upon the wrecked scenes of a home that was once filled with cheer, the continuance of which I had no reason to suspect would be arrested, my heart for the first few years thereafter was filled with a degree of sadness, grief and sorrow which I am incapable of describing. And then with reference to my daughter, who was the pride of my home, but who is now, through a cruel fate, a stranger to the paternal source of her existence. Her lot is cast upon the side of her mother, in consequence of which she had been made a subject to that process of absorption, which is true of so many others, to prevent and avoid which the filial tie is not sufficiently strong.

Being strongly opposed, as a result of a deep-seated religious conviction, to the dissolution of the marriage tie through any other process than that of physical death, I had about come to the conclusion that I should never again seek the heart and hand of another one of the opposite sex. For a period of nine years I was never brought in contact with one whom the sentimental side of my nature, which had remained dormant all those years, was aroused, until I accidentally or providentially met for the first time in August 1909 the elegant and accomplished woman who two years later honored me by becoming the companion of my life. In her I was sure that I saw the possibilities of a bright and delightful future in store for me which would completely eradicate, entirely remove, and effectually destroy the gloom and darkness resulting from my previous domestic misfortunes. I am therefore delighted to find that in the sunset of a life which I hope has thus far been well spent, I am surrounded with that domestic happiness and tranquility which should be the laudable ambition of every man.

The Cleveland Years: Interracial Marriages

In selecting his first cabinet Mr. Cleveland did Mr. Lamar and the state of Mississippi the honor of making him secretary of the interior. Upon the occasion of my first visit to Washington after the inauguration of Mr. Cleveland, which was early in the administration, I called on Secretary Lamar to tender him my congratulations upon his appointment. When I entered his office, he was engaged in conversation with some prominent New York Democrats, Mayor [William R.] Grace of New York City being one of the party. The secretary received me cordially, and, after introducing me to the gentlemen with whom he was conversing, requested me to take a seat in the adjoining room, which was used as his private office, until the departure of the gentlemen with whom he was then engaged, remarking at the time that there was an important matter about which he desired to talk with me.

I had been seated only a short while before he made his appearance. Taking a seat by my side and placing his right hand upon my knee in a friendly and familiar way, he said: "Lynch, you have shown me some favors in the past, and I desire to manifest in a substantial way my appreciation of what you have done for me and the friendly interest you have taken in me. No one knows better than I do, or can appreciate more keenly than I can, the value of the services you have rendered me and the satisfactory results of your friendly interest in me. In saying this I do not wish to even intimate that you have done anything for me that was inconsistent with the position occupied by you as an influential leader of the Republican party of your state. The truth is you were fortunately placed in such a position that you were enabled to render a great service to a Mississippi Democrat without doing a single act, or giving expression to a single thought, that was not in harmony with your position as a leader of your own party. That you saw fit to make me, rather than some other Democrat, the beneficiary of your partiality, is what I keenly appreciate, highly value, and now desire to reciprocate.

"The Republican party is now out of power and it is likely to remain so for the next quarter of a century at least. Fortunately for me and for you, I am now so situated that I can reciprocate, in a small measure, the friendly interest you have taken in me in the recent past, and this I hope you will allow me to do. I have an office at my disposal that I want you to accept. I know you are a pronounced Republican. I neither ask nor expect you to change your politics. Knowing you as I do, it would be useless for me to make such a request of you even if I desired to have you make such a change. All I shall ask of you is that you be not offensively active or boldly aggressive in political matters while you hold a commission from me. In other words I want to render you a service without having you compromise your political standing and without making the slightest change in your party affiliations, but recognizing as you must and do, the delicacy of the situation resulting from the position I occupy and the relation that I sustain to the administration, you will, I know, refrain from saying and doing anything that will place me in an embarrassing position before the public and the administration with which I am identified. The office to which I refer is that of special agent of the public lands. The salary is 1,500 a year and expenses. The place is worth from 2,000 to 2,500 a year. I shall not send you down South, where you may have some unpleasant and embarrassing experiences, but I will send you out into the Black Hills of the West where you will not be subjected to the slightest inconvenience and where you will have very little to do but make your reports and draw your pay. If you say you will accept the appointment I shall give immediate directions for the commission to be made out and you can take the oath of office within the next twenty-four hours."

Of course I listened with close attention and with deep interest to what the honorable secretary said. When he had finished I replied in about these words: "Mr. Secretary, I fully appreciate the friendly interest you manifest in me and what you are willing and anxious to do for me. If I have rendered you any services in the past, I can assure you that they were not rendered with the expectation that you would thereby be placed under any obligations to me whatever. If I preferred you to others in your own party it was because I believed that in you the state would have the services of one of its best, most brilliant, and eloquent representatives. It was the good of the state and the best interests of its people rather than the personal advancement of an individual that actuated me. The exalted position now occupied by you I consider a confirmation of the wisdom of my decision.

"But the fact cannot be overlooked that while you are an able and influential leader in the Democratic party, I am, though not so able nor so influential, a leader in the Republican party, at least locally, if not nationally. While I can neither hope nor expect to reach that point of honor and distinction in the Republican party that you have reached in the Democratic, I am just as proud of the position I occupy today as a Republican, as it is possible for you to be of yours as a Democrat. Even if it be true, as you predict, but in which I do not agree with you, that the Republican party will be out of power for the next quarter of a century, or even if it should never again come into power, that fact cannot and will not have the slightest weight with me. As a member of a national Democratic administration, therefore, I do not feel that you can afford to tender me a position that I can see my way clear to accept. While I fully and keenly appreciate your friendly interest in me and your desire and willingness to serve me, I cannot accept the position you have so gracefully tendered me, nor can I accept any other you may see fit to offer me.

"But if you want to render me a service, I can tell you wherein it can be done and the same will be just as much appreciated as any you can possibly render me. When I was a member of Congress, I secured the appointment of quite a number of young colored men to clerkships in the Pension Bureau of your department. I understand that all of them have excellent records. If you will retain them in their positions I shall feel that you have repaid me for whatever you may think I have done for you in the past."

"That," the secretary replied, "is a very reasonable request. Come to see me again in a day or two and bring a list of their names and I will then see just what I can do along those lines."

I then bade him good-bye and left his office. A few days later I returned with the list. But upon that list I had placed the names of two men who had not been appointed on my recommendation. One was a colored man and a physician; the other was a white man and a lawyer. The physician occupied a position that was in the line of his profession. The lawyer was a clerk in the Pension Bureau. He had been recently appointed upon the recommendation of Senator Bruce. The physician had been connected with the public service a long time.

I knew both men favorably and well and felt that it was my duty to save them if in my power. Both were married and had nice and interesting families. When I placed the list in the secretary's hands he read it over very carefully and then said:

"I think I can safely assure you that the name of everyone on this list will be retained except two." The two referred to were the colored physician and the white lawyer. "This physician," the secretary said, "is a colored man and the husband of a white wife. The lawyer is a white man and the husband of a colored wife. I cannot promise you, therefore, that they will be retained, however capable and efficient they may be. So far as I am personally concerned it would make no material difference. I should just as leave retain them as any of the others. But I cannot afford to antagonize public opinion in my state on the question of amalgamation. One of these men, the white lawyer, is from my own state, where he is well known. His case is fresh in the public mind. So far, therefore, as he is concerned, I can see no power of escape. With the colored physician it may be different. He is not from my state and is not known in the state. I doubt very much if anyone in the state knew anything about him or is aware of the fact that the position occupied by him is in my department. If attention is not called to his case, I shall let him alone.

"But with the lawyer it is different. A representative of a Mississippi newspaper that is unfriendly to me is now on the ground. He has a list of all the Republicans, especially the colored ones, holding positions in this department. The name of this lawyer is on that list. It is the intention of the faction his paper represents to bring pressure to bear upon me to force me to turn all these men out of office for political reasons regardless of their official standing. But, so far as your friends are concerned, I shall defy them except in the case of this lawyer and also in the case of this physician if attention is called to him. In their cases, or either of them, I shall be obliged, for reasons already given, to yield."

Chapter Thirty-three

Strange to say, attention was never called to the case of the physician and he remained in office during the whole of Mr. Cleveland's first administration. I made a strong appeal to the secretary in behalf of my friend, the white lawyer. I said in substance: "Mr. Secretary, you ought not to allow this worthy, deserving, and meritorious man to be punished simply because he was brave enough to legally and lawfully marry according to the forms of law the woman of his choice. You know him personally. You know him to be an able and brilliant young man. You know that he is now discharging the responsible duties of the position which he occupies in your department with credit to himself and satisfaction to his official superiors. You know that you have not a better or a more capable official connected with the public service than you have in this able, efficient, and brainy young man. Under these circumstances, it is your duty, as the responsible head of your department, to protect and save him and his estimable family from this gross wrong and cruel injustice. For no one knows better than you do, Mr. Secretary, that this alleged opposition to amalgamation is both hypocritical and insincere. If a natural antipathy existed between the two races no law would be necessary to keep them apart. The law, then, against race intermarriage has a tendency to encourage and promote, rather than discourage and prevent, race intermixture, because under existing circumstances local sentiment in our part of the country tolerates the intermixture provided the white husband and father does not lead to the altar in honorable wedlock the woman he may have selected as the companion of his life and the mother of his children. If instead of prohibiting race intermarriage the law would compel marriage in all cases of concubinage, such a law would have a tendency to discourage and prevent, rather than encourage and promote, race intermixture, because it is only when they marry according to the forms of law that the white husband and father is socially and otherwise ostracized. Under the common law, which is the established and recognized rule of action in all of our states in the absence of a local statute by which a different rule is established, a valid marriage is nothing more than a civil contract entered into between two personal persons capable of making contracts. But under our form of government, marriage, like everything else, is what public opinion sees fit to make it.

"It is true that in our part of the country no union of the sexes is looked upon as a legal marriage unless the parties to the union are married according to the form prescribed by the local statutes. While that is true it is also true that there are many unions, which, but for the local statutes, would be recognized and accepted as legal marriages and which, even under existing conditions, are tolerated by local sentiment and sanctioned by usage and custom. Such unions are known and yet not known. None are so blind as those who can see but will not see. One of the unwritten but most effective and rigid laws of our section, which every one respects and never violates, is that a man's private and domestic life must never be made the subject of political or public discussion or newspaper notoriety. The man who at any time or under any circumstances will so far forget himself as to say or do anything that can be construed into a violation of that unwritten but sacred law will be likely to pay the penalty with his own life and that too without court, judge, or jury and the one by whom the penalty may be inflicted will stand acquitted and justified before the bar of public opinion. If, then, this able and brilliant young man whose bread and meat you now have at your disposal had lived in concubinage with the mother of his children, no law against custom and tradition would have been violated and no one would suggest that he be punished for what he had done. Knowing these facts as you do, you ought to rise to the dignity of the occasion and protect this good and innocent man from the cruel, unjust, and unreasonable demands that are now being made upon you to dispense with his valuable services. The gentleman, to my personal knowledge, is not only worthy of whatever you may do for him, but his elegant and accomplished wife is one of the finest and most cultivated ladies it has been my good fortune to know.

"She is not only remarkably intelligent, but she is a woman of fine natural ability and of superior attainment. She is such a brilliant conversationalist, so interesting, instructive, and entertaining that it is a pleasure and satisfaction to have the opportunity and privilege of being in her delightful presence and sitting under the sound of her sweet, charming, and musical voice. In physical development she is as near perfection as it is possible for a woman to be. I have had the good fortune of knowing her intimately, favorably, and well for a number of years. I have always admired her for her excellent traits and admirable qualities. She is a woman that would ornament and grace the parlor and honor the home of the finest and best man that ever lived, regardless of his race or nationality or the station he may occupy in life, however exalted, important, or dignified it may be. She married the man of her choice, which marriage was then authorized and allowable even under the local statutes of Mississippi, because in her opinion he possessed everything but wealth that was calculated to contribute to her comfort, pleasure, and happiness.[1]

"In a recent conversation I had with her, her beautiful, large dark eyes sparkled with delight and her sweet and lovely face was flushed with a smile of satisfaction when she informed me that she had never had occasion to regret the selection in the person of her devoted husband. She was then the mother of several very handsome and attractive children, to whom she pointed with pardonable pride and delight. The products of such a union could not possibly be otherwise than handsome

1. The 1870 legislature repealed all laws involving racial discrimination. During the following six years there were several recorded cases of racial intermarriage in Mississippi. In 1876, with the restoration of Democratic control in the states, the legal prohibition of racial intermarriage was restored.

and attractive, for the father was a remarkably fine looking man, while the mother was a personification and exemplification of the typical Southern beauty. The husband and father was intensely devoted to his family. How could he be otherwise? Husband and wife were so strongly attached to each other that both were more than willing to make any sacrifice that cruel fate might have in store for them.

"I therefore appeal to you, Mr. Secretary, in behalf of this charming and accomplished woman and her sweet and lovely children. If you cannot respect the husband and father, spare him, for the present at least, for the sake of his wife and children. In taking this position I am satisfied you will have nothing to lose, for you will not only have right and justice on your side, but the interest of the public service as well. Rise, then, to the dignity of the occasion and assert and maintain your manhood and your independence. You have done this on previous occasions, why not do it again? As a member of the Senate of the United States you openly and publicly defied the well-known public sentiment of your party in the state which you then had the honor in part to represent, when you disregarded and repudiated the mandate of the state legislature instructing you to vote for the free and unlimited coinage of silver. It was that vote and the spirit of manly independence shown by you on that occasion that placed you in the high, exalted, and responsible position you now occupy, the duties of which your friends know will be discharged in a way that will reflect credit upon yourself and honor upon your state, and also in a way that will be beneficial to your country and to the administration with which you are identified.

"You again antagonized the dominant sentiment of the Democratic party of your state when you pronounced an eloquent eulogy upon the life and character of Charles Sumner. And yet you were able to overcome the bitter opposition you had encountered on each of those occasions. You can do the same thing in this case. I therefore ask you to promise me that this competent, worthy, deserving, and meritorious public servant shall not be discharged as long as his official record remains good."

The secretary listened to my remarks with close and respectful attention. When I had finished he said: "I agree with nearly all you have said. My sympathies are with your friend and it is my desire to retain him in the position he now fills with entire satisfaction. But when you ask me to disregard and openly defy the well-known sentiment of the white people of my state on the question of amalgamation, I fear you make a request of me which I cannot safely grant, however anxious I may be to serve you. I could defend myself before a public audience in my state on the silver question and the Sumner eulogy much more successfully than on the question of amalgamation, although I recognize the force and admit the truth of what you have said, in the main, upon that subject. Hypocritical and insincere as the claims may be with reference to maintaining the absolute separation of the two races, the sentiment on the subject is one which no man who is ambitious to have a political future can safely afford to ignore and disregard, especially under the changed conditions and the new order of things about which you are well posted and fully informed. While I am sorry for your friend and should be pleased to grant your request in his case, I cannot bring myself to a realization of the fact that it is one of sufficient national importance and significance to justify me in taking the stand you have so forcibly and eloquently suggested and recommended." This ended the interview.[2]

2. There is no account of this interview in the standard biography of Lamar: Wirt Armstead Cate, *Lucius Q. C. Lamar* (Chapel Hill, 1935). Cate, at one point, comments somewhat gratuitously, "Generally speaking, little or no dependence can be placed on the writings of the Mississippi Negro ex-Congressman, John R. Lynch. . . . [He] perverted the facts . . . in all cases that suited his purpose and in some where falsifying apparently brought him no advantage," p. 434. It should be added that Lynch's regard for Lamar was apparently greater than the bare facts of their relationship justified.

I went to the home of my friend that evening and informed him and his amiable wife of what in substance had been said and done. They thanked me warmly for my efforts in their behalf. They knew that I had said and done all in my power for them, for which they were truly grateful. They declared that there was a future before them and that in the battle of life they were determined to know no such word as *fail.* A few weeks later, my friend's official connection with the public service was suddenly terminated. He and his family then left Washington, destined for some place out West, I think Kansas. About a year thereafter he had occasion to visit Washington on business. I happened to be there at that time. He called to see me and informed me that, instead of regretting, he had every reason to be thankful for what had taken place in his case, for he had done very much better than he could have done had he remained in Washington. I was, of course, very much gratified to hear this and warmly congratulated him. Since that time, however, I have not seen him nor any member of his family, nor have I heard anything from or about them except by indirection, although I have made a number of unsuccessful efforts to find or locate them or some one of them.

I am inclined to the opinion that, like thousands of people of the same class, their identity with the colored race has long since ceased and that they, as the writer firmly believes to be destined for the great mass of colored Americans, have been merged into and absorbed by the white race. It is to prevent any embarrassment growing out of the probability of this condition that has actuated me in not making public the names of the parties in question. No good can come, but much harm might follow if their names were given and their race identity disclosed. The writer can and does most positively assure the public, however, that this is not a fiction—that it is not a mere picture that is painted from the vividness of his imagination—

but that the story as related in all of its details is based upon truthful, actual, and positive occurrences.

With this one exception, Secretary Lamar retained in office every clerk whose name appeared on the list that I gave him. They were not only retained throughout the administration, but many of them were promoted. It can be said to the credit of Secretary Lamar that during his administration, very few changes were made in the clerical force of the department for political reasons, and, as a rule, the clerks were treated with justice, fairness, and impartiality.

34

The Harrison Years

UPON THE INAUGURATION OF A NATIONAL DEMOCRATIC ADministration, I devoted my time principally to my private business, until the opening of the presidential campaign in 1888. The indications were that there was to be quite a bitter fight for the Republican presidential nomination. It was thought that another effort would be made to bring about the nomination of Mr. Blaine. If there had been a strong sentiment in the party in favor of the nomination of the statesman from Maine, he no doubt would have consented to the use of his name. But when it was made plain to him that a well-organized effort would be necessary to secure him the nomination, and even then such an effort might not be crowned with success, he wisely decided not to allow his name to be used as a candidate before the convention. But his friends and supporters were expected to keep the situation well in hand so as to enable them, at the opportune time, to name the nominee of the convention.

Ohio presented the name of Senator John Sherman, whose nomination at one time appeared to be reasonably certain. Indiana presented the name of General Benjamin Harrison, whose ultimate success was not at first seriously contemplated. The state of Illinois presented another son of Indiana in the person of Judge Walter Q. Gresham. Iowa presented the name of a strong and able man in the person of Senator William B. Allison. Michigan presented an aggressive and attractive candidate in General Russell A. Alger, while New York took pride in presenting the name of one of its most brilliant and eloquent statesmen in the person of Chauncey M. Depew.

After looking the field over very carefully, I came to the conclusion early in the campaign that Judge Gresham was the strongest and most available man for the nomination. Consequently, I decided to give his candidacy all the influence I could command. I knew Judge Gresham during the time he was stationed at Natchez, Mississippi, as the commander of the federal troops at that place.[1] I also knew him as postmaster-general and secretary of the treasury during the administration of President Arthur. I knew him to be safe, sound, and sane upon all important public questions, including the tariff, about which some professed to be in doubt with reference to his attitude. While I knew him to be a pronounced protectionist, I knew at the same time that he was not as radical in his views on that subject as some others. I knew him to be about on the order of Senator Allison, General Garfield, and many others of that class. Then, it was believed he had the confi-

1. Gresham was placed in command of the Natchez district in August, 1863, "where he was so successful in dealing with the situation involving cotton speculators and thieves that in the spring of 1864 he was assigned to Sherman's army and was placed in command of the 4th Division of the XVII Corps of the Atlanta campaign." *Dictionary of American Biography* (New York, 1959), 4:608.

dence, and if nominated would have the active and cordial support, of that large element of Independents whose support, particularly at that time, was believed to be essential to the success of the ticket.

While I supported Judge Gresham, I knew that a decided majority of the Republicans of my state were favorable to the candidacy of John Sherman. But this did not prevent my election as one of the four delegates to the national convention from the state at large, nor did it result in the dissolution of the political combination of Bruce, Lynch, and Hill, although the election of the delegates to the national convention at that time was the beginning of the rupture between Bruce and Hill, which finally resulted in the permanent dissolution of the combination. Hill was not only a Sherman man, but he was the leader of the Sherman forces in the state. Mr. Bruce was not in the state. He was at that time engaged in delivering a series of lectures throughout the country on the race question. I was not in direct communication with him, but I knew him to be a Sherman man, and, since Hill had charge of the senator's interests in the state and since his relations with Mr. Bruce were known to be cordial and friendly, I took it for granted that he knew Mr. Bruce's wishes and desires.

The understanding and agreement between Hill and myself was that the Sherman men would support me for a delegate to the national convention from the state at large if I would support the balance of the Sherman slate, including Hill's election as a member of the national committee and that I would make Senator Sherman my second choice. Since I was favorable to the candidacy of the Ohio senator as against anyone except Gresham, and had personally assured the senator of that fact, and since I knew the senator was the choice of a majority of the Republicans of the state, I had no hesitancy in consenting to the plan and accepting the conditions suggested, but with the understanding that the delegates should not be instructed. This was agreed to. I then asked Hill to name his slate, which he promptly did.

"The other two persons on our slate for delegates to the national convention from the state at large besides you and myself," he said, "are Dr. T. W. Stringer and Hon. John McGill." I was very much surprised when he called the name of Stringer instead of Bruce.

"What about Mr. Bruce?" I asked. "You know him to be a Sherman man, and since, according to your plans, the delegation from the state at large is to consist of three colored men and one white man—Hon. John McGill—why not select Bruce instead of Stringer?"

"Bruce," he replied, "is not a candidate and had no desire to be a delegate. He is now somewhere out West lecturing on the race question, and his engagements, I am informed, will extend beyond the sitting of the national convention, so that it is more than probable he will not even be in attendance at the convention. If he expected or desired to be a delegate, I think I would have known it."

"Very well," I replied, "you ought to know whereof you speak, since your relations with Mr. Bruce are more intimate than mine." The slate as thus agreed upon was elected without a hitch. With three exceptions the delegation was for Sherman from the beginning to the end. The three exceptions were the two from my own congressional district and myself. The three Gresham men never got an opportunity to vote for Senator Sherman since Gresham's name remained before the convention until the nomination was made.

One of the first men I met when I arrived at Chicago, the convention city, was Mr. Bruce. To my great surprise I found out from him that he was not only seriously disappointed, but very much incensed at Mr. Hill's action in having Stringer instead of himself elected a delegate to the convention. I then informed him of the interview that took place between Hill and myself before the delegates were elected. He said Hill not only knew that he, Bruce, expected and desired to be a delegate, but from the information he received indirectly from Hill, he, Bruce, was led to believe that his election as one of the four delegates from the state at large was a foregone conclusion. Consequently, his personal presence was not necessary; otherwise he would have been on hand to look after his own interests. It is useless to say that Bruce and Hill were never warm friends after that, although I succeeded in patching up a temporary truce which deferred until the end of the Harrison administration the final and complete dissolution of the combination.

If Mr. Bruce or his friends had been aware of what was in contemplation when the delegates to the national convention were elected, it is safe to say that Bruce instead of Stringer would have been elected. But Mr. Hill had evidently come to the conclusion that Stringer, who was the head of the colored masonic order in the state, with which Mr. Hill had recently identified himself, could be of more service to him in the future than Bruce; hence the substitution of Stringer for Bruce as a delegate to the national convention from the state at large.

The breach thus created between Bruce and Hill and the wound thus inflicted upon Mr. Bruce as a result thereof proved to be so bitter, so deep, and so intense that time could not cure them and distance could not lessen their intensity. Mr. Bruce could not believe otherwise than that it was a deliberate act, the intent and purpose being to lessen, if not destroy, his influence in the future with a national administration of his party. He was apprehensive that his failure to be chosen as a delegate to the national convention from his state at that time would be accepted by the administration, should it be Republican, as evidence of the fact that he was no longer an important factor in the politics of the state. This impression, it was feared, would be strengthened from a knowledge of the fact that the faction with which he was identified was in complete control of the state convention and had elected a delegation that was almost solid in its support of the candidate to whom he was known to be favorable. But, whatever purposes Mr. Hill may have had in contemplation, Mr. Bruce, as will be seen later, was able to more than survive them.

The convention proved to be one of the most interesting and exciting in the history of the party. The final result was the nomination of General Benjamin Harrison of Indiana, through a combination of the Blaine men with the New York delegation, supported by a strong Western following chiefly from Wisconsin and a few other smaller Western states. New York was allowed to name the candidate for vice-president, which was done in the person of Hon. Levi P. Morton of that state. The Democrats renominated President Cleveland, with Senator Allen G. Thurman of Ohio as his running mate. The campaign was an aggressive one from beginning to end. General Harrison surprised his friends and disappointed his enemies by the brilliancy of his campaign. It was soon developed that he was a much stronger and abler man than many of his friends believed or his enemies suspected. He carried the important and pivotal state of New York by over twenty thousand, in addition to his own state of Indiana, and was duly elected. His administration, of which more will be said later, was one of the best with which our country has ever been blessed.

President Harrison's cabinet selections were strong and able men. Mr. Blaine, by the aid of whose friends and active supporters the president was chiefly indebted for his nomination, was made secretary of state. Hon. William Windom, who was President Garfield's secretary of the treasury, was again named for that responsible and important position. An able and brilliant lawyer in the person of General John W. Noble of Missouri was made secretary of the interior. Hon. Redfield Proctor of Vermont was made secretary of war, General Benjamin F. Tracy of New York was selected for secretary of the navy. The successful businessman in the person of John Wanamaker of Pennsylvania was made postmaster general. The president's former law partner W. H. H. Miller of Indiana was made attorney general, while the Department of Agriculture was placed in charge of an able and popular Western man in the person of Hon. J. M. Rusk of Wisconsin. With nearly all of these men I was personally acquainted. With three of them, Messrs. Blaine, Windom, and Rusk, my relations had been both pleasant and cordial, although I had never supported Mr. Blaine for the Republican presidential nomination.

One of the first things the new administration was called upon to determine was the official recognition to be accorded the colored race. The first point decided was that no backward step should be taken in this matter. In other words, the administration would not do less in its official recognition of that race than had been done by previous Republican administrations. If there should be any changes at all it would be in the direction of an enlarged and increased representation of members of that race in the administration of the government, especially in view of the continued and loyal devotion of that race to the party and a material increase which it had made in recent years in the accumulation of wealth and in the acquisition of education. Then again the fact was not overlooked that Mr. Cleveland made an earnest effort to break down the race or color line in the Democratic party and to bring that party up to a recognition of the fact that mere race or color should not be a bar to official recognition even by a Democratic administration.

In other words, that the Democratic party should be brought to a full and complete recognition of the fact that merit and not race, fitness and not color, should be the principal tests for political preferment. It looked for a while as if his efforts in that direction would be crowned with success, but it transpired that the extreme Southern element in the party was too strong and influential to allow it to be done at that time. Still, Mr. Cleveland had made a brave and gallant, though unsuccessful, fight, except in a few minor details—a fight that no Republican suspected would be made by a Democrat. Since Mr. Cleveland, in spite of defeat, had not wholly abandoned his efforts in that direction, there was no telling what the ultimate result would be, or what effect his efforts would have in bringing about a division of the colored vote. The question was one to which it was deemed necessary that the administration should give careful attention.

While it was known that the colored man's loyalty to the Republican party was not measured by the degree of official recognition accorded members of that race—that with them officeholding was looked upon as an incident of party success and not the incentive to party affiliation—still it was necessary for the administration to pursue such a course in the distribution of the patronage at its disposal as to prevent the impression from being created that the administration would recognize, encourage, or countenance opposition or objection to anyone solely on the ground of race or color.

The most important office which had been previously filled by a colored man was that of Register of the Treasury, which had been ably filled by Hon. B. K. Bruce during the Garfield-Arthur administration. Mr. Bruce had been succeeded by General W. S. Rosecrans, who was appointed by President Cleveland. Being an ex-Union soldier himself, President Harrison had a natural weakness for ex-Union soldiers. He therefore decided that General Rosecrans, though a Democrat, should be retained in that office, but that a colored man should have some other of equal dignity and importance.

After a careful consideration by the president and his cabinet, it was decided that a colored man should be made an auditor of one of the bureaus in the Treasury Department. The matter was then turned over to the secretary of the treasury not only to find and recommend a suitable man, but also to select the bureau over which he was to be placed. The president insisted, however, that the man to be selected should have a pretty good general knowledge of the law, since he would no doubt be frequently called upon to consider and decide complicated questions of law as well as fact. I was not an applicant for any position at the disposal of the administration. The only document that had been filed in my behalf, so far as I knew, was a letter written by Senator George F. Hoar of Massachusetts addressed to the president and signed by a majority of the Republican senators, in which attention was called to my merits and fitness, and requesting that I be officially recognized in some appropriate way by the administration.

When Hon. J. M. Wilson, an ex-member of Congress from Indiana and a member of the law firm of Shellabarger and Wilson, heard of what was in contemplation, he wrote and filed with the secretary of the treasury a letter in which he bore testimony to my legal ability, special attention being called to the brief that was written and the oral argument that was made by me in the case before the committee of the House that had before it the celebrated contested election case of Lynch against Chalmers, his firm having represented me in that contest. This seems to have furnished the president and the secretary with all the information they desired on that point at least. The following Saturday I met ex-Congressman Guenther of Wisconsin on Pennsylvania Avenue, who warmly congratulated me on my appointment as Fourth Auditor of the Treasury, now called the Auditor of the Treasury for the

Navy Department. I told him that what he had stated was news to me and requested the source of his information.

"Secretary Rusk," he replied, "I am just from the Secretary's office, and in the course of my conversation with him, he informed me that the appointment was agreed upon at the Cabinet meeting yesterday afternoon."

I called the same day on Secretary Rusk who not only confirmed the report but gave me the particulars about what took place at the cabinet meeting. Of the eight members of the cabinet, five were outspoken for me—Secretaries Windom, Blaine, Proctor, Noble, and himself. The other three, Messrs. Wanamaker, Miller, and Tracy were not particularly opposed to me, but, their knowledge of me being somewhat limited, they were not in a position to express an intelligent opinion with reference to my fitness and qualifications for such a responsible position. They were willing, however, to defer to the judgment of the secretary of the treasury and acquiesce in his decision and recommendation. My commission was signed early the following week, when I took the oath of office and entered upon the discharge of my duties, succeeding General Charles M. Shelley of Alabama.

Nothing thus far had been done for my friend Hon. B. K. Bruce, and since nearly every desirable place had been disposed of, I was somewhat anxious and concerned about him. Before calling on the president in his behalf, I decided that I would first see the president's private secretary, Hon. W. H. Halford, to find out through him, if possible, what, if anything, was in contemplation for Mr. Bruce. From him I learned that Mr. Bruce had not been overlooked and that in course of time he would be appropriately recognized. There were two district offices, he said, yet to be filled: Recorder of Deeds and Register of Wills. The president, he remarked, does not look with favor upon the idea that colored men should be limited, restricted, or confined to any particular class or kind of position at the disposal of an administration. With that end in view the president was disposed to appoint colored men to positions not heretofore held by members of that race. With reference, then, to the two positions referred to, Recorder of Deeds and Register of Wills, the president is strongly inclined to appoint a white man, General Wright, Recorder of Deeds and that the registership of wills will no doubt go to a colored man, and that man he was sure would be Mr. Bruce.

But the office of Register of Wills was then held by a Mr. Claggett, an ex-federal soldier, who had been appointed late in the administration of Mr. Cleveland. Unlike the case of General Rosecrans, it was not the intention of the president to allow Mr. Claggett to remain in the office indefinitely, but he did decide that no change should be made until Mr. Claggett had served out the full four-year term for which he had been appointed. Since his term would not expire until late in the administration, the outlook for Mr. Bruce's early recognition was not bright, in view of the fact that the registership of wills was the place for which he was slated. When these facts became known, strong and successful pressure was brought to bear to induce the president to change his plans with reference to the two positions referred to. The result was that Mr. Bruce was shortly thereafter appointed Recorder of Deeds. General Wright was then slated for Register of Wills, the appointment to be made after Mr. Claggett had served out his four-year term. When Mr. Cleveland succeeded President Harrison, he extended the same courtesy to General Wright that President Harrison had extended to Mr. Claggett, by allowing General Wright to serve out the four-year term for which he had been appointed.

In addition to the appointment of Mr. Bruce and myself to the important and responsible positions named, many colored men were appointed to good positions, not only in the different departments in Washington, but also in the different states, and in the foreign service of the government. In my own bureau, Robert H. Terrell, a talented young lawyer and a graduate of Harvard, was made chief of one of the important divisions of the bureau, which carried an annual salary of two thousand dollars, the duties of which he discharged in an able, creditable, and satisfactory manner. At this writing he holds the important, responsible, and dignified position of Justice of the Municipal Court of the District of Columbia. That he discharged the duties of the same with credit to himself and satisfaction to the public I have not the slightest doubt.

35

Republican Factionalism and the Problem of Disenfranchisement

It was during the administration of President Harrison that another effort was made to secure the enactment by Congress of the necessary legislation for the effective enforcement of the war amendments to the national Constitution—a federal elections bill. Mr. Lodge of Massachusetts was the author of the bill. But the fact was soon developed that there were too many Republicans, in and out of Congress, who lacked the courage of their convictions to secure favorable action. In fact, there were three classes of white men at the South who claimed to be Republicans who used their influence to defeat that contemplated legislation. The white men at the South who acted with the Republican party at that time were divided into four classes or groups.

First, those who were Republicans from principle and conviction—because they were firm believers in, and advocates of, the principles, doctrine, and policies for which the party stood and were willing to remain with it in adversity as well as in prosperity, in defeat as well as in victory. This class or group, I am pleased to say, while not the most noisy and demonstrative, comprised over seventy-five percent of the white membership of the party in that part of the country.

Second, a small but noisy and demonstrative class or group, comprising about fifteen percent of the remainder, who labored under the honest but erroneous impression that the best and most effective way to build up a strong and influential Republican party at the South was to draw the race or color line in the party. In other words, to organize a Republican party to be composed exclusively of white men, to the entire exclusion of colored men. What those men chiefly wanted and felt the need of for themselves and their families was social recognition by the better element of the white people of their respective localities. They were anxious, therefore, to bring about such a condition of things as would make it possible for them to be known as Republicans without subjecting themselves and their families to the risk of being socially ostracized by their white Democratic neighbors. And then again those men believed then, and some of them still believe or profess to believe, that Southern Democrats were and are honest and sincere in the declaration that the presence of the colored men in the Republican party prevents Southern white men from coming into it. "Draw the race or color line against the colored race, organize a white Republican party, and you will find that thousands of white men who now act with the Democratic party will join your party."

Some white Republicans believed that the men by whom these declarations were made were honest and sincere, and it may be that some of them were, but it appears not to have occurred to them that if the votes of the colored men were suppressed, the minority white vote, unaided and unprotected, would be powerless to prevent the application and enforcement of methods and practices which would nullify and render ineffective any organized effort on their part. In other words, nothing short of an effective national law to protect the weak against the strong and the minority of the whites against the aggressive assaults of the majority of that race would enable the minority of the whites to make their power and influence effective and potential; and even then it could be effectively done only in cooperation with the blacks.

Then again, they seemed to have lost sight of the fact, or perhaps they did not and do not know it to be a fact, that many leading Southern Democrats are insincere in their declarations upon the so-called race question. They keep that question before the public for political and party reasons only—because they find it to be the most effective weapon they can use to hold the white men in political subjection. The effort, therefore, to build up a "white" Republican party at the South has had a tendency, under existing circumstances, to discourage and prevent, rather than encourage and promote, a strong Republican organization in that section.

But, even if it were possible for such an organization to have a potential existence, it could not be otherwise than ephemeral, because it would be wholly out of harmony and at war with the fundamental principles and doctrines of the national organization whose name it had appropriated. It would be in point of fact a misnomer and therefore wholly out of place as one of the branches of the national organization which stands for, defends, and advocates the civil and political equality of all American citizens, without regard to race, color, nationality, or religion. Any organization, therefore, claiming to be a branch of the national Republican party, but which had repudiated and denounced the fundamental and sacred creed of that organization, would be looked upon by the public as a close, selfish, and local machine that was brought into existence to serve the ends and seek to gratify and satisfy the selfish ambition of the promoters and organizers of the corporation. And yet there were, and perhaps are, a few well-meaning and honest white men in some of the Southern states who were, and are, disposed or inclined, through a mistaken sense of political necessity, to give such a movement the benefit of their countenance.

But the movement has been a lamentable failure in states where it has been tried, and it cannot be otherwise where it has not been but in which it may yet be tried. Men who were in sympathy with a movement of this sort took a pronounced stand against the proposed Federal Elections Bill and used what influence they had to prevent its passage, their idea being that if passed it would have a tendency to prevent the accomplishment of the purposes they had in contemplation.

The third class or group consisted of a still smaller number who were Republicans for revenue only—for the purpose of getting office. If an office were in sight, or believed to be obtainable, they would be quite demonstrative in their advocacy of the Republican party and its principles and doctrines. But if they were not officially recognized, their activities would not only cease but they would soon be back in the fold of the Democracy. But, should they be officially recognized, they would be good, faithful, and loyal Republicans, at least so far as words were concerned, until they ceased to be officials, when they would cease at the same time to be Republicans. Men of this class were, of course, opposed to the proposed legislation for the enforcement of the war amendments to the Constitution.

The fourth class or group consisted of an insignificantly small number of white men who claimed to be national Republicans and local Democrats, that is, they claimed that they voted for the Republican candidate for president every four years, but for the Democrats in all other elections. Of course they were against the proposed legislation referred to. These men succeeded in inducing some well-meaning and good-intentioned Republican members of Congress, like Senator [William D.] Washburne of Minnesota, to believe that the passage of such a bill would have a tendency to prevent and discourage the building up of a strong Republican organization at the South. Then again the free-silver question was prominent before the public at that time. The Republican majority in the Senate was not large. Several of those who had been elected as Republicans were free-silver men. On that question they were in harmony with a majority of the Democrats and out of harmony with the great majority of Republicans. The free-silver Republicans, therefore, were not inclined to support a measure that was particularly offensive and objectionable to their friends and allies on the silver question. After a careful canvass of the Senate, it was developed that the Republican leaders could not safely count on the support of anyone of the free-silver Republicans in their efforts to pass the bill and since they had the balance of power, any further effort to pass it was abandoned. It was then made plain to the friends and supporters of that measure that no further attempt would be made in that direction for a long time, if ever.

I wrote and had published in the Washington, D.C., *Post* a letter in which I took strong grounds in favor of having the representation in Congress reduced in the manner prescribed by the Fourteenth Amendment, in states where the colored men had been practically disfranchised through an evasion of the Fifteenth Amendment. In that letter I made an effort to answer every argument that had been made in opposition to such a proposition. It had been argued by some fairly good lawyers, for instance, that the subsequent ratification of the Fifteenth Amendment had so modified the Fourteenth as to take away from Congress the optional and discretionary power which had been previously conferred upon it by the Fourteenth Amendment. I tried in that letter and I think I succeeded in answering the argument on that point. It was also said that if Congress were to take such a step it would thereby give its sanction to the disfranchisement of the colored men in the states where that had been done. This I think I succeeded in proving was untrue and without foundation.

The truth is that the only material difference between the Fourteenth and Fifteenth Amendments on this particular point is that subsequent to the ratification of the Fourteenth and prior to the ratification of the Fifteenth Amendment, a state could legally disfranchise white or colored men on account of race or color, but, since the ratification of the Fifteenth Amendment this cannot be legally done. If the Congress had the constitutional right and power under the Fourteenth Amendment to punish a state in the manner and form therein prescribed for doing what the state then had a legal and constitutional right to do, I cannot see why Congress has not now the same power and authority to inflict the same punishment upon the state for doing or permitting to be done what it now has no legal and constitutional right to do.

No state, in my opinion, should be allowed to take advantage of its own wrongs, and thus by a wrongful act augment and increase its own power and influence in the government. To allow the white men or a majority of them in the state of Mississippi, for instance, to appropriate to themselves through questionable methods the representative strength of the colored population of that state, excluding the latter from all participation in the selection of the representatives in Congress, is a monstrous wrong and grave injustice the continuance of which should not be tolerated. For every crime there must be a punishment. For every wrong there must be a remedy, and for every grievance there must be a redress. That this state of things is wrong and unjust, if not unlawful, no fair-minded person will deny or dispute. It is not only wrong, unfair, and unjust to the colored people of the state who are thus denied a voice in the government under which they live and to support which they are taxed, but it also involves a grave injustice to the states in which the laws are obeyed and the national

Constitution, including the war amendments to the same, is respected and enforced.

I am aware of the fact that it is claimed by those who are responsible for what is here complained of that while the acts referred to may be an evasion if not a violation of the *spirit* of the Constitution, yet, since they do not violate the *letter* of the Constitution, the complaining parties are without a remedy and therefore have no redress. This claim or contention is not only weak in logic but unsound in law, even as construed by the Supreme Court of the United States, which tribunal seems to be the last to which an appeal can be successfully made, having for its object the enforcement of the Constitution and laws so far as they relate to the political and civil rights of the colored Americans. That a state can do by indirection what it cannot do directly is denied even by the Supreme Court of the United States.[1]

That doctrine was clearly and distinctly set forth in a decision of the Court rendered by Mr. Justice Strong, which was concurred in by a majority of his associates. In that decision it was held that affirmative state action is not necessary to constitute discrimination by the state.[2] In other words, to constitute affirmative state action in violation of the constitutional mandate against distinction and discrimination based on race or color, it is not necessary that the state should pass a law for that purpose. The state, the Court declared, acts through and by its agents and representative of the state, whose acts are binding upon the state and the effect is the same as if the state had passed a law for that purpose. If a judge, for example, in the selection of jurors to serve in his court, should knowingly and intentionally allow a particular race to be excluded

1. For a discussion of the Federal Elections Bill and an analysis of the votes on it, see Logan, *The Negro in American Life and Thought*, pp. 61–64.

2. Strauder v. West Virginia, 100 U.S. 303 (1880).

from such service on account of race or color, the effect would be the same as if the state, through its legislature, had passed a law for that purpose. The colored men in the states complained of, having been disfranchised in violation of the spirit, if not the letter, of the national Constitution, either by affirmative state action or through and by its agents and representatives, acting for and in the name of the state and by its authority and under its direction and supervision, constitutes state action as fully as if the legislature had passed a law for that purpose.

The defeat or abandonment of the Lodge Federal Elections Bill was equivalent to a declaration that no further attempts would be made, for a good while at least, to enforce, by appropriate legislation, the war amendments to the national Constitution. Southern Democrats were not slow in taking advantage of the knowledge of that fact.

My own state, Mississippi, was the first to give legal effect to the practical nullification of the Fifteenth Amendment. On that question the Democratic party in the state was divided into two factions. The radical faction, under the leadership of Senator George, advocated the adoption and enforcement of extreme methods. The liberal or conservative faction, or what was known as the Lamar wing of the party under the leadership of Senator [Edward C.] Walthall, was strongly opposed to such methods. Senator George advocated the calling of a constitutional convention to frame a new constitution for the state. Senator Walthall opposed it, contending that the then constitution, though framed by Republicans, was in the main unobjectionable and should be allowed to stand. Senator George was successful; hence, a convention was called to meet in the fall of 1890. In order to take no chances and run no risks, the senator had himself nominated and elected a member of the convention.

When the convention met it was found that there were two strong factions, one in favor and one opposed to giving legal effect to the nullification of the Fifteenth Amendment.[3] The George faction or nullificationists were slightly in the majority, resulting in one of their number, Judge S. S. Calhoun, being elected president of the convention. The plan advocated and supported by the George faction, of which Senator George was the author, provided that no one should be allowed to register as a voter or vote if registered, unless he could read and write, or unless he could understand any section of the Constitution when read to him and give a reasonable interpretation thereof. This was known as the understanding clause. It was plain to everyone that its purpose was to so evade the Fifteenth Amendment as to disfranchise the illiterate voters of one race without disfranchising those of the other.

The opposition to this scheme was under the leadership of one of the ablest and most brilliant members of the bar, in the person of Judge J. B. Chrisman of Lincoln County. As a substitute for the George plan, or understanding clause, he ably and eloquently advocated the adoption of a fair and honest educational qualification as a condition precedent to registration and voting, the same to be equally applicable to whites and blacks.

The speeches on both sides were able and interesting. It looked for a while as if the substitute proposed by Judge Chrisman would be adopted. In consequence of such an apprehension, Judge Calhoun, the president of the convention, took the floor in opposition to the Chrisman plan and in support of the one proposed by Senator George. His speech in substance was that the convention had been called for the purpose of insuring the ascendancy of the white race or the Democratic party in the administration of the state govern-

3. For an excellent account of the convention see Wharton, *The Negro in Mississippi*, pp. 206–15. See, also, Kirwan, *Revolt of the Rednecks*, pp. 65–84.

ment through some other methods than those which had been enforced since 1875.

"If you fail in the discharge of your duties in this matter," he declared, "the blood of every Negro that will be killed in an election riot hereafter will be upon your shoulders."

In other words, the speaker frankly admitted what everyone knew to be a fact, that the ascendancy of the Democratic party in the state had been maintained since 1875 through methods and practices which in his opinion should no longer be sanctioned and tolerated. These methods, he contended, were corrupting the morals of the people of the state and therefore should be discontinued, and yet the ascendancy of the Democratic party must be maintained at any cost. The George plan, he contended, would accomplish this result, because if the Negroes were disfranchised according to the forms of law, there would be no occasion to suppress their votes by violence because they would have no votes to suppress; and, having no votes in the ballot boxes, there would be no occasion to commit fraud in the count or perjury in the returns, as heretofore.

Notwithstanding this frank and candid speech, which was intended to arouse the fears of the members of the convention from a party standpoint, the defeat of the Chrisman substitute was by no means an assured fact. But the advocates of the George plan, or understanding clause, were both desperate and determined. Contrary to public expectation, two Republicans, George B. Melchior and I. T. Montgomery, had been elected to the convention from Bolivar County. But their seats were contested, and it was assumed that their Democratic contestants would be seated. Still, pending the final disposition of the case, the two Republicans were the sitting members. Montgomery was colored and Melchior was white. But the George faction needed these two votes. No one suspected, however, that they would get them in any other way than by seating the contestants. The advocates and supporters of the Chrisman substitute were, therefore, very much surprised and disappointed when they learned that Mr. Montgomery, the only colored member of the convention, intended to vote for and make a speech in favor of the adoption of the George plan, which he did. Why this man who had the reputation of being honest and honorable, and who in point of intelligence was considerably above the average of his race in the state at that time, should have thus acted and voted has always been and perhaps will continue to be an inexplicable mystery. It is difficult to believe that he was willing to pay such a price for the retention of his seat in the convention. Still, it is a fact that the contest was never called and Montgomery and his colleague were allowed to retain their seats. The adoption of the George plan was thus assured, but not without a desperate fight.

The opponents of that scheme made a brave and gallant, though unsuccessful, fight against it. But it was soon made plain to the advocates of the George plan that what they had succeeded in forcing through the convention would be defeated by the people at the ballot box. In fact, a storm of protest was raised throughout the state. The Democratic press as well as the members of that party were believed to be about equally divided in support of and in opposition to the ratification of the constitution as thus framed. Since it was well known that the Republicans would be solid in their opposition to ratification, the rejection of the proposed constitution was an assured fact. But the supporters of the George scheme felt that they could not afford to have the results of their labors go down in defeat. To prevent this they decided to deny the people the right of passing judgment upon the work of the convention. The decision, therefore, was that the convention by which the constitution was framed, should declare it duly ratified and approved, the same to go into effect upon a day therein named. The people of that unfortunate state, therefore, have never had an opportunity to pass judgment upon the constitution under which they are living and which they are required to obey and support, that right having been denied them because it was known that a majority of them were opposed to its ratification and would have voted against it.

But this so-called understanding clause, or George scheme, as construed and enforced is much more sweeping than was intended by its author. The intent of that clause was to make it possible to disfranchise the illiterate blacks without disfranchising the illiterate whites. But as construed and enforced it is not confined to illiterates, but to persons of intelligence as well. No man, for instance, however intelligent he may be, can be registered as a voter, in the first place, or vote if registered, in the second place, if the registering officer or the election officers are of the opinion that he does not understand the Constitution.

It is true the instrument is so worded that no allusion is made to the race or color of those seeking to be registered and to vote. Still, it is perfectly plain to everyone that the purpose was to enable the state to do, through its authorized and duly appointed agents and representatives, the very thing which the Fifteenth Amendment declares shall not be done. According to the decision of the Supreme Court, as rendered by Mr. Justice Strong, to which allusion has been made, the effect was and is the same as if the instrument had declared in so many words that race or color should be the basis of discrimination and exclusion.

The bitter and desperate struggle between the two factions of the Democratic party in the state of Mississippi in this contest forcibly illustrates and proves that the national Republican party made a grave mistake when it abandoned any further efforts to enforce by appropriate legislation the war amendments to the Constitution. In opposing and denouncing the questionable methods of the extreme and radical faction of their own party, the conservative faction of the Democrats believed, expected, and predicted that such methods would not be acquiesced in by the national Republican party nor would they be tolerated by the national government. If those expectations and predictions had been verified they would have given the conservative element a justifiable excuse to break away from the radicals and this would have resulted in having two strong political parties in that section today instead of but one. But when it was seen that the national Republican party made no further opposition to the enforcement of these extraneous, radical, and questionable methods, it in fact not only had the effect of preventing further opposition on the part of the conservative Democrats, but it also resulted in many of them who were politically ambitious joining the ranks of the radicals, since that was then the only channel through which it was possible for their political aspirations to be gratified and realized.

The reader cannot fail to see that under the plan now in force in the state of Mississippi, for instance, there is no incentive to intelligence, because intelligence does not secure access to the ballot box, nor does the lack of it prevent such access. It is not an incentive to the accumulation of wealth, because the ownership of property does not secure the owner access to the ballot box, nor does the lack of it prevent such access. It is not a question of intelligence, wealth, or character, nor can it be said that it is wholly a question of party. It is simply a question of factional affiliation. The standard of qualification is confined to such white men as may be in harmony with the faction that may happen to have control for the time being of the state election machinery. What is true of Mississippi in this respect is equally true of the other Southern states in which schemes of various sorts have been invented and adopted to evade the Fifteenth Amendment to the national Constitution.

Chapter Thirty-five

The congressional elections of 1890 resulted in a crushing defeat for the Republicans. This was due, no doubt, to the McKinley Tariff Bill which became a law only about a month before the elections of that year. Congress convened the first Monday in December 1889, and that session did not come to a close until the following October. The Democrats in Congress made a bitter fight against the McKinley Tariff Bill, and, since it was a very complete and comprehensive measure, a great deal of time was necessarily consumed in its consideration and discussion. When it finally became a law, the time between its passage and the elections was so short that the friends of the measure did not have time to explain and defend it before the elections took place. This placed the Republicans at a great disadvantage. They were on the defensive from the beginning. The result was a sweeping Democratic victory.

But, strange to say, the same issues that produced Democratic success and Republican defeat at that election brought about Republican success and Democratic defeat at the presidential and congressional elections of 1896. The McKinley Tariff Bill of 1890 was so popular six years later that the author of that measure was deemed the strongest and most available man to place at the head of the Republican ticket as the candidate of that party for president. His election was a complete vindication of the wisdom of the measure of which he was the author and champion. In 1890 his bill was so unpopular that it resulted in his own defeat for reelection to Congress. But this did not cause him to lose faith in the wisdom and ultimate popularity of the bill which he was proud to have bear his name.

"A little time," he said, "will prove the wisdom of the measure." In this he was not mistaken. His defeat for reelection to Congress ultimately made him president of the United States, for the following year the Republicans of his state elected him governor, which was a stepping stone to the presidency. All that was needed was an opportunity for the merits of this bill to be thoroughly tested. Shortly after its passage, but before it could be enforced or even explained, the people were led to believe that it was a harsh, cruel, and unjust measure, imposing heavy, unreasonable, and unnecessary taxes upon them, increasing the prices of the necessities of life without a corresponding increase in the price of labor. The people were in an ugly and angry mood in anticipation of what was never fully realized.

It is true that the tariff was not the sole issue that resulted in such a sweeping Republican victory in the national elections of 1896. The financial issue, which was prominent before the people at that time, was one of the contributory causes of that result. Still it cannot and will not be denied that McKinley's connection with the Tariff Bill of 1890 was what gave him the necessary national prominence to make him the most available man to be placed at the head of his party ticket for the presidency that year.

36

Cleveland's Reelection

PRESIDENT HARRISON'S ADMINISTRATION WAS ONE OF THE BEST the country has ever had. The president was an able lawyer and a great statesman but he was not what may be called a tactful politician. He was plain, honest, candid, and outspoken. He did not possess the faculty of saying one thing and meaning another. No one could leave his presence and have any doubt about his attitude upon the subject that had been discussed. He was not only emphatic in giving expression to his opinions, but he was sometimes unfortunate in using language that was more forceful than the occasion required. He never failed to consult and confer with the representative men of his party in and out of Congress about making appointments to office, but he would not always accept their suggestions or act favorably upon their recommendations. In fact, such suggestions and recommendations were frequently ignored and disregarded. In this way and on this account he made more enemies than friends among the representative men of his own party.

In his candidacy for renomination in 1892, those men were, of course, against him. Senator [Matthew S.] Quay of Pennsylvania, who had successfully managed the campaign of 1888, as chairman of the National Republican Committee resulting in the election of Mr. Harrison, was one of his bitterest opponents. Ex-Senator [Thomas C.] Platt of New York whose action at the national convention of 1888 it was claimed and believed made the nomination of Mr. Harrison possible, but who had no doubt been very much disappointed through the failure or refusal of the president to carry out the conditions by which it was claimed that result was brought about, was also very bitter in his opposition to the renomination of the president. A majority of those who were known as national party leaders were outspoken in their opposition to the president, while some others were apparently indifferent about his renomination.

But the most difficult task the opponents of the president had before them was to find a fit and suitable man to bring out against him. To find such a man, or one who was believed to be such, the president's own cabinet had to be invaded. Mr. Blaine was President Harrison's secretary of state. While Mr. Blaine's health was known to be poor, he had not entirely abandoned the hope that he might ultimately reach the acme of his ambition—the presidency of the United States. He was urged and finally consented to the use of his name, his resignation as secretary of state being immediately tendered and accepted. This announcement, it was thought, hoped, and believed by the opponents of the president, would be fatal to the president's ambition. The magic name of Blaine, it was thought, hoped, and believed by the opponents of the president, would carry the convention by storm and the statesman from Maine would be nominated by acclamation. But they were sadly disappointed. The Harrison men were too well organized to be stampeded. While Senator Quay was opposed to the president, the anti-Quay faction of the party in Pennsylvania, under the leadership of State Senator [Christopher L.] Magee of Pittsburgh, who controlled about one-third of the state's delegation, supported him. While ex-Senator Platt of New York was against the president, Chauncey M. Depew of the same state supported him. While Senator [Joseph B.] Foraker of Ohio was strongly opposed to the president, Major William McKinley of the same state supported him.[1]

When it became apparent that the Blaine movement was a failure, a move was then made by the Ohio delegation, under the able leadership of Senator Foraker, to swing the convention to Major McKinley. But McKinley, who was a Harrison man and who was president of the convention, threw the weight of his influence against the movement; consequently it was not favorably received. The truth is President Harrison's renomination was an assured fact in any event, but even if it had been possible under any combination of circumstances to bring about his defeat, Major McKinley was determined that his name should not be used in an effort to defeat the nomination of the man who was the unmistakable choice of his party at that time. With the rank and file of the party President Harrison was strong and popular. They were not brought personally in contact with him, but they felt and appreciated the beneficial effect of his able, successful, and brilliant administration; hence his strength and popularity with the masses of his own party.

Under the Harrison administration, as stated in a previous chapter, I occupied the responsible position of Auditor of the Treasury for the Navy Department, then called the Fourth Auditor. Mr. Bruce was Recorder of Deeds of the District of Columbia. In the fight to secure the renomination of the presi-

1. Foraker, who had served three terms as governor of Ohio, was not in public office in 1892. He did not go to the United States Senate until 1896.

dent it was assumed, of course, that Mr. Bruce and I would not fail to bring in a delegation from Mississippi favorable to the president's renomination. I had been chairman of the Republican Executive Committee of the state from 1881 until 1889, my resignation having been tendered and accepted upon my appointment as an Auditor of the Treasury Department. All important appointments in the state, with a few exceptions, as well as many outside of the state, were made upon the joint recommendation of Mr. Bruce and myself. Upon our recommendation Mr. Hill was made postmaster at Vicksburg, the largest, most important and lucrative post office in the state. The appointment was extremely objectionable to some of the white patrons of the office. An indignation meeting was held and strong resolutions were passed protesting against the appointment. In consequence of this it was feared by some that the appointee would be in danger of personal violence should he attempt to take charge of the office.

The objections were alleged to be based upon two grounds. The first, and of course the most serious one, was that the appointee was a colored man. The second was that he was not a citizen of Vicksburg. In consequence of the threats of personal violence some of the chief officials of the Post Office Department at Washington hesitated about having a commission issued. Mr. Bruce and I were called in consultation. The situation as it had been officially reported to the department was explained to us in detail and our advice in the matter solicited. We took the ground that the commission should be issued without delay and that the appointee should be placed in charge of the office, let the consequences be what they may. It would never do, we contended, for the government to yield to the demands of a mob. If this were done in one case it would have to be done in many; hence, it would never do to allow that precedent to be established.

Our advice was accepted, the commission was issued, and a post office inspector was sent to Vicksburg to place the appointee in charge of the office, the duties of which he discharged, without risk, danger, or interference from anyone, for a period of several months, or until the end of the Harrison administration. In the meantime, President Harrison had been defeated for reelection, which fact destroyed all hope of Mr. Hill's confirmation by the Senate. When it became apparent that the nomination could not be confirmed, it was withdrawn, and upon the recommendation of Mr. Bruce and myself a young and aggressive white Republican, in the person of Mr. M. J. Mulvihill, was appointed to fill the vacancy. But, since the end of the Harrison administration was so near at hand, this young man had only a few months to serve when he was succeeded by a Democrat who was appointed by President Cleveland.

In consequence of the fight we made in behalf of Mr. Hill, Mr. Bruce and I believed that we could safely rely upon his active cooperation and assistance in our efforts to secure a delegation to the national convention favorable to the renomination of the president. In this we were somewhat disappointed. Why so? Because Mr. Hill had a pretty strong following in the state, built up under, through, and by the distribution of the federal patronage which was at the disposal of Senator Bruce during the administration of President Hayes. During that administration Mr. Bruce was the only Republican in either branch of Congress from the state; consequently, his influence was potential in the disposition of the patronage of the state.

As explained in a previous chapter, the district in which I lived was the only exception to this rule. The disposition of the patronage in that district Mr. Bruce gracefully yielded to me, although during a part of the time I had no official connection with the administration or with either house of Congress. In all of the other districts the appointments were controlled absolutely by Mr. Bruce, and yet, strange to say, very few of the appointees felt obligated to him for the positions to which they had been appointed. This was because Mr. Bruce made Mr. Hill his referee and representative. It was useless for anyone to make an application for a federal position of any kind, except in my district, without having the endorsement of Mr. Hill. This is what gave Mr. Hill his power, prestige, and influence and secured for him a considerable following in the state.

As between Bruce and Hill, therefore, most of the men who had been thus favored felt that they were more obligated to Hill than to Bruce, and when, therefore, they were called upon to choose between them, they were disposed from a standpoint of gratitude to take sides with Hill. But under the administration of Harrison the situation was materially different. Under that administration I shared with Mr. Bruce in this responsibility and duty, in the discharge of which there was never any friction, dispute, disagreement, or misunderstanding. We were not unfriendly to Mr. Hill. We were not only willing, but determined that he should be appropriately provided for; but we were also determined that neither he nor any other one man should be the sole referee and dispenser of the patronage under this administration as had been the case under the administration of President Hayes. This is what gave mortal offense to Mr. Hill. To him this was a great disappointment. It was so radically different from that to which he had been accustomed that it was impossible for him to gracefully accept the new order of things. He could not become reconciled to the fact that it was no longer necessary for those who were applicants for federal appointments to have their applications endorsed by him as a condition precedent to favorable action.

The first important case that made this plain to Mr. Hill was in the appointment of a federal judge for the southern district of the state. Mr. Hill had a personal friend, in a lawyer by the name of A. M. Lea, whom he desired to have appointed. Lea was a reputable man and a good lawyer and no doubt would have made a fairly good judge, but in the opinion of Mr. Bruce and me, Henry C. Niles was the better man of the two applicants for this responsible position and we supported him and he was appointed. Another case that soon came up was that of United States marshal for the southern district of the state. Mr. Hill had a candidate in the person of a friend by the name of Rosenbaum, but Mr. Bruce and I thought that Frederick W. Collins was a better man for the place and supported him. Collins was appointed. Mr. Hill then decided to throw what influence he might have on the side of the anti-Harrison men in spite of the fact that he was then postmaster at Vicksburg, not on account of any objections to Harrison, but because he hoped and believed that through the defeat of Harrison the power and influence of Bruce and Lynch would be destroyed.

In the fight for delegates to the national convention that year from the state, Mr. Hill used his influence to secure the election of a delegation that would be in sympathy with the anti-Harrison men although he claimed to be favorable to Harrison himself. Of course he was easily defeated in his efforts to select such a delegation, but since he was a member of the national committee of which Senator Quay was chairman, he carried a contesting delegation to the national convention, a part of which, including Hill himself, was placed on the roll by the national committee, a majority of that body being opposed to Harrison. Hon. Thomas H. Carter of Montana was made chairman of the national committee under whose management and direction an aggressive campaign was inaugurated.

The Democrats nominated ex-President Grover Cleveland of New York and Hon. A. E. Stevenson of Illinois for president and vice-president, respectively. The fact soon became apparent that the Republicans were not to have a walkover. It was not only true that many of the party leaders were lukewarm and indifferent, but that the public was still laboring under the impression that the McKinley Tariff Bill was a bad thing for the people, the consumers especially.

As a result of that legislation the Democrats had carried the country by a large majority in 1890. It was hoped that two years would be long enough to enable the people to see the wisdom and begin to feel the beneficial effects of that legislation. Yet the indications were that nothing short of an actual trial of several years' duration of both systems or theories would be satisfactory. The result was another Republican defeat. The Democrats not only elected their candidates for president and vice-president, but the same party had a decided majority in both houses of Congress. The people were thus assured that the McKinley Tariff Bill would not only be promptly repealed, but that a bill in the direction of free trade or a tariff for revenue only would be enacted in its place. But as soon as the elections were over the country was thrown into a disastrous financial panic in anticipation, no doubt, of what was to follow.

In the vain hope of appeasing the silver Republicans and holding them in line, the Republican Congress during the Harrison administration passed a bill authorizing and requiring the purchase by the government monthly of a certain amount of silver to be used for coinage purposes. This legislation was in a large measure experimental, and, under a Republican administration, it would have been harmless, since it could have and would have been promptly repealed should the experiment prove to be a failure. President Cleveland endeavored to create the impression upon the public mind that it was this legislation that brought on the panic, and he therefore recommended that it be immediately repealed, which was promptly done. But no relief came in consequence thereof, which was conclusive evidence that that was not the primary cause of the trouble.

But the promise was held out that the new Tariff Bill, to take the place of the McKinley Bill, would be sure to bring the necessary relief. The Democrats now had the opportunity to put their theory about the tariff into practical effect—to demonstrate the wisdom and beneficial effects of the same. After several months of hard work, what was known as the Wilson-Gorman Bill was all that could be obtained. This was a protective tariff bill—not so protective as the McKinley Bill, but still a protective measure. President Cleveland, who was a true and sincere believer in and advocate of a tariff for revenue only, and therefore much opposed to any bill having protection as its primary object, was so disappointed and disgusted that he publicly expressed himself about it in language that was more forcible than elegant.

The president no doubt represented and reflected the dominant sentiment of his own party, but this sentiment was not strong enough to sway the action and influence the votes of the party leaders in Congress. Those leaders had no doubt come to the conclusion that, since the anticipated passage of a tariff bill, having for its object a tariff for revenue only, had created such a terrible panic throughout the country, the passage of such a bill, they apprehended, would be disastrous. Hence their decision to allow no such bill to pass. Mr. Cleveland's letter in which the bill then pending was so bitterly denounced appeared to have had the opposite effect from that which was intended. Instead of causing the leaders of his party in Congress to change their attitude upon that subject, it appeared to have strengthened them in their determination to pass that bill or none at all. That fact was soon made plain to the president.

When the bill finally passed both houses of Congress and was presented to the president for his signature, he refused to sign it, but he felt that he could not afford to veto it, for in that case no bill would have passed and the McKinley law would have remained on the statute books. As bad as the Wilson-Gorman bill was, it was, from Mr. Cleveland's point of view, an improvement on the McKinley law. Still, since he had so bitterly assailed it, he could not see his way clear to sign it. So the only thing he could do was to allow it to become a law without his signature.

Notwithstanding this legislation, the country experienced no material relief from the effects of the panic, but the same continued more or less throughout that administration. While the Wilson-Gorman Bill was a protective measure, it went far enough in the direction of free trade or a tariff for revenue only to give the people an opportunity to pass judgment upon the merits of the two systems or theories. Their conclusions were that if a bill which went no further in the direction of free trade or tariff for revenue only than the Wilson-Gorman Bill would cause so much mischief, a bill which would go further in that direction they feared might cause still more. The result was a sweeping Republican victory for president in 1896 and at each subsequent presidential election up to and including 1908.

When Mr. Cleveland was inaugurated in 1893, I was Auditor of the Treasury for the Navy Department. Hon. J. G. Carlisle of Kentucky had been made secretary of the treasury. My resignation had been tendered, the acceptance of which I expected to see announced any day, but the change did not take place until August of that year.

While seated at my desk one day, a messenger from the White House made his appearance, by whom I was informed that the president desired to see me in person. When I arrived at the White House, I was immediately ushered into the president's private office, where he was seated at a desk, all alone, engaged in reading a book or a magazine. It was at an hour when he was not usually accessible to the public. He received me in a very cordial and friendly way. He informed me that there was an important matter about which he desired to talk with me—to get the benefit of my opinion and experience. He assured me of his friendly interest in the colored people. It was his determination that they should have suitable and appropriate recognition under his administration. He said he was very much opposed to the color line in politics. There was no more reason why a man should be opposed or discriminated against on account of his race than on account of his religion.

He believed it to be the duty of the Democratic party to encourage the colored voters to divide their votes, and in his opinion, the best way to do this was to accord to that race the same relative consideration, the same treatment, and to give the race the same relative recognition that is given other races and classes of which our citizenship is composed.

The party line is the only one that should be drawn. He would not appoint a colored Republican to office merely for the purpose of giving official recognition to the colored race, nor would he refuse to appoint a colored Democrat simply because he was colored. If this course was pursued and this policy adopted and adhered to by the Democratic party, the colored voters who are in harmony with that party on questions and issues about which white men usually divide, could see their way clear to vote in accordance with their convictions upon such questions and issues and not be obliged to vote against the party with which they may be in harmony, on account of that party's attitude toward them as a race. In other words, he said, it is a well-known fact that there are thousands of colored men who vote the Republican ticket at many important elections, not from choice, but from what they believe to be a necessity. If, he said, the views entertained by him on that subject should be accepted by the Democratic party, as he hoped and believed they would be, that necessity, real or imaginary, would no longer exist, and the gradual division of the colored vote would necessarily follow.

He said he had not hesitated to express himself fully, freely, and frankly with members of his own party on the subject and that he had informed them of the course he intended to pursue, but that he had been warned and advised against appointing any colored man to an office in which white women were employed.

"Now," said the president, "since you have been at the head of an important bureau in the Treasury Department during the past four years, a bureau in which a number of white women are employed as clerks, I desire very much to know what has been your experience along those lines." I informed the president that I would take pleasure in giving him the information desired. I assured him that if my occupancy of that office had been the occasion of the slightest embarrassment to anyone connected with the public service, whether in the office over which I presided or any other, that fact had never been brought to my notice. On the contrary, I had every reason to believe that no one who had previously occupied the position then held by me enjoyed the respect, goodwill, and friendship of the clerks and other employees to a greater extent than was enjoyed by me.

My occupancy of that office had more than demonstrated the fact, if such were necessary, that official position and social contact were separate and distinct. My contact with the clerks and other employees of the office was official, not social. During office hours they were subject to my direction and supervision in the discharge of their official duties, and I am pleased to say that all of them, without a single exception, have shown me that courtesy, deference, and respect due to the head of the office. After office hours they go their way and I go mine. No new social ties were created and none were broken or changed as the result of the official position occupied by me. I assured the president that, judging from my own experience, he need not have the slightest apprehension of any embarrassment, friction, or unpleasantness growing out of the appointment of a colored man of intelligence, good judgment, and wise discretion as head of any office or bureau in which white women were employed.

I could not allow the interview to close without expressing to the president my warm appreciation of his fair, just, reasonable, and dignified position in the so-called race question.

"Your position and attitude," I said, "if accepted in good faith by your party, will prove to be the solution of this mythical race problem. Although I am a pronounced Republican, yet as a colored American I am anxious to have such a condition of things brought about as will allow a colored man to be a Democrat if he so desires. I believe you have stated the case accurately when you say that thousands of colored men have voted the Republican ticket at important elections from necessity and not from choice. As a Republican, it is my hope, wish, and desire that colored as well as white men act with and vote for the candidates of that party when worthy and meritorious, but as a colored American I want them to be so situated that they can vote that way from choice and not from necessity.

"No man can be a free and independent American citizen who is obliged to sacrifice his judgment and convictions upon the altar of his personal safety and interests. The position and attitude of the Democratic party upon this so-called race question have made the colored voter a dependent and not an independent American citizen. The Republican party emancipated him from physical bondage, for which he is grateful. It remains for the Democratic party to emancipate him from political bondage for which he will be equally grateful. You are engaged, Mr. President, in a good and glorious work. As a colored man, I thank you for, and congratulate you upon, the brave and noble stand you have taken. God grant that you, as a Democrat, may have influence enough to get the Democratic party as an organization to support you in the noble stand you have so bravely taken."

The president thanked me for my expressions of goodwill and thus terminated what to me was a remarkable as well as a pleasant and most agreeable interview.

A few days later a messenger from the State Department called at my office and informed me that the secretary of state, Judge Gresham, desired to see me. Judge Gresham and I had been warm personal friends of many years' standing. He had occupied many positions of prominence and responsibility. He had been a major general in the Union army and was with

Sherman's army during that celebrated march through Georgia. He was one of the leading candidates for the presidential nomination before the National Republican Convention at Chicago in 1888, when General Benjamin Harrison of Indiana was nominated.

As stated in a previous chapter, I was a member of that convention and one of Judge Gresham's active supporters. In the campaign that followed Judge Gresham gave General Harrison his active and loyal support, but for some unaccountable reason he supported Mr. Cleveland against General Harrison in 1892. Mr. Cleveland was not only elected but, contrary to public expectation, carried the state of Illinois, a state in which Judge Gresham was known to be very popular especially among the colored people of Chicago, many of whom it was said and believed voted for Mr. Cleveland through the efforts and influence of Judge Gresham. As evidence of that fact and because Judge Gresham was known to be a very able man, Mr. Cleveland paid him the distinguished honor of appointing him to the leading position in his cabinet—that of secretary of state.

When I called at the State Department, the Judge invited me to a seat in his private office. He said there was an important matter about which he desired to talk with me. My name, he said, had been the subject of recent conversation between the president and himself. The president, he said, was well aware of the cordial and friendly relations existing between us, and the president believed that if any man could influence my action, he, Gresham, was that man.

"Now," said the judge, "the president has a very favorable opinion of you. He is anxious to have you remain at the head of the important bureau over which you are now presiding in such a creditable and satisfactory manner. But you understand that it is a political office. As anxious as the president is to retain you and as anxious as I am to have him do so, he could not do it and you could neither ask nor expect him to do it, unless you were known to be in sympathy with, and a supporter of, his administration, at least in the main. Now you know that I am not only your friend, but that I am a friend to the colored people. I know you are a Republican. So am I, but I am a Cleveland man. Cleveland is a better Republican than Harrison. In supporting Cleveland against Harrison I am no less a Republican. As your friend I would not advise you to do anything that would militate against your interests, politically or otherwise. Knowing as you do that I am not only your friend, but also a good Republican, you can at least afford to follow where I lead. I want you then to authorize me to say to the president that you are in sympathy with the main purposes of his administration as explained to you by me and that his decision to retain you in your present position will be fully and keenly appreciated by you."

In my reply I stated that while I was very grateful to the judge for his friendly interest in me and highly appreciated the president's good opinion of me, yet it would not be possible for me to consent to retain the position I then occupied upon the conditions named.

"If it is the desire of the president to have me remain in charge of that office during his administration or any part thereof, I would be perfectly willing to do so if I should be permitted to remain free from any conditions, pledges, promises, or obligations. The conditions suggested mean nothing more nor less than that I should identify myself with the Democratic party. The president has no office at his disposal, the acceptance or retention of which would or could be a sufficient inducement for me to take such a step as that. I agree with what you have said about Mr. Cleveland so far as he is personally concerned. I have every reason to believe that he has a friendly interest in the colored people and that he means to do the fair thing by them so far as it may be in his power. But he was elected as a Democrat. He is the head of a national Democratic administration. No man can be wholly independent of, nor greater than, his party. That fact is recognized in the conditions suggested in my own case.

"I don't think that Mr. Cleveland is what would be called in my part of the country a good Democrat, because I believe he is utterly devoid of race prejudice and is not in harmony with those who insist upon drawing the color line in the Democratic party. In my opinion, he is in harmony with the Democratic party only on one important public question—the tariff. On all others, the so-called race question not excepted, he is in harmony with what I believe to be genuine Republicanism. Still, as I have already stated, he was elected as a Democrat, and, since he holds that the office now occupied by me is a political one, it ought to be filled by one who is in political harmony with the administration. I am not that man. I cannot truthfully say that I am in harmony with the main purposes of the administration."

The judge remarked that my decision was a disappointment to him and he believed that I would some day regret having made it, but that he would communicate to the president the result of our interview. In spite of this, my successor, in the person of a Democrat from the state of Maine by the name of Morton, was not appointed until the following August.

37

Law Firm of Terrell and Lynch

When I retired from office in the summer of 1893, the country was in the midst of a fearful financial panic. Banks were being suspended, factories and mines were being closed, and thousands of laborers were being thrown out of employment. The products of labor, and property of every kind had depreciated in value and there was general industrial prostration throughout the country. Out of my salary as auditor I had saved some money, one thousand dollars of which I unwisely invested in the purchase of stock in a local savings bank at Washington which was under the management and control of colored men and which had been in successful operation for several years. The investment might not have been unwise if it had been made at any other time, but that proved to be the wrong time for an investment of that sort, for it turned out shortly afterwards that only financial institutions whose resources were almost unlimited could successfully tide over the panic which soon fell upon the country. While the credit and resources of the bank were sufficient to prevent its failure during the Cleveland administration, yet it was so badly crippled as a result of the panic that its failure ultimately followed.[1]

While I had made the study of law a specialty since early manhood, I had not settled down to practice that profession at any one place. In fact, I had not even made application for admission to the bar for the reason that the business in which I had been mostly engaged made it impossible for me to remain very long at any one place. In the meantime, the Mississippi legislature passed a law making the admission to the bar much more difficult than it had previously been. When, therefore, I decided to make the application, I found out that I would have to pass a very rigid examination, but I was satisfied I could easily pass it. Prior to the passage of this law, all that an applicant had to do to secure admission to the bar was to make application to any one court of record, by which a committee of about three members of the bar would be appointed to examine the applicant, and if the committee's report was favorable, the admission of the applicant would be ordered by the court and the same made or recorded.

Under the new law this was changed. It was provided that the applicant make an application to the judge of the chancery court of his district, by whom a number of written questions would be prepared covering the different subjects named in the law. The applicant was then required to give a written answer to each question, the same to be done while the court was in session and in the presence of the judge, without suggestions or assistance from anyone and without being allowed to see or examine any book or document during the progress of the examination. Whenever the court adjourned or took a

1. Lynch is referring to the Capital Savings Bank, founded in 1888. It did not close its doors until 1902. Abram Harris, *The Negro as Capitalist* (Philadelphia, 1936), pp. 104–6.

recess the papers were turned over to the judge by whom they would be retained until the court was again opened for business.

The number of questions I was required to answer was about 120, covering every important branch of the law. It took about three days, counting three hours to a day to answer them. While the questions were numerous and comprehensive, I have never believed and therefore cannot and do not charge that there was any prejudice or unfairness shown, nor that any other applicant would not have been subjected to the same sort of an examination. I was personally acquainted with the judge, Claude Pintard, by whom the questions were prepared, and I had and still have the most implicit confidence in his fairness and impartiality. After the examination was over the judge, as required by law, transmitted the papers to the judges of the state supreme court, who were to decide whether or not the applicant has passed a satisfactory examination.

About ten days later Judge Pintard informed me that the supreme court had turned me down. They were of the opinion that I had not correctly answered a sufficient number of questions to entitle me to admission to the bar. He was unable to tell me in what branch or branches I was, in the opinion of those judges, deficient. Shortly thereafter I had occasion to visit Jackson, and while there I called at the consultation room of the justices of the supreme court to find out, if possible, the facts in the case. With the chief justice, T. E. Cooper, I had been personally acquainted for a number of years. My opinion of him was favorable. I could not believe otherwise than that he would be fair, just, and impartial.

When I entered I saw him seated at a desk in a corner of the room. I approached him without hesitation. He received me in a cordial and friendly way and said he was pleased to see me. After passing the compliments of the season and engaging in a brief, friendly, and pleasant conversation, I informed him that the main purpose of my call was to find out, if possible, what the trouble was about my examination for admission to the bar. "I flatter myself," I stated, "that I know as much about the law as the average Mississippi lawyer. Consequently I cannot understand why I was turned down in the examination."

The justice looked at me, smiled, and then replied that he was very glad I had approached him on the subject. "From a careful examination of the questions and answers in your case, it was developed that you have a splendid knowledge of the elementary principles of the law. In fact, taking the questions and answers as a whole, you passed a most creditable and satisfactory examination. But there were just two subjects—equity and pleadings, and the statute laws of the state—in which in our opinion your answers were not sufficiently satisfactory to justify us in authorizing your admission to the bar at this time. I suggest, therefore, that you make another effort, brush up a little more in those two branches, and you will have no trouble in passing a satisfactory examination."

I thanked the chief justice for the information he had given me and the suggestion he had made. I informed him that I had already made up my mind to pass the examination, if it should require a dozen efforts to do so. But, since he had so kindly informed me wherein I was deficient, I was sure it would be necessary for me to make but one more effort. I informed him that with reference to the two branches referred to, the facts, no doubt, were about as he had stated. I had not given very much attention to equity pleadings and in recent years I had not kept myself well informed about the statute laws of the state. "But I shall brush up in these two branches and make another effort to pass the examination as soon as it can be done under the law." This was done.

The answers in the second examination were not only satisfactory to the supreme court justices, but the chief justice wrote me a personal congratulatory letter. In the second examination I pursued a course somewhat different from that pursued in the first one. In the first examination I made brevity an object in answering the questions. In the second I not only answered each question elaborately, but if any one of them were in the least ambiguous, I would restate the question before answering it.

In the meantime, I had formed a law partnership with Robert H. Terrell, under the firm name of "Terrell and Lynch." This firm opened an office and carried on business at Washington, D.C. Terrell was an able and brilliant young man. He was a graduate from the college department of Harvard University and the law department of Howard. He had served as chief of a division in the bureau over which I presided under the Harrison administration, the duties of which he discharged in a most creditable and satisfactory manner. It was during those years that I had become sufficiently convinced of his ability and integrity to be willing to have him associated with me in business as a partner, a decision, I am pleased to say, I have never had occasion to regret having made.

The firm continued in active business until the inauguration of President McKinley, by whom, in June of 1898 I was made a major and Paymaster of Volunteers to serve as such during the Spanish-American War. Subsequently, Mr. Terrell was also called into public service, having been appointed a justice of the peace for the District of Columbia, and later one of the judges of the municipal court of said district.

38

1896: The McKinley Campaign

THE CONTEST FOR THE REPUBLICAN NOMINATION IN 1896 commenced early in the administration of Mr. Cleveland. In 1892 the country had voted to try the experiment of a change in the fiscal policy of the government. So much had been said and written in defense and in explanation of free trade or a tariff for revenue only, especially by Mr. Cleveland, who was one of the strongest and ablest advocates of that doctrine, and who had sent a message to Congress devoted exclusively to it, that a majority of the people decided that the prosperous condition of the country at that time presented a favorable opportunity for trying the experiment of a change. But the result was more serious than had been anticipated. It seemed to be apparent, shortly thereafter, that the people were waiting with impatience for the next election day to come so as to enable them to reverse the decision they had made in 1892. In anticipation of that fact the indications were that the contest for the Republican presidential nomination in 1896 would be a spirited and lively one.

It appeared that the leading candidates would be Major William McKinley of Ohio and Speaker Thomas B. Reed of Maine. I knew both of those gentlemen personally, favorably, and well, having served with them in the national House of Representatives. With Major McKinley my relations were especially friendly and cordial. I had not only served with him as a member of Congress, where I was brought in frequent contact with him, but also as a member of the Committee on Platform and Resolutions in the National Republican Convention of 1888, of which the major was chairman, and with him as a member of the subcommittee that drafted the platform. He was also one of the few men whom I consulted, as stated in a previous chapter, and upon whose judgment and advice I finally acted at the national convention of 1884, when I consented to the use of my name for temporary chairman of that convention. Since he was a Blaine man and I was the candidate of those who were opposed to the nomination of Mr. Blaine, Major McKinley felt in honor bound to vote for the candidate who was supported by the friends of Mr. Blaine. After Major McKinley had been renominated for Congress that year, a number of the colored Republicans in his district threatened to bolt his nomination because he had voted against me for temporary chairman of the National Republican Convention, under the impression that he had done so because I was a colored man. That, of course, was not true, and, at the request of the major, I wrote a strong letter, addressed to the colored Republicans of his district in which the major's position in that matter was fully explained. It accomplished the desired purpose and the major was reelected to Congress.

Shortly after the election, while taking breakfast at the Union Station at Pittsburgh, Pennsylvania, someone approached me from the rear and put his hand on my shoulder. It was Major McKinley. He had been seated at a table near the end of the room. He saw me when I entered. He thanked me for the letter I addressed to the colored Republicans of his district, stating that it had the desired effect. I warmly congratulated him upon his reelection to Congress, but stated it was my sincere hope that a much higher honor than a seat in Congress was in store for him.

Early in 1895 I was one of the few with whom Major McKinley talked and confidentially consulted with reference to his prospective candidacy for the Republican presidential nomination the next year. On the occasion of a visit which the major made to Washington in April 1895 I called on him at his hotel to pay my respects. He received me cordially and said he was especially pleased to have me call on him. He frankly informed me, in the course of the conversation, of his ambition about the presidency and stated that I was one of those upon whom he believed he could depend for support to gratify his ambition in that direction. I informed him that, aside from my personal interest in him and friendship for him, I believed he was the strongest and most available man for the nomination. I was satisfied that the tariff was to be the dominating issue of the campaign, and since the law that bore his name embodied the principles upon which the party was to appeal to the country, it seemed to me that the author of that law was the most available man to put forward as the party leader. I therefore assured the major that he would not only have the benefit of whatever influence I could command, but I felt safe in promising him that he would have practically a solid delegation from Mississippi.

But there were two reasons why I did not desire to have my preference made public until later in the campaign. They are as follows: first, Southern Republicans had been accused of trying to dictate the nomination of candidates for the presidency, to whose election they could contribute nothing. That had been one of the alleged reasons for several efforts to change the basis of representation in the national conventions of the party, with a view to reducing the representation in said conventions from the Southern states. On that point I was somewhat sensitive and was anxious to avoid having the Southern delegates placed in the attitude of attempting to force upon the party a candidate against the wishes and votes of a majority of the delegates from states upon which we must depend to elect the ticket.

I did not believe, therefore, that Southern Republicans ought to be in a hurry about proclaiming their preferences for the Republican presidential nomination. I further stated that I did not want the major to suspect that my purpose was to find out, if possible, who would likely be the choice of the party and then fall in line in support of that man. It had been a rule with me in previous campaigns to make a selection without regard to the probability of success at the convention and stand by the candidate of my choice until a nomination was made.

"That," I said, "is the course I intend to pursue this time; hence, I have no hesitation in telling you freely and frankly what my position is.

"The second reason is there are two factions in the party in my state, one represented by Mr. James Hill, the other supposed to be represented by me. This division is not serious, but it is serious enough to deserve some notice.

"I am inclined to believe that Mr. Hill is so intense in his opposition to me that he will probably be opposed to anyone whose candidacy I am known, suspected, or believed to favor. I therefore suggest that Mr. Hill be sounded, and if possible, committed before my preference is made known. In that event there would be no danger whatever of a divided delegation. Otherwise it might be possible for him to control the delegates from one and possibly two of the seven congressional districts."

The major was very much pleased with my plan and endorsed my position fully and assured me that in the event of his nomination and election no colored man in the country would be closer to, or be more influential with, the administration than myself. That the major was honest and sincere and meant every word he said on that occasion I have every reason not only to believe but to know. That this was not done in my case to the extent that he expected, intended, and desired, especially since every promise made by me had been kept and redeemed in perfect good faith, was due to circumstances which subsequent events made it impossible for him to wholly control.

It developed that in his candidacy for the nomination, he, like Harrison in 1892, was opposed by nearly every party leader of national prominence. Senator Lodge was active and aggressive in the support of Speaker Reed. Mr. Platt of New York, was working faithfully to secure the nomination of ex-Vice-President Levi P. Morton. In order to control the delegation from his own state and to prevent the same going to McKinley, Senator Quay of Pennsylvania announced himself as a candidate. Efforts were also made to have other states bring out "favorite sons," such, for instance, as [Shelby M.] Cullom in Illinois, [Charles] Manderson in Nebraska, [C. K.] Davis in Minnesota, and [William B.] Allison in Iowa; but the fact was soon developed that the popular tide in favor of McKinley was so strong that his defeat for the nomination was well nigh impossible.

But before that stage of the canvass was reached, the major had many moments of doubt and despondency, which at times almost reached the point of hopeless despair. The one upon whom he could look and upon whom he could depend during those anxious and doubtful moments for encouragement, hope, and loyalty was Hon. Mark A. Hanna, who was looked upon at that time as a novice in the conduct and management of political campaigns. But, novice as he was, or supposed to be, he brought McKinley's campaign for the nomination to a successful termination, which brought him into national prominence as a successful party leader. Of course, Major Mc-

Kinley's own personal popularity, as well as favorable conditions, contributed largely to this result. Still, it is no doubt true that it was the skill and ability displayed by Mr. Hanna as a leader and manager that made Mr. McKinley's nomination possible. Then, the beauty of it was that Mr. Hanna was not actuated by any selfish motive or purpose. He was a man of great wealth and did not care for any political distinction or official recognition for himself. It was known that he would not be an applicant for and could not be induced to accept any office that would be at the disposal of the administration he was trying to bring into existence. His chief ambition seemed to have been to make McKinley president of the United States. How well he succeeded in this the reader of these lines need not here be reminded. That Mr. Hanna should be allowed to wield a powerful and potential influence in the disposition of the patronage by an administration which he had been so instrumental in bringing into existence was not only natural but was to be expected. That such conditions would be developed as would produce that situation was not anticipated when the interview between Major McKinley and myself took place at Washington in April 1895.

A few weeks after that interview, Mr. Hanna passed through Washington en route to his summer home in the state of Georgia. While he was at Washington, I accidentally met him just as he was about to enter the elevator at the Senate wing of the Capitol. He said he was glad to see me. He desired, he said, to have a talk with me and requested me to call on him at his hotel that evening. I did so and had quite a pleasant interview with him, but it was evidently not as satisfactory to him as he had expected and desired. He wanted Major McKinley nominated for the presidency the following year, and he wanted me to promise him then and there that I would, from that time on, work and use my influence to bring about that result. I was not as communicative nor as confidential with him as I had been with Major McKinley. In view of subsequent developments, this was, perhaps, a mistake, but I did not think so at the time. He was not then such an important man as subsequent events made him. At any rate, I did not deem it necessary or advisable, at that early date, to take him or anyone else except Major McKinley himself fully into my confidence.

There was nothing at that early date to indicate that future developments would make him the authoritative organ, spokesman, and mouthpiece of the administration in the event that the man of his choice should be at its head. In this interview, therefore, I gave him no positive indication as to what my action would be, but simply promised him that I would take the matter under advisement and when I had arrived at a decision that fact would be communicated to him. I indicated a friendly interest in, and partiality for, Major McKinley, and assured Mr. Hanna that he would hear from me in ample time to enable the necessary steps to be taken to protect the major's interests in Mississippi, regardless of my own decision and action.

About two months later, or just before I left Washington for my home in Mississippi, I wrote to Mr. Hanna and informed him of my decision to support Major McKinley. I further stated that I would soon leave Washington for Mississippi and that it was my purpose to make an active canvass of the state in the interest of Major McKinley's candidacy. In his reply he expressed himself as being very much pleased with what I had written and that in consequence thereof he was satisfied there would be a solid McKinley delegation from Mississippi. Letters frequently passed between us, but in no one of them did he give the slightest intimation of any trade, bargain, agreement, or understanding between Mr. Hill and himself. While Hill and his friends were quite active in their support of McKinley, that made no difference with me. In fact, I was pleased, accepting it as an indication that there would be a harmonious convention and a solid and uncontested delegation for Major McKinley.

In the early part of 1896 it came to my knowledge that

shortly after Mr. Hanna arrived at his Georgia home the year before, he sent for Mr. Hill and entered into an arrangement or agreement with him by which Hill was to secure a McKinley delegation to the national convention from Mississippi. This Mr. Hill thought was his opportunity to get rid of both Bruce and me. That we, or either of us, should be for or against McKinley made no difference with him. His purpose was to personally dominate the party organization in the state and succeed himself on the national committee.

When the fact was brought to his notice that I was supporting McKinley and that there was no reason why we should not work in harmony and both be sent as delegates to the national convention from the state at large, his reply was that if anyone claiming to be a friend of his should make or entertain such a suggestion as that, it would be accepted as evidence of unfriendliness to him and to his interest. He would not consider such a suggestion for one moment. There was not room enough on the delegation from the state at large, he declared, for both Lynch and himself. One or the other must be defeated and his friends and supporters must govern themselves accordingly. No one, he declared, could be favorable to Lynch and at the same time be a friend and supporter of his. He felt that he could afford to be thus independent and defiant on account of the assurances he had received of the support and backing of the national McKinley organization, financially and otherwise.

That Hill received material financial assistance through and from that organization was self-evident. Without it his organization in the state would have amounted practically to nothing. The fact that no requests for assistance came from anyone connected with the Lynch organization had a tendency, no doubt, to confirm the impression that Hill endeavored to create upon Mr. Hanna's mind that my friends and I were not honest and sincere in our support of McKinley. Mr. Hanna knew what the demands had been on the other side and it was difficult at first for him to understand why there was no necessity for any assistance from the other.

He found out later, as he frankly confessed to me, just what the facts were: that McKinley's interests were not involved in the controversy, that the contest was of a local nature, merely for the control of the party organization in the state and for membership of the national committee. If, under such circumstances, I had obtained of him financial assistance in electing a McKinley delegation, it would have been obtaining money under false pretenses; hence, no such requests were made at any time. Still, having made a deal with Mr. Hill, Mr. Hanna felt that he was in honor bound to do what he had promised. He was a man whose word was as good as his bond. It was a fact well known that he never violated a pledge and never failed to redeem a promise. Even when convinced that he had made a bad bargain, he would not allow that fact to furnish an excuse to violate it.

He subsequently talked with me about matters in Mississippi with absolute frankness and candor. His deal or bargain with Hill he admitted was a mistake, especially in view of the fact that it resulted in a grave injustice, for a while at least, to me and my friends, but for that mistake on his part I was not wholly blameless. Had I been wholly frank and as communicative with him when he met me at Washington in 1895 as he afterwards found out I had been with Major McKinley, the deal or bargain with Hill would not have been made, at least to the extent that it was. Both of us, therefore, were somewhat to blame. He for having been too hasty, and I for not having been more frank and candid in the conversation that took place with him at Washington in 1895. He assured me, however, that his deal or bargain with Hill did not go so far as to bind him to do nothing for me and my friends. He would never allow himself to be bound to that extent by anyone. When, therefore, he had done all for Hill and his friends that he believed he obligated himself to do, he would then be both able and willing to render substantial justice to me and my friends. He requested me to be patient and assured me that at the end I would have no occasion to complain. His perfect good faith in what he then declared and promised subsequent events more than confirmed.

Mr. Hanna was not only one of the McKinley managers that found out, after investigation, that a grave injustice had been done through the deal or bargain that was made with Mr. Hill. Hon. Charles Dick, who was one of Mr. Hanna's able assistants, and Judge A. C. Thompson, who represented the McKinley interests before the national committee and the Committee on Credentials of the national convention, also came to the same conclusion, and therefore did all in their power, in cooperation with Mr. Hanna, to see that substantial justice was ultimately done. In fact, I have every reason not only to believe, but to know that it was largely through the efforts and influence of Mr. Dick and Judge Thompson that Mr. Hanna was convinced of the mistake he had made.

The president was determined, of course, that his promises to me should not be wholly repudiated. That they were not, at first, carried out to the extent expected, desired, and intended was due to the subsequent developments which placed him under such deep obligations to Mr. Hanna that he felt in honor bound to redeem and carry out in perfect good faith every one of the pledges made and the obligations incurred by Mr. Hanna so far as the disposition of the patronage was concerned, since he was satisfied that it was chiefly through the efforts of Mr. Hanna that his nomination and election had been made possible. For this he could neither be blamed nor censured, but on the contrary, heartily commended.

39

Contest for Mississippi Delegates

SHORTLY AFTER I HAD FINISHED MY TOUR OF THE STATE IN THE interest of Major McKinley's candidacy for the Republican presidential nomination, the fight for delegates to the state and national convention commenced in earnest. Mr. Hill had made it known to his friends and supporters that Bruce and Lynch should both be eliminated from the future politics of the state, consequently neither should be elected a delegate to the national convention. It was not long, therefore, before the fact was made plain to me that I had before me a very bitter fight. It was to be a life-and-death struggle. I knew that Hill and his friends had not the means with which to make very much of a fight, and yet it was apparent that he was being supplied with whatever was needed in that direction. The first thought that occurred to me was that he was not loyal to McKinley, but that he was doing with McKinley as he had done with Harrison in 1892—claiming to be for McKinley while working at the same time to secure a delegation favorable to some other candidate and receiving assistance from that quarter.

It did not occur to me that Mr. Hanna, who knew my position and attitude, could be induced to pursue such a course, but it afterwards developed that such was the understanding and agreement between Mr. Hill and himself. Mr. Hanna was honestly of the opinion that in aiding Hill he was promoting the interests of McKinley. But, let the facts be what they may, I soon found out that, in consequence of this outside assistance Hill and his friends were receiving, I had a very much harder fight before me than had been anticipated. But the fight had to be made. In consequence of Hill's attitude there could be no compromise. The fact that I and my friends and supporters were willing to compromise was accepted as evidence of weakness on our part. Hill wanted no compromise and would not consider or entertain a suggestion looking to that end. His decision was that the fight must be carried to the bitter end. But this was because he believed he had every advantage. He not only had ample financial assistance, without which nothing could have been done by him, but through an act of Providence he had secured a majority of the state committee.

When the committee was reorganized, growing out of the fight of 1892, an equal number of members had been taken from each faction in the formation of the new committee, the officers of the new committee being apportioned in the same way: the Lynch faction, securing the chairman, a Hill man having been made vice-chairman. In the meantime, three of the members belonging to the Lynch faction died. In accordance with the custom, the chairman made temporary appointments to fill the vacancies thus created. Since the newly appointed members could not vote to confirm their own appointments, this gave the Hill faction a majority. The appointments made by the chairman on vacation were then rejected and three members belonging to the Hill faction were elected in their stead.

The committee as thus organized issued the call for the state convention. It also created a subcommittee to pass upon the credentials and prepare the roll of delegates to the state convention. This was the committee that was to do the necessary work. It was carefully selected with that end in view. The Hill men, of course, were very happy. Being in control of the state committee, they felt that the victory for them had been more than half won. But my friends were a large majority of the delegates to the state convention. That we might be counted out by the state committee was not only possible, but probable, especially if the majority should be small. Our purpose, therefore, was to make the majority so large that the counting out business could not be easily done. We therefore went before the people with a determination to win, but we knew it meant not only hard work but something more. Money had to be raised. Where was it to come from? That was the question. We could not honorably make any demands upon the McKinley national organization because McKinley's interests were not involved, and yet money had to be raised if we expected to win. The other side had a weekly newspaper published at Vicksburg, which was about the center of the Black Belt. It was necessary that we have one there also. But this required money. Not very much but some.

I gave directions to my friends throughout the state to go to work, organize and carry the convention, and leave all other matters to me. I assured them that I would find a way to make ends meet. Mr. Bruce was engaged in the lecture business and therefore could give no personal assistance to the cause. Consequently, the management of the campaign was left entirely to me. I knew that we not only could, but must win. The friendship and support of a weekly newspaper published at Vicksburg was secured. The campaign was not only conducted by me from my home at Natchez, but I was also a frequent contributor to the editorial columns of the paper. But, as already stated, money had to be raised. Some of my friends made liberal contributions, a few of them being friends who lived outside of the state, but the money thus raised was not half enough. I had given instructions to my friends and supporters to proceed and leave all other matters to me. I was obliged to make my word good in some way, but there was only one way in which it could be done, and that was to raise the money myself, out of my own resources.

I owned two cotton plantations. They were worth more than I needed. The money was raised. In consequence of the encumbrance placed upon them at that time for the purpose stated, I was obliged, ultimately, to let them go. In that fight, therefore, I sacrificed the greater part of the accumulations and savings of a lifetime. But it was willingly and cheerfully done. While I regretted that there should have been a condition of affairs which rendered this action on my part necessary, still I have never regretted that the emergency was met in that way. If I had it to do over again, the same course would be pursued, especially in view of subsequent developments which resulted therefrom and to which allusion will later be made.

When the election for delegates to the state convention was over and the smoke of the battle had cleared away, it was found that my friends had elected a large majority of the delegates, but the Hill faction, having control of the state committee, did not concede their defeat. They depended upon that committee to undo the work that had been done at the primaries.

The first step in that direction was to get up bogus contests in nearly all the large counties in which Lynch delegates had been elected. Even in my own county, Adams, where the election was practically unanimous, a few persons were hired to hold a private meeting in a barroom and go through the form of electing a contesting delegation to the state convention. In this way the committee found that it had sufficient material to work upon to enable it to proceed with the election, practically, of a new convention while engaged in the preparation of what was claimed to be a roll of the delegates. This they proceeded to do and thought they had done, but a majority even of the subcommittee that had been appointed for that purpose refused to go as far as Hill desired to have them go. This subcommittee threw out and refused to entertain and consider some of the fictitious contests that had been made for the occasion, the one from my own county being among the number.

But they thought they had enough without these, but in this they were mistaken, for it turned out that on the roll, even as thus agreed upon and adopted by the full committee, the Lynch faction still had a majority. It was small, but large enough to answer the purpose. The discovery of that fact created consternation. Something had to be done and done quickly. The Democratic officials were appealed to for assistance and advice. It was well known that in this contest the Democrats were in sympathy with the Hill faction. This was due to the fact that in my canvass of the state I had bitterly attacked and denounced the new constitution under which the colored men of the state had been disfranchised, while the Hill faction had refrained from any criticism of that instrument. The vice-chairman of the state committee [Isaiah T. Montgomery], who belonged to the Hill faction, was the one solitary colored member of the constitutional convention who had spoken in favor of, and voted for, that instrument. That the Democrats should be in sympathy with the Hill faction, therefore, was perfectly natural.

As a result of the conference with the Democratic officials, including the governor of the state, the following plan was agreed upon: first, the right of the chairman of the state committee to call the convention to order and preside over the same if the temporary organization should be refused. Second, the vice-chairman should enter the hall in which the convention was to meet at least half an hour ahead of the time fixed for the convention to be called to order and take possession of the same in the name of the state committee. Third, admission to the hall was to be by ticket, the tickets to be given out by some mysterious person who could be located only by those whose presence was desired. Fourth, police protection was to be furnished by the mayor of the town, the police being instructed to allow no one to enter the hall who could not produce a ticket of admission.

About ten minutes before the time fixed for the convention to be called to order, the Lynch delegates, constituting a clear majority of those whose names were upon the roll that had been prepared and adopted by the state committee, marched to the hall in a solid body with the chairman of the state committee at the head of the column. We found the door in charge of a policeman who informed us of his instructions and by whom we were denied admission to the hall. We then saw just what the scheme was. When the policeman refused to allow the chairman of the committee to enter the hall, it was plain to us that the purpose was to exclude a sufficient number of Lynch men, including the chairman of the committee, to enable the Hill men, though in the minority, to organize the convention and that the police force of the city was to be used for that purpose.

The chairman, therefore, requested the delegates to follow him to another hall, in which he said the regular convention would be held. This was done. The convention, of course, seated those that had been unseated by the state committee, but the convention, even as thus constituted, contained a majority of those whose names appeared on the roll that had been prepared by the state committee. But the result was two conventions and two sets of delegates to the national convention from the state at large.

Fighting the Hill Organization

TWO SETS OF DELEGATES HAVING BEEN ELECTED TO THE NAtional convention, the fight for recognition was then to be made before the national committee. In this fight my friends were also placed at a disadvantage for two reasons: first, because Mr. Hill was a member of that committee which placed him in the position of being one of judges to pass upon the merits of his own case. Second, because the fact was afterwards developed that the recognition of his delegation was one of the conditions of his deal or agreement with Mr. Hanna. Since the Hanna machine controlled the national committee, the recognition of the Hill delegation was, of course, expected to be the result of the contest.

I had occasion to visit Washington before the meeting of the

In the original manuscript there is a space of several lines at this point. In view of the fact that the author did not provide a chapter numbered 40, it may be assumed that this is the beginning of chapter 40.

committee, or shortly after the election of the Mississippi delegates. Major McKinley, having seen the announcement of my arrival at Washington, wrote me, expressing a desire to have me come to Canton to talk with him in person about the situation in Mississippi. Of course, the invitation was accepted and I left the next day for Canton. The major received me cordially. He said he wanted to learn directly from me the actual situation in my state. His information was that both factions were favorable to him. If this were true, he could not see why they could not come to an agreement and thus prevent a divided or double delegation.

I then went over the situation in detail and explained to the satisfaction of the major just what the facts and conditions were. I assured him that the presidency was not involved in the contest and that he was sure to get the vote of the delegation, regardless of the result of the contest. He was pleased and gratified to learn just what the facts were and that he was sure to have the support of the delegation from the state in any event. He repeated his expressions of gratitude for my friendship and support, and reassured me of his determination, in the event of his nomination and election, to see that satisfactory and appropriate recognition be accorded me and my friends. When I arose to bid him good-bye, I remarked that it might be just as well for me to run over to Cleveland and see Mr. Hanna before returning to Washington.

"No," replied the major, "it is not at all necessary for you to see Mr. Hanna. You have seen and talked with me. That is sufficient."

"All right," I said, "I shall go directly from here to Washington."

The major evidently knew about the understanding between Mr. Hanna and Mr. Hill, and knowing Mr. Hanna's plain, blunt way of expressing himself, he was no doubt apprehensive that should an interview take place at that time between Mr.

Hanna and myself, it might bring out some embarrassing facts. Hence, he advised against it. Then again, he was presumed to be, as he strongly intimated, the important factor in the case anyway, and since his position would be, in the event of his nomination, conclusive and authoritative, it was useless to bring a third party into it.

When the committee meeting took place to pass upon the contests and Judge Thompson of Ohio appeared to represent the Hill delegation, the true situation was for the first time made plain to me. But I could see in Judge Thompson's attitude that, so far as the Mississippi case was concerned, his heart was not in the work. He was selected to represent the McKinley interests in all contests before the committee. His connection with the Mississippi case, therefore, was more in the nature of form than otherwise. Still, it was his presence in that capacity, rather than what he said and did, that gave the Hill delegation a standing and prestige it otherwise would not have had. When the cases had all been decided by the committee, the Hill delegates had been seated from the state at large and from four of the seven districts, the Lynch delegates being seated from the other three. This, under the circumstances that developed at the hearing, was at least one district more than we expected.

Of course, McKinley was nominated, but we were all very much surprised to find that one of the Hill delegates voted for Senator Quay instead of McKinley. This delegate, like all the others on the Hill slate, had been elected through the aid of the Hanna machine, with the understanding that he would support McKinley. This vote was both a surprise and a disappointment, especially to Mr. Hanna. It was one that Mr. Hill could not satisfactorily explain. It was one of the things that contributed to Mr. Hill's political downfall, to which allusion will hereafter be made. Of course, the Hill men were in high glee. Of the eighteen delegates from the state, twelve of the

Hill men had been seated, and Hill had succeeded himself on the national committee.

When he left the convention city for home, he had a Pullman sleeping car for the exclusive use of himself and friends, or such of them as he saw fit to invite, while the discouraged, downhearted, and defeated Lynch men had to find their way home as best they could. It did not occur to Mr. Hill at that time that the attention then being paid him and the material aid and assistance he was receiving was temporary and for that occasion only and that he was not strong enough to stand in the future on his own merits without the assistance of such men as Bruce and myself and that without assistance his downfall was only a question of time. But he had to live only about one year longer to have that fact made plain to him. But when he realized it, it was too late for him to be saved. When he at last saw the error of his way and realized the grave mistake he had made he was both willing and anxious to accept the olive branch of friendship and peace which he had so scornfully rejected in 1896. He held out and maintained an independent and defiant attitude as long as he could. It was not until he plainly saw the handwriting on the wall that he expressed a desire to make terms and have the old order of things restored. But it was too late. The die had been cast and cruel destiny, which had taken advantage of the situation he himself had created, had rendered a decision which could neither be changed nor reversed. Like Haman of old, he was the first to be executed on the gallows which he had prepared for others.

But when we returned from the national convention of 1896, there was nothing to indicate that anything of that sort was even a remote possibility. On the contrary, the indications all pointed in the other direction. With the flush of victory beaming from their pleasing countenances, the Hill men returned to their homes with banners flying as conquering heroes.

"Nothing," they said, "remains for the Lynch men to do but

to disband their organization and gracefully accept the situation, for the victory of the Hill faction is full and complete. "But, it is immaterial with us," they said, "what action the Lynch organization may take. If they do not vote to disband, the disintegration and dissolution of their organization will only be a question of time, since the Hill organization has been fully recognized by the national committee, of which body Mr. Hill is a member."

Some of the Lynch men had, while en route home, hoisted the flag of surrender and announced their decision to accept what had been done as final and that it was their purpose to recognize the Hill organization as the regular one. As soon as I reached the state, I issued a call for the representative men of my organization to meet me at Jackson, the state capital, on a day therein named, for consultation and decision as to what should be done. When the conference met, every man, with three or four exceptions, whose presence was expected and desired, was present. The exceptions were those who had already decided and declared, upon their own responsibility, to give in their allegiance to the Hill organization.

As soon as the conference was called to order and an organization was perfected, all eyes were turned towards me and the call came from every part of the hall for me to come forward and give my opinion and advice as to what course should be pursued. I promptly responded to the call, for it was just what I expected and desired, because I had already fully matured the plan in my own mind which I intended to advise them to pursue, but which I had made known to no one.

I commenced by telling them that we had the best opportunity that had yet been presented. The Hill organization had already placed an electoral ticket in the field, but everyone knew that the state, under existing conditions, was hopelessly Democratic. If it were otherwise, I might advise the adoption of a different line of action. But under the circumstances we had everything to gain and nothing to lose by putting out an electoral ticket of our own. I stated that if they would place me at the head of the ticket, I would make a thorough canvass of the state and endeavor to bring to the polls on election day as large a Republican vote as possible. We had made the claim that we represented a majority of the Republicans of the state and that we had elected a large majority of the delegates to the recent state convention. We now had an opportunity to prove what we had claimed.

It is true the election would be conducted and controlled by the Democrats who, for reasons already stated, were known to be in sympathy with the Hill organization and would, therefore, give that organization every possible advantage. Still, we should make the fight just the same. It was also a fact that could not be denied, that in consequence of what had been done by the national convention and the national committee, there were some Republicans who acted with and supported the Lynch organization at the primaries who would now support the ticket which represented the Hill organization, simply on the ground of party regularity. After taking all of these things into consideration, I was still of the opinion that we could poll for our ticket a large majority of the Republican votes, especially if a thorough and active canvass should be made, such as it was my purpose to make if they desired to have me do so. After a number of others had spoken, all in support of my position, the plan was thus recommended and was unanimously adopted. The electoral ticket was then and there nominated with my name at the head.

The Hill men pretended to make light of what had been done, but they were evidently somewhat worried about it, so much so that Mr. Hill made an earnest appeal to his friend and backer, the Democratic governor of the state, to take a hand in the fight, which he decided to do. Because I had been engaged several years in the practice of my profession, law, at Washington, D.C., this official made that fact the basis for a public declaration that I was no longer a citizen of the state and was therefore ineligible to be elected to or hold any office under the constitution and laws of the state. He therefore instructed his Board of Election Commissioners in my county to erase my name from the registry list of the county, which was promptly done. It was thought, hoped, and believed among the Hill men that this would result in my withdrawal from the ticket if not the withdrawal of the whole ticket itself. But the scheme failed as will be more fully explained in a subsequent chapter.

But before I commenced my canvass of the state, I received a pressing invitation from the National Campaign Committee to take part in the campaign in support of the national ticket, especially in the states of Tennessee and West Virginia. This invitation I felt that I could not afford to decline, but it was accepted upon condition that I should be allowed to devote the last ten days of the canvass in my own state. This was done, but the time was too short to enable me to make a thorough canvass such as I had contemplated. My efforts, therefore, were necessarily confined to the larger towns located on the lines of the principal railroads.

When the election was over and every county in the state had been heard from, it was found that the Lynch electoral ticket had polled a decided majority of the Republican votes in five of the seven congressional districts, and that too, according to the official returns as canvassed, counted, and returned by Mr. Hill's friends and sympathizers, the Democrats. In two districts the Hill ticket had a slight lead. I am satisfied that, had I made a thorough canvass of the state, as had been first contemplated, the Lynch ticket would have polled a majority of the Republican votes in every district in the state.

Another conference composed of the representative members of the Lynch organization was held shortly after the election. This conference was one of jollification and congratulation. We felt that we were in a much better position before the administration and the country than demonstrated and proved. We were therefore in a position to make our demands upon the administration for appropriate and satisfactory recognition. For that purpose a special committee was appointed. We then adjourned, feeling that a substantial victory had been won and that we had by no means made a hopeless fight.

McKinley Appointments: The Postal Service

In about a week or ten days after the president had signed the letter addressed to the postmaster general with reference to fourth-class postmasters, I received a message requesting me to call at the White House. When I arrived, the president handed me a slate containing the names of six persons that had been tentatively agreed upon for six of the most important offices in the state. Three of the six, stated the president, were represented as belonging to what is known as the Lynch organization.

"It is with reference to that fact and about those three that I wish to consult you. I have promised to give you and your friends appropriate recognition. I not only intend to do this, but to do it in a way that will be entirely satsifactory to you and your associates. In other words, in making selections from your organization, only such men as are known to be acceptable to, and the choice of, that organization will be selected. I am reliably informed that one or two of your men have deserted you. I assume that you do not care to have one of those appointed and accredited to your organization. I therefore want you to read this list and tell me whether or not the three that are represented as being identified with your organization are acceptable to, and the choice of, that organization for the positions for which they are slated. You are neither expected nor asked to express an opinion about the other three, or any one of them. It is with reference to your own friends that you are asked to give information and express an opinion."

After looking over the list carefully, I handed it back to the president, stating that so far as the three Lynch men were concerned, they were not only satisfactory but that they were the men selected by the organization for the position for which they were slated. The president was pleased to hear this, remarking at the same time that had it been otherwise, their names would have been erased, and others selected by, or acceptable to, the organization would have been selected. He also stated that he would have Mr. Hill call the next day so as to consult him about the other three. After thanking the president cordially for the courtesy and consideration he had thus shown me, I bade him good-bye.

I then approached an intimate friend, who was officially connected with the White House staff, and requested him to report to me the substance of the interview that would take place the next day between the president and Mr. Hill, which was done. This was merely to satisfy my curiosity.

When Mr. Hill made his appearance, the president handed him the same slate and made substantially the same remarks he made to me the day before. But this was not what Mr. Hill wanted. Instead of giving the president his opinion and advice with reference to the three men about whom his opinion was asked and desired, he commenced by making a vigorous protest against the three Lynch men, but he could plainly see that the president was not in a frame of mind to listen with patience to any objections he was disposed to make of those men. Of course, the three men belonging to his own organization were satisfactory and acceptable to him, but the fact that the president had decided to divide six of the best and most important offices in the state equally between the two organizations was to him a serious blow and a painful disappointment. He could not fail to see the force and effect of this action, for it was thus made plain that it was the settled determination of the president to give neither organization any advantage over the other, but to recognize both on an equal footing. This course was strictly pursued, for when all of the important appointments in the state had been made, it was found that both organizations had about an equal representation.

While the candidate supported by the Hill organization had been appointed postmaster at Natchez, my own home, a man belonging to the Lynch organization had been appointed postmaster at Jackson, Mr. Hill's home. While a Hill man had been appointed United States attorney for the southern judicial district, a Lynch man had been appointed United States attorney for the northern judicial district. While a Hill man had been appointed United States marshal for the northern judicial district, a Lynch man had been appointed United States marshal for the southern judicial district. This proportion was subsequently maintained throughout the state, even in appointments to the most unimportant positions. It came to my knowledge shortly after the first slate was prepared, about which Mr. Hill and I were consulted, that that slate, as well as subsequent ones, was prepared by the president's intimate friend, Judge A. C. Thompson. He acted under the personal directions of the president and saw that the president's wishes were faithfully carried out in every particular. In the preparation of those slates Judge Thompson did not personally consult either Mr. Hill or myself. But he consulted other members of both organizations, from whom he obtained accurate and reliable information about the choice and selections of each organization. When every office in the state had been filled and every one outside of the state to which a Mississippian had been appointed, it was found that no deserter from either organization had been recognized.

42

McKinley Appointments: Army Paymaster Lynch

MR. HILL WAS AN APPLICANT FOR, AND EXPECTED TO BE appointed to, the office of Collector of Internal Revenue for the district composed of the states of Mississippi and Louisiana with headquarters at New Orleans. But it so happened that his own appointment to any particular position was not among the things for which he had secured a direct pledge or promise from Mr. Hanna. Shortly before the Collector of Internal Revenue for the district referred to was appointed, Mr. Hill received an intimation fom a reliable source that his ambition in that direction, in all probability, would not be gratified. This created a great deal of apprehension and alarm at his headquarters. A few days after that, I happened to meet one of his loyal supporters, who insisted upon conversing with me upon the situation, especially with reference to Mr. Hill and myself. He remarked that something was evidently going on that he could not understand and did not like. Nearly every office in the state, he said, had been filled, and that too by men who had been selected in about equal numbers from both organizations, but nothing thus far had been done for the leader of either organization, and no one seemed to know what, if anything, was in contemplation for either of them. He very much desired to know whether or not I was in possession of any information along these lines.

"Yes," I replied, "I can give you all the information you want, but I shall only give you such as I think you are entitled to and ought to have. In the first place, Mr. Hill will not be appointed Collector of Internal Revenue. That office will go to a white Republican from Louisiana."

"You surprise me very much," he replied; "are you absolutely sure of the accuracy of your information on that point? Mr. Hill and his friends have never doubted for one moment that he would be appointed to that office. If he fails to get it, it will be a great disappointment—in fact, a death blow. We cannot understand it. You surely must be mistaken about it."

I assured him in the most positive manner that I was not only not mistaken, but that I knew absolutely and positively whereof I spoke. I further informed him that Mr. Hill might have been, and probably would have been, appointed to the position for which he was an applicant, had he been supported, as in the past, by Mr. Bruce and myself. But for reasons which he knew all about, this influence and support he could not get. On the contrary, it was against him. I further informed him that he ought to know that the administration was, in point of fact, under no obligation whatever to Mr. Hill, because he had done nothing more than to allow himself to be used as one of the mediums through whom certain things had been accomplished and certain results had been obtained, or believed to have been obtained, by Mr. Hanna's national organization. To do the work assigned him he had been amply supplied with whatever assistance he claimed he needed. At the time this was done it was believed that no misrepresentations were being made, but that the assistance thus rendered was used in good faith in the interests of the candidacy of Major McKinley. The fact has since been made plain that this was not true and that deception was practiced and misrepresentations were made.

I further remarked that in spite of that fact, Mr. Hill would be appropriately recognized, simply because Mr. Hanna felt somewhat favorably inclined towards him, but he would not get the office for which he was an applicant. I was then asked what office in my opinion he would get. I replied that he would probably be tendered one of the land offices at Jackson, Mississippi, and furthermore, I remarked that he would be very fortunate to get that.

"But," replied this gentleman, "our organization has endorsed another man for that office and we look for his appointment. If what you say is true, our plans will be entirely upset and we will be completely at sea."

"I cannot help that," I replied, "you will soon find out that I am not mistaken and that I know whereof I speak."

"Well, what about yourself? What is going to be done for you?" I informed him that I had thus far given no attention to anything personal to myself, that my efforts had been, and would continue to be, to secure satisfactory and appropriate recognition of my friends. Until this was done, no efforts would be made in my own behalf. This ended our interview.

A few days later the appointment of Collector of Internal Revenue for the district composed of Mississippi and Louisiana was announced. It was a white Republican from Louisiana. Among the last appointments announced for the state of Mississippi appeared the name of James Hill, for Receiver of Public Moneys at Jackson, Mississippi. This was great disappointment to Mr. Hill, but he was made to understand that it was that or nothing, and since he was very much in need of something, he was obliged to take what he could get and be thankful for it.

In the meantime my warm and loyal friend ex-Senator B. K. Bruce had been appointed Register of the United States Treasury, the most lucrative, important, and dignified position to which any colored man had thus far been appointed. As a result of this appointment, Mr. Hill began to see the handwriting on the wall. He began to see and realize for the first time the hopelessness and helplessness of his own situation. Mr. Bruce was one of the strongest and most influential colored men that our country had produced–able, courteous, respectful, and dignified, yet bold, outspoken, and aggressive in the advocacy and defense of what he believed to be right. He enjoyed and merited the unlimited confidence of his own people and the respect and favorable opinion of all who had the good fortune to know him, without regard to race or politics.

No Republican national administration would be complete that did not have B. K. Bruce officially connected with it. His great ability, his effective influence, and his wide experience were needed and sought after. He was not only the able head of the important bureau over which he presided with dignity, but his influence and services were recognized and felt in many different directions. In fact, he was frequently consulted and his opinion solicited upon many public questions, not only by cabinet members, but by the president as well. Mr. Bruce's official connection with the administration made it unnecessary for me to put forth my efforts in my own behalf. He was not only my friend, but he was entirely familiar with every detail of the political situation. He knew that the president had assured me that I should, in some way, be officially connected with this administration. It was his determination that the president's wishes in this respect should be carried into effect without further delay.

It was now late in the year and it was necessary for me to return to Mississippi to give personal attention to my business interests. I therefore left my affairs at the national capital in the hands of my friend, Mr. Bruce, and returned to my Mississippi home. I had been there only a short while when I received a letter from Mr. Bruce in which I was informed that he had just had an interview with the president, at which it was decided what office I was to have. It was the collectorship of taxes for the District of Columbia. He deemed it important that I return to Washington as soon as possible. I could not return immediately, but I did so much sooner than I otherwise would. The appointment was not one that was made directly by the president, but by the district commissioners. But since the district commissioners were appointed by the president, it was assumed that an intimation from the president relative to the disposition of any office under their control would be respected and carried out. The Board of Commissioners consisted of three members, one Republican, one Democrat, and one army officer.

When I returned to Washington, I found out that Mr. Bruce had been delegated by the president to see the commissioners and have his wishes in this matter carried into effect. The fact was soon developed that the Republican member of the board, a man by the name of Wight, was not as friendly to the colored people as Mr. Ross, the Democratic member. Commissioner Wight was very much opposed to the change. When Mr. Bruce saw him the second time, he informed him that the matter had been turned over to Mr. Ross, the Democratic member of the board, who desired to confer with the president about it. In this the army member of the board, Colonel Black, he said, concurred. Mr. Bruce then called on Commissioner Ross. The commissioner informed him that he knew me personally and favorably and he knew of no one whose appointment would be more agreeable to him, and as he believed, more acceptable to the public. But he wanted to see the president in person and make an appeal to him in behalf of his friend, Davis, who was then in the office and whose circumstances were such that it would be a great hardship on him if he were obliged to give up the office just at that time. He wanted an opportunity to plead with the president to find another offer for me, if possible, and if not possible, to give his friend Davis at least a few months longer so as to enable him to make other business arrangements before going out of office. He promised that he would endeavor to see the president one day the following week. This was the latter part of February 1898.

Early in March Mr. Bruce was taken suddenly sick, and after being confined to his bed about ten days, he quietly breathed his last and peacefully passed away. This brought about at least a temporary suspension of the efforts to give effect to the president's decision in this matter. But the president was determined that the appointment should be made. I found out a few days after Mr. Bruce died that he designated his personal friend, Judge A. C. Thompson, to act as his representative in the place of Mr. Bruce and to see that the appointment was duly made. Judge Thompson immediately took it up with the commissioners, to whom Mr. Ross made substantially the same statement that he had made to Mr. Bruce. Judge Thompson reported this fact to the president, which resulted in an early date being fixed when the interview between the president and Commissioner Ross should take place. It so happened that in the meantime the *Maine* was blown up in the harbor of Havana, and the war with Spain was soon thereafter declared. This resulted in another suspension of negotiations looking to a change in the office of Collector of Taxes for the District of Columbia.

One afternoon shortly thereafter, when I picked up an evening paper and looked over the list of appointments sent to the Senate that day, I was very much surprised to find in that list the name of John R. Lynch for major and Additional Paymaster of Volunteers. I could hardly believe my own eyes. I was not aware that my name had ever been mentioned or thought of in connection with such an appointment. The first conclusion I came to, therefore, was that there was a typographical error or possibly someone of that name had been appointed from Maine, Maryland, Massachusetts, Minnesota, or

Missouri, and that "Mississippi" had been printed by mistake. But when I called at the White House the next day, I found that no mistake had been made. The president had heard that I was in doubt as to whether or not I was the Lynch I had seen announced, which he appeared to enjoy very much. He said that my name had not been suggested by anyone—that it was a personal selection of his own. There was only one person to whom he had mentioned it before transmitting the list of nominations that day to the Senate, and that was Mr. Bruce's successor, Register of the Treasury J. W. Lyons, who happened to call at the White House that day just before the list was sent to the Senate.[1]

The president stated that the appointment was a temporary one which would last only a few months probably. He had been informed that Commissioner Ross was anxious for his friend Davis, the Collector of Taxes, to remain in office a few months longer. This, he said, would enable him to grant Mr. Ross his request without doing injustice to me. In addition to this, he was ambitious to have a colored man a paymaster in the United States Army. He desired, therefore, as a personal favor to him that I accept the appointment. When the war is ended, which he thought would be soon, the collectorship of taxes would again be taken up and the change made if conditions at that time should render it necessary.

I told the president that while I had no ambition to become an army officer, I would take pleasure in accepting the appointment, especially since it come to me in the way it did, which I considered a great compliment and therefore could not help but keenly appreciate the same.

1. Judson W. Lyons, a native of Georgia, had been active in Republican politics for many years. He had been in government service but left in order to study law at Howard University, from which he graduated in 1884. He practiced law in Augusta, Georgia, until his appointment as Register of the Treasury in 1898. J. W. Gibson and W. H. Crogman, *Progress of a Race, or The Remarkable Advancement of the American Negro* (Atlanta, 1902), pp. 631–32.

Chapter Forty-two

Shortly before peace was declared, I had occasion to pass through Washington while on leave of absence and called at the White House to pay my respects to the president. In the course of the conversation the president asked me how I liked the position. I replied that I was better pleased with it than I supposed I would be. He then asked if I should like to be selected to be retained in the regular establishment. I replied to him that since I was now quite familiar with the duties of the position, which I found to be agreeable and somewhat in harmony with work to which I had been accustomed, I would be pleased to have the appointment made permanent, if such should be his desire.

"Then," replied the president, "you shall be retained in the regular establishment," for which I cordially thanked him. The president informed me at the same time that my record at the War Department was one of the best of the Volunteer paymasters, which pleased him very much. This accounts for my connection with the United States Army.

43

Keeping in Politics

Although I had been appointed a Major and Paymaster of Volunteers, yet since the position was known to be a temporary one, I felt that it was not only my privilege but my duty to continue to take an active part in politics. Having secured a greater degree of official recognition for my friends than appeared to be possible during the early days of the administration, the outlook for the future was not only encouraging but more satisfactory than at any time since the beginning of the factional fight in the state. My friends were very much encouraged and elated, not because they had received more than they merited, but because they had received more than they had expected. The friends of Mr. Hill, including Mr. Hill himself, were discouraged and disheartened, not because they had not received all they merited, but because they had not received all they expected and desired.

Having been denied a seat in the national convention of 1896, to which I knew I was justly entitled, I began at an early date to lay my plans for the national convention of 1900. I was determined to be elected a delegate to that convention from the state at large, which would probably be the last national convention I would aspire to be a member of. The first step in that direction was to bring about such an adjustment of factional differences in the party as would prevent a double or contesting delegation. With that end in view, I had several conferences with Judge A. C. Thompson and Hon. Charles Dick, to both of whom I was under deep obligations for their earnest and successful efforts to secure for my friends substantial justice and appropriate recognition in the disposition of federal patronage in the state.[1] I had served a term in Congress with Judge Thompson, with whom my relations had been very friendly.

Since Judge Thompson had been a representative of the administration in the disposition of patronage in the state, I did not see why he should not be selected as the medium through whom the factional differences in the party should be adjusted. This was finally done, with the approval of the administration and the national committee. Shortly thereafter I left Washington for my home, preparatory to assuming the duties of paymaster with station at Atlanta, Georgia. While on that trip, I was requested and authorized by Judge Thompson to have a conference with a few of the representative men of both factions and place before them the wishes and desires of the administration and the national committee with reference to the party organization in the state, which were, that the two rival state committees should be disbanded and a new one created, to be composed of an equal number of members of each of the

1. Charles Dick, an old friend and political aide of William McKinley, helped to plan the strategy to secure the nomination and election of McKinley. For a while he was secretary of the Republican National Committee. After serving in Cuba as a lieutenant colonel of the Eighth Ohio Regiment, he continued to advise the president. Margaret Leech, *In the Days of McKinley* (New York, 1959), pp. 57, 62, 68 ff.

two factions. I assured the judge that, to this plan of adjustment no objections would be made by my friends.

I took the necessary steps to bring about the conference. It took place at Jackson, Mississippi, and was composed of but four persons—Mr. Hill and Hon. A. M. Lea, representing the Hill faction, and Hon. C. A. Simpson and myself representing the Lynch faction. When the plan of adjustment was disclosed, Mr. Hill was strongly opposed to it and declared that he would not under any circumstances agree to it. Since he was a member of the national committee himself, he declared that he would not give his consent to any plan of adjustment that did not carry with it a full recognition of the state committee that was created by his organization. But in this he was not supported by Mr. Lea. Three of the four, therefore, favored the acceptance of the plan. Mr. Hill then yielded, for the reason, no doubt, that Mr. Lea's position made it plain to Mr. Hill that he would not be able to control a majority even of his own state committee in the opposition to the plan.

The two committees were then called to meet a few days later. Both voted to disband, and a new committee was then and there created, composed of an equal number from each faction. This newly formed committee was then organized with a Lynch man as chairman and a Hill man as secretary. Matters were now in satisfactory shape for the contest of 1900. My plans did not include Mr. Hill either for a delegate to the national convention or to succeed himself on the national committee. I assumed that there had been no change in his attitude towards me; hence, it would be useless for me to take him into consideration in the formation of any plans or the making of any slate that I had in contemplation. I was ambitious, in 1896, to succeed Mr. Hill on the national committee, but now I had no ambition in that direction.

Since Judge Thompson had taken such a friendly interest in me and had rendered me such valuable service, it occurred to me that I could not manifest my appreciation of his efforts in my behalf in a more appropriate way than to use my influence to have his brother-in-law, Judge H. G. Turley, postmaster at Natchez, made a member of the national committee to succeed Mr. Hill. Consequently, on the occasion of my next visit to Washington, I made this fact known to Judge Thompson. He thanked me for the friendly interest I thus manifested in his brother-in-law. His brother-in-law, however, he stated, had not very much political experience, for which reason he was not prepared to say that he was the best man for the place, but that he would think the matter over and on the occasion of my next visit to Natchez he thought it would be advisable for me to talk it over with Judge Turley.

About a month later I went to Natchez and while there I had the suggested interview with Postmaster Turley. He had already heard from Judge Thompson about it and had made up his mind to consent to the use of his name. The interview, therefore, was pleasant and in every way satisfactory. In the course of the conversation I remarked that since the postmaster had not, up to that time, taken an active part in politics, I thought it would be a good plan for him to be made a member, and then elected chairman, of the Republican Executive Committee of the county. To this he assented. I then decided to prolong my stay at Natchez for a few days so as to enable me to see that these plans were successfully carried out. The call was then issued for a meeting of the county committee.

Promptly at the time and place indicated in the call, the committee assembled and was called to order by the acting chairman, who had been informed of what was in contemplation. Postmaster Turley and I were present. When the call developed the fact that a large majority of the members were present, the acting chairman announced that the meeting had been called, upon the suggestion and at the request of Major Lynch, who was just from Washington and who had an important matter to put before the committee. I was then called upon for a speech. After I had spoken about thirty minutes, giving an account of what had been done and what we hoped to be able to do in the near future, I closed with the request that Postmaster Turley be elected to fill one of the vacancies on the committee and that he be elected chairman of the same. Judge Turley was then elected a member of the committee without a dissenting vote and was afterwards made the chairman thereof. The plan was thus successfully carried through, and Judge Turley was the recipient of congratulations from many persons, some of them Democrats.

While I was at Natchez on this occasion, I received a message from Mr. Hill requesting me to stop off at Jackson on my return to Atlanta, as he was anxious to see me and have a conference with me. He had evidently heard something about what was going on at Natchez. I was then under orders for a change of station from Atlanta to Havana, Cuba, and therefore did not have very much time to spare, but I decided to stop off for a few hours anyway. I went directly from the depot to Mr. Hill's office, where the interview took place. It continued much longer than I supposed it would; he had heard something about what was on foot.

I knew he was ambitious to remain a member of the national committee. He said he wanted to say to me frankly and candidly that he had come to the conclusion that he had made the mistake of his life in the course that he pursued in 1896. On account of that unfortunate, unwise, and unnecessary fight, the influence of both of us had been weakened, if not destroyed. But for that fight, he was now satisfied that he would have been appointed to the responsible and dignified position to which he aspired and that I would have been, no doubt, at the head of an important bureau at Washington. As it was, he had been obliged to accept a small and insignificant place which he had selected for one of his friends, while I had been practically isolated, politically, by being given a position in the army. It looked to him as if an effort were being made to destroy the leadership of colored men in the party.

As matters then stood, he said, he was afraid he would be succeeded by a white man on the national committee, a white man would remain chairman of the state committee, and those two would control the federal patronage in the state. Hence, no colored man would, in the future, have a controlling voice or commanding influence in such matters. He hoped, therefore, that we could forgive and forget the mistakes of the past and now come together once more so as to save as much as possible from what seemed to be the wreck that was now before us. He declared that he had been deceived and betrayed in the house of his friends, or those who were supposed to be his friends. Many of those in whom he had confided and upon whose loyalty and friendship he confidently relied, had simply taken advantage of the unfortunate situation that resulted from this rupture between us, to undermine his influence, lessen his power, destroy his standing and prestige, and bring about his political ruin and humiliation.

Those words were uttered in a tone that indicated sadness and sorrow, mingled with bitterness and chagrin. In fact, as he spoke I could see that his eyes were moistened with tears, which indicated the deep grief that was in his broken heart, while the quiver of his lips, which interfered with the articulation of his words, was an unmistakable evidence of a deeply wounded pride. I admit that I was deeply impressed with what he said, not on account of what was said, but on account of the way in which he spoke and because I could plainly see that he had at last come to a realization of what was perfectly plain to me from the beginning. I could not, and did not, of course, foresee everything that he had so bitterly experienced, but I foresaw and predicted that it would lessen and perhaps destroy the influence of colored men in shaping the policy of the party and controlling the patronage in the state, regardless of the result of the factional fight.

In my reply to him, therefore, I was perfectly frank and candid. I reminded him of the fact that when he thought he had me in his power, at his mercy, and politically crushed, as he supposed, he was unreasonable, dictatorial, and tyrannical. He would show no consideration and give no quarters. He insisted upon my complete political annihilation and extinction. He would listen to nothing short of this. I was therefore forced to make the fight of my life to save myself and friends from political destruction. I reminded him of the fact that, in making that fight, I was obliged to sacrifice the greater part of the savings of a lifetime. But the fight had to be made, because his attitude, with the backing which he had secured through negotiations with Senator Hanna, made it absolutely necessary. To save myself and my friends, therefore, I determined to fight to the bitter end, regardless of cost or consequences. I not only made a brave and gallant fight against fearful odds, but I had the proud satisfaction of knowing that it was not wholly in vain. In fact, I felt and knew that, from a factional standpoint, my victory was full and complete. It came by degrees but it was no less decisive and satisfactory.

I reminded him of the fact that he was more completely at my mercy now than I was at his in 1896, but, unlike himself, I was charitably disposed and was therefore willing to return good for evil. Life is too short, I said, for one to occupy any part of his valuable time in fighting the battles of the past, or in fighting battles of retaliation and revenge. I was willing, therefore, to let the dead past bury its dead, and look only to the present and the future. I informed him that while I was willing to meet him more than half way, I was afraid he had come to a realization of the true situation too late for very much to be saved from the wreck which his previous work had produced. He had refused to see until now that which was perfectly plain to everyone else. In fact, as I informed him, he had sent for me to meet him on this occasion after he had seen the probable wreck of his own personal and political future.

"Yes," I stated, "you will be succeeded on the national committee by a white man, but you are responsible for the situation that created this necessity. Since you brought about the conditions, I was obliged to avail myself of them to name the man that will succeed you." I then named the man by whom he was to be succeeded and told him that if he wanted to save himself from complete political destruction, it would be necessary for him to join me in support of that man. If he did this, he might possibly be elected one of the delegates to the next national convention from the state at large. At any rate, I could afford to make an excuse for giving him the benefit of my influence and support, otherwise he could not get it, and without it I was sure he could not be elected.

He said it was a bitter pill for him to swallow, but he would take it under advisement and inform me later of his decision. I admonished him that he must not take too long to consider it, because I was soon to leave for Havana, Cuba, from which point I should be obliged to conduct my campaign. He must, therefore, come to an early decision, otherwise his name would not be on the slate that I should ask my friends to support. Shortly after I arrived in Cuba, I received a letter from him in which I was informed that he had been to Natchez and had talked with Judge Turley and that a perfect understanding was reached. He had pledged himself to support Turley for member of the national committee, in return for which Turley was willing to join my friends in supporting him for delegate to the national convention. The slate that was finally made up and supported by both factions contained the names of both Lynch and Hill as delegates to the national convention of 1900 from the state at large. Everything was so harmonious that it was not even necessary for me to attend the state convention in person. I therefore remained at my post of duty in Cuba until the meeting of the national convention. There was peace and harmony all along the line. Judge Turley was made a member of the national committee, and it was then agreed that Mr. Hill should be made chairman of the state committee. This was satisfactory and the party organization in the state was once more in a good condition and upon a harmonious basis.

There being no opposition in the party to President McKinley, his renomination was conceded. Vice-President Hobart having died, it was necessary to name a new man for vice-president. The convention was considerably at sea for a while as to who was the strongest and most available man for that position, but Governor Roosevelt of New York was finally agreed upon, and he was induced, for the good of the party, to accept the nomination, although he was not a candidate for the position and did not desire to have that honor conferred upon him. Mr. Bryan was again nominated by the Democrats, but his defeat was more decisive this time than it was in 1896.

The country had been remarkably prosperous during the administration of President McKinley, in spite of the war with Spain, and it was the desire of the people that there be a continuance of the administration policies for which he stood and for which he was the exponent and typical representative. But, early in his second administration, the whole country—in fact the civilized world—was horrified and shocked by the announcement that this great and good man had been slain by an assassin. This was a sad and serious blow, but since Vice-President Roosevelt had given the people of New York such a satisfactory administration as governor of that great and important state, it was hoped and believed he could and would do the same for the country at large.

But the change was destined to have a very serious effect upon certain persons, some disastrously and some otherwise. Among others who were thus placed upon the anxious seat was my friend James Hill. It was an unfortunate fact that in the discharge of the duties of his office Mr. Hill had not given entire satisfaction to his official superiors. While the office was not so important and not so remunerative as the collectorship of Internal Revenue, yet for Mr. Hill it was a much more difficult one to fill. As Collector of Internal Revenue, his duties would have been merely directory and supervisory. The government provided a sufficient force of clerks and deputies to do the principal work of the office, leaving the head thereof merely the responsible medium by whom this work was to be approved and given official sanction. With the office he then held it was different. No clerks or deputies were allowed, and the income from the office was not sufficient to justify the employment of outside help. The incumbent was expected to do the work himself.

As easy and as simple as this was believed to be, it was an unfortunate fact that Mr. Hill's attainments were hardly equal to what was required of him in the efficient discharge of the duties thereof. The result was that inspecting officers made reports to the department which were not favorable to the head of the office. In consequence of these reports, the secretary of the interior recommended a change during President McKinley's first administration, but, since there was nothing in the reports that reflected upon the honesty of the incumbent, no action was taken at that time. But, it had been decided that a change would be made sometime during Mr. McKinley's second administration when another suitable place for Mr. Hill could be found.

It was hoped by Mr. Hill's friends that President Roosevelt would adhere to this determination and see that President McKinley's wishes therein be carried out. But President Roosevelt could not be induced to take this view of it. While he was committed to and fully intended to carry out the public policies to which President McKinley was known to be committed, this did not include, as he understood it, appointments to or retentions in office.

Shortly after the induction of Mr. Roosevelt into the presidential office, I had occasion to go to Mississippi on leave of absence. En route to Natchez I passed through Jackson where

I spent a day. While there I saw and conversed with Mr. Hill. It was then for the first time that I was made aware of the seriousness of the situation. Mr. Hill informed me that he was satisfied a change in his office had not only been decided upon, but that his successor had already been selected. That person, he had been reliably informed, was his bosom friend and faithful political supporter in the past, Hon. I. T. Montgomery of Mound Bayou. This was the same man, heretofore referred to, who, as a member of the Constitutional Convention of 1890, made a speech in favor of, and voted for, the constitution, the main purpose of which was to disfranchise the colored men of the state through an evasion of the Fifteenth Amendment to the federal Constitution.

In the factional fight in the party in that state he had been a friend and loyal supporter of James Hill. Mr. Hill was not without hope that the change would not be made until he was otherwise provided for, since he was sure that this would be the only condition upon which his friend Montgomery would consent to the use of his name for that office. He had already sent a friend to Mr. Montgomery's home to find out whether or not this was true. On my return from Natchez he would no doubt be able to give me definite information on that point.

On my return, Mr. Hill informed me that his friend Montgomery had been seen and questioned on the point referred to, to which he declined to give a positive answer, but intimated that since he had not sought the office, if it came to him, he would accept it. Mr. Hill was more discouraged and downhearted than I had ever seen him before. He told me frankly that if he were obliged to give up that office, as small as it was, without getting another one, he would be a ruined man. He had now passed the meridian of life, and yet he had not been able to lay aside anything for old age. Since he took charge of this office he had made a start in that direction. Should he now be turned out, he would not only lose the property he had contracted to purchase, on which a cash payment had been made, but he would lose what he had already paid, some of which he had borrowed from personal friends. He urged me, therefore, to go to Washington and see the president in person and make a strong plea in his behalf.

I confess that I was deeply touched. My heart went out in sympathy for him. I could hardly realize what a marked change had taken place in so short a time. Now the wheel of fortune had turned; I could hardly believe my own eyes as I looked upon this man who, only a few years previous, was proud, haughty, defiant, and independent, now weak, dependent, helpless, and apparently friendless, pleading for help and assistance at the hands of the one man whom he had sought to crush and destroy. Could this be possible? Yes, it was not only an actual fact, but the one whom he sought to ruin and destroy was now to use what little influence he may have left in an earnest effort to save his would-be destroyer.

I promised that I should do all in my power to save him. The second day after I arrived in Washington I was fortunate in securing an audience with the president. After passing the compliments of the season, I inquired of him what action, if any, had been taken with reference to the office at Jackson, Mississippi, then held by Mr. Hill. He replied that a change had been decided upon and that the appointment had been tendered to Mr. I. T. Montgomery. Mr. Montgomery, he said, had been recommended by Professor Booker T. Washington. I replied that I knew Mr. Montgomery personally and well and had known him for many years. Officially I had every reason to believe he would make a capable and efficient officer, but politically the appointment would not be a strong one. When he pressed me for the reasons upon which that opinion was based, Mr. Montgomery's speech and vote as a member of the Constitutional Convention of 1890, in support of that constitution, under which the colored men of the state had been disfranchised, were given. The president was surprised to hear this. It had not been brought to his notice. Still, since his competency and efficiency were conceded and the case had gone that far, he would allow the appointment to be made. I then asked him what, if anything, was in contemplation for Mr. Hill.

"Nothing," was his prompt reply. "I know Jim Hill personally," he said, "and while I have nothing against him, I do not feel obligated to provide for and take care of him. Men should be appointed to or retained in office not for purposes of charity or merely on account of some political service rendered, but on account of character, fitness, honesty, and ability and efficiency. As a public official, Mr. Hill's record is not good. He must therefore give way to one who can and will discharge the duties of the office in a satisfactory manner."

I replied that I was in perfect accord with the president in the enunciation of the views to which he had given expression. Still, it could not be denied that a well-qualified man might not be able to fill a certain office in a creditable and satisfactory manner, and yet one less qualified in point of education might fill the same office acceptably and well. This, I thought he would find to be true of Mr. Hill if he would give him a chance. I was of the opinion that the office now held by him was not one for which he was best fitted, but it would be unjust and unfair to him to assume that, in consequence of that fact, he could not render satisfactory service in some other.

I then made a most pathetic appeal to the president in Mr. Hill's behalf. I called attention to the fact that he and I were radically different in every important particular. We were different in temperament, disposition, and even in personal habits, and as the president well knew, we were different in political methods. My plea for him, therefore, was not based upon obligations I was under for services rendered me, politically or otherwise, at least in recent years, but it was based upon the fact that in spite of his faults and shortcomings, he had some merit and some claim upon a Republican administration that should not be ignored, but suitably recognized.

"Personally he may not be your ideal or your type of a man,

but he has a claim upon you as a Republican president—as the head of the party in the service of which he has given the best years of his life—which I hope you will not disregard. Dismiss him from the public service at this time, when the same had not been anticipated by him, and therefore unprepared for it, he will not only be crushed, but positively ruined. I know whereof I speak. I plead with you, therefore, to spare this man. Do not, at this time at least, strike this cruel and fatal blow. I do not ask you to retain him in the office he now holds, but to provide for him somewhere and in some way."

But the president's heart was hard. It could not be touched and his sympathies could not be aroused. When I left him I had not received the slightest encouragement that anything would be done, and it turned out that nothing was done. Mr. Hill was deposed and his late friend Montgomery was appointed and took charge of the office, but he too, strange to say, for reasons satisfactory to the president, soon gave it up, thus making another appointment necessary. A young man by the name of T. V. McAllister, who had also been one of Mr. Hill's friends and supporters in the factional fight, was appointed. He was the one that was originally slated for the office by the Hill organization in the early days of Mr. McKinley's administration. He was an intelligent and capable young man and proved to be an acceptable and satisfactory official.

But what became of Mr. Hill? He was there, but he was both crushed and ruined. He was brought to a sad realization of the fact that when he had no power, he had few if any friends. As the days passed the fact was more and more apparent to him that, like the Savior of the world, he would soon have nowhere to lay his head. He had already gone to his own and his own received him not. With a heart full of sadness and sorrow, broken in health and spirit, his pride crushed, he could not face the humiliating ordeal that he knew was before him. Consequently, he soon passed away, a discouraged, disappointed, and broken-hearted man. Peace to his ashes!

44

Controversial Convention Procedures

As a delegate to the National Republican Convention of 1900, I was honored by my delegation with being selected to represent the state on the Committee on Platform and Resolutions, and by the chairman of said committee, Senator [Charles W.] Fairbanks, I was made a member of the subcommittee that drafted the platform. At the first meeting of the subcommittee, the Ohio member thereof, Senator J. B. Foraker, submitted the draft of a platform that had been prepared at Washington, which was made the basis of quite a lengthy and interesting discussion. This discussion developed the fact that the Washington draft was not at all satisfactory to a majority of the subcommittee.

The New York member, Hon. L. E. Quigg, was especially pronounced in his objections, not so much to what was declared, but to the manner and form in which the declarations were made. In his opinion, the principles of the party were not set forth in the Washington draft in language that would make them clearly understood and easily comprehended by the reading public. After every member who desired to speak had done so, it was agreed that those who desired changes or additions would submit the same in writing and that these with the Washington draft be turned over to Mr. Quigg as a subcommittee of one, by whom a platform, to be in harmony with the views expressed by members of the committee, was to be carefully prepared and submitted to the subcommittee at an adjourned meeting to be held at an early hour the next morning.

The only amendment I suggested was one which was to express more clearly the attitude of the party with reference to the enforcement of the war amendments to the national Constitution. When the subcommittee met the next morning, Mr. Quigg submitted an entirely new draft which he had prepared the afternoon and night before, using the Washington draft and the amendments submitted by members of the subcommittee as the basis of what he had done. His draft proved to be so satisfactory to the subcommittee that the same was accepted and adopted with very slight changes and modifications. Mr. Quigg seemed to have been very careful in the preparation of his draft not only to give expression to the views of the subcommittee, which had been developed in the discussion and as had been set forth in the suggested amendments which had been referred to him, but the manner and form of expression used by him impressed the committee as being a decided improvement upon the Washington draft, although the subject matter treated of and elaborated upon in both drafts was substantially the same. Mr. Quigg's draft was not only accepted and adopted, as already stated, with very slight changes and alterations, but he was the recipient of the thanks of the other members for the excellent and satisfactory manner in which he had discharged the important duty that had been assigned to him.

The full committee was then convened by which the unanimous report of the subcommittee was adopted without opposition and without change. But I had anticipated a renewal of the effort to change the basis of representation in future National Republican Conventions, and had, therefore, made some little mental preparation to take a leading part in opposition to its adoption. Such a proposition had been submitted at nearly every national convention of the party since 1884. That an effort would be made at this convention I had good reason to believe. In this I was not mistaken. It was introduced by Senator Quay of Pennsylvania. His proposition, like the others, was that in the future, delegates to the national convention should be apportioned among the different states upon the basis of the votes polled for the party candidates at the last preceding national election, instead of upon the basis of the state's representation in Congress, as at present.

On the first view this proposition seems to be both reasonable and fair, but it cannot and will not stand the test of an intelligent analysis. As soon as I sought and secured the recognition of the chair, I offered an amendment in the nature of a substitute, declaring it to be the judgment of the party that in all states in which there had been, or might hereafter be, an evasion of the Fifteenth Amendment by state action, there should be a reduction in the representation in Congress from such state or states in the manner and for the purpose expressed in the Fourteenth Amendment.[1] A point of order was immediately made against the amendment, but the occupant of the chair, Senator Lodge, stated that he would hold his decision in reserve, pending an explanation by me of the amendment I had submitted.

At that time a suggestion was made that the whole subject be postponed until the next day, to which I assented and then yielded the floor, but it was not again called up; hence, my

1. *Official Proceedings of the Twelfth Republican National Convention Held in the City of Philadelphia, June 19, 20, and 21, 1900* (Philadelphia, 1900), p. 100.

speech was never delivered. Since it may be of some interest to the reader to get an idea of what I intended to say on that occasion, had the opportunity been presented, I shall here produce the substance of what I intended to say.

"Mr. Chairman, while there may be some doubt, in a parliamentary sense, as to whether or not the amendment I have submitted can be entertained as a substitute for the original proposition, it cannot be denied that it relates to the same subject matter. I hope, therefore, that the convention will have an opportunity in some way of voting upon it in lieu of the one that has been presented by the distinguished gentleman from Pennsylvania. It is a well-known fact that under the present system each state is entitled to double the number of delegates that it has senators and representatives in Congress. The plan now proposed is that the apportionment in future conventions be based upon the number of votes polled for the candidates of the party at the last preceding national election, according to what is known as the *official* returns, although it may be a fact, as is unquestionably true in some states, that the *official* returns may not be free from fraud—that the same may represent in some instances not the actual party vote polled, but the party vote counted, certified, and returned. This plan, therefore, means that representation in future National Republican Conventions from some states will not be based upon Republican strength nor determined by Republican votes, but will be fixed and determined by Democratic election officials. In other words, Democrats, and not Republicans, will fix and determine in a large measure representation in future conventions of the Republican party.

"The proposed change is predicated upon the assumption that elections are fair and returns are honest in all the states and at each and every national election. If that were true the difference in the representation from the several states would be unimportant and immaterial, even under the proposed change;

hence, there would be no occasion for the change. The fact that this assumption is not true furnishes the basis for the alleged inequality in representation and the apparent necessity for the change proposed. In addition to this, it is a fact well known that in several of the Southern states, my own, Mississippi, among the number, the Fifteenth Amendment to the national Constitution has been practically nullified and that the colored men in such states have been as effectually disfranchised as if the Fifteenth Amendment was not a part of the organic law of the land.

"If the plan that is now proposed by the distinguished gentleman from Pennsylvania should be adopted, the national Republican party will have thereby placed itself on record as having given its sanction to, and approval of, the questionable methods by which these results have been accomplished, by accepting them and making them the basis of representation in future national conventions of the party. I frankly confess that the plan I have presented is based upon the humiliating confession that the national government is without power under the Constitution as construed by the Supreme Court to effectually enforce the war amendments to the national Constitution, and that, in consequence thereof, nothing is left to be done but to fall back upon the plan prescribed by the Fourteenth Amendment, which is to reduce the representation in Congress from such states in the manner and for the purposes therein stated.

"It is true that the Fourteenth Amendment having been proposed and submitted prior to the Fifteenth, the provision with reference to reduction of representation in Congress was predicated upon the assumption that the different states could then legally make race or color a ground of discrimination in prescribing the qualification of electors. Still, it occurs to me that if a state could be thus punished for doing that which it had a legal right to do, the same punishment can now be inflicted for doing that which it can no longer legally do. If the plan proposed by the distinguished gentleman from Pennsylvania should be adopted, the National Republican party will not only have placed itself on record as having acquiesced in, and given its sanction to, the methods by which these results will have been accomplished, but it will be notice to the different states, North as well as South, that any of them that may see fit to take advantage of their own wrongs will have no occasion to fear any future punishment being inflicted upon the state for so doing, for under the plan thus proposed the state that may thus take advantage of its own wrongs will not only receive no punishment in the reduction of its representation in Congress, but its methods and practices will have been approved and adopted by the national Republican party.

"On the other hand the plan I propose is one which is equivalent to a notice to the different states that, while the national government may not be able to enforce by appropriate legislation the war amendments to the national Constitution, the legislative department thereof can and will prevent a state from taking advantage of its own wrongs, through the infliction of a punishment upon the state in the reduction of its representation in Congress. Since representation in the national convention is based upon the states' representation in Congress from such states, representation should be reduced in the national convention. The main purpose, therefore, which the distinguished gentleman from Pennsylvania seems to have in view will have been practically accomplished, but in a far different and in a much less objectionable way. It will be some satisfaction and consolation to Southern Republicans who are denied access to the ballot box through an evasion of the national Constitution, to know that if they are to be denied a voice in future national conventions of the party to which they belong, because they are unable to make their votes effective at the ballot box, the party through or by which they are thus wronged will not be allowed to take advantage of and enjoy the fruits thereof. They will at least have the satisfaction of knowing that if they cannot vote themselves, others cannot vote for them, and thus appropriate to themselves the increased representation in Congress and in the electoral college to which the state is entitled, based upon their representative strength.

"The strongest point in favor of this proposed change, as I have endeavored to show, grows out of the apparent inequality in representation in the national convention due to the denial of Republican access to the ballot box through an evasion of the Fifteenth Amendment. I cannot believe, Mr. Chairman, that this convention can be induced to favorably consider any proposition, the effect of which will be to sanction and approve the questionable methods by which the colored Republicans in several Southern states have been disfranchised. I cannot believe that this convention can be induced to favorably consider any proposition, the effect of which will be the sending of a message of sympathy and encouragement to the Democrats of North Carolina who are now engaged in an effort to disfranchise the colored Republicans of that state.

"The colored Americans ask no special favors as a class and no special protection as a race. All they ask and insist upon is equal civil and political rights and a voice in the government, state and national, under which they live, and to which they owe allegiance and to support which they are taxed. They feel that they are entitled to such consideration and treatment, not as a matter of favor, but as a matter of right. They came to the rescue of their country when its flag was trailing in the dust of treason and rebellion and freely watered the tree of liberty with the precious and patriotic blood that flowed from their loyal veins.

"There sits upon the floor of this convention today a distinguished gentleman whose name is upon the lips of every patriotic American citizen. The gentleman to whom I refer is the member from the great and important state of New York,

Theodore Roosevelt, who, as the brave leader of the American troops, led the charge upon San Juan Hill. In following the lead of that gallant officer on that momentous occasion, the colored American again vindicated his right to a voice in the government of this country. In his devotion to the cause of liberty and justice the colored American has shown that he was not only willing and ready at any and all times to sacrifice his life upon the altar of his own country, but is also willing to fight side by side with his white American brother in an effort to plant the tree of liberty upon a foreign soil. Must it now be said, that, in spite of this, the colored American now finds himself without a home, without a country, without friends, and even without a party? God forbid!

"Mr. Chairman, the colored American has been taught to believe that when all other parties and organizations are against him, he can always look with hope and encouragement to conventions of the Republican party. Must that hope now be destroyed? Must he now be made to feel and to realize the unpleasant fact that, as an American citizen, his ambition, his hopes, and his aspirations are to be buried beneath the sod of disappointment and despair? Mr. Chairman, the achievements of the Republican party as the friend and champion of equal civil and political rights for all classes of American citizens constitute one of the brightest and most brilliant chapters in the history of that grand and magnificent organization. Must that chapter now be blotted out? Are you now prepared to confess that in these grand and glorious achievements the party made a grave mistake?

"It was a most beautiful and imposing scene that took place yesterday when a number of venerable men who took part in the organization of the Republican party occupied seats upon the platform of this convention. The presence of those men brought to mind pleasant and agreeable recollections of the past. Until the Republican party was organized, the middle classes, the laboring people, the oppressed and the slave, had no channel through which to reach the bar of public opinion. The Democratic party was subservient to, and controlled by, the slave oligarchy of the South, whilst the Whig party had not the courage of its convictions. The Republican party came to the front, with a determination to secure, if possible, freedom for the slave, liberty for the oppressed, and justice and fair play for all classes and races of our population. That its efforts in these directions have not been wholly in vain are among the most glorious and brilliant achievements that will constitute a most important part of the history of our country, for it was the unmistakable determination of that party to make this beautiful country of ours, in truth and in fact, the land of the free and the home of the brave. Surely it is not your purpose now to reverse and undo any part of the grand and noble work that has been so successfully and so well done along these lines.

"And yet, that is just what you will have done if you adopt the proposition presented by the distinguished gentleman from Pennsylvania. While I do not assert and cannot believe that such was or is the purpose and desire of the author of that proposition, no one that will give the matter careful consideration can fail to see that the effect of it will be to undo, in part at least, what the Republican party has accomplished since its organization. As a colored Republican speaking for and in behalf of that class of our fellow citizens who honor and revere the Republican party for what it has accomplished in the past, I feel that I have a right to appeal to you not to cloud the magnificent record which this grand organization has made. So far as the colored man is concerned, you found him a slave; you made him a free man. You found him a serf; you have made him a sovereign. You found him a dependent menial; you have made him a soldier. I therefore appeal to the members of this convention, in the name and on behalf of the history of the Republican party, and in behalf of justice and fair play, to vote down this unjust, unfair, unwise, and unnecessary proposition which has been presented by the distinguished gentleman from Pennsylvania."

In addition to what is stated above, there are many other reasons that can be given against the proposed change. In the first place the plan was based upon the sound and stable principle upon which the government itself was organized. Representation in Congress is not based upon votes or voters but upon population. The same is true of the different state legislatures. All political parties, or at any rate the principal ones, adopted the same system or plan in the makeup and composition of their state and national conventions. The membership of the national convention being based upon each state's representation in Congress, the state conventions, with perhaps a few exceptions, are based upon the representation in the state legislature from each county, parish, or other civil division. It was the fairest, safest, best, and most equitable plan or system that can be devised or adopted.

Under this plan or system, no state, section, or locality could gain or lose representation in any party convention through the application or adoption of extraneous, doubtful, or questionable methods, either through the action of the government or a political party. The representation in Congress and in the different state legislatures, which is based upon population, fixes the representation from each state in the different national conventions and in many of the state conventions. Any other plan or system, especially one based upon the number of votes cast for the candidates of the party as officially ascertained and declared, would have had a tendency to work serious injustice to certain states and sections. In fact it would have had a tendency to sectionalize the party by which the change was made.

Under the present system, for instance, Pennsylvania and Texas had the same representation in a National Democratic

Convention that they had in a National Republican Convention, although one was Republican in national elections and the other Democratic. And why should not the representation from those states have been the same in both conventions? Why should Texas, because it was believed to be safely Democratic, have had more power and influence in a Democratic convention on that account than the Republican state of Pennsylvania? The answer may be because one was a Democratic and the other a Republican state—because one could be relied upon to give its electoral votes to the candidates of the Democratic party, while the other cannot. But this is not in harmony with our governmental system. Representation in Congress being based upon population, every state, section, and locality has its relative weight and influence in the government in accordance with the number of its inhabitants.

That this is the correct principle will not be seriously questioned when it is carefully considered. What was true of Pennsylvania and Texas in a National Democratic Convention was equally true of the same states in a National Republican Convention and for the same reasons. The argument that Pennsylvania should have had, relatively, a larger representation in the National Republican Convention than Texas, because the former was reliably Republican while the latter was hopelessly Democratic, is just as fallacious in this case as in the other. But it was said that delegates from states that could not contribute to the success of the ticket should not have had a potential voice in nominating a ticket that other states had to be dependent upon to elect. Then why not exclude them altogether, and also those from the territories and the District of Columbia?

The argument is unsound and unreasonable. A state may be reliably Republican at one election and yet go Democratic at the next. In 1872 General Grant, the Republican candidate for president, carried nearly every state in the Union, South as well as North. Four years later Governor Hayes, the Republican candidate for president, came within one vote, in the electoral college, of being defeated, and even then his election was made possible through the decision of the electoral commission. In 1880 General Garfield, the Republican candidate for president, carried New York and was elected, while four years later Mr. Blaine, the candidate of the same party, lost it and was defeated. In 1888 Harrison, the Republican presidential candidate, carried New York and was elected. Four years later he not only lost New York, but also such important states as Indiana and Illinois and came within a few votes of losing Ohio. This was due to a slump in the Republican vote throughout the country, which would have made a very radical change in the national convention of 1896, if the apportionment of delegates to that convention had been based upon the votes cast for Harrison in 1892. While McKinley, the Republican presidential candidate, was elected by a large majority in 1896, he lost such important western states as Kansas, Nebraska, Colorado, Montana, Washington, and Nevada. While he was reelected four years later by an increased majority, he again lost some of the same states. While Roosevelt, the Republican presidential candidate in 1904, carried every state that McKinley carried in 1900 and several others besides, Mr. Bryan, the Democratic candidate in 1908, though defeated by a large majority, regained some of the Western states that Roosevelt carried in 1904, notably his own state of Nebraska.

There was a time when such states as Delaware, Maryland, West Virginia, Kentucky, Missouri, and Tennessee were as safely Democratic as Texas and Georgia. Will anyone assert that such is true of them now? There also was a time when such states as Nebraska, Colorado, and Nevada were as reliably Republican as Pennsylvania and Vermont. Is that true of them now? In addition to these, taking into consideration important elections that have been held since 1880, the Republicans cannot absolutely rely upon the support of such states as Massachusetts, Maine, Connecticut, New York, New Jersey, Indiana, Illinois, Kansas, and even Ohio. Even the strong Republican state of Pennsylvania has occasionally gone Democratic in what is called an off year. Other Republican states, or states that usually go Republican, have gone Democratic when it was not an off year—Illinois for instance in 1892. All of this goes to prove how unreliable, unsafe, unsatisfactory, unjust, and unfair would be the change as thus proposed on the basis of representation in future national conventions of the party.

Another argument in support of the proposed change is that delegates from Democratic states are, as a rule, controlled by the administration then in power, if Republican, and that such delegates can be depended upon to support the administration candidate whoever he may be, regardless of merit, strength, or availability. This argument, of course, is based upon the assumption that what is true of Democratic states in this respect is not true of Republican states. The slightest investigation will easily establish the fallacy of this assumption. The truth is that the federal officeholders, North as well as South, especially those holding appointive offices, can always be depended upon, with a few exceptions, to support the administration candidate, whoever he may be. The only difference between the North and the South in this respect is that in some of the Southern states where but one party is allowed to exist, and that the Democratic party, the Republican officeholders can more easily manipulate and control the conventions of their party in such states. But that the officeholders constitute an important factor in the election of delegates to national conventions, in all parts and sections of the country, will not be denied by those who are familiar with the facts and are honest enough to admit them.

For purposes of illustration we will take the National Republican Convention of 1908, which nominated Judge Taft. It was known that Judge Taft was the one whose candidacy was supported by the administration. The proceedings of the convention revealed the fact that outside of five states that had what was called favorite-son candidates of their own, there were, perhaps, not more than fifty votes in the whole convention that were opposed to the administration candidate, although it is more than probable that Judge Taft would not have been nominated but for the fact that he was the choice of the administration.

I am sure no fair-minded person will assert that in thus voting the delegates from the Democratic states were influenced by the administration, while those from Republican states were not. It is not my purpose to assert or even intimate that any questionable methods were used to influence the election or control the votes of the delegates in the interest of any one candidate. Nothing of that sort was necessary, since human nature is the same the world over.

That the officeholders should be true and loyal to the administration to which they belong is perfectly natural. That those who wish to become officeholders should be anxious to be on the winning side is also natural, and that too without regard to the locality or section in which they live. It is a fact, therefore, that up to 1908 no candidate has ever been nominated by a Republican National Convention who did not finally receive a sufficient number of votes from all sections of the country to make his nomination practically the choice of the party without regard to sectional lines.

If it be a fact that in 1908, for instance, delegates to the National Republican Convention were elected and controlled through administration influences in the interest of any one candidate, such influences were no less potential in Republican than in Democratic states. Outside of the administration candidate there were, at that convention, five very important states that presented candidates of their own. They were New York, Indiana, Illinois, Pennsylvania, and Wisconsin. That the delegation from each of said states was practically solid in the support of its favorite son was due largely to the wise decision of the managers of the administration candidate to concede to each of said favorite sons the delegation from his own state without a contest. But for this decision, which was wisely made in the interest of party harmony, no one of said favorite sons would have had the solid delegation from his own state. As it was, a large majority of the delegates from the five states named were not unfriendly to the administration candidate. They voted for their favorite sons simply because they knew that in doing so they were not antagonizing the administration.

There never was a time, therefore, when they could have been united upon any one candidate in opposition to the one that had at his back the powerful influence and support of the administration. Our government has reached that point in its growth where it is not only possible, but comparatively easy, for an administration to secure the nomination of the one by whom it desires to be succeeded, especially under the present system of electing delegates. It was in anticipation of this and to prevent any one man from perpetuating himself in power that Washington established the precedent against a third successive term.

If the advocates of this proposed change are to be believed and they wish to be consistent, they should include the national committee. The composition of that body is somewhat similar to that of the United States Senate. In the Senate, Nevada and Delaware have the same representation as New York and Pennsylvania. In the national committee, each territory and the District of Columbia has one vote. If any change, in the interest of reform, is necessary, the National Republican Committee is the organization where it should first be made, for it often happens that said committee can not only shape the policy of the party, but control the nomination as well, especially when the result between opposing candidates is close and doubtful. In such a contest the candidate that has the support of a majority of the national committee has a decided advantage over his rivals for the nomination. If the result should be close, that advantage will be more than likely to secure him the nomination. The national committee prepares the roll of the delegates to the convention, and in doing so it decides, primarily, every contested seat. If the contest thus decided should give any one candidate a majority, that majority will be sure to retain the advantage thus secured. It will thus be seen that if any change is necessary this is the place where it should first be made. It occurs to me that the most effective remedy for the evils now complained of is to have the delegates to national conventions elected at popular primaries instead of by state and district conventions.

In Cuba

DURING THE THREE YEARS THAT I WAS STATIONED ON DUTY in Cuba, it was my good fortune to be required to visit not only every province, but nearly every important city and town on the island. While doing so I made it a point to carefully study the country and people—the character and fertility of the soil, the habits and customs of the natives. During the first year I made very little progress, because only a few of the natives could speak or understand English and I had no knowledge of Spanish. But during the second and third years, the third especially, I made satisfactory progress, because I had mastered the Spanish language sufficiently to understand, in the main, what was said in conversation and to make myself understood. In fact I could carry on a conversation in Spanish whenever I could get a person with whom I was talking to speak slowly and deliberately and articulate clearly and distinctly. But I succeeded in getting all the information I wanted, except in a part of one province–Puerto Principi.[1]

I found that the soil was fertile and very productive. On account of the mildness of the climate, whatever can be produced during the summer can be produced equally well during the winter. The weather is never cold enough, even in the western end of the island, to make it necessary to wear winter clothes or to have a fire in the house for heating purposes. The rainy season usually begins in May and continues almost daily for about six months. In the month of September the rains are usually more copious than in any other month. In November they usually have very severe wind storms. For that reason the farmers, as a rule, do not plant until the danger from wind storms is over. Earthquakes are of frequent occurrence, but they are seldom severe and therefore do very little and often no damage at all, except to tall buildings that may be of brick or stone. On account of the earthquakes, the buildings are usually made of wooden material and most of them have but one story. Very few of them have more than two stories.

There is, or was when I was there, some very valuable timber in certain parts of the island, but it is fast disappearing, and unless steps are taken to prevent its destruction and exportation, the island will soon be without native timber. Although the soil, as a rule, is rich and productive, there are certain things that can be profitably produced in the United States that cannot be produced there. In the fruit line, peaches and figs, for instance, cannot be produced in large quantities there–too much rain. Oranges, pineapples, bananas, coconuts are produced in large quantities. Cotton is another article that cannot be profitably produced on account of the rain–that is, they have too much rain during the rainy season and not enough

1. Since there is no province in Cuba called "Puerto Principi," Lynch could have been referring to an area around the Bay of Puerto Madre in eastern Camagüey.

during the dry season. Even if it could be produced during the dry season, the rains would set in before it could be gathered; hence the most of it would be destroyed. Corn can be produced in great abundance, but very little of it is raised for any other purpose than to feed stock in its green state. On account of the dampness, if the corn were allowed to mature, it would soon decay and would also be destroyed by insects. Very little cornmeal is used by the natives, because it can be kept on hand only for a short while. Even that which is imported is kept in store only a brief period before it will begin to mold and be infested with bugs of different sorts and thus be worthless as an article of food. What is true of corn and cornmeal is equally true of cereals.

The principal products of the island, outside of the fruits above mentioned, are sugar and tobacco, which are annually produced in great quantities. Cuba is especially noted for the superiority of its sugar and tobacco, tobacco especially. The soil, especially in certain sections, as well as the climate, seems particularly adapted to the profitable cultivation of those articles.

There is no good reason why the island should not be perfectly healthy the year around. The reason that yellow fever was liable to break out at certain times in the larger cities and towns was on account of the unsanitary conditions. I found that in no one of those cities and towns was there a proper drainage and sewerage system. The accumulated filth, therefore, must necessarily breed disease. Nearly everything was thrown into the streets, sometimes including dead animals, which were allowed to remain there for hours if not days, thus poisoning the atmosphere that the people breathed. At many places the bay is nothing more than an island lake of stagnant and polluted water.

Another point upon which I tried to secure accurate and reliable information was with reference to the native population—

its origin and racial composition. Like America, the original inhabitants were Indians, who were conquered and driven out by the Spaniards. For a long time thereafter the population was composed chiefly of Spanish soldiers and some other unmarried men of the same race. But, after the country had somewhat developed and it was found to be rich and productive, the population was soon augmented not only from Spain, but from different European countries and some from America.

Slaves were subsequently imported from Africa and other countries and islands to be utilized in cultivating the large sugar and tobacco plantations. It is from these different countries and races that the present native Cuban population sprang. In the main, therefore, the native population is a mixed one. This is especially true of those living in the cities and towns. While, therefore, there can be and is what may be called a sort of color question, there is not and cannot be a *race* question in Cuba, for the reason that no one can tell where one race begins and the other ends. There again, it is true of Cuba, as of all other tropical countries, that there are many persons who, perhaps, have no African blood in their veins, but who in complexion are much darker than many who have. All persons in Cuba, therefore, who are not black are white if they want to be, and nearly all who can want to be.

A census of the population was taken while I was there, which revealed the fact that about sixty percent of the population were whites, but I am satisfied that not less than ten percent that were classed white would have been classed colored in the United States. But in Cuba they are white people, recognized and treated as such, hence it cannot be said that the census was inaccurate because they were thus enumerated. Although the population is nearly equally divided between what may be called white and colored people, the color or race question, at least prior to American occupation, has never been the slightest occasion of any political or social friction. On the contrary, the two races lived and I am sure are yet living in peace, union, and harmony upon terms of absolute and perfect civil and political equality. Whatever difference if any may exist between the two races is due largely to some other than race differences.

During the three years that I was in that country I never heard or read of an assault upon a white woman by a colored man, and I am sure nothing of the sort took place. If it were true, as some people in the United States profess to believe, that this is a crime peculiar to the colored man, regardless of country or locality, Cuba is the place of all others where that fact could be and would be easily established, for there is no country on earth where there is more freedom and less restraint with reference to the mixing of the races than in Cuba. And yet we not only hear of no such occurrences, but so far as the eye can detect, we find less evidences of race intermixture in Cuba than in the Southern states of America, where there are rigid laws against race intermarriage and for race separation at public places and on public conveyances.

In Cuba there are no such laws. On the contrary every person, regardless of race, color, religion, or nationality, is not only allowed to enjoy his civil and political rights upon terms of absolute equality, but he is allowed access upon the same terms to all places that are intended for, and supported by, the public. Consequently, in the public schools and military organizations, and in the churches, hotels, restaurants, and theaters, and on railroad trains, no distinction or discrimination is made or allowed to be made based merely upon race or color. And yet, under their system objectionable persons are less liable to be thrown in contact with decent and well-to-do persons at such places and on such occasions than in the Southern states of America.

On the railroad cars, for instance, there are three different classes with corresponding rates of fare. If a seat in a first-class coach would cost, for instance, one dollar for a certain distance, a seat in the second-class coach would cost seventy-five cents, and in the third-class coach fifty cents for the same distance. The result is that the common laboring people are seldom brought in contact with the opulent, cultivated, and refined, even on public conveyances, for the reason that the common or laboring people always select a seat in the coach that will cost them the least money. And then they, like the same class in any country, prefer to ride in such a coach anyway. The "jim-crow" laws of the Southern states of America are based upon an unjust and absurd theory, which is that all white people, because they are white, regardless of character or condition, are equals socially and otherwise and therefore fit and suitable for association and companionship upon terms of absolute equality. Nothing can be more ridiculous than this.

There can never be such a thing as *social* equality even among people of the same race and blood. It is impossible for wealth and poverty, intelligence and ignorance, vice and virtue to mix upon terms of equality even if all should be of the same race and blood. Society is something that is stronger than, and superior to, the statute law, so far at least as the home is concerned. Social companionship is the outgrowth of the mutual and voluntary choice of individuals and families. In the selection of his social companions—those whom he may desire to mingle with him and share the hospitality of his home—a man is not supposed to include all of those whom he may know personally and who may be his equals in point of wealth, intelligence, and virtue.

It does not follow, therefore, that because a white and a colored person, for instance, should be equals in the particulars above named that they will necessarily find mutual and desirable social companionship in each other. These are matters about which all persons are or should be at liberty to suit their own tastes and act upon their own judgment. While this is the law, the unwritten law with reference to social rights, it is not the law and cannot be the law with reference to civil and political rights. These are rights that belong to, and should be enjoyed by, the public, subject only to such rules and regulations as may be necessary to insure safety, health, and comfort. While every person is, or should be, at liberty to suit his own taste and exercise his own judgment in the selection of his own private associates, he has no right to set up any standard of his own for the government or the public in the exercise and enjoyment of civil and political rights. Such rights are those which define the relationship which the individual sustains to his government, for the support of which he is taxed.

Taxation without representation or a voice in the government by which he is taxed is a denial or curtailment of one's civil and political rights. These rights are those which his government is presumed to guarantee to him in exchange for his support and allegiance, in addition to affording him ample protection in the enjoyment of life, liberty, property, health, and reputation. Any law, rule, or regulation which denies, curtails, or abridges any of these rights, such, for instance, as the "jim-crow" law, which is intended to degrade and proscribe one race of which our citizenship is composed, is a gross denial of the civil rights of that race.

The fallacy and absurdity of the "jim-crow" laws were illustrated on a train on which I was a passenger en route from Chicago to my home in Mississippi. At a point between Chicago and Cairo, a contractor brought aboard about fifty common laboring men with whom he had made a contract to work on a railroad in Texas. They were rough and indecently clad and had an unpleasant odor. The contractor knew that they should not occupy seats in a coach with first-class passengers; hence, with the consent of the conductor, they were assigned to seats in a coach to themselves, which was the front one, next to the baggage coach.

But when Cairo was reached this had to be changed, because

the train was then about to cross the Ohio River and into a state that is cursed with the "jim-crow" law. The contractor was notified by the conductor that the coach then occupied by his men must now be transferred into a coach for colored people, and, since his men were white, they must go back into the first-class coach, which was then transformed into a coach for white people. The contractor protested against this because the men were not really fit to be thrown in contact with first-class passengers, but he was informed that neither the conductor nor the company had any discretion in the matter. It was the law that he was obliged to enforce. So this horde of undesirable and offensive humanity was marched into the first-class coach with the white passengers simply because they were white. Had it been left to the discretion of the company or even of the white passengers, it is safe to say that it would have been much more satisfactory to all concerned if the few decently clad colored passengers had been allowed to occupy seats in the first-class coach, rather than this mass of objectionable white humanity.

The Cubans have some strange customs which it would be difficult for Americans to follow. One of them is that the sabbath is not only a day for divine worship, but for recreation and pleasure as well. That is the day they select for having their parties, balls, entertainments, and sports of different kinds. The prevailing religion is Roman Catholicism, but if one wants to worship in the church he must be an early riser, for it is a rare thing to see a Catholic church open after nine o'clock in the morning except on special occasions and feast days, such, for instance, as Easter Sunday, when nearly the whole day is devoted to religious worship. But ordinarily the churches are closed by nine o'clock, and by about noon, preparations are under way for the festivities of the day. From about noon until a late hour at night these festivities are going on. They are a great people for having clubs composed exclusively of men, under the auspices of which these parties and balls are given.

When I first went to Cuba I was under the impression that it was only the laboring people that utilized the sabbath for such purposes, since on account of being otherwise engaged during the other days of the week it was the only day they had for recreation and pleasure. But in this I soon found I was mistaken. Those in opulent circumstances did the same thing. It is a custom of the country. It is on these occasions that the ladies turn out in large numbers, wearing the best and finest that can be found in their wardrobes.

With reference to the religion of the Cubans, I much say that while I was raised a Protestant and am now too old to change even if I were so disposed, my respect for, and admiration of, Roman Catholicism were materially increased and strengthened during my stay in that country. They convinced me that they practice what they preach and preach what they practice. The impression they made upon my mind was that in their religious professions and practice they were thoroughly honest and consistent. They do not, for instance, allow or tolerate the color line or any other mark of distinction or discrimination to enter the church. They preach and teach that God has no respect of persons and that in his house all are upon an equal footing. They give all to understand that whatever lines of distinction and discrimination they may see fit to draw outside the church of God, when they enter that holy and sacred edifice, they must leave them on the outside. They insist that any religion that does not teach the fatherhood of God and the brotherhood of man is hypocrisy. They insist that Christ suffered and died, not for the redemption and salvation of any particular race or class, but for every race and all classes—not for the rich and powerful alone, but for the poor and lowly as well.

I learned that these were not only their professions, but their acts were consistent with the same. Then, one cannot help but be impressed with their devotion and sincerity, especially during their religious celebrations on special occasions, such, for instance, as Good Friday and Easter Sunday. Every church is open during the whole of those two days; and on Good Friday until a late hour at night. During the afternoon of that day, the people flock in great crowds to the churches in different parts of the city, some of them visiting nearly every church, for the purpose of looking upon the typical remains of the crucified Savior which they will find in a coffin on the altar of the church. The priest stands at the front door and reviews the crowd as they pass in and out of the church. It is a most beautiful and magnificent sight. In the crowds are to be seen people in all grades and walks of life. Old and young, rich and poor, white and black, employer and employee are seen in the immense crowds making their way to the church of God to manifest their devotion to, and faith in, the crucified Savior of the world. On Easter Sunday morning the same crowds will see the Savior whose lifeless body they looked upon the Friday before, situated upon a high pedestal, with a crown of glory upon his head, indicative of victory, and a scepter in his hand, and the words printed in large letters "He is risen." The sign, in connection with the ceremonies that follow, is not only impressive and beautiful, but it is one that can never be forgotten.

In the treatment of their women the Cubans have not kept pace with the other civilized countries. Women have no voice in anything outside the home and not very much there. Except for school teaching, very few remunerative places are open to them. There are no women employees in the stores and offices except those conducted by Americans and other foreigners. They are not even allowed a voice in church. Women, for instance, are seldom seen in any of the church choirs. The only time that I heard the voice of a woman in a church choir was at the evening service once on Good Friday. A woman was allowed on that occasion to sing a solo. I was told it was unusual and out of the ordinary. They seem to think that a woman's proper place is at home, looking after domestic matters and administering to the wants and needs of the husband and children. If she should not be blessed with a husband and children, it is her misfortune for which the public is not responsible. It is her place to have them, the husband anyway. It is her sphere in life and she must not expect to occupy any other. Everything outside of the home must be looked after and attended to by the husband and father—the head of the home.

Political parties are not at all like those in the States. They appear to be organized on a different basis and for a different purpose. But I found while there that they had two principal parties just as we have in the States—one called the Conservative and the other the Liberal. The Liberal party represented at that time a considerable majority of the people, comprising as it did, and perhaps does, the major part of those that compose the Cuban army and their supporters and sympathizers. The Conservative party, however, was and perhaps is composed of some of the best and most substantial citizens in the country. In fact it was claimed, and perhaps truthfully, that it represented a majority of the wealth and intelligence of the country. Whatever sentiment existed in favor of annexation to the United States was found in that party. But annexation to the United States I found to be very unpopular throughout the island. No political party would dare openly advocate it.

I was there when the presidential election took place in the United States in 1900. While I believe it can be truthfully said that fully ninety percent of the colored voters in the United States supported McKinley and the Republican party at that time, I found that the colored Americans did not influence the Cubans in the least. They were Cubans and were looking out for what they believed to be the interest of Cuba and the Cubans. On that point they had no sympathetic feeling for the colored Americans on account of race, for they have no race issue there such as we have in the States. As against the colored

American and the white Cuban, the colored Cuban was for the white Cuban. As against the colored Cuban and the white American, the white Cuban was for the colored Cuban. With the Cubans, white and colored, it was not a question of race or color, but of country. With them the paramount question or issue was immediate, unconditional Cuban independence. On this question they had a suspicion that McKinley and the Republicans were not sincere and that Bryan and the Democrats were. For that reason and that alone, the Cubans, white and colored, with a few exceptions, were in sympathy with Mr. Bryan and the Democratic party and were extremely anxious to have that party carry the election. When the news came that McKinley had been elected, it cast a gloom over the whole island. To them it was bad news, and they were sadly disappointed.

46

In Nebraska

MY NEXT STATION AFTER BEING RELIEVED FROM DUTY IN Cuba was Omaha, Nebraska. When I crossed the Missouri River at Council Bluffs, Iowa, I realized that for the first time in my life I had put foot on what may be called historic soil. It was the first time I had been that far west. I had frequently passed through a number of the Western states, but had never before been as far west as the state of Nebraska. As a young man I had read about the Missouri Compromise, the Dred Scott Decision, the Wilmot Proviso, the Kansas and Nebraska Bill, and the Fugitive Slave Law, all of which contributed in no small degree to what finally culminated in the War of the Rebellion.

When I reached the state of Nebraska, therefore, those important historical events were brought vividly to my memory. The fight over the great questions growing out of, and connected with, that section will always be fresh in the minds of those who were and are interested in the important events that were connected with that period. It was a desperate struggle between the slave power on the one side and the advocation of freedom on the other. The slave power secured, shortly after the war with Mexico, and as one of the results thereof, what to it was an important point in the acquisition of Texas; but this proved to be the rock upon which the Whig party finally went to pieces.

The slave power of those days dominated and controlled the Democratic party and through it the national government for many years. The Whig party was composed of two hostile and bitterly antagonistic elements, proslavery and antislavery. While those two factions or elements could be harmonized on the tariff and other minor questions, when it came to the slavery question, which was then the paramount one, they were hopelessly divided, the Northern Whigs, as a rule, being opposed to the extension of slave territory while the Southern Whigs strongly favored it. The Northern Whigs at the same time did not have the courage of their convictions. While they were not friendly to their Southern allies, they seemed to be afraid to openly antagonize them. The slave power was the one that all political parties stood in fear of until the antislavery party came to the front, which was subsequently absorbed by, and merged into, the Republican party, the primary purpose of which was to oppose the extension of slave territory.

But it was plain to everyone that public sentiment in the free states was rapidly growing in opposition to the aggression of slave power. A desperate conflict, which could not be indefinitely postponed, was inevitable. It was in reality a fight between free labor on one side and slave labor on the other. Wherever slavery existed free labor could not prosper, because the slave owner utilized his slaves for every branch of labor, skilled as well as unskilled. The Republican party came to the front as the friend, champion, and advocate of free labor and, as an incident thereof, freedom for the slave, should that be necessary. While the abolition of slavery, where it then existed, was not at that time the primary object, it was to be brought about should it be necessary to accomplish the purpose desired and intended. In other words, the primary purpose of the party was to oppose and antagonize the further aggressions of the slave power and prevent its growth and expansion. It was to contend for free labor, free speech, and the freedom of the press, which necessarily meant free men. For in the language of Mr. Lincoln, the government could not exist half free and half slave.

This new, vigorous, and aggressive organization soon absorbed nearly all of the antislavery Whigs and free-soil Democrats of the North, as well as the members of the antislavery party. The principal source of its strength and popularity at that time, however, grew out of its advocacy and championship of free labor. That it was opposed to slavery as an institution was a well-known fact, but it was also known that its strength before the public was due not so much to a moral sentiment upon that question as to the material interests involved.

As soon as I entered the state of Nebraska those historical facts were brought fresh to my memory. It was upon the territory which now comprises the states of Kansas and Nebraska that the preliminary battles in the interest of freedom were successfully fought. This is especially true of that part of the territory which now comprises the state of Kansas. That state had occupied a prominent place before the public not only for the reasons above given but because of other important events which attracted public attention. It was that state, for instance, that furnished one of the Republican United States senators [E. G. Ross] who voted against the conviction and thus secured the acquittal of President Andrew Johnson, who had been impeached by the House of Representatives for high crimes and misdemeanors in office.

That state also furnished one of the most remarkable men that ever occupied a seat in the Senate of the United States, in the person of John J. Ingalls. I distinctly remember him as an able and brilliant young senator in 1875 when, under the leadership of Senator George F. Edmunds of Vermont, he took an active part in the successful fight that was made in that body to secure the passage of the Sumner Civil Rights Bill. It was this fight that demonstrated his fitness for the position he subsequently occupied as one of the distinguished leaders on the Republican side of the chamber. He had a most wonderful command of the English language. In fact he was a natural-born orator. While he was somewhat superficial and not always logical, he never failed to be interesting, though seldom instructive. For severe satire and irony, he had few equals and no superiors. It was on this account that no senator was anxious to get into a controversy with him. But for two unfortunate events in the career of John J. Ingalls, he would have filled a more popular position in the history of this country than it is now possible for the impartial historian to give him.

Kansas, unfortunately, proved to be a fertile field for the growth and development of that ephemeral organization known as the Populist party, which had secured a majority in the legislature that was to elect the successor to Mr. Ingalls. The senator evidently had great confidence in his oratorical ability. He appeared to have conceived the idea that it was possible for him to make a speech on the floor of the Senate that would insure his reelection even by a Populist legislature. In this he was, of course, mistaken, which he soon found out, to his bitter disappointment. He no doubt came to the same conclusion that many of his friends and admirers had already come to, which was that in bidding for the support of the Populists of his state, he had made the mistake of his life. The impression he made upon the public mind was that he was devoid of principle and that he was willing to sacrifice his own party upon the altar of ambition.

But it was neither known nor suspected that he contemplated making a bid for the support of the Populist members of the legislature until he delivered his speech. When, therefore, it was announced that Senator Ingalls would address the Senate on a certain day, he was greeted as on previous occasions with a large audience. But this was the first time that his hearers had been sadly disappointed. This was due more to what was said than how it was said. Then, it was plain to those who heard him that his heart was not in what he was saying; hence, the speech was devoid of that fiery eloquence which on previous occasions had charmed and electrified his hearers. But after that speech when one would ask another what he thought of it, the reply invariably was a groan of disappointment. When the immense crowd dispersed at the conclusion of the speech, instead of smiling faces and pleasing countenances as on previous occasions, one could not help but notice marked evidences of disappointment in every face. The impression that had been made was that it was an appeal to the Populist members of the legislature of his state to return him to the Senate, in exchange for which he was willing to turn his back upon the party which he was then serving. It was almost equivalent to an open declaration of his willingness to identify himself with them and champion their cause if they would reelect him to the seat he then occupied. From the effects of that fatal blunder the senator never recovered.

Another thing that lessened the distinguished orator and senator in the estimation of the public was his radically changed attitude upon questions affecting the political, social, and industrial status of the colored Americans. From a brilliant and eloquent champion of their civil and political rights he became one of their most severe and harsh critics. From his latest utterances upon that subject it was clear to those who heard what he said or read what he wrote that, in his opinion, the colored Americans merited nothing that had been said and done in their behalf, but nearly everything that had been said and done against them. Why there had been such a strange and radical change in his attitude upon that subject has been and no doubt will continue to be an inexplicable mystery.

The only explanation that I have heard from the lips of some of his former friends and admirers was that it was in the nature of an experiment, the hope and expectation being that it would give him a sensational national fame which could be utilized to his financial advantage upon his retirement to private life. This explanation would have been rejected without serious consideration but for the fact that some others have pursued the same course and for the same reason and their hopes and expectations have been, in a large measure, realized. In his bid for the support of the Populist members of the legislature of his state, the senator had established the fact that he did not have very strong convictions upon any subject and that those he had could be easily changed to suit the time and the occasion. It may be, therefore, that in taking this stand upon the race question, he did so with the hope and expectation that it would not only give him a national fame, as it had given others of far less note and ability than himself, but that it might open the door for him to easily acquire considerable wealth.

Nebraska, though not very strong politically, is one of the most important states in the West. It has sent a number of men to the front who have made an impression upon the public mind. For many years no state in the Union was more reliably Republican than Nebraska. A large majority of its voters, I am sure, are not now and have not been in harmony with the Democratic party, but it is true at the same time that thousands of those who for many years acted with the Republican party and voted for its candidates, national and state, have become alienated, thus making Republican success at any election in the state close and doubtful and that too regardless of the merits of opposing candidates or the platform declarations of opposing parties.

For this remarkable change there must be a good and sufficient reason. The state, in its early history, was sparsely populated and stood very much in need of railroads for the development of its resources. In those days railroads were very popular and the people were in a mood to offer liberal inducements to those who would raise the means to furnish them with the necessary transportation facilities through the medium of railroads.

For the same reason the national government made valuable concessions in the interest of railroad construction in the Western states. Since the railroads thus aided were, in a large measure, the creatures of the state and nation, they thereby acquired an interest in the administration of the national and state governments, especially those of the state, that they otherwise would not have had. The construction of the roads went on with such a rapid rate that they soon acquired such a power and influence in the administration of the state government that the people looked upon it as being dangerous to their liberties. In fact it was claimed, which was no doubt largely supported by the facts, that the state government was actually dominated by railroad influence. No one, it was said, could be elected or even appointed to an important office who was not acceptable to the railroad interests. This state of affairs produced a revulsion among the common people, thousands of them deciding that they would vote against the Republican party, which was then and had been for many years in control of the state government, for allowing such a state of affairs to be brought about.

Edward Rosewater, editor and proprietor of the *Omaha BEE*, the most influential Republican paper in the state, took sides against the railroad interests. The result was that Nebraska, for the first time, elected a Democratic governor. But many of the Republicans who acted with the Democrats on that occasion could not see their way clear to remain in that party, and yet some of them were not willing to return to the ranks of the Republicans. So they decided to cast their lot with the Populist party, which in the meantime had made its appearance upon the field of political activity. While the Democratic party remained the minority party in the state, it was seldom for a number of years that the Republicans could poll more votes than the Democrats and Populists combined, and since, under the then leadership of the Democratic party in the state, that party and the Populists stood practically for the same things, it was not difficult to bring about a combination or fusion of the two parties against the Republicans. This gave the fusionists control of the state government for a number of years.

In the meantime a brilliant, eloquent, and talented young man came upon the stage of political activity in the person of William J. Bryan. His first entry into public life was his election to Congress [in 1890] as a Democrat from a Republican district. While a member of the House, he made a speech on the tariff question which gave him some national notoriety. As a speaker he was plausible and captivating. He could clothe his thoughts, ideas, and opinions in such beautiful and eloquent language that he seldom failed to make a favorable impression upon those who heard him. It was this wonderful faculty that secured him his first nomination for the presidency. His name was hardly thought of in connection with the nomination by that convention. In fact his right to a seat as a member of the convention was disputed and contested. But after he had delivered his "cross of gold and crown of thorns" speech before that body, he carried the same by storm. His nomination was then a foregone conclusion.

It was under the leadership and chiefly through the influence of Mr. Bryan that the fusion between the Democrats and Populists of his state was brought about. But for his advocacy of free silver and his affiliation with the Populists, he might have reached, at that time, the goal of his ambition. The result showed that while he commanded and received the support of not less than eighty percent of his own party, the remaining twenty percent proved to be strong enough to insure his defeat. In fact the business interests of the country were almost solid against him, and it is safe to say that no man can ever hope to become president of the United States who cannot at least divide the substantial and solid business interests. The businessmen were apprehensive that the election of Mr. Bryan would bring about financial and commercial disaster. Hence they, almost regardless of previous party affiliations, practically united in an effort to defeat him.

The state of Nebraska, therefore, will always occupy a prominent place in the history of the country, because, though young, small, and politically weak, it has produced the most wonderful and most remarkable man of which the Democratic party can boast. It has also produced a number of very able men on the Republican side, such men, for instance, as C. F. Manderson and John M. Thurston, both of whom have served the state in the United States Senate and made brilliant records. But Mr. Bryan had an advantage over both of them when before a popular audience in Nebraska, because they had been identified with the railroad interests while he had not.

That Mr. Bryan was a strong man and had a wonderful hold upon his party is shown by the fact that he was three times the party candidate for the presidency. While it may be true that he could never be elected to the presidency, it is no doubt equally true that no other Democrat could be, while Bryan lived, who was not acceptable to Bryan and his friends.

At least in one respect Mr. Cleveland and Mr. Bryan were very much alike. As already stated, Mr. Bryan was a Democrat, at least in name and action. The same was true of Mr. Cleveland, and yet they were as radically different as it is possible for two men to be. They were not only different in temperament and disposition, but also in their views and convictions upon public questions, at least so far as the public is informed, with the exception, possibly, of the tariff. Another question came to the front after the Spanish-American War called "imperialism," upon which they may have been in accord, but this was not positively known to be a fact. The tariff is such a complicated subject that they may not have been in perfect accord even on that. Mr. Cleveland was elected president in 1892 upon a platform pledged to a tariff for revenue only. The Democrats had a majority in both houses of Congress, but when that majority passed a tariff bill it fell so far short of Mr. Cleveland's idea of a tariff for revenue only that he not only denounced it in strong and bitter language, but refused to sign it. Whether or not Mr. Bryan was with the president or the Democratic majority in Congress in that fight is not known, but judging from his previous public utterances upon that subject, it is to be presumed that he was in accord with the president.

It is claimed by the friends and admirers of both Mr. Cleveland and Mr. Bryan that they were what is called Jeffersonian Democrats, which means that they were strong advocates and defenders of what is called states rights, and this constitutes one of the principal differences between the Republican and Democratic parties. And yet, President Cleveland did not hesitate to use the military force of the government to suppress the domestic violence within the boundaries of the state of Illinois and that too against the protest of the governor of the state, for the alleged reason that such action was necessary to prevent the interruption of the United States mail. Mr. Bryan's views upon the same subject appeared to be sufficiently elastic to justify the national government, in his opinion, in becoming the owner and operator of the principal railroads of the country. His views along these lines were so far in advance of those of his party that he was obliged, for reasons of political expediency and party exigency, to hold them in abeyance during the presidential campaign of 1908. Jeffersonian democracy, therefore, seems now to be nothing more than a meaningless form of expression.

The South has been a fertile field for political experimental purposes by successive Republican administrations since the second administration of President Grant. The solid South, so called, has been a serious menace to the peace and prosperity of the country. How to bring about such a condition of affairs as would do away with the supposed necessity for its existence or continuance has been the problem, the solution of which has been the subject for political experimental purposes. President Hayes was the first that tried the experiment of appointing Democrats to many of the most important offices, with the hope that the solution would thus be found. But he was not given credit for honest motives or honorable purposes in doing so, for the reason that the public was impressed with the belief that such action on his part was one of the conditions upon which he was allowed to be peaceably inaugurated. At any rate the experiment was a complete failure; hence, so far as the more important offices were concerned, it was not continued by Republican administrations that came into power subsequent to Hayes, and prior to the Taft administration.

I do not mean to say that no Democrats were appointed to important offices at the South by the administrations referred to, but such appointments were not made with the belief or expectation that they would contribute to a solution of the problem that was involved in what was known as the solid South. Political and social conditions in that section of the country are such that the appointment of men who are not identified with the Republican party to some of the federal offices is inevitable and unavoidable. The impression that the writer desires to make upon the mind of the reader is that between the administrations of Hayes and Taft no Republican administration made such appointments with the expectation that they would contribute to a breaking up of the solid South. President Theodore Roosevelt tried the experiment of offering encouragement and inducements in that direction to what was known as the gold-standard Democrats, but even that was barren of satisfactory results. President Taft seems to be the first and only Republican president since Mr. Hayes who allowed himself to labor under the delusion that the desired result could be accomplished through the use and distribution of federal patronage.

The chief mistake on the part of those who thus believe grows out of a serious lack of information about the actual situation. In the first place, their action is based upon the assumption that the solid South, or what remains of it, is an outgrowth of an honest expression of the wishes of the people of that section, whereas, in point of fact, the masses, even of the white people thereof, had very little to do with bringing about present conditions and know less about them. Those conditions are not due to the fact primarily that colored men are intimidated by white men, but that white men are intimidated by the Democratic party. They are not due primarily to the fact that colored men are disfranchised, but that white men are prevented from giving effective expression to their honest political opinions and convictions.

The disfranchisement of the colored men is one of the results growing out of those conditions which would not and could not exist if there was absolute freedom of thought and action in political matters among the white people. The only part that the so-called race question plays in this business is that it is used as a pretext to justify the coercive and proscriptive methods thus used. The fact that the colored man is disfranchised and has no voice in the administration of the government under which he lives and by which he is taxed does not change the situation in this respect. His presence, whether he can vote or not, furnishes the occasion for the continuance of such methods, and, as long as intelligent persons, especially at the North and particularly in the Republican party can be thus fooled and deceived they will not be discontinued.

The announcement of President Taft's Southern policy, therefore, was received with satisfaction and delight, not on account of the official recognition that members of their party were to receive, for that was of secondary importance, but on account of the fact that they could clearly see that their contention about the so-called race question was thus given national sanction and countenance, which would have the effect of making that question serve them for several more presidential campaigns. It was giving a new market value to this "watered stock," from which they would derive political dividends for a much longer period than they otherwise would. They could thus gleefully see that if a man of President Taft's intelligence and experience could thus be fooled and deceived about conditions at the South, they would not have very much difficulty in deceiving others who were not believed to be so well informed.

To solve the problem, therefore, the disposition of the federal patronage will cut a very small figure. The patronage question is not half as important, in a political or party sense, as many have been led to believe. It really makes very little difference by whom the few offices are held, whether they be all Democrats, all Republicans, some white and some colored, provided they be honest, capable, and efficient. For political, personal, or party reasons some feeling may be created and some prejudice may be aroused on account of the appointment of a certain person to an office, but if no attention should be paid to it and the fact should be developed that the duties of the same are being discharged in a creditable and satisfactory manner, the public will soon forget all about it.

But the fact remains that the disposition of the federal patronage will not produce the slightest change in the political situation in such localities. If a national Republican administration should refuse to appoint colored men, for instance, to any office in any one of the Southern states for the alleged reason that it might be objectionable to the white people of the community, and therefore might have a tendency to prevent white men from coming into the Republican party, the fact would be demonstrated at the very next election in that community that the Republican party had not gained and the Democratic party had not lost a single vote as a result thereof, for the reason, in the first place, that the excuse given was insincere and untrue, and in the second place, because the incumbent of the office, whoever he might be, would produce no effect whatever in the local situation in consequence of his appointment to, and acceptance of, the office. If there should be any change in the situation at all, it would doubtless be to the loss and detriment of the Republican party, for there would no doubt be someone who would be disposed to resent what would seem to them to be political or party ingratitude.

So far as the colored Republicans are concerned, they have been in the past and must be in the future nothing more than party allies. They have never dominated a state nor have they controlled the Republican organization of any state to the exclusion of white men. They have simply been allies of white men who could be induced to come forward and assume the leadership. This is all they have been in the past; it is all they desire to be in the future. They are perfectly willing to follow where others lead, provided they lead wisely and in the right direction. All they ask, desire, and insist upon is to be recognized as political allies upon terms of equality and to have a voice in the councils of the party of their choice and in the administration of the government under which they live and by which they are taxed and also fair and reasonable recognition as a result of party success, based, all things else being equal, upon merit, fitness, ability, and capacity.

Even in states where it is possible for them to wield a sufficient influence to make them potent in party conventions and in shaping the policy and selecting the candidates of the party, they never fail to select the strongest and best men among the white members of the organization. If it be true that they were sometimes the victims of misplaced confidence, it cannot and will not be denied that the same is equally true of white men of far more experience in such matters.

If there is ever to be again, as there once was, a strong and substantial Republican party at the South, or a party by any other name that will openly oppose the ruling oligarchy of that section, as I have every reason to believe will eventually take place, it will not be through the disposition of federal patronage, but in consequence of the acceptance by the people of that section of the principles and policies for which the national organization stands. For the accomplishment of this purpose and the attainment of this end, time is the most important factor. Questionable methods that have been and are still being used to hold in check and in abeyance the advancing civilization of the age will be eventually overcome and effectually destroyed. The wheels of progress, intelligence, and right cannot and will not move backward, but they will go forward in spite of all that can be said and done. In the meantime, the exercise of patience, forbearance, and good judgment are all that will be required.

Another fact which seems to be overlooked by many is that the so-called solid South of today is not the menace to the country that it was between 1875 and 1888. During that period the solid South included the states of Delaware, Maryland, West Virginia, Kentucky, and Missouri. Those states at that time were as reliably Democratic as Texas and Georgia. Such does not seem to be true of them now, and yet I venture the assertion that the disposition of the federal patronage in them had very little if anything to do with bringing about the change. What has been done and is being done in those states can and will be done in others that are located south of them. As strong as the Republican party is there is one thing it cannot afford to do, and that is to encourage or tolerate the drawing of the race or color line in any efforts that may be made to break and dissolve what now remains of the solid South.

One of the cardinal principles and doctrines of that party—the one that has, more than any other, secured for it the loyal and consistent support of those who represent the moral sentiment of the country—is its bold and aggressive advocacy and defense of liberty, justice, and equal civil and political rights for all classes of American citizens. From that grand and noble position it cannot afford to descend in an effort to find new and doubtful allies.[1] If it should, in an evil moment, allow itself to make such a grave blunder and criminal mistake, it will thereby forfeit the confidence and support of the major part of those upon whom in the past it has relied, and never in vain, for its continuance in power. There is nothing in the situation that would justify the experiment, even if it were thought that a little temporary and local advantage would be secured thereby.

The Fifteenth Amendment to the national Constitution was not intended to confer suffrage upon any particular race or class of persons, but merely to place a limit upon the national government, and that of several states, in prescribing the qualification of electors. Whatever power the national or any state government may have had in prescribing the qualification of electors prior to the ratification of the Fifteenth Amendment, they still have, except that they cannot make racial identity the basis of discrimination.

1. In 1928, before Lynch wrote the final version of this chapter, the Republican party sought to build its Southern support among prospective white members and seemed quite willing to sacrifice the interests of its Negro members.

47

In Puerto Rico and San Francisco

After having spent about three years and six months at Omaha, Nebraska, I was relieved from duty there and assigned to a station at San Francisco, California, where I was to remain only about six months and then proceed to the Philippine Islands for a tour of duty which was to cover a period of two years. But instead of remaining at San Francisco only about six months, I remained there sixteen months. I had never been to California before. I left Omaha on 29 December 1905 and arrived at San Francisco on 1 January 1906, where I remained until 6 May 1907. I was charmed with the country as soon as I saw it. It brought to my mind the beautiful island of Puerto Rico, which is one of the most attractive countries it has ever been my good fortune to visit.

I spent only about ten days at Puerto Rico while I was stationed on duty at Santiago, Cuba. That was in November 1901. I was directed to go there to pay the troops then stationed on the island, for one month only, the paymaster that was stationed there being temporarily absent. While en route I saw from a distance the historic city of Santo Domingo, where the boat on which I was a passenger remained several hours.

The first landing place on the island of Puerto Rico was Ponce. From there I went overland to San Juan, the capital. It was during this overland trip that I was enabled to see the most beautiful and attractive country on the face of the globe. The climate is as near perfection as it is possible for it to be. I was informed by people who lived there for years that the temperature is about the same the year round. It is never disagreeably cold nor uncomfortably hot. Of course one will feel the heat during the middle of the day if he is exposed to the sun, but it does not have a depressing effect upon the system. It is a real pleasure to sit in the parks and on the front porches in the early evenings and enjoy the lovely and healthful sea breezes and then retire to bed under a light covering and sleep soundly, comfortably, and well and get up the next morning feeling refreshed and ready for a hard day's work. While it is never cold enough to need a fire in the house for heating purposes, it is necessary to sleep under cover the year round, otherwise one will be uncomfortably cold, especially about the middle of the night.

The road from Ponce to San Juan was in splendid condition, which made the ride exceedingly enjoyable. For several hours we would be passing, apparently at least, around immense mountains, from which we could look down and see the beautiful streams of running water. The sweet odor from the blooming flowers and the cheerful songs of the native birds made one feel that he was surrounded by everything that is calculated to contribute to the comfort and happiness of mankind. The green foliage could be seen for miles and miles and the fruit trees of different sorts were laden with fruits. The gardens were well worked and the farms appeared to be in good and satisfactory condition. In fact, there was every indication of thrift and industry, prosperity and happiness among the people in spite of the hardships the country had recently experienced as a result of the late war.

But, notwithstanding what is here said, it is a country to which only two classes of people should be encouraged to go. First, those who have ample means and who may be looking for an opening for the profitable investment of at least a part of their capital. Second, those who may be in good circumstances, financially, and may wish to go there only for health and recreation. For all others it is not a desirable place to go, because the island is small and the population is dense. In spite of the fact that the island is what its name indicates, rich port, the poor people there are largely in the majority. This is due chiefly to the fact that the industries are not sufficient in number and volume to afford profitable employment to labor the year round. The island can, and no doubt will, in the course of time, be developed to such an extent that it can and will support profitably and comfortably considerably more than double the present population, but to accomplish this, outside capital must precede that of labor. That this will eventually be done there can be, in my opinion, no reasonable doubt, especially when a sound, safe, and stable government is an assured fact.

San Juan, even at that time, had the appearance of being a modern American city. It had first-class and up-to-date hotels, banking institutions, and a number of large, important, and wealthy commercial houses. It also had telephones, electric lights, and a splendid trolley-streetcar system. In fact there was every indication that all who were engaged in business were in a prosperous condition and were entirely satisfied from a business standpoint.

I was sorry that I could not see more of Santo Domingo, but the boat on which I was a passenger, en route to Puerto Rico, did not remain at the port of Santo Domingo city long enough to make it worthwhile for me to go ashore. But I got a pretty good view of the city from the boat, and then I saw the natives that came on board. I was surprised to find that the language spoken by them was Spanish. I had been under the impression that the prevailing language among them was French. I learned afterwards that this was true of the adjoining island of Haiti, but not of Santo Domingo.[1] I was anxious to see more of the island, not only on account of what I had read and heard about it, but on account of the great fight that took place during President Grant's first administration between the president and Senator Charles Sumner over the proposed annexation of that island to the United States.

As previously stated, the president had negotiated a treaty with that end in view, but Senator Sumner, who was at that time chairman of the Senate Committee on Foreign Relations, bitterly opposed it and secured its rejection by the Senate. This fight finally resulted in the deposition of Senator Sumner from the chairmanship of that important committee and the support by the senator of Horace Greeley for the presidency against Grant in 1872. While my ship was lying in port at the harbor of Santo Domingo, those stirring scenes and incidents were made fresh in my memory, but it was not possible at that time to satisfy my curiosity by going ashore and visiting the different points of interest and of historic note. I hope to be able some day in the future to do this.

But it was Puerto Rico of which I was reminded when I reached California. I was not there very long before I came to the conclusion that it was about centrally located between the extreme cold of the East and the intense heat of the tropics. In point of fact it is what may be called semitropical. While it is cold enough during the winter season to need a fire in the

1. No doubt the author intended to say that Haiti was on the western part of the same island instead of "the adjoining island."

house to enable one to feel comfortable, especially before nine o'clock in the morning and after six in the evening, it is seldom hot enough any time during the summer season, particularly in the cities and towns located on the ocean and bays or near them, to make it necessary for anyone to go to the seashore or any other summer resort to escape the intense heat.

I did not have the opportunity, prior to my departure for the Philippines, to visit many parts of the state, but the most beautiful and attractive section visited by me was the valley bordering on the ocean between San Francisco and Los Angeles. Except for Puerto Rico, it is the most charming and beautiful country I have ever seen. The most surprising thing to me was to find that the wonderful resources of such a remarkable state have not been more rapidly developed. During the sixteen months between my arrival there and my departure for the Philippines, I never once saw a flash of lightning nor heard a clap of thunder. This was something that was both remarkable and strange to one who had witnessed some of the most fearful and terrific storms that can be imagined or described. The dense fogs on the bay during certain months render navigation somewhat dangerous, and yet very little property has been destroyed and very few lives have been lost as a result thereof. In fact the transportation facilities both by land and water are so perfect that the risk and danger of the loss of life and destruction of property have been reduced to a minimum.

But, in spite of what is said above, California has its disadvantages as well as its advantages—some things that are unpleasant and disagreeable as well as many that are pleasant and agreeable. The great earthquake that took place in the state and the disastrous fire that nearly destroyed the city of San Francisco in April 1906 is a case in point. I was there when that calamity took place and am therefore entirely familiar with what occurred at that time and place. The first shock was felt about 5:15 A.M. I lived on the Oakland side of the bay.

sent to that country to remain any considerable length of time. Prior to American occupation, it is safe to say that the islands, or at least some of them, were never entirely free from cholera and smallpox. Those diseases were always prevalent in some of the islands, though not often in epidemic form. In consequence of improved sanitary conditions inaugurated by the Americans, these diseases are not now so prevalent or so fatal as heretofore. The natives as a rule pay very little attention to sanitation and never observe the laws of health and hygiene. They live for to-day and let tomorrow take care of itself.[7]

7. This disregards the immunities which the indigenous population inevitably develops.

Chapter Forty-seven

The family I was living with occupied the lower flat of a well-constructed two-story frame building. The shock was something terrific. The sound was something like that of thunder or heavy artillery at a great distance. While I was still in bed, I happened to be awake at the time. Shortly after the sound I felt the house move like a vessel on the ocean. The falling of dishes, bottles, pictures, and chimneys and the cracking of walls, ceilings, and windows made one feel that there was no place of safety inside or outside of the house. The situation at that particular moment can better be imagined than described.

And yet when it was all over it was seen that the damage done to property by the earthquake was not one-half of what one would naturally have supposed it would be, judging from the severity of the shock, especially the first one—for there were several, each some hours apart—which was the worst and most severe of them all. I am satisfied that the shocks were just as severe at Oakland as at San Francisco, and yet the serious damage done to property at Oakland was confined chiefly to poorly constructed buildings of brick and stone and some very old and weak frame structures, and the chimneys, windows, and plaster on the walls of nearly all the frame houses. One could not fail to notice that the damage done to the modernly constructed houses was very slight, and some of them did not seem to be damaged at all. I noticed one building especially that was about ten stories high and located on the corner of two of the principal streets of the city that did not seem to have a crack in its walls at any point. It was the recently and modernly constructed buildings that were both fire- and earthquake-proof. The fact was made plain that buildings can be erected that will stand the test of severe shocks of earthquakes.

I rode over the principal parts of San Francisco a few days after the disaster and made a careful examination and study of the situation. The conclusion I came to was that nearly all of the reports published in Eastern papers about the disaster had been largely exaggerated. That it was a great disaster cannot and should not be denied, but that it was not as great as the public had been led to believe is also true. It was the fire and not the earthquake that did the great damage to San Francisco. The earthquake was, of course, the primary cause of the fire, but if the city had escaped the fire, it would have been found that the damage done by the earthquake was comparatively light. In my investigations I endeavored to get some idea of what the damage would have been if there had been no fire. I found out that in the first few blocks between the ferry and the business section of the city, the buildings had been erected on what is called made land, on which it is a difficult matter to secure a solid foundation without making deep and expensive excavations. Then again in other sections of the city, especially in what is known as the mission district, the soil is sandy and soft, presenting the same difficulty in securing a solid foundation for building as is found in the section where it is made land.

That the earthquake did considerable damage to buildings in those sections is true. It was in the mission district where no doubt the fire started, and as most of the buildings in that section, large and small, were frame structures, the fire gained great headway, and as the water mains had been broken by the earthquake shocks, the fire soon got beyond the control of the fire department. But it could be easily seen that nearly every large and modern building in the city, such, for instance, as the Flood, the Call, the Chronicle, the Mills and many other similar buildings, were very slightly damaged by the earthquake. It was the fire that did the great damage to such buildings. The solid and substantial walls that were left standing after the buildings had been gutted by the fire were conclusive evidence of that fact.

Some buildings that were supposed to have been solidly

built according to modern and up-to-date plans were greatly damaged by the earthquake. This was especially true of the new city hall, which had cost the taxpayers a large sum of money. But it was asserted and believed by some that there was graft connected with the construction of that building, in consequence of which some inferior material was no doubt used in its construction; hence, the building was not as strong and solid as it was supposed and believed to be. The new city Post Office was also damaged more by the earthquake than it should have been, but this no doubt was due more to its location than to any other cause. It was located in the mission district. The earth under the end of the building fronting on Mission Street had sunk down several feet below the bottom of the stone steps, which showed that the main building had been erected, partly at least, on a defective foundation.

These impressions were strengthened and confirmed by a careful examination and inspection of the unburnt part of the city, located between Market Street, Van Ness Avenue, the waterfront, and the Presidio. This is largely on an elevated location. Hence the buildings, as a rule, were erected on a safe and solid foundation. No building in that section was found to be seriously damaged by the earthquake. The extent of the damage consisted of a few cracked walls and plastering and some broken windows and demolished chimneys. What was true of that section was no doubt true of all the other sections of the city, so far as the earthquake was concerned, except in the low or made lands and in what is called the mission district.

But the people of that great and wonderful state and of that remarkable and progressive city deserve and merit a great deal of praise and commendation for their pluck, push, energy, and determination. That great and awful calamity, which was asserted by some and believed by others to have been a special visitation of divine displeasure, inflicted as a punishment upon the place and its people on account of alleged wickedness, did not discourage them in the least. Hence, I believe it can be safely predicted that inside of a quarter of a century from the date of that great and disastrous calamity, a better, a more beautiful, and a more imposing city will have made its magnificent appearance upon the ruins of the old one.

Political conditions in California I found to be difficult to understand. Of course I took no part in politics, not even to the extent of giving public expression to any views or opinions I might have entertained upon public questions. My information, therefore, was obtained from private conversations and from what was published in the newspapers. At that time there were three political parties in the state—Republican, Democratic, and Union Labor. In addition to these, another one came into existence under the name of the Independence League. It was the product of William R. Hearst. The Union Labor party was strong only in certain parts of the state, San Francisco being the principal source of its strength.

Shortly before I went to California, I had seen that the Republican and Democratic organizations in San Francisco had united upon a ticket to make sure the defeat of Mayor Schmitz, the Union Labor mayor, who was a candidate for reelection. I took it for granted, as perhaps the public did, that the Union Labor party would be defeated, for it was hardly conceivable that the Union Labor party, even in San Francisco, was stronger than the Republican and Democratic parties combined. That the Union Labor ticket was successful, in spite of the union or fusion of the Republican and Democratic organizations, was to me a very great surprise. I could not understand it. But, after I had been in the state a short while, I found out how it happened and how to account for it. It was not because the Union Labor party was stronger than the Republican and Democratic parties combined, but because the Union, or fusion, ticket did not command the solid support of the two principal parties. While it was a fusion of the two organizations, it was not, in point of fact, a fusion of the voters belonging to those organizations.

San Francisco, as is true of most of the large cities in the United States except Philadelphia, is usually Democratic in a straight party fight between Republicans and Democrats. The Union Labor votes in San Francisco came principally from the Democrats. With but two parties in the field, Republican and Democratic, the Democrats would be sure to win. But if the Union Labor party should have a ticket in the field, the Democrats would be reasonably sure to lose. At previous elections when there were three tickets in the field—Republican, Democratic, and Union Labor—many Democrats voted the Union Labor ticket to make sure the defeat of the Republicans, while some Republicans voted the same way to prevent the possible success of the Democrats. Under these circumstances the Union Labor party received considerable support from the other parties.

When the fusion movement was inaugurated, the idea that occurred to many Republicans was that it would be better for their party to allow the Union Labor party to retain control of the local government of the city if the Republicans would be allowed to control the state. Then, some of the influential corporations were opposed to a change since they did not have very much difficulty in getting what they wanted from that administration. These things accounted for the success of the Labor party at that election. From a Republican standpoint it cannot be said that this was bad politics, for the corruption that prevailed under the local administration that was subsequently brought to light and exposed was not then known or even suspected. Politically, the local Labor machine was more friendly to the Republicans than to the Democrats, for the reasons above given, and if the administration of local affairs had remained decent, the Labor organization could have and would have been retained in control of the local government for an indefinite time, under what was supposed to be a sort of reciprocal agreement or understanding between the two parties to the silent compact—Republican and Union Labor. But when the rottenness existing under the local government had been thoroughly exposed, there were very few honest men who felt that they could afford to advocate a continuance of an administration under which such things had been tolerated and permitted.

But with reference to the principles and policies of the different political parties in California, I did not remain there long enough to find out what they represented or for what they stood. Judging from the editorial utterances of the newspapers I read, I am afraid I would not have been much better informed if I had remained there a good while longer. According to my conception of the fundamental principles and doctrines of the Republican party, it must represent, stand for, and advocate equal rights, equal privileges, equal opportunities, and exact justice for all classes of American citizens without regard to race, color, nationality, or religion. But the presence in California of a considerable number of Japanese and Chinese seems to have caused confusion and to have brought about a material change in the attitude of the Republicans thereof with reference to the fundamental principles and doctrines of their party. I found out that the situation with reference to the Japanese and Chinese is not so much racial as it is industrial.[2] The apprehension is that, as competitors in the field of labor with the American man, they are liable to bring about, if they should be there in large numbers, a reduction in the wages of the American laborer or throw him out of employment and thus degrade the American standard of wages and of labor. These are questions and problems that deserve and merit the thoughtful and careful consideration of the American people.

2. The author seemed not to be familiar with the laws and discriminatory practices designed to degrade the Chinese and Japanese in California.

Those conditions do not exist between the white and colored people in the South or in any part of the United States, as they did at one time. It was as slaves that the colored people in the South represented a degraded standard of labor. There is, therefore, very little opportunity along race lines for friction between the white and colored American laboring man for the reason that the colored American is gradually reaching that point where he insists upon the same rate of wages for himself that is paid to a white man for the same kind of service.

I feel that I should not close this chapter without again alluding to the labor question in politics. It has been said that the Union Labor party was strong in certain parts of the state and this was especially true of San Francisco. That it is both right and proper for laboring men to form themselves into union organizations for their protection and to promote their interests in legal and legitimate ways no one, I am sure, will seriously question. But experience has shown that they are just as liable as other organizations to go to extremes, to make unjust and unreasonable demands and do some of the very things and commit some of the same acts which they so justly complain of in others.

One of the most serious mistakes made by the labor unions in San Francisco, and in some other parts of the state, was in going into politics as a Labor party. The proper and legitimate function of such organizations should be to agree upon and formulate fair, just, and reasonable demands in the interests of labor and take the necessary steps to influence public opinion to support them. No political party will disregard such demands or ignore such organizations when they are supported and sustained by public sentiment. But when they allow their organizations to be converted into a political party, they not only expose their own weakness, but they thus forfeit any claim they might otherwise have upon the successful party. And, even in localities where they may be occasionally successful, as in San Francisco for instance, they thus throw upon their organizations the responsibility for the local administration, which is liable to be manipulated and controlled by selfish, designing, and dishonest men, thus bringing the labor organizations into public disfavor. This was clearly shown in the case of the Schmitz government of San Francisco, for the existence of which the Union Labor organizations were primarily responsible.

Then again, the formation or organization of a political party in the interest of any one race, class, or sect is contrary to the spirit of our institutions. Under a Republican form of government no one race or class of people can have, or should have, any rights or privileges that are not common to, and enjoyed by, all alike. No political party that seeks to create, encourage, or countenance class or race distinction in the exercise and enjoyment of public rights and privileges, can ever secure the endorsement and support of the American people, or retain it very long if once secured.

A political party, to merit the confidence of the people and be successful at the polls, must be one that is committed to the fair and impartial enforcement of the laws that are equally applicable to all alike, and to protect all in the exercise and enjoyment of their political, civil, and religious rights and privileges without regard to race or class. A political organization, therefore, that is created in the interest of labor is no less repugnant to the spirit of our institutions than one that is created in the interest of capital. In either case, class legislation will be contemplated, which the good sense of the American people, I am sure, will never tolerate. Our government is not and never shall be administered in the interest of any one class, race, or religion, but it is or should be, and should continue to be, administered in the interest of the whole people, thus making it in truth and in fact a government of the people, by the people, and for the people.

The word *people* is so broad and comprehensive that it includes, as it should, all classes, races, and nationalities of which our citizenship is composed. The organization or formation, therefore, of a political party to promote and protect the exclusive interests of one particular class was one of the grave errors, if not fatal mistakes, that the Union Labor organizations of San Francisco and some other sections of the same state allowed themselves to make. But it is hoped that the unsuccessful experiment which has been made in San Francisco of utilizing labor organizations for political purposes will prove to be a blessing in disguise and that such organizations will be confined in the future to the legitimate objects and purposes for which they are brought into existence.

48

In Hawaii and the Philippines

On the sixth day of May 1907 I took passage on the army transport *Logan* for a tour of two years duty in the Philippines and arrived safely at Manila on the thirty-first day of the same month. The transport stopped at only two points between San Francisco and Manila—Honolulu and Guam. We remained several hours at each place but much longer at the former than the latter. While at Honolulu I visited many points of historical note and interest. The fact was brought to mind that as a member of Congress I witnessed the ceremony that took place in the national House of Representatives on the occasion of an official visit paid to the United States by the then king of the Hawaiian Islands.[1] The Demo-

1. In November 1874 King Kalakaua, accompanied by several Hawaiian dignitaries, began a visit of three months in the United States. Sylvester Stevens, *American Expansion in Hawaii, 1842–1898* (Harrisburg, 1945), pp. 118–19.

crats had a large majority in the House, but that did not appear to lessen in the slightest degree the intensity of the enthusiasm by which this ruling monarch was received and entertained, notwithstanding the fact that he was identified with, and a member of, one of the dark races.[2] He was received and entertained as the official representative of his country, and as such he was made the recipient of the honor and distinction that all admitted to be due his distinguished and exalted position. There was no thought at that time of those beautiful and fertile islands becoming a part of the territory of the United States.

Honolulu, the principal town of the Hawaiian archipelago, is a charming and beautiful place. The climate is known and admitted to be one of the very best on the face of the earth. While American capital has done much in developing the resources of the country, very much more in that direction remains to be done. At this writing, the labor problem is the most serious that remains to be solved. Sugar is now, and has been for years, the principal product, but there are many other articles, in addition to sugar and the native fruits, that can and eventually will be profitably produced.

All that is needed is labor that can be relied upon both as to quantity and stability. In these particulars the natives cannot be wholly depended upon. They are not only insufficient in numbers but they are also deficient in stability. Then again they do not seem to be adapted in any respect for the purposes desired and required. On the contrary, they are not very much more adapted for producing sugar in their own country than the Indians were for producing cotton, rice, and sugar in the United States. Some of the large landowners have tried the experiment of importing labor from Japan, but the experiment does not seem to have been entirely satisfactory. While the

2. The House of Representatives still had a Republican majority, since the Democrats who were elected in November 1874 and who would constitute a majority did not take office until 6 March 1875, by which time King Kalakaua had returned to Hawaii.

Japanese is a good worker and a fine producer, he is also an apt pupil. It does not take him very long, for instance, to fall into American ways, ideas, habits, notions, and customs. Hence he soon begins to make demands for higher wages than the employer is able or willing to pay. When such demands are refused, strikes are liable to follow, thus producing confusion and demoralization in the labor market. Some of the large landowners, it is said, contemplate trying the experiment of introducing labor from the Philippines, while others may try to get desirable labor from different parts of Europe. Whether or not any or all of these efforts will produce the desired results remains to be seen. At any rate, the possibilities of the country are wonderful, the remarkable production of which will surprise and astonish the commercial world as soon as the labor problem shall have been satisfactorily solved.

Annexation to the United States took place during the administration of President Harrison.[3] Some Americans believed at the time that this result was brought about through methods that were indefensible from a moral and equitable standpoint and possibly of questionable legality. President Cleveland, who succeeded President Harrison, was one of that number, but the work of annexation had gone so far when he took office that he found himself powerless to undo what had been done. Besides, it was well known that annexation was strongly supported by public sentiment in this country. The public believed that, regardless of the methods that had been used and employed to bring it about, the result itself was the best thing for both countries. While this was no doubt true, it cannot be denied that, had that question been submitted to a popular vote of the natives and citizens of that country, such a result would not have been an accomplished fact, at least at that time.

3. President Harrison sent a treaty of annexation to the Senate on 15 February 1893, but the Senate did not ratify it. Hawaii was finally annexed to the United States on 12 August 1898 during the administration of President McKinley.

Upon the death of the king, which occurred prior to annexation, his widow became the ruling monarch.[4] Her administration seems not to have been strong enough to prevent the successful organization of a rival government with white Americans practically in control of it, through whose efforts and negotiations annexation was brought about. It was really an accomplished fact before the queen realized that she had been deposed, her government overthrown, and her country no longer free and independent. Those facts were not only soon made clear to her, but she was also made to realize that she was at the mercy, and subject to the will of, a strong and powerful government against which it was useless for her to make the slightest resistance.

Peaceful submission and quiet acquiescence, therefore, soon became the settled policy of the natives and their deposed rulers. While this may not have been gracefully done, it was done just the same. They saw that they had no other alternative and that hence they might as well accept the situation gracefully and without making wry faces. The former queen was not only thus deprived of power, prestige, and influence, but she was also deprived of what had been the principal source of her income—the revenue from the public, or crown lands—which she had persistently claimed and contended she could not be deprived of equitably, morally, or legally during her lifetime. Her contention was that, although they were public, or crown lands, the title to which descends from one ruler to another, yet when the title is once passed, it thus becomes a vested right which can be legally terminated only by death—hence, she has been an applicant at the doors of the American Congress to have that body recognize the justice of her claims and demand.

The probabilities are that, from a purely legal standpoint, she would have no standing in court, notwithstanding her con-

4. King Kalakaua was succeeded by his sister, Lilioukalani, and not by his widow as Lynch claims.

tention, for the reason that, according to the customs of the country, the income from the public lands belonged to, and constituted a part of, the income of the head of the government whoever that head might be. Neither title in fee nor a life tenure could pass to any one ruler, but must, according to the rule of succession, pass from one ruler to another, and finally, when the government passed from one sovereign to another, everything belonging to the government, including the title to the public lands, must pass also. Notwithstanding this fact, many Americans believed that, from a standpoint of equity and justice, the claim of the former queen should be, at least in part, recognized through a direct appropriation out of the public treasury as a compensation in part for the losses thus sustained by her through the action of this country. The justice of such a claim may be some day recognized, but whether or not it will be done during the lifetime of the former queen is extremely doubtful.

When we entered the harbor of Manila the mind was carried back to the eventful Sunday which was made memorable by the destruction of the Spanish fleet by Admiral Dewey. The day we entered the harbor was bright and beautiful, which made it easy for all on board to see the different points of interest as they were pointed out and explained by those who were familiar with the country and had a thorough knowledge of the important events that were connected with that famous naval battle. But the city of Manila was a disappointment. It was not what the imagination had pictured. It is neither beautiful nor imposing. The buildings, especially those inside of what is called the walled city, are old and some of them in a state of dilapidation and decay. The Spanish appear to have acted upon the assumption that the right of the Spanish government to retain possession of that country would some day be contested by other powers; hence the precaution they took and the great expense they incurred in having nearly every important city, town, and village converted into a military fortification by having them enclosed in an immense wall, the said wall being utilized as a fort. They were not only constructed for that purpose, but they were so arranged as to make it a very difficult matter for an invading army to gain access to the city, or at least that part of it inside of the wall fortification.

The principal or main part of the city of Manila is enclosed within one of those immense walls which must have been in process of construction for a number of years and which evidently cost a very large sum of money. It was almost impossible, therefore, for an invading army to get into the city except by scaling this immense wall and fortification, to prevent which a large ditch or canal was dug in front of the wall, thus making the approach to the wall itself extremely difficult if not impossible. Even after the destruction of the fleet in the bay, the American army could not have safely marched into the city if it had been garrisoned by a strong and well-disciplined army which had the active, moral, and physical support of the people of the city and locality. Under such circumstances the place could have been captured in no other way than by a long siege, resulting in a complete cutting off of the source of supply, thus forcing a surrender from starvation or physical exhaustion. But the Spanish army or what there was of it was not only insufficient in point of numbers, but very deficient in discipline. And then again the government did not have the sympathy and support of the native population.

These things made American occupation a comparatively easy matter. It is true that what the great majority of the natives wanted and still want was and is absolute independence and self-government. With that end in view, they did all in their power to assist the Americans in ridding the country of Spanish rule, but when the fact was subsequently made known to them that the United States was to step into the shoes of Spain—that there was to be a transfer of sovereignty from Spain to the United States and not from Spain to the natives—their joy was turned into sadness, sorrow, and bitter disappointment.

The Americans claim, of course, that the natives are not yet capable of self-government and will not be for some time to come, but the natives contend that they are better judges of that than it is possible for the Americans to be and that if they are given the opportunity they would soon demonstrate that fact to the satisfaction of the civilized world. But the probabilities are that they will not have that opportunity for many years to come.

It is a rich and fertile country and its future possibilities are great. Certain parts of it are now being developed with American and European capital, and very much more capital would seek investment there if the question of the future relations of the island to the United States was definitely settled and permanently fixed. But this will never be done as long as one of the two principal parties in the United States is in favor of, and the other opposed to, turning the country over to the natives and recognizing their independence. I am of the opinion that it is best for the natives and for their country that they remain, for at least one generation, under the control and sovereignty of the United States, and yet it must be frankly admitted that this is not in harmony with the declaration promulgated by the Americans in that instrument called the American Declaration of Independence, to the effect that all just governments derive their power from the consent of the governed.

That the Philippine Islands are being governed by the United States against the will of the people thereof, will not, I am sure, be denied by anyone. And yet that is nothing unusual for the United States, for there are thousands of American citizens living upon American soil contributing to the support of the government, state and national, who are governed against their will and contrary to their wishes. They are thus taxed without representation. It is a fact well known that in several states of the American Union the colored citizens thereof are not allowed to have even a voice in making or enforcing the laws by which they are governed. They are not allowed to enjoy the civil and political rights upon terms of equality with other American citizens.

Notwithstanding these things, the colored American is much better off in his own country than it is possible for him to be in any other. He is aware of the fact that his own deficiencies, for which he is not wholly responsible, are among the alleged causes of the conditions of which he complains. He is therefore hopeful and confident, and he has every right to be, that the wrongs to which he is now subjected will eventually cease to exist. What is true of the colored American in the states referred to is equally true of the inhabitants of the Philippine Islands, but with reference to the latter in a much more marked degree, for it will not be denied by those who are familiar with the facts and will look at the situation from an unprejudiced standpoint, that the colored American can and does exercise the elective franchise and discharges the duties and responsibilities of citizenship with much more intelligence, wisdom, and discretion than the average "Filipino."

Then again, the colored people in the States constitute a very small minority of the population of the country, and consequently, their votes cannot be potential or decisive except in certain localities and on some occasions when the whites are so divided as will make the colored vote a deciding factor. But in any case and under all circumstances the whites in America are and will continue to be the ruling class. That is not true of the Philippine Islands. The probabilities are that the natives of those islands will continue to be largely in the majority for many years to come if not indefinitely. All that the Americans can hope to accomplish is to gain and retain the goodwill and friendship of the natives by kind treatment, good administration, and an honest and efficient government.

Considerable progress has already been made in this direction. The splendid school system which has been inaugurated and is being efficiently maintained is doing more good in this respect than anything, the churches not excepted. I found out that, along religious lines, very little improvement or progress has been made. The natives are willing and even anxious to have their children attend the public schools and learn to speak and write the English language, but they do not seem to have a very strong desire to embrace the white man's religion. In that respect their inclination is to let well enough alone. Still, the missionary is making some little progress and accomplishing some good along the lines of morality and religion, but they are hardly enough to justify the energy and money spent for such purposes.

The *Negritoes*, which is the Spanish word for "little Negroes," are supposed to be, like the Indians of America, the aborigines of that country, but who were overpowered, driven out, and almost exterminated by the Malays who took possession of the country, but who, in turn, were overpowered and subjugated by the Spanish. The "Filipinoes" belong to the Malay race. They are called "Filipinoes" simply because they are the inhabitants of the Philippine Islands, the islands being thus named in honor of Philip, the ruling monarch of Spain when the islands were acquired by that country. If the Spanish government had treated the natives as they are now being treated by the United States, they would now be fully capable of organizing and maintaining a free and independent government of their own. Instead of seeking to improve and elevate them along lines of modern civilization and enlightenment, it appears to have been the policy of the Spanish government to hold them in subjection by keeping them in a state of ignorance, poverty, and superstition.

Very many years, therefore, must necessarily pass before the desired and essential changes along these lines can be brought about. These facts will be made plain to anyone who will carefully examine the industrial and commercial situation. It will be seen that very few of the natives are thus engaged. The principal business is carried on by foreigners—Americans, Europeans, Chinese, and Japanese, especially the Chinese, who seem to be the principal commercial people of the country. Many of these businessmen have become citizens and have identified themselves with the people in every important particular. Still they are not of the manor born and might not stand well with the powers that be in the event of independence. But under the existing order of things they feel that they can safely remain there and carry on their business.

The principal products of the islands are sugar, tobacco, and hemp. Coconuts are also produced in large quantities, as are certain other fruits that are indigenous to the country and climate, such as mangoes and nuts of various kinds. Manila hemp has a worldwide reputation. It is the finest hemp produced in the world. Another important industry that is practically in its infancy is the manufacture of a material called "penio" and another called "jusie." Both are used largely by ladies for dress skirts, shirtwaists, and veils. Though delicate, the material is fine and very popular with the ladies, especially Americans and Europeans. The manufacture of it is in its crude state. At this writing it is manufactured by the natives at their homes, small machines being utilized for that purpose. To see the people engaged in manufacturing it reminds one of the early days of the Republic when cotton cloth and thread were woven and made by small machines that were worked by human hands. The industry is destined to become a large and important one.[5]

The removal of the tariff duties from products of the Philippines imported into this country will add materially in the prosperity of the islands and the people thereof, and at the same time will work no hardship on the American manufacturer, for the reason that the importation from the islands will hardly be sufficient to make the supply very much, if any, in excess of the demand. Philippine importations therefore will hardly be a

5. For a discussion of weaving see Hamilton M. Wright, *A Handbook of the Philippines* (Chicago, 1909), p. 63, and Gladys Zabilka, *Customs and Culture of the Philippines* (Tokyo, 1963), p. 97.

drop in the bucket as far as they may have a bearing on the law of supply and demand, and yet they will have a very important bearing and influence upon the country from which they are exported. But, another reason why the importations from that country are not likely to make any material impression on the American market is because they are not likely to be sufficient in volume to produce such a result.

The labor supply in that country is not now and is not likely to be equal to the demand. While the average Philipino is periodically industrious and produces whatever is produced, the probabilities are that no other race or class can be relied upon to take his place in that line. The climate is such that only those who are to the manor born can stand it and there is a limit even to their powers of endurance. The climate is severe and has a very debilitating effect upon the average American and European, even though they be not exposed to the burning heat of the tropical sun. The climate seems to develop whatever is latent in the system. Many Americans have gone there who were apparently in the enjoyment of perfect health at the time but who returned physical wrecks, although they remained there only about twenty-four months. This is especially true of the women upon whom the climate seems to be more severe than upon the man. No American over fifty years of age ought to go there or be sent there to remain longer than about six months. While going through the period of acclimatization the chances are decidedly against the person that has passed the fifty-year milepost.[6]

Even young men who have been careless and followed habits of dissipation cannot safely go there and remain as long as two years. Only young men in good health, a strong constitution, and in a sound and perfect physical condition should go or be

6. The author's point of view is strikingly similar to the arguments used by white Americans who insisted that only persons of African descent could stand the harsh and debilitating effects of the climate of the deep South.

49

Retirement and Remarriage

SHORTLY AFTER MY ARRIVAL AT MANILA, I WAS ASSIGNED TO duty at Iloilo, S. Panay, as paymaster. During the summer of that year the order was promulgated requiring all commissioned army officers to be subjected to a physical examination to determine their fitness for active military service. The test spoken of was to ride or walk a specified number of miles within a given time. If as the result of the physical examination a serious physical defect was detected, he would not be required to take the test, but he would be a suitable person for retirement on account of physical incapacity.

I was apprehensive that I would be pronounced physically incapable of making the test, on account of a slight heart ailment which no doubt was somewhat aggravated by the climate. I had suffered from this ailment slightly for many years. But whether or not it was organic or functional I was not absolutely sure. I happened to be personally acquainted with and enjoyed the friendship of a very eminent army physician to whom I applied for personal physical examination to satisfy myself as to whether or not it would be safe for me to take the test officially or otherwise. This was done, and he made a verbal report to me in which he stated that there was a slight heart ailment which he was satisfied was not organic, but if he were on the official board by which I was to be examined, he would no doubt be one who would report against allowing me to take the test for the reason that while he was sure it was not organic, it might be possible for him to make a mistake. If the board's recommendation were that I could safely take the test and fatal results would follow, the board would be to blame. To be on the safe side, therefore, they would advise against having me subjected to the test.

As a result of his own personal examination, however, he did not hesitate to advise me that I could safely take the test, officially or otherwise, because in his opinion the ailment was not organic. There are very few doctors who can tell the difference between an organic and a functional heart lesion, because the symptoms in both cases are practically the same. If, therefore, I should take the test upon his recommendation and a fatal result would follow, no one would ever know that the test was taken on my recommendation, because this examination was private and confidential, no one being aware of the examination which he had made. It transpired, as I was satisfied it would, that the official board of examiners by whom I was examined reported that it would not be safe for me to take the test, on account of the existence of organic heart disease. In spite of this I decided to take the test myself, unofficially, not because I was opposed to being put on the retired list, if their report were true, but because I was satisfied in my own mind that the report was inaccurate.

Major Walter H. Loving, chief of the Constabulary Bank of Manila, was then a visitor at Iloilo and a guest of mine. I requested him to accompany me in taking the riding test which he kindly consented to do. The morning that the test was to take place I had the quartermaster send me two horses to enable Major Loving and myself to take that test. This was done. We not only rode the prescribed number of miles within the time specified, but five miles further than we were required to ride. On our return we passed the commanding general's home. He was seated on the front porch and saw us as we passed by.

Shortly after I reached my home a messenger from headquarters made his appearance. He stated that he was just from headquarters and the department commander desired to have me report at headquarters without delay. I did so. He expressed himself as being very much surprised when he saw me pass by on horseback at a rapid gait. From the official report made by the examining surgeons in my case, he was of the opinion that I could not ride safely a distance of five miles without fatal results. He stated, therefore, that he would make a special report in my case, which I am sure he did, for the reason that I heard nothing from it until I returned to the United States. This was in the summer of 1907, and these lines are being written in 1937, a period of just about thirty years, and I am not only still alive, but in comparatively good health, and I have only to live a few months longer to reach the age of ninety.

Early in 1909 I had about completed my tour of two years foreign service and was relieved from duty in the Philippine Islands in order to return to the United States, and was assigned to duty at San Francisco, California. Shortly after my arrival at San Francisco, I was subjected to another physical test, but this time it was a walking, instead of a riding test. There was no preliminary examination in this case, but the test was safely made just the same. In the meantime Judge William Howard Taft was elected president of the United States to succeed President Theodore Roosevelt in November 1908 and was inaugurated in March 1909.

Chapter Forty-nine

Early in his administration an order came from the War Department by which I was directed to appear before a retiring board based upon the report that was made by the army doctors at Iloilo in 1907. I appeared before the board at the time and place designated, the board consisting of about five members, two of whom were doctors. The first question put to me was whether or not I desired to be represented by counsel, to which I gave a negative answer, stating that being a lawyer I would represent myself. The papers from the department in my case, therefore, were turned over to me. I then saw for the first time the report of the army doctors by whom I was examined in 1907.

When I read it I could hardly believe my own eyes. For that report would indicate that I was not only afflicted with a clearly developed case of organic heart disease, but that the disease had made such headway that I probably had only a few months longer to live. And yet two years had then passed since that report had been made. Of course, in my argument I ridiculed the report and contended vigorously that it was untrue and inaccurate. Still, this retiring board reported that I was thus afflicted and should be retired on account of physical incapacity. When I heard that, I immediately made application for a leave of absence to enable me to take a trip to Washington City to see the president in person to protest against the confirmation of that report. When I arrived at Washington, my next step was to take whatever step was necessary to secure an audience with the president.

A colored Republican from Ohio by the name of Tyler was then Auditor of the Treasury for the Navy Department, the same position held by me under the Harrison administration.[1]

1. Ralph W. Tyler was a journalist from Columbus, Ohio. After serving as Auditor of the Treasury for the Navy Department, he was to see service during World War I as a war correspondent for the Committee on Public Information. John Hope Franklin, *From Slavery to Freedom: A History of Negro Americans* (New York, 1967), pp. 475–76.

While I occupied that position I usually had no difficulty in securing an audience with the president for any friend of mine, or any other person visiting the capital who would see fit to utilize my services for that purpose. All that was necessary to be done was for me to get in touch with Hon. E. W. Halford, the president's private secretary, through whom an audience would be secured, usually within twenty-four hours, whether the purpose of the visit was to merely pay respects or on business. I therefore decided to take the same course in this instance. Auditor Tyler was the man through whom I expected to secure this audience. When I approached him, he was more than willing to serve me. He immediately called up the president's private secretary requesting that a time be named when he could accompany Major Lynch to call on the president. He was informed that the president could be seen by the public only two days in each week, Tuesdays and Fridays, and if he would appear with the major the following Tuesday at 10:00 in the morning he was satisfied an audience could be secured.

The following Tuesday about 9:30 Mr. Tyler and myself were on hand at the White House and, after remaining there for about an hour, we were notified that the president could not be seen that day, but we must return another day. We did this with the same result. This was continued from week to week covering a period of five weeks. I then came to the conclusion that a scheme had been concocted by which I should not have an opportunity to get in touch with the president personally. I therefore informed Auditor Tyler that I would make no further demands upon him nor consume any more of his valuable time, in what seemed to me to be a vain effort to reach the president. I decided nothing more remained for me to do but to return to my post of duty, having made the trip in vain, unless I could get in touch with some other official who could bring about the desired result.

I found out afterwards that Senator William O. Bradley, a Republican United States senator from Kentucky, was accessible, with whom I got in touch. By appointment I called on him at his office at the Capitol. I knew the senator personally and favorably. He and I were warm personal as well as political friends. In fact he was largely responsible for my election as temporary chairman of the National Republican Convention of 1884. I informed him of the purpose of my visit to Washington and of my disappointment up to that time. He said he was satisfied that he could secure an audience with the president for me; and he would take the necessary step to bring about that result. I cautioned him, however, not to let it be known for what purpose he desired to see him, because I had become convinced that a scheme was on foot to prevent me from seeing the president; and that if he would let it be known that the purpose was to secure an audience for me, it might be frustrated. He said he would bear that in mind.

He then called Mr. Carpenter, the president's private secretary, and stated that it was very important for him to see the president for about five or ten minutes the next morning. He was asked to make his appearance at the White House the next morning at 10:00 and that the secretary might be able to arrange an interview. He stated, however, that the president was not ready yet to take up Kentucky appointments. The senator replied "I said nothing about Kentucky appointments and that is not the purpose of my call. The purpose of my call is a very important matter which will not consume more than five or ten minutes. Make the arrangements."

"All right," replied the secretary, "be here at 10:00 tomorrow morning."

The senator requested me to meet him there at 10:00 the next morning. At 9:30 I was at the White House, but merely mingled with the crowd without letting my presence be known. A few minutes before 10:00 Senator Bradley made his appearance and he immediately notified Mr. Carpenter he was ready to see the president. When the door was opened, the senator stepped in and I stepped in immediately behind him.

Mr. Carpenter seemed to be very much surprised when I entered with the senator, but I was then in the president's presence and the contemplated interview could be postponed no longer.

The president received me very cordially and expressed himself as being pleased to see me. I briefly stated the purpose of my visit, which was to protest vigorously against the confirmation of the report of the Retiring Board in my case, because I was satisfied that what was therein contained was inaccurate and untrue. If it were true, I would not only make no objection to its confirmation, but I would ask to be retired. What I objected to was being forced upon the retired list upon statements which I knew to be inaccurate and untrue. "In fact, Mr. President, I want you to see me yourself and determine to your own satisfaction whether or not I look like an invalid." "Very well," said the president, "the matter will receive immediate attention and consideration." I then thanked him and retired.

I went to the War Department to see parties upon whom I could depend to keep me informed as to what was being done in my case. First information received by me was that the Secretary of War had been directed by the president to have the Retiring Board reconvene and, if possible, reconsider their report. This was done. In their second report they declared that their first report was accurate and therefore could not be changed, but, notwithstanding the facts therein contained, if I were allowed to remain on duty in a climate like California, no unfavorable results would probably follow prior to the time I would be retired by law, which covered a period of only a little over two years. This ended the case and nothing more was heard of it.

The trip referred to above proved to be an eventful one in the history of my life. During my strenuous fights in the state of Mississippi, I had one true, faithful, and loyal friend and supporter in the person of a successful cotton planter located at Round Lake, Bolivar County, Mississippi, by the name of Calvin Miller. Whenever I would pay a visit to the state, even after I was in the army, he would insist upon my spending a few days at his home, which I usually did. On one of those occasions he had me draw his will. He was the father of two sons by a prior marriage and a son and a daughter by a second marriage. He provided quite liberally both for his present wife and the children of both marriages. He died while I was on duty in the Philippine Islands. The children of the first marriage were not satisfied with the will after the contents were made known and therefore contested it and were not successful.

While at Washington City I received a letter from his widow urging me to pay her a visit on my return to California, or if necessary, she would meet me at her sister's home in Memphis, Tennessee. She desired to see me on business. In view of my long stay at Washington, I wrote her that I would not have time to meet her on this trip at all, unless she could arrange to meet me at Chicago. This she decided to do and made the necessary arrangements for me to meet her at the home of a dear friend and namesake of hers, Mrs. C. W. Miller, who lived on Champlain Avenue in Chicago near 70th Street. It was not very far from the first station at which the train would stop after reaching Chicago. I decided to meet her there. The train arrived at that station at an early hour in the morning, and I walked from the depot to Mrs. Miller's residence, but arrived there before breakfast. I was cordially received and invited to take a seat in the front parlor until the arrival of Mrs. Emma Miller, widow of my deceased Mississippi friend, which consumed about an hour. The house was so constructed that the bedrooms could not be entered without going through the parlor. While I was seated there, a very accomplished looking lady passed through the parlor in going to her bedroom. I had no idea who she was, but with her personal appearance as she passed through I was profoundly and favorably impressed, and as a result thereof my stay in Chicago was prolonged several days.

I took advantage of every occasion and opportunity to get in touch with this accomplished lady. She and her sister, Mrs. Cora Williamson, were then getting ready to go east on their summer vacation, and therefore I could not see them as often as I otherwise would, but I saw them often enough to have my first favorable impressions of the lady referred to strengthened. The lady in question was the widow of a successful businessman of Memphis, Tennessee. Upon his death, she joined her sister, Mrs. C. W. Miller of Chicago, and together they carried on a successful beauty parlor business. They left Chicago on vacation before I departed. But I succeeded in securing a promise from Mrs. Williamson that she would do me the honor of replying to any letter that I might see fit to write to her. I remained in Chicago several days after Mrs. Williamson and her sister departed, but since I had a nephew in Chicago connected with the Post Office Department, I spent those days under his roof.

My purpose in remaining there was to procure, if possible, some information relative to Mrs. Williamson and her family connections. Why I had become thus impressed was a question I could not answer to my own satisfaction, because I had been divorced from my daughter's mother about ten years and had about made up my mind not to remarry, but that I would endeavor to get my sister and her amiable and accomplished daughter to keep house for me during the balance of my days at a home which I probably would select in California. After I saw Mrs. Williamson, these plans, I thought, might possibly be changed. Why, I did not know and could not explain. At the same time, if my investigations did not convince me that she would be one for me to cultivate, I would dismiss the thought from my mind. But the more I found out, the stronger those favorable impressions grew on me. My Bolivar County friend, Mrs. Emma Miller, was one who spoke of the family in the highest terms. At any rate, the more I heard of her, the more I found out about her, the more favorably impressed I became. She promptly answered every letter I wrote her, but nothing I could say in any one of my letters, however complimentary I might be, could draw from her any reply which I could construe as manifesting any interest in me other than that of an ordinary friend. Still, I was satisfied that a negative answer to any question I might put would not result.

One sentence in one of my letters, therefore, I have always believed made a deep and favorable impression upon her. That sentence was, "The happiest moments that it was my good fortune to spend on my recent trip east were those that I spent when I was surrounded by the sunshine of your charming presence." At any rate the correspondence continued for more than a year before it was my good fortune to lay eyes upon her again. In one of the letters written in 1910, I invited her and her accomplished sister, Mrs. C. W. Miller, to come to California the following year, 1911, instead of going east. This invitation was accepted. Hence, in August 1911, when Mrs. Williamson and her sister, Mrs. C. W. Miller, left Chicago on their usual summer vacation, they made Oakland, California, their destination. It was not until I was brought personally on that occasion in contact with Mrs. Cora E. Williamson that I succeeded in getting a positive and satisfactory answer to questions I deemed vital and important relative to her future status with me. She stated that her principal reason for declining to be more specific in answering my letters was that she preferred to wait until she was brought in contact with me personally. At any rate it was on that occasion that we decided to get married. I told her that it was useless to wait for some day in the future, however near it might be, and I suggested that we marry while she was there on that occasion. To this she assented.

Consequently, we were married within the next few days, but we agreed that she should return to Chicago to wind up her affairs, and then return to California as Mrs. Lynch. This was done, but inside of twelve months Mrs. Lynch came to the conclusion that she would rather live in Chicago than Oakland, California. She hoped that I would be willing to make the change. I told her that if that was her wish it would give me pleasure to comply with it, since I was satisfied that having lived in the tropics for several years without having developed any serious physical ailment, I was sure I could endure the climate of Chicago, however severe the same might be. Hence, the following year, 1912, we came to Chicago and have lived there ever since.

I have never had any occasion to regret making this change. I am pleased to be able to say that my chief ambition to make the closing years of my eventful life happy and cheerful is being fully realized. I am being convinced more and more every year that in the selection of my present wife, I made no mistake. On the contrary, I find in the person of my present wife I have one who is more than willing to gratify every wish, satisfy every want, and comply with every request. No sacrifice is too great for her to make upon the altar of my personal happiness. Hence, during the closing years of my eventful life, I am experiencing no hardships and no unpleasantness of any kind whatever. I am now living a quiet, happy, satisfied, and contented life, with no unpleasant experiences of any kind or nature. Hence I am looking forward with pleasure and satisfaction to the ending of an eventful life in peace and happiness.

Then again, from a business standpoint, I am proud to be able to say that I have succeeded in establishing myself upon a creditable and satisfactory basis with many of the best and most successful business and professional men in Chicago. When I came to Chicago, though sixty-four years of age, I was too young and too active to spend my days in idleness.

Hence, in 1915 I secured admission, by reciprocity, to the Chicago Bar, and although I did not go into active practice but confined myself to civil business such as real estate, contracts, and abstracts which could be attended to out of court, I succeeded in building up quite a business in that line, from which I realized, prior to the Depression, an amount which netted me on an average considerably more than the difference between my active and retired pay. Though nearly ninety years of age now, I have not fully retired from the practice of my profession. In fact, from a standpoint of health, I cannot say that I am afflicted in any particular with the exception of slightly defective hearing and eyesight. I have never aspired to be a millionaire, and hence have not accumulated a massive fortune; but I am satisfied that should my wife outlive me, which is more than probable since I was about twenty-seven years of age when she was born, she will not be reduced to poverty and therefore will not be dependent upon the charities of the public.

Democrats in the South: The Race Question

As stated in the preceding chapter, when I came to Chicago I was still too young to be wholly inactive, but whether or not I should take an active part in politics was one of the first questions that occurred to me. I had no intention of actively participating politically in local matters, but it occurred to me that like some other retired army officers, I could, with propriety, take an active part in national matters. But after going over the field very carefully, I found that conditions nationally as well as locally were not such as would justify me in doing so. In fact, beginning with the unfortunate administration of President William Howard Taft, the colored American had no standing with either of the two major parties. The Democratic party, nationally, was still a white man's party and, beginning with the Taft administration, the Republican party was no longer a champion of human rights. In fact, the policy inaugurated by President Taft was equivalent to transforming the

Republican party, as far as it was in the power of an administration to do so, into a race proscriptive party. In other words, racial identity regardless of merit was made a bar to official recognition.

In his inaugural address Mr. Taft went so far out of his way as to declare that no colored American would be officially recognized under his administration where white people objected. He not only refused to officially recognize them where white people objected, but he accorded them no recognition where white people did not object. His policy was equivalent to a declaration that the presence of colored Americans in the Republican party was a liability instead of an asset and that their continued identification with the party should be discouraged. This declaration was not only unnecessary and unwise, but from a party standpoint it was inexcusable, indefensible, and reprehensible. The failure to officially recognize colored Americans was not of itself a justifiable cause for dissatisfaction and resentment but it was the reason for the failure to accord this recognition that caused dissatisfaction and resentment.

It was thought by some of Mr. Taft's friends and supporters that this new policy was not in harmony with his own personal convictions, but that he was lacking in courage to give forcible expression to his own convictions. He was neither positive nor aggressive. He preferred to move along lines of the least resistance and was therefore anxious to avoid a contest or controversy. Unlike Theodore Roosevelt, he preferred to follow, rather than resist, what was believed to be popular, whether it be right or wrong. He evidently labored under the mistaken and erroneous impression that Southern Democrats were honest and sincere in the assertion that the suppression of the colored vote at the South was necessary to prevent "Negro domination." Had he been well informed he would have known that there has never been the slightest foundation for that assertion, but it served the purpose of the existing Southern oligarchy as long as they could make men of Mr. Taft's caliber believe that it was true. There was never a time during, nor since, Reconstruction when colored Americans drew the race or color line in politics. There was never a time when they supported colored men because they were colored and opposed white men because they were white, but they did draw party lines. Hence, they voted against Democrats, both white and colored, because they were Democrats, and for Republicans, white and colored, because they were Republicans.

Mr. Taft evidently realized the weakness of his position on this issue when he made an effort to convince genuine Republicans that his new policy did not involve a surrender or abandonment by the party of the fundamental principles and doctrines which characterized the Republican party as the champion of equal civil and political rights for all American citizens, regardless of race, color, nationality, or religion. Hence to deceive and mislead the public on that point he made Washington City and the foreign service, the Hawaiian Islands being classed foreign, temporary exceptions to its application; therefore, quite a number of colored Republicans were appointed to important positions in Washington City, including Register of the Treasury, Auditor of the Treasury for the Navy Department, and several others. A number of colored men in the different states were holding important federal positions when Mr. Taft was inaugurated, no one of whom was reappointed, except the small and unimportant land offices, one in Mississippi and one in South Carolina, the incumbent in each case being reappointed.

That took place while the national convention was going through the form of renominating him to succeed himself. In the other cases he simply allowed the incumbents to hold over without being reappointed until each and every one of them was finally succeeded by a Democrat. From a colored American standpoint there is no difference between a "Lily White Republican" and a White Line Democrat. No colored American can support either; it matters not what party may nominate him, or what the platform declaration may be upon which he is a candidate. If a colored American should vote for either a White Line Democrat or a "Lily White Republican," he will be giving his own approval to his unfitness to be an American citizen simply on account of his racial identity.

In going carefully over the situation, therefore, I found that there had been a retrogression along political lines for the colored Americans. In fact, the colored American had been practically outlawed. I found that he was still persecuted by one of the major parties and deserted by the other. The Democratic party was still a white man's party, and the Republican party under the Taft administration had ceased to be the friend and champion of human rights. Hence, the colored American had nowhere to lay his political head. So far as the two major parties were concerned he had no claim upon either and had no right to expect any consideration from either of them. In fact he was without friends. This was a very discouraging outlook. I therefore abandoned every idea of taking any part at all but to wait for developments. But this situation confirmed that to which I had frequently given expression: that I hoped to see the day come when the colored man's identification with any one political party would be solely one of choice and not one of necessity.

Even when the Republican party was recognized as the champion of human rights, the colored American could then be a Republican from choice, and those who were not in harmony with that party upon many important issues were compelled to act with that party from necessity, the national Democratic party being responsible for the existence of conditions which made this necessary. This was unfortunate for the colored American because it was a limitation upon his political discretion.

Every American citizen regardless of race, color, or nationality should be at liberty to affiliate with any party or support or oppose any candidate, it matters not what the candidate may stand for or the party may represent. This condition will be an accomplished fact when the two major parties will accord to the colored American the same rights and the same discretion that is accorded to other groups of which our citizenship is composed. In other words, every American citizen should be safe and secure in the enjoyment of life, liberty, and property, it matters not what political party may be in control of the government. This result will be an accomplished fact when the so-called race question is no longer in politics—when colored Americans, like other Americans, can affiliate with any party they want to without jeopardizing their civil and political rights.

During the administration of President Wilson, an unsuccessful effort was made to have the Democratic party in states north of the Mason-Dixon Line adopt the same policies that had been inaugurated in the Southern states by members of that party to bring about a complete elimination of the colored American simply on racial grounds. The effort failed for two reasons: first, because the sentiment among Northern Democrats on the race question is not as antagonistic toward the colored man as it is in the South, and secondly, because the colored race being so largely in the minority in the North that the average white man north of the Mason-Dixon Line cannot be made to believe that there is any danger of "Negro domination," to prevent which it is necessary that his vote should be suppressed. This was also the dominant sentiment of a majority of Southern Democrats prior to the sweeping Democratic victories throughout the country in the state and congressional elections of 1874. Nearly every state in the Union at that time went Democratic, the rock-ribbed Republican state of Massachusetts not excepted.

The principal cause of that political revulsion, it is believed, was due to the disastrous financial panic of 1873. At any rate, let the cause be what it may, it not only resulted in the death of the Republican party at the South, but it also resulted in placing the radical element of that party in control of the Democratic organization of that section. Prior to that disastrous result, some of the best and most substantial white men of the

South were rapidly coming into and assuming the leadership of the Republican party. But that election resulted in a radical change. White men in that section who were ambitious for political recognition and distinction came to the conclusion that the same could not be accomplished through any other channel than the Democratic party. Hence, nearly all of the white men of that section who had affiliated with the Republican party identified themselves with the Democratic party. This not only deprived the colored Republicans of the aid and assistance of the white men that they had affiliated with, but the liberal and fair-minded white Democrats could no longer dominate and control their own organization. The radical element in the Democratic party felt that the change had been authorized by the verdict of the voters of the nation and they had been thus authorized to take whatever steps they might deem necessary, legal or illegal, to insure the ascendancy of their organization in every one of the reconstructed states.

The mythical race issue was then inaugurated, the principal purpose of which was to hold the white voters in political subjection to the Democratic organization. The result was that the average white man at the South was a slave to a party fetish. The result is that there has been no such thing as a real and genuine election in the extreme Southern states since that time. Every Republican national administration, however, the Hayes administration not excepted, has never drawn the color line within the Republican party until the inauguration of the Taft administration. This left the colored American, as already stated, practically without a party. But during the Hoover administration, a hopeful sign was indicated when the Northern Democrats decided to drop the so-called race question and seek to win the colored vote instead of suppressing it. The unwise policy inaugurated by the Taft administration made the success of this movement possible. Hence, a much larger number of colored Americans voted the Democratic national ticket in 1936 than at any presidential election since the Civil War. As between a Republican of the Taft type and a liberal and fair-minded Northern Democrat, the latter was the least objectionable and most acceptable of the two.

The situation thus created is more hopeful and encouraging to the colored American than anything that has occurred since the Civil War. Notwithstanding this, the masses of the colored Americans adhered to the Republican party, nationally, at least, at subsequent presidential elections until 1936. This was due chiefly to the fact that the national Democratic party was still a white man's party and the colored Americans believed that Mr. Taft's disastrous defeat in 1912 resulted in the defeat of the policies for which he stood. In other words, they concluded that he had betrayed the Republican voters in the policy inaugurated by him on the race question, and that the Republican party as a whole was still the champion of human rights.

Regardless of the effect that this change in policy may have upon the average colored voter, it is a fortunate thing for the race to have the race question completely eliminated from politics so that the colored voter's identification with any political party will be solely one of choice and no longer one of necessity. With both of the major parties conceding to the colored voters the same rights and privileges enjoyed by the other groups of which our citizenry is composed, the colored American can then support or oppose the candidates of any party without running the risk of jeopardizing the civil and political rights of his race. It does not necessarily follow that the colored Americans will rush pell-mell into the Democratic party, since a large number of them are prejudiced against that party historically and traditionally.

But the elimination of the race issue cannot result otherwise than contributing to the political emancipation of the colored American. It not only results in the political emancipation of the race, but it contributes to the inculcation of a more friendly, amicable, and cordial relationship between the races. White and colored Americans will then meet as friends and not as enemies. They will greet each other with a smile instead of a frown. The white aspirants for political recognition regardless of their political affiliations will seek to win the friendship and support of colored as well as white voters. With the race question eliminated, beneficial results will necessarily follow, because the colored voter will know that his rights as an American citizen will not be contingent upon the result of an election. Hence, he can act in accordance with his views upon whatever questions may be under consideration and discussion.

Colored Americans smarted under the restrictions and limitations to which they were subjected, by being obliged to act practically in a solid body in support of one and in opposition to the other party. Even if they were compelled to act practically in a solid body with any one political party, as long as it was the result of a voluntary choice and not one of compulsion, no material harm would result. The colored Republicans who are still in good standing as Republicans are nevertheless in favor of having the color question done away with in politics, so that their action politically will be influenced by their unbiased decision upon questions that are presented for their consideration.

Even when the race question was the dominant issue the colored Americans, Republican as well as Democrat, refused to draw party lines in local elections. As long as the Democratic party was the white man's party nationally and the Republican party was the champion of human rights, the colored voters ignored party lines in local elections. In all local contests they voted for and against individuals and in national elections for and against parties. That attitude has since been changed. They now vote for and against individuals in national as well as local elections. In other words, in the future, party lines will be practically eliminated. The vote of the colored American will be determined upon the attitude of the individual candidate upon certain questions rather than upon his party affiliations. This is as it should be.

Notwithstanding the hardships and injustices to which colored Americans are subjected in many parts of the United States, still this is a better country for the colored man to live in than any others of which we have any knowledge. In view of what is written above, the same being based upon indisputable facts, the outlook for the future covering the civil rights of the colored American is growing better every year. This is due especially to the fact that the feeling of tolerance and respect for human rights is slowly but surely developing. The abandonment of the race question from politics will ultimately result in the political emancipation of the white men of the South and as the result thereof, two vigorous and aggressive political parties, instead of one, will exist at the South as well as at the North. In other words, the existing Southern oligarchies which have prospered upon the mythical race issue for the past sixty years will ultimately decay and pass out of existence. The two parties which will then be brought into existence will vie, each with the other, in an effort to win the friendship and support of colored as well as white citizens. The spirit of tolerance and deference which once existed in that section will return which will result in the protection of every American citizen in that locality in the enjoyment of life, liberty, and property.

The great bane of our country has been due to the doctrine of states rights, especially when the same is strictly and not liberally construed. States rights when strictly construed is why many lynchings have taken place in that section. The public does not seem to understand that the prevalence of this evil is due largely, if not wholly, to the fact that those who are in authority and whose duty it is to punish mob violence are the official products of the mob they are called upon to punish. It is contrary to human nature for an official who owes his official existence to the mob to prosecute and punish those to whom he is indebted for the position he occupies. The only effective way to remedy this evil, which is now being done, is to do away with the vicious and pernicious doctrine of states rights, or at any rate the strict construction thereof, and have the national government invested with sufficient power and authority to protect its own citizens against domestic violence when the state cannot, does not, or will not afford that protection. As already pointed out, the tendencies are in that direction.

After all, the supreme and prevailing law is the law of public opinion. That law is now being crystallized, vitalized, and nationalized. The day is not far distant, therefore, when an American citizen will be safely secure in the enjoyment of his rights and privileges as an American citizen, it matters not of what state he may be a resident. In other words, those who are the creatures of mob violence will no longer be the tribunals called upon to punish those who merit punishment imposed by law. That this is being done by the cooperation of both major parties is being set forth by influential leaders of both parties. That fact was clearly set forth in a letter addressed to the late Arthur Brisbane by Hon. William Randolph Hearst. I have not always agreed with Mr. Hearst in his attitude upon public questions, but the utterances contained in the letter herein referred to are meritorious and commendatory and ought to meet with the approbation and approval of every true American. The paragraph referred to reads as follows:

> Equality before the law is the primary protection of the little man. It is the fundamental guaranty of his rights and liberties. As soon as discrimination is introduced it leads eventually and inevitably to the discrimination in favor of the big fellow and against the little fellow. It may not start this way, but it ends this way and the only safeguard against discrimination against the little fellow is freedom from discrimination. . . . You cannot have the benefits of equality unless you have equality. You cannot discriminate in favor of one class or against one class and have equality. You cannot have unequal privileges and unequal obligations and maintain a government based upon equal rights. . . . When the torch of liberty is extinguished our era of enlightenment is ended and we return to the dark ages of force and fear.

INDEX

Index